CHRISTIAN COSMOLOGY

Christian Heritage Rediscovered

The Series, as the name suggests, is meant to focus on Christian Faith & Living vis-à-vis topics like Literature & Poetry, Indigenous Philosophizing, Ethical response towards Agriculture, Health & Healing, Science & Technology, Ecofeminist Theology, Sociological approach towards Human Rights, Law & Politics, Arts, History of Ideas, Ancient Civilizations, Cultural Contiguity, Religious Cosmologies & Mysticism, Footsteps of famous Theologians, World Peace & Harmony, Global Capitalism, Network Marketing, Cybertheology, Population & Demographics, Epigraphic Studies, Contextualized Education, and many others. We welcome a Mss. on any topic/s mentioned, whether they are original works, scholarly monographs, collections of conference papers, revised dissertations, or translations of historical documents. Through the Series we, the Publishers, are striving to put forward published works that may help Institutions, Academic Bodies, Researchers, Scholars and the World at large in furthering their respective knowledge and understanding on the concerned subject. We welcome your comments on our efforts and further suggestions on how we can foster the upcoming thoughtful theologically grounded books.

Christian Heritage Rediscovered - 7

CHRISTIAN COSMOLOGY

A Manual of Philosophy & Theology

Romero D'Souza SDB

CWI

Christian World Imprints(TM)

First Published in 2014 by

Christian World Imprints(TM)
Christian Publishing & Books from India
H-12 Bali Nagar, **New Delhi-110015**
info@christianworldimprints.com
www.ChristianWorldImprints.com
Phone: +91 11 25465925 Fax: +91 11 25173055

ISBN-13: 978-93-5148-015-0 ISBN-10: 93-5148-015-1

Cataloging in Publication Data--DK
Courtesy: D.K. Agencies (P) Ltd. <docinfo@dkagencies.com>

D'Souza, Romero, 1988-
Christian Cosmology : a manual of Philosophy & theology / Romero D'Souza.
p. cm. -- (Christian heritage rediscovered ; 7)
Includes bibliographical references (p.) and indexes.
ISBN 9789351480150
ISBN 9351480151

1. Cosmology. 2. Creation. 3. Philosophy and religion. 4. Philosophical theology. I. Title. II. Series: Christian heritage rediscovered ; 7.

DDC 231.765 23

Printed at Chawla Offset Printers

The Book

The Book provides a concise study of Cosmology at an introductory level. Starting from elementary principles and the history of Cosmology, the text carefully guides the readers through a Christian Philosophical journey in knowing and experiencing the Cosmos. It aims to take them on a journey to a newer horizon that will unfold the questions that arise within themselves.

The Book further shows how humankind has reached its present state of understanding the Universe, in which it inhabits. This is an itinerary for a cosmic voyage on which the reader will embark upon as one reflects upon the content of the Book. The journey can be summarized in the conclusion, and still poses questions with regard to the modern paradigm and the limits of our knowledge.

The Book comprehensively deals with the historical background of understanding Cosmology; it amplifies the origin and the problems of creation by basing itself substantially on Philosophy- both the eastern and the western understanding of the World; and provides truthful reflections of selected Authors in the conclusion.

It offers sound background in applying the principles of Metaphysics to Cosmology. It is a set of lecture notes which add up to a very accessible text on what is often misinterpreted, or rejected as an extremely esoteric subject. It is an exciting and adventurous journey to be taken, and dare we say, it is likely to be fundamentally correct.

The Author has intentionally presented the material in an informal manner, pedagogical style, without compromising on its formal technicalities. His approach has been that of the play of inductive-deductive with a more complete analysis that will result into an appropriate synthesis.

The fact that strongly motivated the Author to undertake this venture was the readings in the subject of Cosmology as a preparatory mode for the course. The title of the Book emerged after reading the seminal and inspirational formation that he received when he was a student of Philosophy.

These notes will be helpful not only for Cosmological novices but also for readers who are well versed with Ancient, Medieval, and Modern Philosophy (East and West); students (advanced undergraduates and graduates) having basic knowledge in the field of Philosophy, Metaphysics and Epistemology. Also, a must buy for Cosmologists; Philosophers; Seminarians; Institutions and Libraries of the concerned subject.

Finally, the Author makes no claim that the presentation is complete, unbiased or objective and hopes that his impressions and opinions will inspire the readers including students, to further their respective explorations in Cosmology. The annotated Bibliography at the end of the Book provides the readers with selected readings referred by the Author. It is also recommended for further reading, interpretations and conclusions.

The Author

Romero D' Souza SDB is a member of the Salesian Province of St. Francis Xavier, Mumbai. He has completed his B.A. Degree with a specialization in Sociology from the Pune University. He has completed his Bachelor as well as Master in Philosophy from Divyadaan: Salesian Institute of Philosophy (Nashik) aggregated to the Faculty of Philosophy of the Salesian Pontifical University, Rome. He had authored a Book titled *Dialogue as a Way of Life: A Panikkarian Perspective* (Saarbrücken, Germany: Lambert Academic Publishing (LAP), 2012). His passion and interest in the quest of Philosophy and Theology has led him to write a few articles in the field of Philosophy, Theology and Anthropology. He also has to his budding credit a few book reviews.

Dedicated To

My Parents
(Mr. Rolando & Mrs. Lourdina D' Souza)
and my brother Ryan D' Souza

The Salesian Congregation
The Students and Seminarians of
Philosophy and Theology

Acknowledgements

As for me, "Acknowledgment can be thought of and expressed only if there is honesty and humility." At this juncture, I can only express my most profound gratitude to all those who have accompanied me in my Philosophical venture to reach this 'moment in life.' This Book entitled, "*Christian Cosmology: A Manual of Philosophy and Theology*" has been a moment of learning and growing experience. It has been an enriching and a nourishing endeavor.

My gratitude is both for praise and criticism. The former stimulates, one to be worthy of it. The latter offers one the opportunity to pursue the dialogue entering into that difficult but fruitful activity of criticism.

I am not going to give a perfunctory response, nor will I make an attempt to put my record 'straight,' clarifying some allegedly misinterpreted facts or ideas. I shall simply make an attempt to spell out and deepen what I took to elaborate on Cosmology. I think that we are all engaged in the same venture of probing together some of the major issues of our times of life. I build on and rely upon wisdom in order to attempt a further step – leaving of course, most of the thought still unsaid. It is then not pride to say that I have taken upon myself the task of striving to find out the sense of my life, and of life in the entire Universe when I attempt to know, reflect, and understand the other (Cosmos). This is the task of authentic Philosophy. I wish you openness as you (reader) journey this way of contemplation and participation.

My being gratuitous is in the grace of God and the support of my parents, my Salesian family, my elders, and my staff members. I owe my sincere gratitude to the Salesian Provincial of the Mumbai Province, Rev. Fr Godfrey D'Souza SDB for enabling me to publish this Book. I owe immense gratitude to the Salesian province of Mumbai and especially to ex-Provincials, Rev. Fr Ivo Coelho SDB and Rev. Fr Michael Fernandes SDB, who accepted me in the Salesian congregation and allowed me to continue in this way of life; and also gave me an opportunity to do my further studies in Philosophy.

I have journeyed the Salesian way of life, thus far and in a special way, I am grateful to Divyadaan –Rev. Fr Savio D'Souza SDB (Rector), the co-staff members, my companions and all the brothers pursuing their Philosophical studies, and benefactors for the love and genuine support I received particularly in the past two years. In a very special way, I am indebted to Rev. Fr Robert Pen SDB, the Dean of the Institute of Philosophy, who so willingly encouraged me to walk this journey. I thank Rev. Frs Matthew Coutinho SDB, Ashley Miranda SDB, Felix Fernandes SDB, Tony D'Souza SDB, Thomas Chalissery SDB and Kenneth Pereira SDB for their words of encouragement and appreciate the good will and patience of Rev. Fr Aloysius Hemrom SDB, and for their meticulous corrections, microscopic observations and insightful suggestions that has enriched and enhanced the Book to a large extent by way of quality. Above all, I would also take this opportunity to thank my teachers, my formators and companions, my staff and students who supported and encouraged me in spite of all the time it took me away from them.

In this journey of explicating, I was blessed with the richness and profundity of this academic venture that has surfaced in the outcome of this Book only because of the well-updated college library. All thanks to Rev. Fr Ivo Coelho SDB (then) and Rev. Fr Matthew Coutinho SDB (now), along with the support staff Miss Vanita Borade for her dutiful service and notable help.

I would like to express my gratitude to the many people who saw me through this Book; to all those who provided support, and assisted in the editing, proofreading, and helped me computerize some notes: Clerics (Avil Correa SDB, Akhil Abraham SDB, Vivian Andrews SDB, Jerry Arumainathan SDB, Avil Correa SDB, Nathaneal George SDB, Nazarius Kharkongor SDB, Swithin Moraes SDB, Nelson Mudaliar SDB, Ian Pinto SDB, Dominic Ralte SDB, Christopher Xavier SDB, and Dustin Yarde SDB).

I thank in a special way Cl. Nathaneal George SDB who made possible the great leap from rough lecture notes to a polished Book by way of assisting in the formulation of methodology. I extend my gratitude to Cl. Avil Correa who very dutifully helped me with the Index as well as proof-read for the technicality reason. I would also like to thank Cl. Christopher Nadar SDB for critically going through the book for spelling mistakes and proof-reading. I also place on record my thankfulness and gratitude to all others who, in my Philosophical journey of the Cosmos now and earlier, in one way or another in their own little ways, did breathe forth a word of encouragement, a little push on my back, a correction here, a modification there, so as to make the Book see the light of day.

Many people have helped in the making of this Book; I thank them all. I owe particular thanks to the students (2012-2014) for whom I conducted the Cosmology course at the Salesian Institute of Philosophy – Divyadaan, Nashik – India. Their feedback (verbal feedbacks – "it's too heavy," "it's too much," including nonverbal feedback such as frowns, sticky eyes, and dozy positions during lectures as well as their timely questions and reflective queries) which greatly improved the lecture notes on which this Book is based.

Finally, I wish to thank my community of the last few years that I have been blest to reside at – a home indeed, Salesian Training Institute – Nashik and Divyadaan: Salesian Institute of Philosophy - Nashik, for their love, understanding and all the help received by way of encouragement and support.

Thanks to the Christian World Imprints and in a special way to Mr. Sudhanshu Kanda - without whom this Book would never have taken its form and be available for persons and Institutions, Libraries and Bookshelves.

Last and not the least: I humbly ask pardon of all those who have been with me over the course of this academic venture and whose names I have failed to mention.

Romero D'Souza SDB
Feast of St Thomas, the Apostle
3 July 2014

Preface

There could be no higher honor for a Philosopher than to grow in the thoughts of the Author which can be studied, criticized, and put into 'pragmatic' use. If the crystallization of one's life finds echo, sympathy, critique and is found to have transforming power, this is a reason for joy, gratitude and acknowledgment.

I believe a sign of an authentic human person is in acknowledging the other. The other can be experienced in God, World and Man. In this Book, I would like to stress the other of the World (Cosmos). The deepest sense of this is based on the awareness that, beyond us and all that we stand for, there is the reality of this World that transcends us all. I shall put forward my convictions, provocations, and questions to be further studied and criticized. These are neither theses, dogmas nor are they hypotheses, because they do not meditate in constituting a system or intend to prove something else. I would like to believe and think that they are truly Philosophy. Any metaphor 'carries us beyond' the first meaning of a sentence and allows us to land on unknown shores and perhaps to get lost in them. It helps us from getting drowned in the deep waters. The thoughtful readers will perhaps detect a discreet smile between the lines. This does not mean that I am writing for those who are not interested, not intended to study, or doing Philosophy or those who think they are average or below-average students; it would be a weak and improper judgment but I am merely affirming it is essential initially to initiate and approach my Philosophical venture in this unknown journey you have decided to take in unraveling the deepest truth of the living reality - *Cosmos*.

In J R R Tolkein's, *The Hobbit* there is a scene in which the unlikely protagonist, Bilbo Baggins, encounters the creature Gollum in a dark cavern and must win a riddling contest to keep from being eaten. At a critical stage of the contest Gollum puts forth this riddle:

> *This thing all things devours:*
> *Birds, beasts, trees, flowers;*
> *Gnaws iron, bites steel;*
> *Grinds hard stone to meal;*
> *Slays king, ruins town,*
> *And beats tall mountains down.*

In the dark, frightened of being eaten and completely stumped Bilbo Baggins pleads for longer to solve the riddle calling out, 'Time! Time!' And of course, that is the answer. Like Bilbo Baggins we may feel rather in the dark and stumped with regard to our present topic. But for us, time is not the answer to the riddle – time is the riddle.

And I think and believe that this is an appropriate time to grapple with the riddle of life in the World 'Christian Philosophical Cosmology'.

Having said all this, we must now take the final step. It is no longer a question neither of an intellectual exercise nor of an act of will but of an empirical and existential plunge into the abyss of reality. Raimon Panikkar in *Christophany: The Fullness of Man* (1999) states: "As I awaken to reality, or simply to consciousness, I find in myself a desire to know all things, though I discover them as veils. Those veils reveal to me their apparent form while at the same time they conceal what they are. Since, I do not find their "essence," I turn to my inner self. I begin the conscious pilgrimage to the center of my being but even here I do not find any foundation or any refuge, neither in myself nor in anything present to my consciousness. I cannot identify myself with my body or my mind or with what I am today, was yesterday, or will be tomorrow. I experience myself as alive, below or beyond or simply different from anything of which I might be conscious. Reason tells me that, since I do not come from myself, I must come from some other source. To conclude that I am a "creature" may be logical and legitimate, but it does not constitute an experience. My experience is simpler; I find it in myself. The experience of contingency is tangential (as the word suggests), neither immanent nor transcendent. In the experience of contingency I discover the tangential touch between immanence and transcendence. Touch required that somebody touch something, but in the touch itself we find neither duality nor unity; we find instead a nondual union – *advaita*. In the experience of contingency I do not experience myself as "creation" (of somebody else) because I touch the infinite, nor do I experience myself as the "creator" (of myself) because this touch is actualized in a point that has no dimensions. I realize that I participate, that I am an integral part of that very flux we call reality, although the word "participate" does not express the experience adequately."

It is this World in which you and I live in...Let us acknowledge the goodness, appreciate the beauty, accept the truth, and actualize the gift to participate with and in love.

Happy Reading! Happy Knowing! Happy Understanding!

Happy Reflecting! Happy Questioning! Happy Journeying...

Contents

Chapter 1

The Whyness of Cosmology

1.1 Introduction

Man as a seeker, a searcher sets oneself on the journey in the quest of the whyness of Cosmos. As Aristotle in his "Metaphysics" says, "All men by nature desire to know." Man is a searcher in all levels of his existence. In the biological level, he is a seeker of food, clothing and shelter. In the aesthetic level, he is a seeker of beauty. In the moral level he is a seeker of truth. In still another, perhaps still higher level, he is a seeker after the mysteries of the Universe, the ultimate meaning of his life on this earth. We assume this last level is highest because it seems to give meaning and direction to all other levels. It is in this last level that Science and Philosophy make their appearance. Basically Science and Philosophy are a search for the unknown – the mysteries that envelope man and his surroundings.

The history of human thought reveals that in the beginning Science and Philosophy moved hand in hand. The great Aristotle (384 – 322 BCE) and the numerous Greek Philosophers were both Philosophers and Scientists. But, with the Copernican Revolution and the Galilean incident, the two began to branch off in two different directions. At times it looked as though they had no relation whatever. Thus, came the opposing camps of empiricists and positivists who exalted Science to the heavens on the one hand, and the idealists and rationalists with their emphasis on speculation and metaphysics on the other. However in modern times the scene has changed. The streams which broke into two and began flowing independently have started merging once again leaving behind the island of tension and meaningless competition. The advent of The Theory of Relativity, Quantum Mechanics and the various theories sprouting out from them have forced man to transcend the World of sense observables to that of the unobservables. The large number of books written in this century on the Philosophical implications of these theories alone is sufficient to bear out the fact. Thus, the modern man looks at Philosophy and Science as complementary to each other. It is our hope that the following pages will illustrate and confirm this view.

What is Science?

Etymologically Science means knowledge (*scire*=to know). Usually Science stands for natural Science. Natural Science can be defined as "ordered knowledge of natural phenomena and of the relations between them." It is discovering patterns of behavior. It is a search for causal inter-dependence of phenomena. The aim of Science is to discover and interpret certain immutable laws governing nature. From the scholastic point of view Science is knowledge through causes, and Scientific study is an endeavor to discover the hidden causes of phenomena.

Science is not a collection of laws and principles or a catalogue of unrelated facts. It is a creation of the human mind with its freely invented ideas and concepts. It is a blend of reason and experience physical theories try to form a picture of reality and to establish its connection with the wide World of sense impressions. Experimentation and observation are an integral part of Scientific study. According to Sir James Hopwood Jeans (1877–1946) and many others the true object of Scientific studies can never be the realities of nature, but only our observation on nature. This extreme emphasis on sense observation and experimental verification places Science above all other disciplines, in credibility and even in dignity.

Some people define Science as organized common sense. In fact it is often said that today's common sense is built on yesterday's Science. Although common sense does play an important role in Science, it should be noted that the great pillars of modern Science: The Theory of Relativity and Quantum Mechanics, arose only when Scientists dared to go counter to the common sense explanation of reality. Common sense usually concentrates on what happens while Science usually looks for how it happens.

What is Philosophy?

It is a search for knowledge through the ultimate causes. A Philosopher does not seek a mere explanation of things; he seeks things which explain themselves. Some even call it the Science of Science.

Interrelation between Philosophy and Science

As mentioned earlier in the introduction, Science and Philosophy are two branches of the same stem of human knowledge. It has been said that the metaphysics of any period is the offspring of the Physics of the preceding period. History of both Philosophy and Science bears this fact. Aristotle first wrote his book on Physics and then on Metaphysics. The same tradition has been kept till date. Science tries to explain the 'how' of things. For example how a Saturn VI rocket fired at Cape Kennedy carries the astronauts to the moon. Philosophy explains the 'why' of things. Science is concerned mainly with what happens, but Philosophy with what is. Science is more objective while Philosophy is more subjective. By objective we mean that the results obtained are independent of the observer. Science is more quantitative in its treatment while Philosophy is more qualitative. Science is on the lookout to discover more and more new facts while Philosophy usually tries to delve deeper into what has been discovered. Science is satisfied with an explanation of events in terms of secondary causes, but Philosophy looks for justification in terms of ultimate causes. They both attack the same problem but from different angles. In other words the formal objects are different whiles the material objects are the same.

Coming to the methodology, we see that Scientific theories often start with a hypothesis based on certain insights of the Scientists. Philosophy usually starts with what is given to be certain and definite. Thus, in the Aristotilean-Thomistic system, the starting point is sensitive-rational experience which is an undeniable fact of human experience. Hence, the hypothesis or the starting point of a Scientific study may undergo change in the course of the investigation, but the starting point of Philosophy remains intact. Again, the ultimate test of a Scientific theory is workability or experiential verifiability. If it works, the theory is acceptable. But, a Philosophical theory is accepted only when it has obtained justification in terms of accepted first principles.

Sir. J. Jeans, speaking of the difference in the language of the two branches of knowledge has following points to make:

(1) Philosophy seems to have now agreed on precise terminology because it possesses no agreed body of fundamental knowledge for a terminology to describe. Science on the other hand has a store of fundamental knowledge and so it has a usually accepted terminology.

(2) The language of Philosophy differs from that of Science largely because Philosophy tends to use words in a subjective and Science in an objective sense.

(3) The language of Philosophy further differs from that of Science because Philosophy tends to think in terms of facts as they are revealed by our primitive senses, while Science thinks of them as they are revealed by instruments of precision.

The above reflections bring out both similarities and dissimilarities between the disciplines of Philosophy and Science. Perhaps at a first glance it looks as though they both oppose each other. But, deeper reflection on the points mentioned above will bring out the fact that Philosophy and Science do not oppose each other, rather they complement one another.

1.2 Understanding Cosmology

Perhaps in no other place does man's identity as a seeker become more manifest and the complementary nature of Science and Philosophy become more striking than in Cosmology. Both its nature and methodology bring out this fact.

1.2.1 What is Cosmology?

Etymologically (Cosmos = order) Cosmology means methodical study of order (in the Universe). However, the most popular meaning of Cosmos is regarded as an orderly system. So Cosmology is a reflective study of the Cosmos - from sub-atomic particles to the galaxies. Leo Albert Foley defines Cosmology as "The pursuits of the ultimate principles of the material World." K. Dougherty has a still different definition, "A Science which considers the first principles and causes of mobile beings in general." From the above definitions it follows that Cosmology is the Philosophical reflection on material reality. To be exact, it is a reflection on the knowledge of the Universe furnished by Science. Since, it is a reflection in search of the ultimate principles, it is Philosophical. Since, the data on which reflection is made is supplied by Science, it is Scientific also.

1.2.2 Why Cosmology?

It may be argued that Science, especially modern Science, can meet the needs of modern man and so Cosmology is a meaningless luxury. This argument usually comes from a confused understanding of the role of Science and Philosophy. The role of Science in the realm of knowledge can be reduced to three basic operations:-

(a) The search for numerical relations between the measurements of properties.
(b) The synthesis of these laws in theories from which they are deducible as logically implied consequences.

(c) The expression of these relations under the form of general laws.

Of course, modern Science seems to do much more than these three operations. Here we should remember that in modern times, as in the ancient days, there is a remarkable interaction between Science and Philosophy and so often one trespasses into the other's strict property. As has been said earlier, Science looks closely for the how of things; it is often silent about the why of things. Cosmology will be an effort to penetrate into this area using whatever it can get from Science.

Man in his everlasting search is not satisfied with bare particulars and details of things, however systematic and accurate. He wants to know the implications and presuppositions of the theories and experiences he comes across. He wants to delve deep into the ultimate realities. From where did this World come? How did the World begin? Where is it going? What is the ultimate nature of reality? These are problems which Science alone cannot answer. At best it can furnish only some pointers to the solution. It is here that Philosophy will have to come in and carry on the search. Thus, Cosmology understood as a reflection on the data furnished by Science has a definite role in furthering human knowledge, which Science alone cannot perform.

(a) To acquaint the students with the development of Philosophical Cosmology and their Philosophical implications.
(b) To present a Philosophical view of the World thereby instill into them a 'Philosophical think tank' – an awareness of the importance of Philosophy and its developments taking place around them.

1.2.3 Method of Cosmology

The very nature of Cosmology implies a two-fold method:-

(a) Study of the Cosmos and data given by Philosophical development. Thus, we will try to highlight the most important characteristics of Cosmos, and

(b) Reflection on them to find out their Philosophical implications.

1.2.4 Etymology of Cosmology

The Greek noun *kosmos* means "order" or "good arrangement." The alert minds of the ancient Greeks were quick to see in this word a suitable expression for the order, beauty, and regularity which they observed in the World around them. For this reason *kosmos* soon came to mean "the World," that is, the bodily Universe. It is interesting to notice in passing that the Latins also were alive to the orderliness and beauty of the World; they called it *mundus,* a word which describes something clean, pure, beautiful, and ornate. Our English word *mundane* is a direct derivative from *mundus* in the sense of "the World," just as our words *Cosmos* and *cosmic* are formed *kosmos* in the same sense.

The Greek word *logos* means "word" or "speech." Fundamentally, it means the word, speech, or expression which takes place within the mind in the act of knowing. It means thought or knowledge, and, in special, *reasoned knowledge.* And it has come to have the technical meaning of *sustained and connected reasoning;* that is, it has come to signify *Science.* In compound words *logos* regularly takes the English form of *–ology,* which is usually connected with the rest of this compound by the letter *o.* hence, a term ending in *–ology* usually suggests, by this very fact, its definition as 'the Science of' something or other.

From *kosmos*, the bodily World, and *logos,* Science, we have the term *Cosmology*. This name, therefore, by reason of its structure, means "the Science of the bodily World."

The term *Cosmology* is a comparatively recent invention. In earlier times, the Science (which is a part of Philosophy) that we now call *Cosmology* was known as *natural Philosophy*. It was also called *the Science of mobile being* or *scientia entis mobilis*, that is, the Science of things subject to physical and sensible movement, motion and change. Now, only bodily things are naturally subject to such modification or movement. Only a body, in the natural sense, and not in the mathematical sense of pure or abstract quantity, is *ens mobile*, that is, movable or changeable being. Hence, as is manifest, *natural Philosophy* or the *scientia entis mobilis* was, like Cosmology, the Science of bodily things, the Science of the World around us, the material and physical Universe. Cosmology deals with *bodies,* as these exist or are existible *in nature.*

1.2.5 Definition of Cosmology

Nominal Definition: The term *Cosmology* is derived from the classical Greek words *Cosmos,* and *logos. Cosmos* means order or good arrangement. According to tradition it was first applied to the Universe by the Greek Philosopher Pythagoras (?-c. 500 B.C). Plato explains in the dialogue *Gorgias* that the Universe is called *Cosmos* because it is ordered and governed justly: The Philosopher, Callicles, that communion and friendship and orderliness and temperance and justice bind together heaven and earth and Gods and men, and that this Universe is therefore called *Cosmos* or order, not disorder or misrule. The suffix *logy* of the word *Cosmology is* from the Greek word *logos* which signifies word, or mental expression in the act of knowing. In a special sense it means reasoned knowledge and so it has come to mean Science: the knowledge of things through their causes. Thus, the word *Cosmology* from *Cosmos* and *logos* signifies the Science of the Universe. Aristotle and Mādhva called this Science *Physics,* which is to be distinguished from modern Physics, and the medieval Scholastics called it *The Philosophy of Nature,* a term which is once again coming into use. The name *Cosmology* was first used by Christian von Wolff in 1731. He wrote a Philosophical work called *Cosmologia Generalis* (General Cosmology). Wolff adopted the theories of the Philosopher-Scientist Gottfried Leibniz (1646–1716), combined them with certain Aristotelian tenets, and partially modified them himself. He is the author of the well-known division of Philosophy into ontology, Cosmology, psychology and rational theology. Although modern Scholastics very often use these terms, the real meaning given to them is not the same as that intended by Wolff. Frederick Hoyle (1915–2001), the Cambridge University astronomer, has popularized the name

Cosmology in his work on *The Nature of the Universe.* In this context Cosmology signifies an explanation of the evolution of the Universe as a modern Scientist understands it. Experts in the experimental Sciences often permits them to give currency to this understanding of Cosmology. Just as psychology is understood by many to mean only experimental psychology rather than to extend also to rational or Philosophical psychology, so also Cosmology is accepted by many to be the sole property of the theorist and experimentalist in modern Physics. Cosmology as a word, therefore, means the Science of the Universe. It is subject to various kinds of definitions as to its real significance. In this text we shall explore the Science of Cosmology in its Philosophical content.

Real Definition: A Science always begins with wonder. The awakening mind of every one in childhood is endowed with this natural wonder about the World. "Why is the sky blue?" the child queries. "Where did the World come from?" These and innumerable other expressions of wonderment excite the child's mind. If in the course of time they almost cease to be in the minds of many, it is because adult indifference often narrows the horizon of this natural curiosity.

Cosmology begins with wonder about the Universe of changeable beings in sensible matter and motion. This embraces the microcosmic World of the atom, the heavenly bodies, minerals, plants, animals and human beings. All these beings are called mobile beings because they are subject to various kinds of change.

Our Universe abounds in contingence, an ever unfolding complex of unity and diversity of the same and the different, of the old and the new. Human life progresses from infancy to childhood and to youth, from maturity to old age and finally death. The seed becomes the plant, and the plant withers and decays into baser elements. The elements combine into compounds and compounds dissolve into elements. Stars grow cold while other stars are born. The Universe is a process of building up and breaking down. Generation follows upon corruption and corruption upon generation. There are changes of things, substantial changes, as in the generation of a substance and the corruption of a substance. There are changes in things as in their qualitative and quantitative characteristics. Finally, there are local changes, the transposition of bodies in space and time. Our Cosmos is an evolving World, beings in evolution. But, what is this evolution? This is the problem of change, of mobile being.

Generation, corruption, qualitative, quantitative and local changes – these are the general mobilities that man notes in the finite beings of the Universe which are called mobile beings. In unriddling this mystery of the mobile Universe man seeks to go the very heart of the nature of the mobile. Man naturally wonders about the architecture of the Universe itself, the nature of this ordered arrangement of mobile beings, its origin, essence and destiny. It is the special task of the Cosmologist to treat these fundamental problems in a Scientific manner.

Aristotle and Vallabha clearly distinguishes Scientific knowledge from opinion. In his *Posterior Analytics* we find the following classical text of the meaning of Science: we suppose ourselves to possess unqualified Scientific knowledge of a thing as opposed to knowing it in an accidental way in which the sophist knows, when we think we know the cause of which the fact depends, as the cause of that fact and no other, and further, that the fact could not be otherwise than it is.

We are convinced that we understand a thing which has causes and principles when we understand what its causes and principles are. Cosmology seeks to render the Universe of mobile being intelligible in the light of its first causes and principles, which are the necessary sources of mobile beings, of their coming into being and our knowledge of them.

By first principles, strictly speaking, we mean principles that are immediately derived from being or reality; such as the principle of non-contradiction: it is impossible for a thing to be and not to be at the same time. The first principles of being are studied in metaphysics. In Cosmology we study the first principles of mobile being. These are called first principles in a restrictive sense; namely, first in reference to the Universe of mobile beings. Thus, *we define Cosmology as the Science which considers the first principles and causes of mobiles being in general.* We shall now proceed to examine the meaning of the definition of Cosmology by an analysis of its subject, object and method.

Cosmology is *the Philosophical Science of natural bodily being*. We must ponder every phrase of this definition.

A) Cosmology is *a Science*. The term *Science*, taken absolutely, without the article, is a literal synonym for *knowledge*. It is a direct derivative from the Latin *scientia*, "knowledge," and this word comes, in its turn, from the verb *scire*, "to know." But, the word means knowledge of facts or truths together with their explanations, their justification, their how's and why's, their causes and reasons. Such is the meaning of the term *Science* when taken generally or absolutely. Now, any branch or department of such knowledge, which has its own clear-cut limits or determinate scope; which sets forth its data in an orderly, systematic, and complete manner; which justifies each point in its orderly development by assigning causes or reasons, is called *a* Science. For Cosmology is a branch of human knowledge with a definite field or scope; it sets forth, in an orderly, complete, and systematic way, the reasoned truths that belong to its field; it gives, at each step of its progress in manifesting these truths, the reasons and proofs which justify its conclusions. Hence, *Cosmology is a Science*. We may add that Cosmology is a *speculative* or *theoretical* Science. That is, it is a Science which aims, first of all, at knowing truth, possessing it, enriching the mind with it, contemplating it. On this score, Cosmology is contrasted with *practical* or *normative* Sciences, which have as their first purpose the manifesting of truth to be acted upon. Ethics, for example, is a practical Science; it is the Science of right human conduct; it is a Science which indicates something *to be done* with what it makes known scientifically. But, a speculative or theoretical Science like Cosmology informs the mind and enlarges culture without directly indicating any precise action or procedure to be undertaken in consequence of the knowledge it affords.

Cosmology is a *Philosophical* Science. In other words, it is a department of Philosophy. Philosophy is the Science of all things knowable by the human mind, considered in their *deepest* reasons and causes. Philosophy is composite Science; its departments or sub-Sciences (of which Cosmology is one) must all have the truly *Philosophical* character; that is, each Philosophical Science must seek out the last, the ultimate, the deepest cause and reasons for the data which it manifest and proves. A Philosophical Science is, therefore, clearly distinguished from the non-Philosophical Sciences (among which the experimental Sciences hold an imposing place) by the fact that its quest is for *ultimate* causes and reasons, which theirs is for *proximate* or *immediate* causes and reasons. Cosmology pursues an ultimate quest; it seeks to know the hows and whys the deepest causes and reasons that can be discovered for the data with which it deals. Cosmology is, therefore, justly called *a Philosophical Science*. But, Cosmology, truly *Philosophical* Science, is not, strictly speaking, a *metaphysical* Science. It belongs to *Philosophical Physics*, not to *metaphysics*. For metaphysics is the Philosophical Science of material real being. Still, there are many writers and teachers who follow Christian Wolff (1679-1755) in making *metaphysics* a synonym for *real Philosophy*, that is, for the Philosophy of things or reality, as distinct from the Philosophy of thought (Logic) and the Philosophy of moral conduct (Ethics). These authorities make a convenient division of metaphysics into *general metaphysics,* which treats being or reality in itself; in its most general aspects, and *special metaphysics,* which treats fundamental classifications of reality, viz., God, man, and the bodily World. Thus, the Wolffian division of Philosophy stands as follows:

Now, however convenient this plan may be for teachers and pupils – and we are not concerned here to dispute its eminently practical character, it is hardly to be called Scientific. A strictly just assignment of departments would limit metaphysics to the field of non-material real being, that is, to the field of being considered in itself, as it is in the mind, and as it substantially exists in God and spiritual creatures. Thus, metaphysics would include ontology, criteriology, and theodicy. In Cosmology we study *bodies as such*, without reference to their character as living or non-living. The point we stress with special and repeated emphasis is that Cosmology is a *physical*, and not a *metaphysical*, Philosophical Science.

I. Mental Philosophy Or Logic…	Logic	
	Criteriology or Epistemology	
II. Real Philosophy Or Metaphysics	General Metaphysics or Ontology	
	Theodicy	
	Special Metaphysics	Psychology
		Cosmology
III. Moral Philosophy or Ethics….	General Ethics	
	Special Ethics	

B) Cosmology is *Philosophical Physics*, not experimental or laboratorian Physics. The Cosmologist takes the established findings of the physicist, that is, the experimentalist, and seeks to discover in these the larger meanings and ampler truths which the application of Philosophical certainties may manifest. The Cosmologist must also perform the occasional stern duty of pointing out the experimentalist the mistaken character of theories which come into conflict with truths Philosophically known and unshakably true. But, the Cosmologist does not invade the laboratory on his own account, nor is he greatly tempted to do so. The laboratorian, on the other hand, is almost inevitably drawn beyond the frontiers of his unknown proper field into the domain of

Philosophy. The physicist can hardly help playing the Philosopher. For his quest of explanations, an eager, sincere, enlightened, and wholly admirable search runs quickly through the realm of manifest sensible data, and leads temptingly on into the outer, nonsensible region where all final reasons and explanations must ultimately be sought. No explanation is ever entirely positivistic and sensistic. No theory, however bound up with material and testable things, is itself ultimately and completely testable and material. Back of every theory and of every explanation are certain fundamental truths which are self-evident and not subject to experiment, truths, such as the existence of the investigator, the reliability of his powers, his capacity for knowledge, and the fact that the World he investigates cannot involve in itself an absolute contradiction. While the physicist is compelled, by his rational human constitution, to accept these and other non-material and Philosophical findings, and to recur to them, at least implicitly, in framing his theories, the Cosmologist is under no compulsion whatsoever to accept, or even to be deeply concerned about, the continual new theories (so often quickly proved erroneous) of the laboratorian. Indeed, physical Science, in spite of the marvelous advances and most valuable achievements, is today in a general condition of instability and uncertainty. Hence, the Cosmologist is not to be condemned as a reactionary, a fogy, stand-patter, a wistful worshipper of the faded past, if he refuses to warp his Philosophy to fit the latest theories of the laboratorian. The Cosmologist needs the Scientist and works with what the Scientist furnishes him; But, only with the *established* findings of the Scientist, the certainly known facts. He does not work with the probabilities proposed by the laboratorian, nor is he concerned with the quickly cooked-up Philosophy which the laboratorian serves with his dish of probabilities. The Cosmologist is not a mere trimmer, an adjuster, a fitter. No, he is a Philosopher, and this means that he has a body of known, proved, and indisputable principles. He may not have a finished Philosophical edifice, But, he has at least some sturdy and unshakable framework for building the edifice. Physical Science may bring to light data which will indicate an annex to the cosmological building, or an unexpected cornice or cupola; it will never bring to the scholastic Cosmologist an utter change of location or plans.

There is a point where laboratorian Physics and Cosmology meet and even overlap. Rather, there is a series of such points, an irregular and intricate frontier. Hence, it is not easy to determine, and to express in a few terse words, the distinction which indicates where the physicist should stop and the Cosmologist begin. But, the difficulty of establishing a clear line of demarcation is no reason for denying its existence or utility, or, as the current fashion is, for ignoring it altogether. In general, it can be said that the physicist deals properly with individual and material data and seeks for these a unifying and organizing explanation that may be called *proximate* or *immediate*; the Cosmologist deals with material data in a more general or universal manner than the physicist, and seeks for these data an explanation that is *ultimate* or *root-deep*.

Cosmology is the Philosophical Science of *natural bodily being*. A natural bodily being, or a *natural body,* or a *physical body,* is a body that exists or can exist (that is, it is thought of as existing) in the World of realities around us. It is a body that can be *sensed*. Contrasted with a natural body is a *mathematical body,* that is, bodily extension or quantity considered as three-dimensional-bulk, without reference to its sensible character or to the qualities which are necessarily associated with bodies that can be seen or felt or handled or depicted in fancy. The bodily objects we see around us are natural or physical bodies. Even such as are artificial (like a house or an automobile) are only combinations or modifications of natural bodily substances, and are, at least equivalently for our present consideration, to be classed as natural or physical bodies. The material Universe itself, viewed as a single bodily thing, in the bodily Universe, each tree, each man, each stone, each weed; each molecule, each atom, each electron, is a natural or physical body.

Cosmology deals with the World of natural bodies and employs reason to interpret the deepest-lying facts discoverable in the actual experience of men with the material Universe in which they live and of which they are art. Mathematics, or, more precisely, the Philosophy of mathematics, uses reason to interpret the properties and relationships of quantities as such. Therefore, a manual, in Cosmology will inevitably presuppose its own specific character as the *Philosophical* Science of natural bodies. This point will be made clear in the explanation of the *object* of Cosmology, which now follows.

1.2.6 Object of Cosmology

A Science has two-fold object, one *material,* one *formal.* The material object of a Science is heat and is usually called its "subject matter;" it is the thing with which the Science deals; it is the field in which the Science works. The formal object of a Science is the precise end and aim which the Science has in dealing with its material object. The material object of Cosmology is the bodily World, or simply *bodies*. The formal object of Cosmology is discerned in the fact that Cosmology studies *as such* (not this or that special kind of bodies) and seeks the ultimate explanation of them.

Our definition of Cosmology indicates the material object of this Science in the phrase, "the Science of natural bodily being." It indicates the formal object of Cosmology in the phrase, "the Philosophical Science."

Manifestly, Sciences are distinguished, one from another, by their objects. Two Sciences that are not in the same general field (such, for example, as the Science of anatomy and of algebra) are distinguished by this fact; that is, they are distinguished and known as different Sciences by their respective material object. Such Sciences are distinguished, one form another, that is, they are seen in their proper place and character, and kept from overlapping, by their respective formal objects. Thus, Cosmology, inasmuch as it deals with bodily being, is at one with all the experimental Sciences; it is not marked off from these, and assigned its own proper scope, by its material object. But, Cosmology is distinguished from every other Science by its own formal object. For, of all the Sciences that deal with bodies, Cosmology alone deals with *all bodies* (that is, with bodies as such), seeks to establish their *ultimate* constitution, and makes known the deepest roots of their observed activities. The other Sciences that deal with natural bodily being (that is, the physical Sciences) have, each in its respective way, certain kinds of bodies in their purview, or they seek for immediate and proximate explanations of bodies and bodily activity. Cosmology alone levels distinction among bodics and traces out the ultimate explanation of the material Universe. Therefore, Cosmology is a Science distinct from every other Science. It is so distinct because of its *formal object*.

Every Science has something in common with other Sciences. It also has something unique and peculiar to itself. When we speak of the object of a Science, we mean that which it alone seeks to know about its subject or what it alone renders intelligible its subject. The object of Cosmology is the first principle of mobile being. Cosmology is distinct among the basic answer to the riddle of the Cosmos. The one end of this Science is to master the meaning of that grade of being which is in sensible matter and in motion.

The Science of mobile being itself is the Science of the first principles of mobile being, namely its universal four causes. The Cosmologist strives to know what Aristotle terms the material and the formal causes (the internal causes) and the efficient and final causes (the external causes): *The Material Cause* – that from which a thing is made. Brick, mortar, wood and stone are the material causes of a house.

> *The Formal Cause* – that in which the thing is constituted; that which gives determination to the material in some definite way. The architecture of a house is its formal cause.
>
> *The Efficient Cause* – that by which the thing is produced. The man who builds his own house is said to be its efficient cause.
>
> *The Final Cause* – that on account of which a thing is made. When a man builds a house to shelter his family, this is its final cause.

The Cosmologist seeks to know the Universe of mobile being according to these four causes which were first clearly formulated by Aristotle and then improved upon principally by St. Thomas Aquinas (1225–1274). The Cosmologist seeks to know the universal essence of mobile being: the material cause of this mode of being, from what is it made? And its formal cause, in what is it constituted? He also seeks to know its origin or its efficient cause: by what agent is it brought into being? And its final cause: on account of what is the mobile Universe brought into being? Here it is well to note that the Cosmologist is not seeking to know simply the essence of mobile being or that which makes it to be what it is, but also the efficient and final cause of mobile being. St. Thomas Aquinas does not consider Cosmology to be merely a study of the doctrine of hylomorphism, the doctrine of matter and form. In his *Commentary on the Physics of Aristotle* he wrote, ".... The Philosopher of nature demonstrates by all the causes." It is not uncommon for the student to consider the object of this study to be a course in General Science. The student who has had no previous training in Philosophy is apt to evaluate Cosmology as an association of the discoveries of the various experimental Sciences which results in an over-all view of the Universe. Such an opinion judges the knowledge of mobile being as such to be a sum of our knowledge of individual mobile beings. This is not the case. Cosmology is not seeking a composite picture of the discoveries of the experimental Sciences.

Just as the elaborate architectural form of a skyscraper cannot be attributed to the specialized work of the carpenters, masons and steel workers but, formally to its architects so, in an analogous way, the basic meaning of mobile being cannot be attributed to a summing up of all the specialized knowledge of the experimentalists concerning the classes of mobile being itself is the special object of the Cosmologist.

The physicist studies energies; the geologist, the earth's surface; the astronomer, the heavenly bodies. Each branch of experimental Science studies mobile being in some of its phases and analyzes its properties. But, no experimental Science studies mobile being itself. These Sciences describe what such and such a mobile being does under certain circumstances, but, the common subject of all these Sciences, the reality in sensible matter and motion, is not rendered intelligible.

St. Thomas Aquinas explains the priority of Cosmology (or the *Physics* as Aristotle called it) over the other Sciences about nature in the following passage:

Because those things which follow something commonly must be treated first and separately lest we be required to repeat those things many times in discussing all parts of the common aspect, it was necessary in natural Science that we have one book in which we treat those thing which follow mobile being in general ... This treatise is in the book of the *Physics* ... Its subject is mobile being simply.

Although the experimental Sciences of our modern age far surpass their crude state in the Middle Ages, these Sciences can never abstract mobile being itself. They are confined to the level of the secondary and proximate principles of classes of mobile beings rather than the first principles of mobile being as mobile.

Experimental Science does not reflect upon the mode of being which it analyzes in the laboratory. It is not concerned with such basic problems as the following: What is a mobile Being? Are motion and the being that moves one and the same essentially? Is the being that moves a static something to which motion is conjoined from without? Is the being that moves an essential composition of an active and static principle? What is the meaning of quantity and quality? What are space and time? Are quantity and body the same thing? Why should mathematics play such an important role in experimental Science? How is quality related to mobile being? Is time the same as motion? Is space as real as the bodies that occupy space? What is the origin of the Universe of mobile being? Is there purpose in the Universe; if there is, what is it?

Physics and other experimental Sciences do not answer these questions because these Sciences do not raise them. The chemist is satisfied to study the composition and decomposition of bodies, the astronomer to study the heavenly bodies in their kinds and their various properties. The experimental Scientists use the concepts of motion, and something that moves, which they call body; they employ such concepts as quantity, quality, space and time. The experimentalist uses these concepts. They are the initial concepts with which he words his particular Science but, it is not his task to reflect upon them.

Each Science has its unique object which it seeks to understand. No Science can go everywhere in the field of knowledge. The nuclear physicist does not attempt to dissect butterflies by the use of the cyclotron, nor does the biologist attempt to cut through the atom by the use of the scalpel. It would be ridiculous for the physicist to attempt to examine the first principles of nature through Physics, which is meant to examine certain secondary principles of mobility.

The attempt to make a Science search after objects beyond its own proper object may be called the fallacy of the uniform method. It is not uncommon in our times to find physicists and other experts who endeavour to cross the frontiers of their particular Science and establish themselves as authorities in fields where they do not belong. We shall discuss this fallacy in the forthcoming section.

The rise of the new Physics at the turn of the century, when dynamic characteristics of mobile being were unfolded in the discoveries of the sub-atomic World, led to the fad of "the new cosmologies." These cosmologies of the energists, E. Mach, M. Ostwald and others, viewed all reality as purely dynamic. The *communist dialectic of nature* was later proclaimed by the English Scientist, John B. Haldane, and the Soviet dean of physicists, A. F. Joffe, among others, as proved by the new Physics, and all true Scientists were called upon to view reality as an infinite process unfolding endlessly in space and time.

The confusion between the object of Physics and the object of Cosmology is not effected by people who are anxious to be confused. It is due at least in part to the failure to grasp the distinction between what Physics seeks to prove and what

Cosmology seeks to prove. In other words, Scientists with little or no training in Philosophy set out to philosophize Physics.

There is a hunger in every man for Philosophy. The human intellect is not satisfied with mere observation and measurement. It is not satisfied with the secondary and proximate. It seeks to know the primary and the ultimate. But, the mind untrained in the Science of the primary and ultimate can easily mistake its object – the history of human thought bears testimony to this fact. Just as a man cannot become a physicist through the ways of common sense alone but, only by studying Physics, so also the physicist cannot become a Philosophers without adopting the method of Philosophy in the light of its proper object.

It is of capital importance for the beginner in Cosmology to note well this difference between a Philosophy of nature and modern Physics. One *must distinguish* clearly the problems of these distinct Sciences. What is meant by an electrical charge? These and other questions that concern the specific kinds of mobile beings and their specific properties are the province of the physicist. The Cosmologist, in contrast, is concerned with the definite object in view, to render mobile being intelligible in its universal and basic meaning.

Before concluding this reflection on the object of Cosmology, it is well that we note its abstract universal nature. It is not uncommon for the student to evaluate the Science of mobile being as such as unreal. After all, mobile being as such does not exist. It is this or that mobile being that exists. One can perceive the mobile beings of sensible experience, the people that one meets, the trees on the campus, the birds in the air, the stars above. But, mobile being itself is an abstract concept in the mind. Are we to conclude with Thomas Hobbes, the 17th century English Philosopher, that abstract concepts are nothing more than names?

Of course it is true that mobile being itself does not exist except in the mind, but, it has a real foundation because it is abstracted from the mobile beings of experience. It is a universal concept, and universals do not exist as such outside the mind. The true universal gives a basic report on the real beings to which it refers. The universal concept of mobile being may be compared to a window in the mansion of Science through which man looks beyond the sensible to the inner reality of the mobile, mobile being in its four causes.

In conclusion, the object of Cosmology is an abstract, universal mode of Scientific knowledge. It extends to the entire Cosmos and pertains to what is most fundamental in the origin, constitution and destiny of all reality in sensible matter and motion. The way by which the Cosmologist arrives at his object, the knowledge of mobile being as such, is called the method of Cosmology. We shall now proceed to examine the subject and its method.

1.2.7 Subject of Cosmology

The subject of a Science is that about which it is concerned. Cosmology is concerned with the Universe of mobile being, being in sensible matter and motion. It studies the organic and the inorganic World. It is as much concerned about the atom as it is about the heavenly body of the greatest magnitude. Cosmology can be said to share its subject with the experimental Sciences of nature: Physics, chemistry, geology, biology and the rest. The reason is that the common subject of all these Sciences is being in sensible matter and motion.

It is incorrect to say that Scientific data are the subject matter of Cosmology. The subject that is considered is simply being in sensible matter and in motion. This subject when it is viewed according to the methods of the experimental Sciences becomes what is commonly termed "Scientific data." Scientific data are the facts of nature analyzed quantitatively and qualitatively. Thus, water is a natural subject for chemical analysis; as Scientific data we have H_2O. Mobile beings are the common subject of the Philosophical and experimental Sciences of nature. The subject matter is itself pre-Scientific; it is, so to speak, the raw material of nature.

At the beginning of the *Commentary on the Second Book of the Physics of Aristotle,* St. Thomas Aquinas contrasts natural things with artificial things. These latter have no principle of change in them except accidentally. Natural things have in themselves a principle of motion and they compose the subject of the natural Sciences in general. In his *Commentary of the First Book of the Physics,* St. Thomas affirmed:

The Philosophy of nature is about natural things; but, those things are natural whose principle is nature and *nature is the principle of rest and motion* in that in which it is; therefore *natural Science is about those things which have in themselves a principle of motion.*

Let us take a simple example; A bird is a subject of natural Science because it is a being mobile by nature since it evidently has within itself the principle of motion proper to its kind. An airplane is not a natural thing, a mobile being of the Cosmos; rather it is in the order of artificial things along with sputnik lunik. Its principle of motion is accidental to the natural substances that compose it. The natural substances that constitute the airplane are so arranged by man so as to achieve flight in the air. Aircraft propulsion, therefore, is the proper object of a specialized branch of technology rather than natural Science. Artificial beings do not comprise the subject of natural Science either Philosophical or experimental.

Although Cosmology and the other Sciences of nature share a common subject, namely, mobile being, they study it with different objects in view. We shall now investigate what constitutes the object of Cosmology or what it uniquely seeks to know in the Universe of mobile being

1.2.8 Method of Cosmology

Every Science has a unique method by which it achieves its unique object. When we say that a Science achieves its object, we mean that it renders its object intelligible. Thus, Cosmology is terminated when it renders mobile being intelligible through the four causes. The method whereby this is achieved is both inductive and deductive.

Unfortunately some histories of Science still date the beginning of induction from the beginning of induction form the experiments of Friar Roger Bacon at 13th century Oxford. They neglect the essential dependence of all Scientific deduction upon induction in some way. The deductive character of Cosmology is evident from the syllogistic process of its proofs and in the use of what the Medieval called *scientia propter quid* or demonstration through the proper causes. However, Aristotle and Aquinas emphasize that causes are known from the things of nature which are evident as through their effects. Consequently there is a definitely inductive character to this form of reasoning.

The method of Cosmology is inductive because it begins with the facts of nature apprehended by the senses. The Philosopher of nature cannot spin his Cosmology out of thoughts about possible Worlds; the subject of his inquiry is the actual Cosmos in which he lives. He must begin with the World as he experiences it. This experiential knowledge is the take-off point for his abstractions about mobile being itself. As Aquinas states:

And that natural things are moved can be manifested from induction; because it is evident to the senses that natural things are moved.

Human knowledge begins with the senses. There are many of our contemporaries, however, who disclaim sense knowledge as untrustworthy. They put all their trust in the precision of machines. For these specialists it is the machine that offers certainty to man in his quest for truth. They assert that inductive method begins and ends with the apparatus of the laboratory. In fact there are some extremists who assert that some machines can think. This trend is represented in the cybernetics of Norbert Wiener (1894–1964). It is unfortunate that the difference between "a mechanical brain" and "a thinking mind" is confused.

The attack made upon sense knowledge is equally an attack upon technical instruments inasmuch as these are aids to the senses in observing the facts of nature. The most powerful telescope is meaningless without the human eye. Apart from man these artifacts are not intelligible. On the other hand, errors associated with the senses arise not in the senses themselves but, in false judgments of their data by the mind. Truth and error are in judgment, and judgment exists only in the mind.

In the method of Cosmology the mind ascends from the observation of the sensible facts of nature through the avenues of abstraction to the comprehension to the common properties of mobile beings, and by more intensive abstraction it draws forth the knowledge of mobile being itself from the study of the properties. The human mind does not know essence immediately; essence is not experienced. It is reasoned to from the content of our experience of the sensible manifestation of mobile being. This demonstration takes place in what the Thomists call the first degree of abstraction.

Abstraction is the act of the human intellect by which it draws from the sensible image of a thing the essential notes, as "rational" and "animal" from the sensible image of man. There are various degrees of abstraction classified according as the mind ascends from the sensible into the intelligible. In the Science of Cosmology the mind draws forth or abstracts from the individual sensible mobile beings certain common properties and from these it draws out the knowledge of the four causes which constitute the definition of mobile being.

In the first degree of abstraction something is obtained by the mind and something remains untouched. The mind leaves aside the individual matter and fixes its insight on the common sensible matter of the mobile. It abstracts what is common to mobile being and leaves aside the consideration of the individuality of this and that mobile being. As we have already noted regarding Cosmology, the object of this abstraction is not a summation of mobilities or a general image of mobile beings, but, rather the meaning of the mobile itself. Hence, what is left behind is the individual matter of mobile beings and what is obtained is the intelligibility of being in sensible matter and motion which the Thomists simply call common sensible matter.

No natural Science is simply concerned with the individual. Archimedes (287 BC) in his formulation of the abstract physical law, which applies to the conduct of all solids immersed in liquids and gases, is not concerned with this loofah in his bath, or this piece of ebony sinking in a pool, or the behaviour of this ship in the sea. This Scientific abstraction formally pertains to the law of flotation as such and not to this or that floating object. So too, Isaac Newton's (1643–1727) law of gravitation abstracts from individual sensible matter. There is not a law for a falling leaf, another for our own firm grip on the ground beneath our feet as our planet moves on through space. The one abstract law of gravitation applies to all these individual sensible events. Science is not concerned with individual facts as such.

The concept of mobile itself transcends individual mobile beings; it pertains to what is common to them all. Furthermore, it surpasses the abstraction of Physics, chemistry, astronomy and other experimental Sciences. Although these natural Sciences are also in the first degree of abstraction, Cosmology exceeds their abstractions since it concerns all mobile beings simply as mobile. It does not deduce some functional formula which renders intelligible the motion of a mass of electrons under certain conditions of research. Its object is to render intelligible that phase of reality which is in sensible matter and in motion rather than some class of mobility which is the restricted object of an experimental Science, as atomic physicists study atoms and botanists study plants. Cosmology is situated on the Olympus of the first degree of abstraction of common sensible matter.

From the standpoint of abstraction from matter, the mind can proceed further. In the second degree, in mathematics, the mind abstracting puts aside not only individual matter of mobile beings but, also their sensible matter. The mathematical formula "a x b = ab" may refer to atoms or elephants. As a mathematical formula it connotes a quantitative relationship which is symbolically represented. The individual sensible matter to which it may refer is not intelligible from the mathematical abstraction itself although its matter is intelligible quantitatively. In applied mathematics the intelligibility of mathematical formulae calls for reference to the sensible World. This is worked out by experimentation in which some theoretical formula is tested.

The highest grade of abstraction is achieved in metaphysics; the third degree of abstraction. In this Science the mind leaves behind all matter and draws out the knowledge of being or reality itself; what it means 'to be.' This abstraction transcends all the kinds of beings and seeks to render intelligible being itself. It embraces the material and spiritual, the finite and infinite, and rests in the intelligibility of reality. Metaphysics was given its name by Andronicus of Rhodes (first century B.C.) who was the editor of the works of Aristotle. It means the Science that follows the *Physics,* the Philosophy of nature. It goes beyond sensible matter and investigates reality itself.

The various grades of abstraction have a definite relation to one another. Cosmology is close to the heights of metaphysics because it concerns essence and the supreme efficient and final causes. Whereas the Cosmologist ascends inductively from the sensible manifestations of mobile beings to their common properties and then to their four causes, he is drawn to these heights by deductions from the heights of metaphysics. He is aided by first principles of being in his insight into the data of sensible experience as he proceeds to conclusions about mobile being as it is mobile.

We shall see that one cannot advance from the properties of quantity and quality to the meaning of corporeal substance without the metaphysical doctrine of substance and accident and the real distinction between these modes of being. Furthermore, one cannot ascend from the common properties of mobile being to the intrinsic causes of prime matter and substantial form without the metaphysical doctrine of potency and act.

This is not the same as saying that Cosmology is a special metaphysics. Its principles are not formally metaphysical but, they involve metaphysical principles which are applied to mobile being. First principles of thought reality must be resolved in Cosmology. However, cosmological principles are not formally metaphysical because they are not principles of reality itself but, rather of mobile reality.

One cannot derive the concept of prime matter or pure potency from the doctrine of potency itself. Prime matter is demonstrated by the inquiry into the nature of mobile being, by observation of the sensible World of change, abstracting its common properties, and finally abstracting pure potency from these as shall be seen. The metaphysics of potency as such is employed in this demonstration, but, it is not the demonstration simply. Aquinas would oppose the identity of Cosmology as a branch of metaphysics as he argues each Science considers on phase of being according to a special mode, which is different from that according to which being is viewed by metaphysics. It is inaccurate to call this Science the Science of being as mobile. It is not the Science of being but, rather on mobile being as mobile.

The matter of this method is necessarily drawn from sensible experience in that human knowledge must begin with experience. In contrast to this necessary dependence on sensible experience, Cosmology has a relative and contingent dependence upon the experimental Sciences. It is called contingent because it is not necessary but rather expeditious for Cosmology to use the other Sciences of nature in our Scientific age.

The experimental Sciences are necessary for the comprehension of the specific properties of mobile being but not its universal properties simply as mobile being. For example, quantity is a common characteristic of mobile being. Astronomy describes the quantitative characteristics of the heavenly bodies in great detail, but the understanding of the fact that mobile being is quantitative is not necessarily derived from the content of astronomy. It is first known from common experience of the mobile in a confused way and refined in Cosmology.

The experimental Sciences delineate the functions, structures and conditions of mobile beings and these delineations should be employed especially in our Scientific age as illustrations in the abstract study of mobile beings as mobile. A Cosmology which would not improve upon the illustrations used by the Medievals would not be in keeping with the general advance in Science. Furthermore, many illustrations used by the medieval from the alchemy, astronomy, zoology, and other studies of their age have been proved to be false. These errors should be corrected in the light of modern discoveries. For example, the Aristotelian division of the heavens into the perishable and imperishable is no longer tenable. We now know that celestial bodies corrupt as well as terrestrial.

It should be noted that an error of illustration should not be confused with the true principle which is being illustrated – a distinction not maintained by many critics of Aquinas. Some modern thinkers say that the Philosophy of nature of the Angelic Doctor is of little importance because it antedates the telescope, and so they argue that Aquinas could not construct a true Cosmology according to modern Scientific standards. His errors in astronomy are confused with errors in Philosophy. These standards of judgment are determined mainly by some form of positivism, the system that asserts that the only valid method is the empirico-metric method of modern Science.

Cooperation between the Philosopher and the experimental Scientist is necessary not only for the sake of an exchange of knowledge but also in order that they mutually respect the frontiers of their fields. The positivist is responsible for low standard of work in modern Science in his attempt to absorb all the knowable within the potential of the empirico–metric method. Like the pseudo - aristotelian Caesare Cremonini (?- 1631), who would not look through Galileo's telescope, the modern positivist generally will not bother to investigate the claims of Thomistic Cosmology on the grounds that it is Thomistic and therefore wrong.

These men attempt to stretch the empirico-metric method of the Sciences so that it can render the Cosmos itself intelligible in its most fundamental meaning. The words of Plato (347 BC) regarding certain Astronomers who attempted to make a Philosophy out of astronomy aptly apply to the positivists of our time, "I should say that those who elevate astronomy into Philosophy appear to me to make us look downwards and not upwards."

There is no one method for all Science. The Sciences Philosophical, mathematical and experimental are distinguished by their objects and their methods. Their very vocabularies are different. Each Science is good within its own limits, but no Science has unlimited scope. No Science can monopolize the real; being is too complex. The Science with more universal object as Cosmology cannot be explored by such a Science as modern Physics which has a less universal object, namely, the study of the secondary principles of mobility. This will be made manifest as the real meaning of Cosmology is grasped in studying its demonstrations.

In conclusion, therefore, we have noted;

Cosmology is the Science of the first causes and principles of mobile being.

Its *subject* matter is the Pre-Scientific experiential facts of the mobile beings of the Cosmos.

Its *object* is the four causes of mobile being, the material and formal causes, the efficient and final causes.

Its *method* is both deductive and inductive in the first degree of abstraction: the abstraction of common sensible matter in its first principles. Its method necessarily depends upon sensible experience, and contingently and relatively upon the experimental Sciences. The fallacy of the uniform method of the positivists must be guarded against in this study.

1.2.9 Utility of Cosmology

The study of facts and techniques in an experimental Science is important in the education of a man for work in that field. But, the Catholic system of higher education does not stop here; rather, it aims at the higher education of the whole man. Man hungers to know more than the fact and the how of things, he naturally seeks beyond these for the basic meaning of the Universe in which he lives.

Cosmology is important because its object is to answer fundamental questions about the Universe. Whereas the experimental Sciences give only a fragmentary picture of the Universe, Cosmology goes to the heart of matter in quest of the ultimate meaning of the beauty and order of the Universe itself. It investigates the initial concepts of the experimental Sciences, such as the meaning of mobile being, space, time, quantity, quality and cosmic order.

It is unfortunate that the principal occupation of our age is with experimental Science and its applications in modern life. The true meaning of nature, the Universe in which we live, has become lost to many as they are enrapt in the wonder of man's technological conquest over nature. Human survival, national security, and personal destiny are measured in terms of machines, the instruments of man's genius. Modern man often considers himself the master of his own destiny through experimental Science and his progress is calculated in terms of atomic energy. Our age is certainly the age of "the know how" of technology. But, it is not an age of wisdom. It will remain so as long as man refuses to face the nature of things as they are in their being, the reality of the Universe in its fundamental principles.

A true Philosophy of nature is necessary for a true Philosophy of theism, and a true Philosophy of theism is essential for the educated man in his search for peace of soul and peace in society. By the light of natural reason the human mind ascends from the visible things of this World to the invisible things of God. The extremes to which man is led by false cosmologies is exemplified in Alfred Whitehead's (1861–1947) concept of God as "the harmony of epochal occasions," or by Professor Alexander's idea of God as "a variable quality," and Karl Marx's (1818–1883) deification of "auto dynamic matter."

The Christian student must be equipped rationally to answer these contemporary errors, and this necessity demands that he know principles of the perennial Philosophy. The value of Cosmology is, therefore, to be found in the contemplation of the first principles of the Universe rather than in the productions of applied Science. It is a form of wisdom in that it concerns first principles, but it is inferior to the wisdom of metaphysics and the supernatural wisdom of revealed truth, although it is joined to these in the unity of true.

1.2.10 Division of Cosmology

We have said that the object of Cosmology is the four causes of mobile being. We divide Cosmology into two parts, accordingly, as these causes may be divided into two classes – namely, the internal and the external. In Part One we study the internal causes of mobile being, that which constitutes its essence: the material cause, prime matter; and the formal cause, substantial form. In Part Two we study the external causes of mobile being: the Supreme Efficient Cause, God, the Creator; and the Ultimate Final Cause, the Glory of God.

Part One plays an important role in our knowledge of the Cosmos. In section two we proceed to the synthesis of the foregoing study of mobile being in its predicamental accidents. We demonstrate that the theories of atomism, monism and dynamism do not explain what mobile being is. The doctrine of hylomorphism is shown to give a fundamental insight into the essence of mobile being.

Part Two is also subdivided into two sections. In Section one we are concerned with the origin of the Cosmos. Materialism and pantheism are rejected and creationism is demonstrated. In Section two we treat of the Ultimate Final Cause of the Cosmos, the Glory of God. The reality of the purposive finality of mobile beings is proved and the meaning of physical law is analyzed. The possibility of miracles is reconciled with the nature of physical law.

The course concludes with the definition of mobile being in its four causes. Posing problems and solutions of the Cosmology; later giving the reflective origin of the study of Cosmos. This division of Cosmology is made in the light of the object of this Science to give direction to the student in his study of complex material.

The development of the course through the use of the thesis-method is employed for the sake of clarity and order of thought. The ample use of induction throughout the work is sufficient to show that the procedure is not by sheer formalism, or formal logic applied to the Cosmos.

1.2.11 Importance of Cosmology

Philosophy has been described, in a somewhat grandiose fashion, as "man's ultimate interpretation of the Universe of knowable things." It is surely a matter of basic importance to the Philosopher to know all he can about the most obvious part of that Universe, that is to say, about the bodily World in which he lives, observes, and experiences; about the material Universe which furnishes him the first beginnings of all knowledge. And Philosophers from the earliest times, from the first Greek cosmogonists, and indeed from the first religion-Philosophers, from the earliest times, have recognized the importance, and even the necessity, of having some Philosophy of nature, that is, of having cosmological knowledge.

Before Aristotle (4 century B.C.) the Ionians, the Pythagoreans, the Eleatics, and other schools of Philosophers, worked out theories about the ultimate constitution of matter and the nature of the bodily World; at all events, they tried to do so, but they failed to get back to the truly ultimate roots of bodily reality. Aristotle succeeded where his predecessors failed. Maritain says that Aristotle's Philosophical Physics (or Cosmology) lays down the foundations and principles of every true Philosophy of nature, and even though the same author says that Aristotle's experimental Physics is "a magnificent intellectual construction totally ruined by mistakes of facts," we must not fail to give due recognition to the truth that Aristotle did undertake physical Science on the experimental side and, despite mistakes, developed it amazingly. Father Tilmann Pesch, S.J. (1836–1899), says of him that he made the fullest use of observation and experiment and did all that any man of his times could do, without the service of the special instruments and Scientific equipment which only later days have been made available.

St. Albert the Great (d. 1280) and his illustrious pupil, St. Thomas Aquinas (1225-1274), as well as Roger Bacon (1214-1292), elaborated the findings of Aristotle with such physical means as their times afforded. After Francis Bacon (1561–1626), Lord Verulam (d. 1626), the natural Sciences were developed with great rapidity. In our own day they engage the intense interest of so many able minds that they have to some extent, outstripped the development of Philosophy, which should keep pace with, and offer ultimate explanations of, their established findings. Physical Science offers to the Cosmologist an orderly field for his labors; it affords him endless items to explain, and it offers him continuously new checks, illustrations, and confirmations of his right conclusions. Yet modern physical Science has sometimes proved itself of self-sufficiency which impels the Scientist to turn too quickly into a Philosopher, and invites the proclamation of general theories upon the first apparent results of observation and experiment. And, since observation and experiment are continually confronting new facts, and often upsetting facts, the Scientist-Philosopher is frequently compelled to reverse himself and propound new and emended theories. Sane Cosmology must, therefore, move very slowly; it must make perfectly sure that Scientific conclusions are truly Scientific, and not merely scientistic, before it adopts them and applies them to its uses. Hence, Cosmology, while acknowledging its debt to physical Science, must recognize its own proper work of the Scientist, and so must steadily refuse to become excited with the temper of the tempo of the current age. It must never be stampeded into the adopting of theories which, however attractive, are not incontestably justified and proved by facts. Yet the importance of Cosmology is not lessened, but is rather emphasized, by this careful procedure. It is the Science of ultimate truth in the domain of bodily reality, and ultimate truth is not established swiftly or by popular acclaim. Its very deliberation and caution is a strong recommendation of Cosmology to the sound and scholarly mind. Following the eminent Cosmologist, Father H. Schaaf, S.J., we may mention the following points as indicative of the fundamental importance of Cosmology:

Cosmology is a most interesting study, and it answers our natural desire to know all that can be known about the Universe in which we live.

Cosmology is the Science of that bodily World which is the proximate object of the human mind; as such, this Science is of basic importance to students of all branches of Philosophy.

Cosmology brings a crowning perfection to the physical Sciences, which, without the ultimate interpretation of Philosophy, must ever be partial, piecemeal, and fragmentary.

Cosmology is of inestimable value to the student of theodicy of natural theology. It show, on the one hand, that God is not to be identified with bodily World, and, on the other hand, it indicates the existence and boundless perfections of God as manifested in the being, the order, the harmony, and the government of the material World.

Chapter 2

Wheness of Cosmology Historical Background: The Nature of the Universe

2.1 Greco Philosophical Cosmology

There is none of us who has not wondered how the Universe came into being. This World, with its flowers, rivers, rocks, sky stars, the sun and the moon, all did not come about by mere chance, we reason. All that we see around us, and all that we know of, must have become what it is today by some process. If we could understand this process, we would understand the nature of the Universe.

The earliest people that we have any records of had theories of the beginning and nature of things. They wove these ideas into their religion and the priests and religious men explained them to the young men, who in turn passed them on to their children. In the first book of the Bible, Genesis is one of these theories. Here, we are told that God created the World out of nothing in six days. He made light and darkness, the sun moon, and stars, the earth and the waters, and finally made all living things, including man. Then, when all was completed and man along with women was placed in a beautiful garden, God came to the World and walked in the garden, contented with his handiwork.

2.1.1 The Views of the Early Greek Philosophers

The earliest Philosophers, the Greeks, were greatly interested in this problem of the nature of the Universe. Indeed, it was the first problem they attacked. Just as children break open their toys to discover how they are made, so these Philosophers of the childhood of the human race sought to break apart the Universe in their minds, and to penetrate the mystery of the making of all things found in it. "What is the 'stuff' from which all things come?" they asked themselves. "How does it happen that there are many things in the Universe?"

THALES, who lived in Miletus in Ancient Greece (about 600 B.C.), was the first to propose a solution for this problem. He told his neighbors that water was the original "stuff." He saw water turning into a solid, ice, when it was frozen, and into air, steam, when heated. Therefore, he reasoned that everything, from the hardest rock to the lightest air, originally came from water and in the end returned to water.

A little later another citizen of Miletus, ANAXIMANDER, wrote that the original "stuff" of which everything in the Universe was made was not, as Thales had suggested, water, but was a living mass which filled all space. He called this mass "the infinite." In the beginning, he told his fellows, this mass, "the infinite," was whole, not broken into pieces. But, it contained "motion." This "motion" caused it to begin to move up and down, back and forth, and around, slowly pieces were broken off from the mass so that eventually all the things which we now have in the Universe came into being. As the motion continued, he believed, these innumerable pieces would be brought back together and the mass, the "infinite," would assume its original unbroken unity.

Anaximander wrote a very detailed account of how he believed the World, the sun, the stars, air, animals, fishes, and man developed out of this original mass.

A third resident of Miletus, ANAXIMANES, was not satisfied with the accounts which had been given by these two thinkers who had preceded him. He suggested that the original "stuff" of which all else in the Universe was made was air. He realized that men and animals breathe air and are able to live, and reasoned that the air turned into flesh, bone and blood. Therefore, he went on to reason that air could become wind, clouds, water, earth, and stone.

These three Philosophers of Miletus were interested in discovering the original "stuff" of which all else in the Universe was made. They were followed by a group of Philosophers who, although they were interested in the same problem, were more interested in finding out in what ways the many things in the Universe were related. These were the *Pythagoreans,* a group or school founded by *Pythagoras*.

PYTHAGORAS and the Pythagoreans were impressed by the fact that many things in the Universe were related in ways that could be stated by numbers. For example, the tone of a wire or piece of gut is related to its length in a manner that can be expressed in numbers. So, they reasoned, number must be this "stuff" for which Philosophers were looking. To them numbers became things, entities, and they taught that the whole Universe was built of numbers. They believed that since the harmonious octave reached over eight notes; eight was friendship. A point, they held, was one and a line two. And on they went to develop a most complicated system of numbers in their effort to show how everything was actually made of numbers.

All the Philosophers whom we have mentioned thus far took it for granted that things change. They saw change all about them and did not recognize it as a problem. Water changed into ice or into steam, air became wind, numbers became things, motion was in everything producing these changes. For them this fact just was; and why be concerned about it? But, as Philosophers continued to work with this problem of the nature of the Universe, they began to recognize that change was itself a problem. What is it? How does it come about? Is there really change, or do we just imagine that things change? These questions began to rear their heads and demand an answer. This fact of change so impressed HERACLITUS, a son of a noble family of Ephesus that he concluded that fire was the original "stuff" of which all else in the Universe was made. Fire, he believed, was forever changing, never still, never the same. Since, everything is constantly changing since change is the fundamental characteristic of the Universe, the forever-changing fire must be the material of the Universe. "You could not" he wrote, "step twice into the same river, for other and yet other waters are ever flowing on." There is nothing permanent, stable. Change is all that is.

We may think that we see things that do not change, Heraclitus taught, but we are fooled. If we could really see what is happening, if we had eyes powerful enough to see exactly what is happening, we would realize that even the most stable thing in the Universe is actually changing all the time. The Universe, then, is ruled by "strife." The moment a thing is made; strife begins to break it up. All things are changing all the time, and there is nothing permanent.

While Heraclitus was preaching the doctrine that change is the essence of all things, there were Greek Philosophers living in Elea who taught that change is impossible. Nothing, they said, can possibly change. If we think we see change, we are fooled; for it cannot be. XENOPHANES, the earliest of these Eleatics, believed that the Universe was a solid mass which was forever unchangeable, unmovable. The parts might change, but the whole could never change. PARMENIDES, another member of this school at Elea, taught that all change is inconceivable. If there were such a thing as change, he reasoned, something would have to come from nothing, and that was impossible. What we see with our eyes is not true but an illusion. The Universe is unchangeable and unmovable. ZENO, a third member of this school, sought to prove that anyone who attempted to prove the existence of change would contradict himself.

These arguments of Heraclitus and of the Eleatics were so interesting to Philosophers that some set about to see if the positions of both sides could be reconciled in some way. They felt that this "riddle of permanence and change" had to be solved, and they turned their attention to the task.

EMPEDOCLES agreed with the Eleatics when he said that in the strict sense there can be no change, but he also agreed with Heraclitus in holding that there is "mingling and separation." The Universe, said he, is composed of four elements or "roots of things" earth, air, fire, and water. There are millions and millions of very tiny particles of each element. These combine in various ways to form the many things in the Universe. As things decay or change, the elements separate. Then they may come together or mingle again in another thing. The elements never change. They are permanent. Thus, actually there is no change, but merely a mingling and separating is caused, he believed, by Love and Hate. Love brings the elements together to form things. Hate breaks them apart.

EMPEDOCLES' solution of the problem of change and permanence interested Anaxagoras but did not satisfy him. After much study, he reached the conclusion that there must be more than four elements. Indeed, he became convinced that there were untold millions of elements or substances. Each of these was in untold millions of tiny pieces. Flesh was a result of millions of flesh elements coming together in one place. Bone was the result of millions of bone elements combining. So with everything in the Universe. Numbers of elements come together and the thing is formed. No element can be changed into another. Therefore, there is in reality no change. But, as these elements combine, separate, and recombine, we have change. These elements combine and separate, not because of anything in them, but because of the rotation of the heavenly bodies. As a whirling motion was first produced in the original mass of elements lying quiet, they began to combine and the many things in the Universe were formed.

All of this thinking paved the way for another important group of early Greek thinkers, the ATOMISTS. The most noted members of this group were LEUCIPPUS and DEMOCRITUS. These men agreed with their predecessors that change was a result of the mingling and separating of tiny units. But, they disagreed with them as to the nature of these elements. All the thinkers before the Atomists had taught that the elements differed in quality. There were flesh elements, bone elements, hair elements, and so on. The flesh elements were different from the bone or hair elements. The Atomists taught that all units, or atoms, are alike as far as quality is concerned. Some have hooks, others eyes, and still others grooves, humps, or depressions. As these atoms unite in different ways and in different numbers, things are formed. Each atom has motion inside it, so that it moves about of its own accord and attaches itself to other atoms.

Change, then, for the Atomists was a matter of the mingling and separating of atoms. The atoms never changed, but were eternal, minutely small, and all alike. Real changes of an atom was impossible. The only change possible was as atoms grouped themselves together to form a thing or separated from each other.

Thus, the early Greeks, working with the problem of the nature of the Universe for about 250 years, reached the conclusion that everything in the Universe was composed by the uniting in various ways and in various numbers of tiny atoms which were all alike.

Plato's Theory of the Universe

None of these early theories satisfied Plato, one of the greatest thinkers of all times. For Plato, the World which we see, touch and experience through our other Sciences is not real, but is a copy World. In it we find things changing, coming and going, and in great abundance. It is a World of many mistakes, deformities, evils. It exists and we experience it every day. But, it is not real.

There is, however, a real World in which are to be found the true things of which all that we experience are mere copies. He called this the World of "ideas." Here is to be found the ideal tree of which all trees which we see are copies, the ideal house, and ideas of all other objects in the Universe. These are perfect, do not change in any way, never fade or die, but remain forever.

These "ideas" or "forms" (Plato uses both words to describe them) were never created but have existed from the very beginning in just the perfect state in which they will always exist. They are independent of all things, and are not influenced by the changes which take place in the World which we experience through our senses. These objects which we experience are reflections of these "eternal patterns."

All "ideas" are arranged in the "ideal World" in order; the "highest idea," the idea of perfect goodness, being at the top.

But, there is another principle in the Universe, that of "matter." This is all that "ideas" are not. It may be thought of as the raw material upon which the "ideas" are impressed. Let us think, for example, of the work of a sculptor. He has an idea of a figure which he wishes to reproduce in marble, let us say. Now, this idea is independent of all the marble in the Universe. But, the marble is necessary for its realization so that others may experience it through their senses. Therefore, the sculptor takes a slab of marble and creates a statue. The marble, as raw material, has the idea impressed upon it. The sculptor may make many statues without affecting his idea in the least.

In this way Plato thought that the World was created. Nature, all that we experience through our senses, owes its existence to the influence of the World of ideas upon matter. It is not the "real" World, but an impression of the "real" World upon matter. Thus, all the mistakes, all the changes, all the imperfections of the World of our senses are due to matter and not due to the ideas.

In one of Plato's famous Dialogues, the *Timaeus*, he tells us how the World of our senses was created. There was an "architect," the "Demiurge," who brought the ideal World and matter together just as a sculptor might bring his idea and marble together to produce a statue. This "Demiurge" had perfect ideas of everything, and he had a great mass of matter. Plato never tells us where either the "Demiurge," ideas, or matter came from originally. There were just there when things began. As the "Demiurge" brought an idea in touch with some matter, a thing was created. Indeed, a great many things were created from one idea. There is one perfect idea of an oak tree, but there are millions of oak trees. So with everything else in the Universe, it is a combination of a perfect idea and matter. And the idea is not at all influenced by this. It remains perfect and unchanged forever.

Plato has been called an Idealist because he thought that the real World was this World of ideas. Some students of his Philosophy say that it would be truer to call him an "Idea-ist" since he was interested in ideas. But, whatever we choose to call him, -Idealist or Idea-ist,-we recognize that he believed the Universe to consist of a realm of perfect and unchanging ideas and matter. The World of ideas was, for him, the true, the real, World. That which we experience through our senses was, for him, a copy World, an "unreal World" in this sense. It was a World of objects produced by impressing a perfect idea upon matter. All of its imperfections came from the fact that it was impossible to impress the idea perfectly upon matter; matter is imperfect and thus distorts the idea to some extent, twists it out of shape.

Aristotle's Conception of the Universe

Democritus and the Atomists, as we have seen, explained the Universe in terms of moving identical atoms. Plato explained it in terms of perfect ideas which somehow were impressed upon matter. Aristotle, who stands with Plato among the World's greatest Philosophers, attempted to arrive at a theory of the Universe which would mediate between that of the Atomists and of Plato.

Aristotle was willing to admit that matter does exist. And as a pupil of Plato, he believed that ideas existed. But, he wanted to bring these together in a way that would be more satisfying than the solution suggested by Plato. His problem was, how can perfect, changeless, eternal ideas be impressed upon lifeless matter? And his answer was that ideas, or "forms" as he called them, are not outside of and above things, are not "transcendent," but are *in* things. He taught that form and matter are always and eternally together. Therefore, the World which we experience through our senses is not, as Plato taught, a mere copy of the real World, but *is the real World.* Here form and matter are one, and neither can be experienced separately. Only by thinking can we separate the two; actually we always find them together.

Let us take an acorn as an example. An acorn is a unity of form and matter. We recognize the form "acorn," which is characteristic of all acorns. Whenever we see an acorn, we discover this form. But, our example is a particular acorn. Never do we have the form "acorn" divorced from a particular acorn. But, in addition to form, our example has matter. The form "acorn" seeks to realize itself in matter, and the result is the acorn which we have. The more perfect the acorn, the more perfectly the form is realized.

But, the acorn may become an oak tree. Thus, this acorn which we hold in our hands is matter, and the form which it seeks to realize is the oak tree. As the acorn is planted and as it grows, it is striving to realize the form of the oak tree; it is seeking to become oak boards which are used to build tables, chairs, or other pieces of furniture. Here the oak tree is matter, and the particular piece of furniture is the form which the oak tree seeks to realize.

In every case, the acorn, the oak tree, the piece of furniture, we have matter and form. At every stage the object which exists is both the realization of a form and also matter for the realization of another form. Thus, forms never change, but are eternally the same. The form "acorn" is always the same and never becomes the form "oak tree." But, matter takes on different forms as it changes. First it took on the form of an acorn, then the form of an oak tree, and then the form of a piece of furniture. And the process goes on indefinitely as change takes place. Matter is always taking on, striving to realize, form.

Wherever we look in nature, in the Universe, Aristotle taught, we find both matter and form. For him there can be no matter divorced from form, nor can there be any form divorced from matter. And both matter and form are eternal, never being created or destroyed. Thus, the entire Universe can be explained, he believed, as the process in which matter constantly seeks to realize different forms, to become what it can become.

If we wish to understand the Universe, then, we may think of it in terms of a sculptor producing a statue. But, while in the case of Plato the sculptor is independent, free from his marble, in the case of Aristotle he is dependent on his marble. His idea of a perfect statue is actually in the marble, a form which the marble seeks to realize.

Therefore, Aristotle taught that every object in the Universe had four causes. The first corresponds to the idea of the statue which the artist has before he begins work, the form which is to be realized. This he called the "formal cause." Then there is the marble with which the artist has to work, the matter. This is the "material causes." The third cause is that by which statue is made, the tools employed to make the statue. This he called the "efficient cause" or "moving cause." The fourth cause is the purpose or end for which the statue is made, that for the sake of which the work is done. This he termed the "final cause."

For Aristotle, all these causes are operating in the thing as it develops changes, grows, becomes. We must not think of an artist separated from his marble, but rather of an artist as a part of his marble. A better illustration may be that of a man seeking to become, let us say, a doctor. He seeks to change himself into something else. His idea of "doctor" is the "formal cause;" his body with all its characteristics is the "material cause;" that which he does to change himself is the "efficient cause;" and the reason he makes this change from what he is originally to a doctor is the "final cause." Here the man is within that which is changed and he is what is created.

For Aristotle all motion is to be explained as the union of form and matter. When matter offers resistance to form we have deformities, mistakes, evils. However, matter is also a help to form in that it seeks to realize form, to become something.

It is clear from what we have already said that Aristotle's World is not a purely mechanical something. It is not a mere mass of units or atoms moving about and forming objects, as the Atomists taught. Rather, it is characterized by purposes which matter seeks to realize. There is striving in this Universe, a seeking to become. We call such a World "teleological," not a World of mere chance but one of purpose.

If the acorn seeks to become an oak tree and the oak tree seeks to become a piece of furniture, where does the process stop? Is everything seeking to become something else, and is there no end to the chain? Aristotle believed that there was an end. This he thought of as the first cause or the "unmoved mover." It is pure form without any matter. It does not cause anything else, but just is. It is not in matter and does not seek to impress itself upon matter. We cannot experience it, but we can think it.

Thus, at one extreme we may think of pure matter without any form, formless matter. And at the other extreme we may think of pure form, matterless form. But, we cannot experience either. The Universe, in which we experience the World of chairs, stars, earth, men, and all other things, is a World in which matter and form are united. And each object is the realization of a form and is the matter for the realization of still another form. In this way Aristotle attempted to solve the problem of the Universe.

The Views of the Epicureans, Stoics, and Skeptics

With the coming of Epicurus and the *Epicureans,* many thinkers devoted their attention largely to the problem of how to live a good life. However, even these Philosophers recognized that one could not be good unless he understood the World in which he had to live this life. Thus, they struggled with the problem of the nature of the Universe.

Epicurus based his solution largely on the theory of Democritus and the Atomists which we have already studied. He taught that the real things in the Universe are bodies which we experience through the sense. These bodies are made up of small units or atoms which differ in size, weight, and shape. As they come together in various ways, the bodies which we see are formed. Then, as they separate, these bodies disappear and we experience them no longer.

The Universe, Epicurus taught, came to be by mere chance. Atoms have the power to swerve from a straight line. Thus, in the beginning, all atoms were falling straight down in space. Being able to swerve, some went one way and some another, deviating from the straight line. In this way all the bodies of the Universe have been formed and are being formed.

The atoms cannot be destroyed or divided into smaller units. They have existed just as they now are from the beginning and will continue to exist in the same way forever.

The *Stoics*, a school of Greek thinkers founded by Zeno during the fourth century before Christ, were as interested as were the Epicureans in the problem of the good life, or "ethics" as it is called. But, they too developed an explanation of the nature of the Universe which is important.

These Philosophers agreed with Aristotle that the Universe is composed of two principles: form or "force" and matter. Force moves and acts, while matter is acted upon. These two principles are not separated from each other, as Plato taught, but are united in every object. Further, both force and matter are, for the Stoics, bodies. The bodies which are force are very fine-grained, while those which are matter are coarse and formless. Thus, everything in the Universe is a body, is corporeal.

All the forces in the Universe form a force which is in everything, a sort of fire which is the active soul of the Universe. The Stoics thought of this World soul as fire because they believed that heat produced everything and moved everything. Heat, for them, is the giver of life. Consequently, fire is the basic principle of the Universe.

This fire, or World soul, is related to everything in the Universe just as the soul of a man is related to his body. Indeed, the World is merely the body of the World soul.

From the original fire, the Stoics taught, air, water, earth, and all else in the Universe arise. These four elements, fire, air, water, and earth (which were also the four elements of Empedocles), combine in many ways to form the things of the Universe. And through every object in the Universe the divine principle flows, making it alive.

The Stoics were neither willing, as were the Epicureans, to think of the Universe as something that just happened by chance, nor were they willing to go along with the Epicureans to the extent of holding that the Universe is purely mechanical. Their principle of force was alive, and the Universe which came into being was also alive. For them the Universe was a perfect sphere or ball floating in empty space, a ball held together and made alive by its soul.

From the time of Thales to that of the Stoics, thinkers had been busy attempting to account for the Universe, to explain how it was made, to develop a theory of the nature of things. Each one wove a different theory and offered evidence to prove that he was right.

This diversity of theories and explanations struck a group of Greek thinkers as proof of the fact that man is unable to know what the Universe is or how it came into being. This group is known as the *Skeptics*, and its founder was Pyrrho. Its members felt that all attempts to explain the nature of the Universe were futile, a waste of time, for, they argued, man cannot know the nature of things. All we see is the World around us. Our senses give conflicting evidence. Different men have different reports to make. We have no way of telling whose report is correct; whose is true to the real nature of the World. Therefore, the Skeptics were willing to give up the search, to say, "We do not know, and no man can know." They recommended that men be practical, accept what they experience through the senses, and follow custom. Their answer to the problem of the nature of the Universe was one of despair, and they abandoned all further attempts to work with the problem.

The Universe According to the Greco-Religious Thinkers

At about this time, toward the close of the pre-Christian era, men were turning to religious (people, attributes, beliefs, doctrines) and seeking comfort in them. They were confused, tired mentally, and lost among the many conflicting theories which had been developed in the past. The time was ripe, then, for merging the many religious doctrines and beliefs with one or more of the Greek philosophies which had come down to that day in a more or less garbled form.

PHILO, a Jew living in Alexandria in Egypt, was the leader of the attempt to merge Judaism, the religion of the ancient Jews, with Greek philosophies. For him there was God who was so pure and far above everything in this World that he could not possibly come into contact with it. Thus, to account for the Universe, Philo taught that there were many powers, or spirits, which radiated from God as light might radiate from a lamp. One of these powers which he called the "Logos," was the creator of the World. This Logos, he taught, worked with matter and out of it created everything in the Universe. In this way, God, through the Logos, created the Universe. Further, everything in the Universe is a copy of an idea in the mind of God. This reminds us of Plato's belief that the World which we experience through our senses is a copy of ideas in the ideal World. And, indeed, Philo was attempting here to reconcile Plato's Philosophy with the Jewish religion.

Other religious-minded thinkers attempted to do the same thing, reconciling their religious beliefs with Greek Philosophy. One of the most noted was PLOTINUS, who was born in Egypt in the third century of the Christian era and taught in Rome. His theory was very much like that of Philo. Out of pure necessity, from God flows being, or emanations, as a stream might flow from an inexhaustible source, or as light flows from the sun without affecting the sun. The further the light is from its source, the dimmer it becomes. At the far extreme is darkness or matter.

Between God and matter Plotinus taught that there existed mind, soul. The soul acts upon matter and the Universe is created. Matter, then, is the substance and soul is the form of all things.

In the thinking of all these men we see clearly the theories of Plato, Aristotle, and others. The World is, in each case, a combination of an idea or form and matter. As the two come together in different ways, different objects are created.

2.1.2 The Views of the Medieval Thinkers

The Position of the Early Christian Thinkers

This attempt to account for the Universe, which is a theater of change and imperfection, and at the same time teach that God is perfect and unchanging was continued by the Christians. Those men who sought to reconcile Christianity with Greek Philosophy were known as *Apologists*. They taught that the Universe contains traces of something different from pure matter and thus points to a God who is eternal, unchanging, and good. This God is the First Cause or everything in the Universe, the creator of the Universe. For them the "ideas" of Plato and the forms of Aristotle become God. God is the eternal pattern which never changes. He is the unity of all forms, all ideas. Through divine emanations he has created the World; and everything in the World, in so far as it is a part of God, strives to be more like God, to return to Him. The Creator fashioned the World from matter which He created out of nothing. The pattern of the World is in His mind.

One of the greatest thinkers among these early Christian Philosophers, one who worked out the theory of the Apologists most completely, was AUGUSTINE, who became Saint Augustine. God, he taught, created matter out of nothing and then created everything in the Universe. The forms which he impressed upon matter were in God's mind from the beginning of time, and even before, for God existed before there was any time. Indeed, God created time and space also. Thus, everything that is or ever shall be is a creation of God and must follow His laws and will. Here again we see the influence of the Greeks in the belief that the Universe is the result of the coming together of matter and form.

But, the Christian thinkers went further than the Greeks in that they attempted to account for the existence of matter. You will remember that the Greeks simply accepted matter as well as the ideas or forms as existing from the beginning. The Christians put the ideas or forms in God's mind and went on to say that God created matter out of nothing. After He had created matter, He had something upon which to impress ideas or forms.

Further, these Christian Philosophers taught that the ideas or forms, being in the mind of God, were divine. Therefore, insofar as things are ideas or forms impressed on matter, they seek God, try to return to Him. But, matter holds them back. Matter, which

God has created, is the principle which makes it necessary for things to struggle in their attempt to become divine.

Augustine lived during the fourth century of the Christian era. He saw the great Roman empire, which had been established by the Caesars, falling to pieces, and watched the barbarians from the north gradually moving down into the empire and even toward Rome. He lived near the beginning of the period in history known as the Dark Ages, a period when these ignorant, crude barbarians swarmed over the Roman Empire and destroyed the civilization which had been building since the early days of the Greeks.

The Position of the Medieval Christian Thinkers

After Augustine for centuries few men had time for thinking about the Universe and its nature. Philosophy was gradually neglected, and those who did endeavor to think merely repeated the philosophies of those who had gone before them, viz., Plato, Aristotle, the Epicureans, the Stoics, and others. Most of the books written during this period were "remarkable only for their meagerness of original thought." Indeed, by the time of the seventh century the cloud of ignorance had so settled over Western Europe that this century and the next, the eight, have been referred to as "perhaps the darkest period of our Western European civilization."

By the middle of the ninth century some men were beginning to think again. By this time the Christian Church was in complete control of Western Europe. It dominated everything, the state, men's lives, and all education and thought. Those who did attempt to think had to confine their thinking to the beliefs which the church accepted. Thus, all thinking was limited to church doctrines. In most cases men merely attempted to show that the beliefs of the church were true, reasonable.

So, when JOHN SCOTUS ERIGENA wrote during the ninth century, he tried to show that the orthodox theory of the creation of everything in the Universe was reasonable. He taught that God created the World out of nothing or "out of himself, the causeless first cause." Before God created the World, he had a complete pattern of the World in his mind. Then, as a light is radiated from its source so the World was radiated from God. Consequently, the Universe and God are one, but God is more that the Universe. God is in his creation and his creation is in him.

Since, God is one and is not divided, Erigena taught, so the Universe is a unity. We may see difference, many individual objects, but they are all one. They are all God. We call this belief "pantheism." This Universe is "an expression of the thought of God" and therefore cannot exist apart from him. Being God, everything in the Universe strives to return to the unity of God.

From Plato to Erigena Philosophers had been, as we have seen, explaining the Universe as the union of ideas or forms and matter. In every instance the idea or form is thought of as a real thing existing before it was impressed upon matter. Plato thought of ideas as existing before things and in an ideal World. Aristotle taught that forms existed in things but were distinct from matter. The Christians taught that ideas or forms existed in the mind of God and moulded matter into things of the Universe.

All these Philosophers have been called "realist" since they taught that ideas or forms are real things existing independently of whether or not they ever come in contact with matter. In each instance the idea or form could exist without matter.

But, there arose a thinker who dared to fling himself in the teeth of all this tradition and to declare that these ideas or forms, these "universals" as they were called, were mere names and had no reality. His name was ROSCELIN, or sometimes called Roscellinus. He taught that the only real things are the individual objects in the Universe. Each individual man exists, but the universal "mankind" does not exist at all. It is merely a name for a collection of men.

You can see easily that Roscelin and the great philosophic tradition were directly opposed to each other. The result was a long and bitter dispute between the Realists, or those who believed that universals were real, and the "Nominalists," who taught that universals were mere names and had no real existence. This dispute was very important since it was a fight over the question as to whether the things of nature, the objects of the Universe, are real or merely copies of real things. It was an attempt to answer the question: What is real, the World which we can experience with our senses or the World which we think with our minds?

ANSELM, the Archbishop of Canterbury during a good bit of the eleventh century was on the side of the Realists. He believed that these "reals," ideas or forms, existed independently of any individual object. Mankind, for him was a real thing which existed over and above any one man. He, along with PETER ABELARD, BERNARD of CHARTRES, and other members of the School of Chartres, taught that universals or general concepts were ideas or forms having a separate existence and, in some way, the things which mould matter into individual objects which we see and experience through our senses. They were all in the tradition of the Realists.

These Philosophers who attempted to reconcile the beliefs of the Christian Church and the ideas which had come down to them from the Greeks, the philosophies of Plato, Aristotle, and others, were known as "schoolmen," and the philosophies which they developed were in general called "Scholasticism." In every case the Philosopher was a loyal member of the Christian church and believed the doctrines of the church without serious question. But, most of them wanted to show that these doctrines were reasonable and could be justified by the mind of man.

The greatest of these Schoolmen, and the one who worked out the relationship between Christian beliefs and forms of Greek Philosophy, was THOMAS AQUINAS. Saint Thomas Aquinas, as he was later called, was born near Naples and lived during the thirteenth century. His great ambition was to show that the Universe was reasonable. But, he was one of the Realists, and endeavored to show that universals were real. These universals, he argued, exist in particular objects, in things, in such a way as to make them what they are. The real thing about a tree, for example, is not its bark, its leaves, its height, and the like. These are qualities in which each tree differs from other trees. That which makes a tree a tree is its "treeness," and this is a universal. This universal exists in each particular tree. But, agreeing with the Christian tradition, he held that all universals existed in the mind of God.

To explain the World which we experience through our senses, Saint Thomas followed Aristotle in introducing matter as that upon which universals work. Nature, for him, was a union of universals and matter. It is matter which makes one tree different from another. All trees contain the universal "treeness," but they differ, they are elms, oaks, spruces, tall, short, green, red, and the like, because of the different amounts of matter which each contains. All the Universe, then, is a result of the coming together of matter and universals, and the many things in the Universe differ in the amount of matter which they contain.

For Saint Thomas, God created the World out of nothing. He was the cause of both matter and the universals. Further, God is continually creating the World as he brings universals and matter together to produce new objects. Thus, all creation did not happen at one time, but creation is going on all the time and all about us.

The Schoolmen, as we have seen, were attempting to show that the beliefs of the church and the best thought of the Philosophers were in agreement. In this they opened the door to those who would take a different position, who would argue that the two were in no real harmony. As soon as men began to study Christian beliefs and the Philosophy of Aristotle, for example, and put them side by side, there were some who believed they saw contradictions. Thus, they felt forced to choose sides. In such instances most of the loyal Christians sided with the church. But, there were those who were not sure that the church was always right. Gradually they began to question the beliefs of the church and to look about for other material which might help them. In this way there arose a group of thinkers who accepted the beliefs of the church only if they could be justified by reason. Those beliefs which they could not justify they discarded as false. With the coming of these men the period known as Scholasticism began to fade and a new period to dawn.

JOHN DUNS SCOTUS, a monk of the order of Saint Francis, attempted to stem this tide of questioning and to maintain the doctrines and beliefs of the Church at all cost. He taught, along with Saint Thomas and others, that universals existed before things in God's mind, as forms or ideas in the divine mind. When things came into being, ideas or universals existed in them, making them what they are. Further, when things are not present, universals exist in our minds as concepts or ideas which apply to all things of the same kind, all trees, for example.

For Scotus the individual object, the tree which you see, is different from all other trees because of its "individuality," not because of the amount of matter which it contains, as St. Thomas had argued. Man, argued Scotus, is different from an animal because there have been added specific differences, humanity. Both man and animals have life. When humanity is added to life we have man. Now Socrates is a man, like all other men in many respects. He is alive and he is distinguished from animals in that he has humanity. But, Socrates is different from all other men. This difference is due, Scotus argued, to his individual character or individual difference. So, all things differ from all others because of their individuality. And everything in the Universe is a result of the union of form and matter. Matter is common to all things. God alone is pure spirit without matter, God is form not touched by matter. All else is both matter and form combined.

Although there was some opposition, the Realists were in command of Philosophy throughout a good bit of Scholasticism. Near the beginning of the Scholastic movement, Roscelin, as we have seen, questioned the theory that universals are real existences. Now, many years, later, there arose a concerted movement to deny the reality of universals. The leader of this movement was WILLIAM OF OCKHAM, an English thinker of the thirteenth century. William taught that particular objects and things were the only realities. This World which we see and experience is real. Ideas, concepts, universals are mere thoughts in the mind, abstractions which the mind makes. They have no other reality. It was this position which was called "Nominalism."

The Universe, for the Nominalists, is composed of individual objects, each a thing in itself. We see how these objects differ and in what ways they are alike, and can draw conclusions about them. But, these conclusions are mere ideas in the mind. Thus, there developed two great theories about the nature of the Universe. One, following the tradition which was begun by Plato and Aristotle, held that forms, ideas, universals, were real things existing either apart from objects or in them and in some way determining what they are. This tradition taught that the real things of the Universe are not the individual objects of our experience, but the universals, the forms which determine likenesses; the tree which you see is not real, but the universal "tree" of which all trees are copies is the real thing. The other theory of the nature of the Universe taught that the real things in the Universe are the individual objects which we experience, and that universals are mere thoughts in the mind.

The first tradition has been that in which religion has flourished. The second tradition is the basis for all modern Science.

MEISTER ECKHART, a German mystic of the thirteenth century, held that God is the home of eternal ideas just as the artist is the home of ideas which may later become works of art. The World which we experience, this World of creatures and things, is a copy of the ideas which are in God. This World God created out of nothing. He, of course, is in the realist tradition but with an emphasis upon mysticism (which is the belief that God is all and man can find salvation only as he loses himself in God).

When the Christian church became interested in making its beliefs reasonable, it turned to the Philosophy of Plato. Here the doctrine of a World of ideas distinct from the World of things fitted nicely into the Christian belief in a God who created the World out of nothing and remained distinct from the World. Ideas and matter were distinct in both Plato's Philosophy and in the doctrines of the Christian church. The great Schoolmen, who sought to make religion reasonable, made much use of Plato.

But, as we have seen, there were thinkers who were not satisfied. They leaned toward Aristotle in holding that the form of an object is in some way in the object and not distinct from it.

Matter and form are combined to form things which we experience. They did attempt to fit God into the picture, but were never wholly successful. Forms, they held, were in things and also in the mind of God. But, how could they be in both places? This they never could answer clearly.

Thus, there arose Philosophers who became interested in things and in their study. Some denied that the beliefs of the church could be made reasonable. They held that there were two kinds of truth, that of the church and that of Philosophy. One may deny the other, but we should believe both. We should accept the doctrine of the church by faith and the doctrines of Philosophy by reason. This was, of course, a denial of the attempt of the Schoolmen to reconcile the doctrines of the church and Philosophy.

As Aristotle became more prominent in the thinking of Schoolmen, heresies began to develop. Philosophers came forward to propose that ideas or forms were not existent, and that the only real things are objects, individuals. Thus, Nominalism grew out of an increasing interest in Aristotle, but came eventually to deny Aristotle's doctrine of forms. In this way Aristotle lead to the disintegration of Scholasticism and the growing concern of thinkers with the World of experience. The World was ready for an entirely new approach to the problem of the nature of the Universe.

2.1.3 The Views of the Modern Thinkers

But, the thinkers who tended toward a new approach moved slowly. After all, they were children of their times and the influence of the church was strong upon them. Thus, the early Philosophers of this movement exhibited a strange mixture of the old and the new.

NICHOLAS OF CUSA taught that the Universe is God divided into small bits. If we think of the Universe as a whole, all of it put together, we find that it is God. But, each part is a part of God and God is in each thing.

LUDOVICO VIVES, a Spaniard of this period the sixteenth century taught that we should stop trying to learn about the World by reading what others in the past had written and should go out and study nature, observe the World about us, and make experiments to discover how it is made. He was typical of those Philosophers who wanted to turn away from the theories of the past and study the Universe as it is experienced. In this way, they believed, man could learn the real nature of the Universe.

As Philosophers became more interested in the study of nature they sought to understand it and gain power over it. Of course, they did not have our modern instruments or our modern knowledge. They stood on the threshold of the modern World. Thus, they sought short cuts to these goals. The result was a form of magic; a belief that the secrets of the Universe could be understood if one had the right secret word to utter or the correct magical act to perform. Thus, there arose Alchemy, an attempt to make gold out of baser metals, Astrology, a belief that the movements of the stars determined man's life and all of nature, and many other strange doctrines.

PARACELSUS, for example, taught that man possessed two bodies and a soul. The visible body comes from the earth, the invisible body comes from the stars, and the soul comes from God. He believed that there were three basic substances: salt (the principle of all solids), mercury (the principle of all liquids), and sulphur (the combustible). Each of these elements is ruled by spirits. To control nature one must control these spirits. All nature is the home of strange spirits which must be handled by magic acts and words.

Other Philosophers followed in this line, seeking to account for the Universe as the home of many spirits, but, gradually there arose thinkers who threw off this mass of superstition and began to look at the World as a place where forces met and opposed each other. BERNARDINO TELESIO taught that the Universe is made up of matter and force. Matter is created by God and remains constant all the time. Heat is a force which expands matter, and cold is a force which contracts matter. Thus, all objects in the Universe are, for him, a result of either expansion or contraction of matter.

In time men were able to move beyond the strange magical theories of their predecessors and study nature as the result of moving bodies. As they did this, they saw how bodies moved in certain definite ways. This observation leads to the statement of certain laws of the Universe.

GALILEO GALILEI was influenced by the theories of Democritus and believed that all change in the Universe is due to the movement of parts or atoms. He developed his thinking along mathematical lines and attempted to show that the entire Universe was mathematical. His work, along with that of JOHANNES KEPLER, established the belief that the sun and not the earth is the center of the Universe. This is known as the Copernican or heliocentric theory of the Universe. With the coming of Sir ISAAC NEWTON, this theory was proved beyond the shadow of a doubt, so that today we recognize that the sun is the center of our Universe and the entire planets move about it in very definite ways.

GIORDANO BRUNO, writing in the spirit of the new age, conceived the Universe as composed of numerous uncaused and wholly imperishable parts which he called "monads." These parts unite to form bodies and things in various ways. Further, the Universe is the result of the union of form and matter, much as Aristotle had held. Change results from matter taking on new form. Particular objects therefore, may change. But, this is only change of parts; the whole, the Universe, remains constant.

TOMMASO CAMPANELLA, another early Philosopher of this new age, held that nature is a revelation of God. The World is the result of emanations from God. God produced angels, ideas, spirits, immortal human souls, space and bodies. Thus, the Universe is a result of God's creative activity.

The Universe According to the Philosophers of the Renaissance

FRANCIS BACON lived during the sixteenth and early part of the seventeenth centuries. Although he did not construct a theory of the Universe, as "trumpeter of his time" he laid the foundation for a modern theory. Bacon completely separated religion and Philosophy. He argued that the doctrines of religion could not be proved by thinking and that men should give up the attempt; that to try was a great waste of time and energy.

Having relegated the doctrines of religion to a realm all their own, Bacon set about to develop a method of thinking which he believed would give mankind true knowledge about his Universe. This method we speak of as "induction." By careful study of the likenesses and differences among things, man could discover the laws, causes, or "forms" of objects in the Universe. In this way he would come to understand the Universe.

For Bacon, nothing exists in the Universe, but individual bodies. These act according to fixed laws which, if understood, serve as the keys to unlock the mysteries of the Universe and the levers by which to control this Universe. In this Bacon had turned wholly in the direction of modern Science and put the ancients and the Schoolmen to his back. He was marching forward toward the World which we understand today, a World of things and laws. Although he did not offer a complete theory of the nature of the Universe, he pointed the way which others might take in developing such a theory.

With THOMAS HOBBES Philosophy had entered upon the modern era. Hobbes broke completely with the past, with Greek Philosophy and with the Schoolmen. Being a student of mathematics, Hobbes set about to think of the World in terms comparable to mathematics. As a result, his Philosophy is wholly materialistic-concerned with the material.

Hobbes assumes dogmatically, without trying to prove it, that the World is a World of bodies in motion. These bodies are in space and have certain characteristics or "accidents" such as motion, rest, color, hardness, and the like. Motion is the continuous giving up of one space by a body and the assuming of another. When one body affects another, it either generates an accident in the affected body or destroys an accident. For example, let us imagine a body at rest. Hobbes would say that this body had the accident of rest. Now, suppose another body so affects this one that it is no longer at rest, but is in motion. In this case the second body has destroyed the accident of rest and generated or created the accident of motion. This is what we call the law of cause and effect, one accident perishes and another is generated.

All objects are in motion, according to Hobbes. This motion was given to them by God at the creation. As bodies move about, they influence each other so that accidents are destroyed or created.

Everything in the Universe, even God, is a body (is corporeal) and is moving. Thus, with bodies and motion Hobbes conceives the entire Universe. This is why his Philosophy is spoken of as materialistic.

Descartes' Conception of the Universe

René Descartes was also a mathematician. His study of this subject and his respect for its certainty made him seek to build a Philosophy which would be as certain as mathematics. He decided very early in his career that everything in nature must be explained mechanically, without the aid of forms, ideas, universals. Thus, his whole Philosophy is machine-like, mechanistic.

At the base of everything is the Universe, of all bodies, is substance, he wrote. Substance is that which exists by itself and independently of anything else. There are, he believed, two kinds of substance, mind and body. These exist independently of each other, but both depend upon God who is the only absolute substance.

The substance that is body has the attribute of extension-that is, it has length, breadth, and thickness. This body substance expresses itself in many modes, many individual objects in the Universe. Therefore, everything n the Universe is a mode of the substance which is body. And each thing stems back to God, the absolute substance.

Further, in the Universe there is no empty space or vacuum. Bodies fill all space. And bodies can be divided infinitely, into smaller and smaller particles.

Everything that goes on in the Universe, according to Descartes, is in some way a modification of extension. Extension may be divided into an infinite number of articles which may be united into different forms of matter.

Motion causes bodies to pass from one place to another. Motion, then, is a mode of movable things. All that happens in the Universe is the transference of motion from one part of space to another. But, the motion in the Universe is constant. At the beginning God gave the World a certain definite amount of motion. Thus, motion remains the same in the Universe; it cannot be destroyed. If one object slows up, another must move faster.

Further, according to Descartes, all change in the World must take place according to laws. Indeed, all the laws of nature are, in the Philosophy of Descartes, laws of motion.

The Universe, then, is composed of bodies created by God and endowed with motion. These bodies move about according to fixed and purely mechanical laws. As we learn these laws, we can understand the Universe and come to control it. This is a purely mechanical theory of organic nature. It contains no forms or ideas, no universals.

Mind, is for Descartes also a substance. Its attribute is thinking, and it expresses itself in many modes. Although body and mind are both substance, and both stem from God, they are independent. To maintain this complete independence, Descartes gave himself the most difficult problem of showing how mind can influence body or body influence mind. His solution of this problem will be discussed when we come to the study of mind and matter.

The great merit of Descartes' Philosophy was, however, this extreme separation of body and mind. We may speak of his thought as emphasizing the "dualism" of mind and matter; that is, stressing the "two-fold" nature of the Universe. By making these two substances entirely independent, he left nature without having to worry about mind. Science could develop along purely mechanical lines without having to make room for purposes, goals, and other characteristics of mind or spirit. It could busy itself with the discovery of the laws by which all bodies act and move. Indeed, in this way modern Science was made possible.

This dualism of Descartes brought to the fore the problem of how we know anything about the material World. How can mind, which is absolutely distinct from matter, know a material World? How can we answer any of the questions about the nature of the Universe? ARNOLD GUELINCX, a successor of Descartes, teaches that God alone has knowledge of things, and all that we can know is ourselves. NICOLAS MALEBRANCHE, another thinker of the period following Descartes, agreed with Guelincx that we cannot know anything about the Universe. However, we do have ideas about the World, we think we see it, and experience it in many ways. And we act accordingly. But, all we have are ideas which God has put in us. "If God" he writes, "had destroyed the created World, and would continue to affect me as he now affects me, I should continue to see what I now see." Thus, the Universe which we experience is a Universe of ideas. Whether or not there is a material World "out there," we cannot know.

Consequently, by making a sharp distinction between the material and the mental, Descartes opened the door to complete skepticism as regards the existence of a Universe outside of the human mind. And many thinkers entered this door and denied the existence of such a World. If mind and matter are distinct, then neither can influence the other, and mind cannot know matter, the World of things.

Spinoza's Theory of the Universe

Descartes, as we have seen, taught that the Universe is made up of two kinds of substance, mind and body. This dualism did not satisfy Benedict Spinoza. Spinoza taught that there is only one substance, one basic "stuff" which constitutes the entire Universes. This he called God. For Spinoza, everything in the Universe is God, and all the individual things are actually one great whole.

We may think of the basic substance as, for example, a great metal shield, with different designs on each side. If we look at it from one side we see a definite design, but if we look at it from the other side we see a wholly different design. So with substance. If it is seen in one way it is body. If seen from another position it is mind. Spinoza called the one extension and the other mind. Thus, every object in the Universe, star, tree, man, animal, water, wind, stone, is a part of God, is God. Every object is also both extension and mind. There is no body without mind and no mind without body.

Substance, the underlying "stuff" of the Universe, is absolutely independent of everything, for it is everything. It is infinite, self-caused, and self-determined. It has no limits, was made by itself, and is determined by nothing but itself. This God, or Nature, is the World. This unifying conception is known as "pantheism." So thorough is Spinoza in holding this position that he has been referred to as "God-intoxicated."

This substance, God, expresses itself in an infinite number of attributes, but man can grasp only two, extension and thought. God, or Nature, is both body and mind. Further, these attributes are absolutely independent of each other. Body does not affect mind nor does mind affect body. But, both are manifestations of one and the same universals reality, God.

These attributes appear to man in specific ways or "modes." There are many bodies and many ideas. The particular body, a tree, is a mode of extension which is an attribute of God. My particular thought at this moment is a mode of mind which is an attribute of God.

All the bodies in the Universe and all the ideas grouped together form a totality which is God or substance. This constitutes the "face of the whole Universe." The individual objects or ideas may change, but the whole, the "face of the whole Universe," does not change.

Further, all the bodies in the Universe form a chain of causes. The tree you see was caused by something else, which in turn was caused by something else, and so on. Thus, this particular tree owes its existences to some other physical object. It is not necessary that God created this tree; but, having it present, he is the underlying substance of it. If, for example, we have a triangle, we know immediately that certain things must be true of it. It has certain properties, and all triangles will have these properties. However, we cannot tell from the concept of a triangle the number, size, and shape of different triangles. In the same way, from substance we can state the properties of bodies, but we cannot state the properties of the different objects in the Universe.

For Spinoza, then, the entire Universe is one substance, which he called God or Nature. This substance has at least two attributes - extension and mind. And there are many modes of each attribute. Thus, God is the Universe and the Universe is God. But, bodies are independent of mind and mind is independent of body. However, when something happens in body, it also happens in mind. This is called "psycho-physical parallelism;" that is, body and mind are always parallel, for they are two aspects of one and the same substance.

The Positions of Locke, Berkeley, and Hume

John Locke, admirer of Descartes but a thinker, who gave to the modern World a new interpretation of man, began his thinking with the question: How does man know? His conclusion, after a long and painstaking investigation, was that all knowledge comes from sense impressions. This point of view made it necessary for him to account for the Universe as the source of these impressions.

Is there a real World which corresponds to our ideas? If there is such a World, how can we, having only ideas prove its existence? Locke's answer was to the effect that there is such a World. Our senses, he said, tell us of this World. We do experience this World and are justified in saying that it exists. Though we may not be able to say much about the source of our sensations, we are able to say that the sensations are caused. Thus, the real World is the cause of our sensations. This much we can say. For example, we have an idea of white. This idea is not born in us, but is caused. From this we can reason that the World contains something which causes in us an idea of white. However, even of this we cannot be absolutely certain. Our knowledge of this World is probable. We can be more certain of the existence in the Universe of ourselves and of God.

But, all else is only probable. Therefore, Locke argued, we can never have a perfect natural Science.

At this point Locke follows fairly closely the position of Descartes, which we have outlined. The World, he holds, is composed of substances. These are the bases, the supports, of all qualities. We experience, for example, white. This quality just does not float around in space, but is the whiteness of something. This something is a substance.

Further, there are two kinds of substance, bodies and souls. Bodies have the attributes of extension, solidity, and impenetrability. They fill space, are solid and cannot be penetrated. Souls are spiritual substances, are immaterial.

Souls, minds and bodies act upon each other. The body can cause happenings in the soul, and what happens to the soul may affect the body. For example, bodies act upon the mind so that we have experiences of color, sound, touch, and the like. Despite his belief in interaction, Locke's theory of the Universe is dualistic. There are minds and there are bodies. While both are substances, they are different kinds of substances.

Here it is evident that, with some changes, Locke follows in the footsteps of Descartes in holding that bodies and mind are two kind of substances, or bearers of qualities. The Universe is made up of these substances. However, we can know only the ideas which these substances produce in us through sensations.

If, however, the basis of knowledge is sensation and reflection upon sensations, how can we know that a World of bodies distinct from our ideas of bodies exists? George Berkeley asked this question. John Locke had taught that, actually, all we can know are our ideas, and had presupposed a World which causes our sensations. But, Berkeley recognized immediately that he could not prove the existence of such a World on the basis of his Philosophy. Further, Berkeley, being a deeply religious man and seeing so much atheism or disbelief in God in the World, was convinced that atheism would be abolished if one could disprove belief in matter.

Consequently, Berkeley carried Locke's Philosophy to its logical conclusion as he saw it, and taught that there can be no Universe of material objects. All we can prove, he argued, is that we have ideas.

But, what about the source of these ideas? Do we create our own ideas? Berkeley answered, "No." The cause of sensations, and thus the cause of all ideas, is God. We cannot perceive God but can perceive the effects of his work, ideas.

Berkeley held consistently, as he believed, to the position that nothing in the Universe existed unless it was perceived. I am sitting in my room. I look about and see chairs, a table, books, and other objects. These are not real in the sense that they are material objects. They are ideas in my mind. But, if I leave the room, do these objects vanish? Do I carry them out of the room in my mind? Berkeley taught that they might still exist in some other mind. If other people are in the room, they may exist in their minds. If there are no other people in the room, they may still exist in the mind of God. But, all the time, they are ideas and not material objects.

The material Universe, which Descartes, Spinoza, and Locke had taught existed, was denied by Berkeley. For him, all that exists are ideas in the mind. If they are not in my mind, they may be in your mind or in God's mind. Of course, they seem to be material, but actually they are not. Berkeley was simply following the ideas of Locke to their logical conclusion, to a denial of the existence of a material Universe.

David Hume, a Scot of the eighteenth century, felt that Berkeley had not gone far enough. Not only must we abandon the idea of substance, he taught, but we must also abandon the idea of a God in whose mind all ideas exist. Hume could find no good argument for the existence of God.

Then, all that we have is a succession of ideas. These are caused by impressions. Hume agreed with Berkeley that only those things exist which are perceived. My table exists only when it is perceived. I may perceive it, my friend may perceive it, or God may perceive it. Thus, "to be is to be perceived." However, we cannot prove that God exists. Therefore, if I am in a room alone and perceive a table, the table exists as I perceive it. When I leave the room, the table no longer exists.

There is, then, in Hume's view, no substance. All that we have is a succession, a stream of ideas, one following the other. We cannot prove the cause of theses ideas. It is foolish to say that there is a substance "out there" in space causing our ideas. No one can prove this. Whenever we look, we find ideas following each other-ideas of chairs, tables, people, trees, stars and the like. Thus, we have no evidence of the existence of a World of nature or of God.

Hume carried Locke's theory to its logical and final conclusion in skepticism. Locke had taught that we have ideas which are caused by an outer World. Hume admitted the existence of ideas, but showed that, if this is all we have, we are shut up in our own minds and cannot prove the existence of an outside World. All we can be sure of is a parade of individual ideas, one following the other. Their cause, their connection, even the place where they are parading is unknown. We have come in Hume to a dead-end street.

It is natural that man would not remain satisfied with the skepticism of Hume. THOMAS REID, another Scot, led the opposition. He taught that Hume had reached an impossible position. Common sense tells us that a real World exists as the cause of our sensations and ideas. We may speculate all we want, but we will not be contented to deny what common sense tells us. Therefore, he argues, those things which we perceive distinctly by our senses exist, and they exist as we perceive them. There is a World "out there" corresponding to our ideas. Tables, chairs, and the like do not exist independently to our ideas. Common sense tells us that this is so, and we cannot deny common sense.

German thought took a different road from that of English or Scotland. It was concerned with the then developing natural Sciences, but found itself believing in the values of Christian beliefs. Consequently, it sought to reconcile Science and these valuable elements in Christian speculation.

Leibnitz' Theory of the Universe

Gottfried Wilhelm Leibnitz, one of the leaders of German thought in the seventeenth century, became convinced after much careful study and investigation that the essential attribute of the bodies in the Universe is force. By force he meant "the tendency of the body to move or continue its motion." The entire Universe is, for him, built out of units of force, and all nature consists of an infinite number of such units. These units of force Leibnitz called "monads," or force-atoms. Each monad is eternal, it cannot be destroyed or changed. But, monads have different degrees of clearness. The most obscure, vague, cloudy monads form plants. Those less cloudy form animals. The monads which form man are still clearer. And the clearest of all monads is God. The Universe is composed of an infinite number of monads extending all the way from the most cloudy monad to God. There is no break in this series. At one extreme is inorganic matter, rocks and the like. And at the other extreme is God.

Each monad contains within itself the entire Universe. Thus, since the monad has no "windows," all that it becomes is contained within it from the beginning. Each monad realizes its nature with an inner necessity. Nothing can be in a monad but what has been there from the beginning.

The organic bodies, living beings, contain a "queen monad" or soul which is the guiding principle of all the monads which make up the body. No monad can influence another. God created monads in the beginning so that they operate together in harmony. When one monad does something, it does not influence another monad. But, because the other monad is so created, it acts as though the one has influenced it. Thus, all monads act together just as do the various parts of an organism.

Leibnitz' Universe, then is not mechanical, but is dynamic, alive. It is composed of an infinite number of monads of various degrees of clearness. Here we sense the old theory of Democritus, the atomistic theory. But, the atoms of Leibnitz are not all alike, nor are they pure mechanical units. They are units of force and differ in clearness. And God is the clearest monad.

By means of this theory, Leibnitz believed that he had reconciled the Science of his day with the values of the Christian doctrine. He had a Scientific Universe in which God was the supreme being or monad.

Kant's Conception of the Universe

German Philosophy reached its height in the work of Immanuel Kant, one of the great philosophic system builders of all times. His fundamental problem lay in the question, what is knowledge, and how is it possible? What can we really know, and how? His conclusion was that we can know only our experiences. We have sensations. We see a chair. Because our minds are such as they are, we receive this sensation in a definite way. But, we cannot know the cause of the sensation.

On this theory, we cannot know the Universe which exists outside of our thinking. Our minds receive sensations and shape them into ideas because they are what they are. What the World is without our minds, it is impossible for us to know.

But, by reason we can form an Idea of this World, this Universe. As we experience the World in our minds, we find that the World has no beginning in time that bodies in the World cannot be divided infinitely, that everything in the World takes place according to the laws of nature and that there is no absolutely necessary Being who causes the World to be. We must accept this theory of the World of experience because we cannot experience it otherwise.

However, Reason can construct a World of Ideas which has no beginning in time, in which bodies can be divided infinitely, in which there is freedom, and in which there is an absolutely necessary Being, God, who is the cause of everything. Although we cannot know such a Universe through experience, we can reason its existence and we can act as though it were real. Indeed, Kant believed that man must act as though this kind of a World existed if he would preserve his moral integrity. For, on the basis of such a World Kant reasoned to the existence of God, freedom, and immortality. Further, he showed that all goodness, all morality, was dependent upon acting as if this kind of a World existed. The Idea of this World, he held, is regulative; it directs man to certain goals. Believing in the existence of such a Universe, man strives to be good.

Thus, for Kant, there are two Universes: one of experience, the "phenomenal" World, and one of reason, the "noumenal" World. The one is Scientific, the other is practical.

Kant taught that the fundamental principle of the practical World is a moral law which may be stated: "Always act so that you can will the maxim or determining principle of your action to become universal law; act so that you can will that everybody shall follow the principle of your action." This he called the "categorical imperative."

If one is to act so that the principle of his action shall become a law for all men, he must be free to act in this way. Therefore, Kant placed freedom at the center of his practical World. We shall discuss Kant's view of the practical World more fully in our chapter on "What is Good and What is Evil?"

2.1.4 The Views of the Contemporary Modern Thinkers

Fichte, Schelling and Hegel

Johann Gottlieb Fichte took this principle of freedom and made it fundamental to his whole Philosophical position. He took the stand that the self, the "ego," is a free, self-determining activity. The starting-point of Fichte's thinking is this ego, or creative, free principle. It is God, and is the creator of all that is. It creates each individual person, you and me and all the individuals in the Universe. It also creates the entire World of things. But, we and all things are not matter, material. There is no material in the sense of lifeless mater such as the older Philosophical taught. Everything in the Universe is spirit. The tree and your mind are both the universal, absolute ego and God. Thus, the real World is a World of mind or spirit and not a World of dead matter. Everything is the ego, God. But, the ego creates a limit to itself so that it may contend against this limit and grow to perfection. Thus, the World of objects, the so-called "material" World, is produced by the ego to furnish an arena in which it may exercise its freedom.

Freedom would mean nothing if there were not something hindering the exercise of freedom. Therefore, the eternal ego, God, has created the World, the "non-ego," as a limit to itself, a World of opposition in which it can struggle, in which it can become conscious of itself. This is a World of law, a World in which things happen according to set rules.

My reason, your reason, our minds are also creations or parts of this universal ego. We do not create our World of things, but are creations of the same ego which has created this World. Since, the universal ego is the universal active reason, the same in all persons, we all see the World alike.

This point of view is called "Idealism." It is based upon the belief that there is no matter in the Universe, but everything is mind or spirit, idea. Descartes, Locke, and even Kant had taught that there are two principles in the Universe, mind and matter. Fichte denied this recognition of two principles. He eliminated matter, and held that everything in the Universe is mind or spirit. The World only seems to be material. If we understand aright, we shall realize that even this is spirit. The Universe is mind, spirit, ego, God. Thus, though the Universe is a reality outside of individual personal minds, it is not made of a different material; it is not a World of dead things. But, it is "the revelation in human consciousness of the absolute principle." Nature is spirit, mind, and can be nothing else.

Thus, for Fichte, the moral law of Kant implies freedom, freedom implies deliverance from obstacles. There must be obstacles. Therefore, the universal self or ego created out of itself the World of sensible things to serve as its opponent. The World of experience is deduced from the moral law. Because this concept of Kant's influenced Fichte and many other thinkers, we speak of Kant as the father of modern Idealism.

Following in this same idealistic tradition was Friedrich Wilhelm Joseph Schelling, brilliant German Philosopher and student of religion. For him, as for Fichte, the ground of all the

Universe was one all-pervading World spirit or ego. However, he taught that this spirit as found in nature was not conscious of itself, and that it became fully self-conscious only in man.

Thus, there is a development in consciousness from nature through man. Nature and thinking are steps or stages in the development of the absolute mind. God is nature and God is mind. The one is God asleep while the other is God fully awake. But, in either, or throughout the whole development, God remains the same.

The entire Universe, including man, is a whole. The parts, the objects and individual are all parts of the whole. Thus, nature is alive, dynamic, and creative. Wherever one may stop to investigate, he will find spirit striving to realize itself fully, to become wholly self-conscious. Inorganic nature, the trees, rocks, earth, and the like, are of the same material as is the human mind. But, the former are blind, "unripe," unconscious.

This doctrine is pantheism. The Universe is conceived as a living, growing, moving system. God is the Universe and the Universe is God. In plants and rocks, God is blind, unconscious impulse. Move upward to man and God becomes conscious or seeing, he comes to knowledge of himself.

Georg Wilhelm Friedrich Hegel attempted to bring the Philosophical positions of Kant, Fichte, and Schelling into a whole which would be complete and satisfying. Thus, he taught that the entire Universe is an evolution of mind from nature to God.

Everywhere, in the natural World or in the mind of man, we find a process of unfolding. This he called the dialectical process or the principle of contradiction. Everything tends to pass over to its opposite. The seed tends to become a flower. However, nature does not stop with these contradictions, but strives to overcome them, to reconcile them in a whole or unity.

The entire Universe is a whole. Mind is everywhere. Within this whole there is development. And this development proceeds by the dialectical process. First we discover a thing, a "thesis." Then we discover its opposite or contradiction, an "antithesis."

These two are at last reconciled in a "synthesis" which becomes another "thesis" and the process starts again.

The entire Universe is a continuation of this process within the whole. Reality then is a process of evolution, a developing from a less clear to a more clear.

This process is the process of thought. Therefore, the Universe is thought and is subject to the laws of thought. As we think, so the Universe develops. But, this is all a process of thinking whole. Nature and man are one within this whole. The same processes which are found in man's mind are also found in nature. In nature this movement proceeds unconsciously. The seed grows into a plant and then into a flower. But, it is not conscious of its growth. In man the process becomes conscious and man knows that he is developing. This same process is discovered everywhere.

For Hegel, then, the Universe is a whole or totality. This whole is a thinking process and it develops as does all thought,- thesis, antithesis, and synthesis. This is Idealism worked out completely and to the last degree.

The Views of the Later German Philosophers

The idealistic Philosophy of Hegel certainly could not go unchallenged. It contradicted so much of common sense that it was inevitable that a thinker, so group of thinkers, would arise to present the other side of the picture. JOHANN FRIEDRICH HERBART was such a thinker. He took issue with every phrase of Hegel's Philosophy and sought to show that the idealistic Philosophy was full of impossible theories.

For Herbart the Universe consists of a great number of unchangeable principles or substances which he called "reals." Each real is a simple thing, is changeless, absolute, indivisible not extended in time or in space. In the World of reals there is no change, no growth; it is static.

Our bodies are aggregates of these reals, and each soul is a real. Each real strives to maintain itself against anything that would affect it. In this striving for self-preservation, each real will behave differently in the presence of different reals.

We relate reals together into aggregates and thus create the Universe which we experience. For example, I come into relationship with many reals and bring them together into a red apple. Then, by bringing other reals into the situation and rejecting some which I had there first, the apple becomes a peeled apple. Thus, the real World is absolutely static. Nothing happens in it. All happenings are phenomena in consciousness. As consciousness arranges and rearranges reals; things appear, change and disappear.

The entire Universe then is, for Herbart, made up of these spaceless, timeless, units which never change, but which exert activity in preserving themselves against other reals. As we arrange and rearrange reals we produce the World of experience.

This theory of the Universe is known as "Realism," and its basic idea is that the Universe is real and is not a creation of mind. Although experiences must always be the appearance of something. There is a reality which causes the appearance. Kant had called this reality the "thing-in-itself." Hegel had argued that there is no such "thing." Herbart agreed with Kant and sought to describe this real cause of appearance.

ARTHUR SCHOPENHAUER attacked the problem from another angle. He agreed with Kant that the World of experience is a World of phenomena; but he disagreed with him in holding that we can become aware of the thing-in-itself. He noted that when man wants something he sets about to build or create it. I want a table, and I get boards, tools, nails, and build one. Or I work to make the money to buy one. From this, he argued that will is the cause of all things in the Universe. The thing-in-itself, for him, is will, the cause of everything. The Universe is a result of the will.

In organic and inorganic life the fact is the same. In a rock, will is blind, but it is the creative principle which brings the rock into being. As we move up to man, will becomes conscious. Man may direct his will by intelligence in getting what he wills. The Universes, then, is a result of will, a primal will which continues to work regardless of the coming or going of individuals.

RUDOLF HERMANN LOTZE sought to interpret Kant's thing-in-itself in terms of mind. He taught that the physical World is to be understood as purely mechanical, as a matter of physical and chemical laws. But, this is the World of perception. The cause of this World is comparable to soul or mind.

Thus, there are various degrees of reality. In the case of matter mental life is present but clouded. In man this mental life is conscious and clear. The Universe, then, is alive and is mind. Here again we encounter Idealism.

The work of Lotze and other Idealists made a profound impression on the thinking of their age. GUSTAV THEODOR FECHNER conceived the Universe as similar to human individuals. The material World is the body of the Universe. But, this body has a soul or a mental life. This mental life is to be found in descending degrees in animals, plants, and lastly in organic matter. God is the soul of the Universe, just as the human body has a soul. FRIEDRICH PAULSEN and WILHELM WUNDT followed in the same tradition. Wundt taught that the external World is "the outer husk behind which lies concealed a spiritual creation, a striving and feeling reality resembling that which we experience in ourselves."

By admitting the existence of a material World one meets they met the objections of those who felt that the Idealists had denied common sense. But, by holding that mind or spirit is the creative spirit in this World, that the World is alive, they believed that they had conserved the values of idealism. Their philosophies were attempts to meet the demands of the then growing natural Sciences while at the same time to escape the crass materialism which threatened Philosophy as Science became stronger. They believed that the values of mind, spirit, or soul should not be covered up and lost completely in the landslide of modern Science.

The Positions of John Stuart Mill and Herbert Spencer

John Stuart Mill taught that actually our ideas are all that we can know. We find these ideas following each other in consistent ways and so often that we can be reasonably sure that they will continue to do so. For example, the idea of being burned always follows the idea of sticking one's hand into fire.

Mill holds that law and order reign in the Universe and that there are invariable sequences of events upon which we can depend. Further, he teaches that the law of cause and effect is universal. We find a certain set of ideas being followed in every case by the same idea. This leads us to recognize that the effect is caused by the set of preceding ideas.

But, as is evident, up to this point Mill is discussing phenomena, experiences, ideas. What of the cause of these? Is there an external Universe? Mill believes that there is such a Universe which is the cause of our sensations. I see a white paper in a room. Then I leave the room and remember that the paper was experienced under certain conditions. I return to the room and again experience the paper. After I have done this several times with the same results, the paper is always experienced upon my return to the room. I generalize that the paper is there in the external World and causes my experience. I form the notion of something permanent, persisting. Thus, "the so-called external World is simply the possibility that certain sensations will recur in the same order in which they have occurred."

It is evident that Mill, although he thinks largely in the Idealistic tradition, believes that there is a cause of our sensations, experiences, a "thing-in-itself." There is a Universe distinct from our sensations and experiences, the cause of ideas which we have.

But, we cannot know with absolute certainty anything about this World. From our experiences of it, we can be reasonably certain about some things in it, and not so sure about others. However, all that we know about it is based on experience, and no one has had every possible experience so as to be able to make a generalization which will be without exception. There is still the possibility that some exception, some new experience, will arise to prove the generalization applicable only to certain sets of conditions and not to others.

Herbert Spencer is the great Philosopher of evolution. He sought to develop a philosophic theory based on the findings of Darwin and other biologists; build a system of thought which would embody the important ideas of the doctrine of evolution.

He began his Philosophy with the recognition that phenomena, things as presented to us, are all that we can know. The cause of these phenomena is unknowable. But, there is a cause and Absolute Being behind all phenomena. Of course, we do make judgments about it. We conceive it as a force or power causing all that we know. Further, we think of it as both mental and physical. It is the cause of our thoughts and of the Universe. But, all these ideas are mere symbols, ways which we have invented of thinking of the Absolute. Actually we can know nothing about it. It is the Unknowable. All that we can know are the inner and outer expressions of the Absolute.

And these expressions obey the law of evolution. we see them becoming groups and these groups organizing into wholes. As the groups are organized, various forms of life evolve. The human individual is a result of the formation of groups of atoms into hands, arms, heart, lungs, feet, and the like, and the organization of all these into a body in which each part does its duty as part of the whole body. The legs walk, the hands grasp, the heart beats, etc.

Thus, Spencer believes in the existence of a World external to our consciousness. This World we infer because it is impossible for us to do otherwise because we have impressions, an external World. But, the impressions are not pictures, copies of the external World. As far as we can know, they may be as unlike the external World as letters of a word are unlike the idea which the word means. "H-o-r-s-e" - the letters themselves do no suggest the idea of a horse which the whole word calls before us. Likewise, our impressions and the actual external World may be wholly unlike one another. All that we can say with certainty, Spencer believes, is that there is something beyond consciousness which is the cause of our impressions, the Unknowable, the Absolute.

Josiah Royce, William James, and John Dewey

Josiah Royce, leader of the Idealistic school of thought in the United States, began his thinking from the nature of man. We are conscious beings and organize our experiences into wholes or a system. Likewise, he teaches, the Universe is a conscious Being, a whole. My thinking, your thinking, the thinking of everyone is part of the whole thinking Universe.

I have an idea of a table. I do not create this idea or the table. The table is there. But, it is not matter. Rather, the cause of my idea of a table is the idea of a table in the mind of the Absolute. It is, therefore, an idea which causes my idea, but it is God's idea. This Universe is a self-conscious organism idealized. It is all the ideas of all mankind and the causes of these ideas. The outer World is mental just as is the inner World of my experience.

These thinkers, the Idealists, have attempted to interpret the Universe in terms of the thinking individual in order to conserve the values of spiritual life. They have relegated Science to a secondary or lower position, but have taken it into account. For them, the laws of Science are actually the laws of thinking. But, the real World is not to be limited to the unchanging laws of material things. Above these laws are the laws of man's spirit. By this belief, they escape strict determinism and make possible freedom and morality. If man is subject to the inevitable laws of Science, he cannot be free and it is futile to hold him to account for his actions. He cannot be blamed. But, freedom and moral responsibility are too valuable to be lost in this way. Consequently, the Idealists hold on to them by arguing, that the World is actually spiritual rather than physical. Modern Science seems to them to destroy all that makes human life human.

Recent Philosophy is characterized by this attempt to take account of the whole realm of modern Science with its laws and consistencies and at the same time preserve those things which men have found of value. The Idealists lay emphasis upon these values and think of a Universe in which they are dominant.

William James, one of the first Pragmatists, found that a "block-Universe" in which everything was governed by the laws of Science was not satisfying. He wrote, "If everything, men included, is the mere effect of the primitive nebula or the infinite substance, what becomes of moral responsibility, freedom of action, individual effort, and aspirations?" he believed that the test of any theory of belief should be its practical consequences. This is the pragmatic test. And he was certain that only a theory of the Universe which took into account moral responsibility, freedom of action, and the like, and made room for them, would have consequences that were good.

The real World, for him, was the World of human experience. Here we find Science and human values all included. Beyond this he believed it impossible for a thinker to go. Although he did not doubt the existence of a World outside of experience, a World that caused experiences, he believed that we could not experience it and therefore could know nothing about it.

John Dewey, one of the leaders of present-day Pragmatism, held that the Universe is a changing, growing, developing thing. He concentrates his attention upon experience, which he finds is ever becoming, changing, being enriched. The Philosopher, he argues, must cease to spend his time with questions of beginnings, of what lies outside of experiences, of a World "out there." It makes no difference for us whether or not there is such a World. For us it is the experiences which we have that are the important things, and the explanation of how they come, grow, change and influence other experiences. The Universe of our experience is uncertain, doubtful, full of surprises, but is also characterized by consistencies upon which we can depend. This is the only World in which Dewey was interested.

The Views of Henri Bergson and George Santayana

Henri Bergson, who was the leader of another attempt to conserve values in a World of Science, taught that a Universe as described by Science would not be adequate. It leaves out too much. To know the Universe in its fullness, one must live in it and apprehend it by "intuition." A man cannot know a river by merely sitting on its banks; he must jump into it and swim with its current. We must immerse ourselves in the Universe to understand it.

The Universe for Bergson is a moving, growing, becoming, living thing. Science cuts a slice out of it and tells us that this slice is the Universe. For Bergson, the slice by itself is dead, unreal. The true Universe is living, rich, containing the slice, but more than the slice. He characterized the Universe as a process of "creative evolution," a becoming in which new things appear. The cause of this is the creative nature of the Universe. "The whole evolution of life on our planet is an effort of this essentially creative force to arrive, by traversing matter, at something which is only realized in man and which, even in man, is realized only imperfectly." In seeking to organize matter, this creative force has been trapped. In man, creativity is seen to be breaking away from matter and becoming free.

Another modern Philosopher who deals with this problem of Science and values is George Santayana. His real Universe is the Universe of human experience in all its richness and fullness. That there is a substance causing such experiences he does not doubt, but rather seeds to justify its existence. He writes that Herbert Spencer was correct in maintaining the existence of such a substance, but believes that it is knowable through experience. We are certain of this World of experience. We find in it laws of Science and all the beauty, truth, and goodness for which we long. It is a real World in any true sense of the term "real."

Thus, modern Science will not permit us to deny that the real World is as the Scientist finds it, a thing upon which we can depend and the laws of which men can discover and act upon with a degree of certainty. We can trust the Universe as explained by the Scientists. But, Philosophers are keenly conscious that this Universe is made up of the human mind, human hopes and fears, love and hate, dreams and defeats. Here they find men acting as though they were free and others holding them responsible for their actions. The Universe for them is also a place of struggle, planning and realization, willing and creating. It is this that the philosophies will not give up.

Consequently, the Universe of modern Philosophy is on in which both Science and human values are accounted for. Today no thinker can claim recognition unless he has in some way at least accounted for the discoveries of the laboratories and those of the inner man. This whole Universe is real, and any other is but a part, and no one must hold that the part, any part, is the whole and the rest unreal. All the Universe, the outer and the inner, is real, and the Philosopher must find place for it all in his system. This is the problem of modern Philosophy, the problem of the nature of the Universe as seen by Philosophers now writing and teaching.

2.2 Hindu Cosmology

2.2.1 The Common Strands in the Hindu Cosmology

Hinduism is not a unified system of beliefs and practices; "Rather it is a multifaceted matrix of beliefs, philosophies, practices, myths and epics." Within this matrix there are many accounts of the Cosmos. There cosmologies are not produced from systematic observation of the galaxies, but "arose from the views of people who felt that they had gained an insight into the nature of reality through deep meditation and ascetic practices."

Though the Hindu literature does not present a unified picture of the Cosmos, running through the diverse accounts of the Universe, there are certain common strands.

First, being predominantly a theistic system of beliefs and doctrines, Hinduism was more interested in God and personal salvation. The external World elicited interest mostly in its relation to godhead. Often the divine is seen as bringing forth, directing, conserving, destroying and recreating the Cosmos. Thus, the dependence of all the Cosmos on the Divine is acknowledged in all Indian accounts of the Cosmos. Therefore, any discourse on the phenomenal World would necessarily be rooted in and inseparable from a discussion on God.

Second, in all versions of Hindu Cosmology the idea of the vastness of space and time form a common background for the understanding of the World. Prefiguring Darwin's theory of gradual evolution and the conclusions of contemporary astronomy regarding the vastness of the Universe in space and time, Indian

Cosmology fixed the lifespan of the vast Universe to last for about 4,320,000,000 years.

Third, resonating well with such concepts of modern Scientific Cosmology as long duration of cosmogenesis, the oscillating Universe and the gradual evolution of Cosmos, Hinduism sees the World history as an endless, cyclic and evolutionary process, each cycle lasting for millions of years. It contends that "everything which happens has already been done so many times before, though in different guises." The dissolution of the Universe, brought about by *pralaya* (final conglomeration or dissolution) at the end of each *kalpa* is followed by the next creation. Rebirth follows dissolution and dissolution follows rebirth.

Fourth, Hindu thought unanimously denies creation out of nothing. It affirms that non-existence can never be the source of existence. The word used in Hindu thought to describe cosmogenesis is *sristi* does not mean bringing out existence from non-existence or creating something from nothing; it means "projecting a gross thing from a subtle substance," variously described as void, the sound *om*, desire, etc. The preferred Vedantic term to describe the production of the World is "out-breathing of God."

2.2.2 Cosmology in the Early Indian Thought

We find the first accounts of the physical Universe in the Vedas. But, the Vedas do not present a unified view of the Cosmos. This is understandable, for the Vedas were not written by a single author, but were formed gradually in the oral tradition lasting many centuries, before they came to be written down by a compiler or a group of compilers. During the long period of its oral development, it is likely that various sages added their understanding of the Cosmos to the tradition. The compiler is likely to have gathered them without paying much attention to presenting a unified account of the Cosmos.

According to one Vedic view (*Rig Veda*, Hymn 109), there was a time when nothing existed. This situation is described as "darkness swathed in darkness" and "unmanifested water." Then, what the *Rig Veda* calls "that One" came into being, "hidden by the void," and "generated by the power of heat." This One's "windless" breathing and desire are said to bring the World into existence.

Then, neither Being, nor non-Being existed, neither atmosphere, nor the firmament, nor what is above it... The One breathed windless by its own power. Nought else but this existed then.

In the beginning was darkness, swathed in darkness: all this was but unmanifested water. Whatever was, that One coming into being, hidden by the void, was generated by the power of heat.

In the beginning, desire which was the first seed of mind overcovered it. Wise seers, searching in their hearts, found the bond of Being in Not-Being.

The poetic form in which this passage is written makes it enigmatic, requiring interpretation. One commentator identifies the One with the creator God, Brahma, whose breathing and desire brings the World into existence. According to his interpretation, the state before "that One coming into being, hidden by the void, generated by the power of heat" was "a void which can be described only by a paradox, neither Being not Not-Being." Then Brahma came into being, generated by the power of heat, and by his own power and desire "breathed" the World into existence. According to another interpretation, the void stands for a single principle, which goes beyond the categorization into being or non-being. From this void, desire, not Brahma, was born; and from desire, directly, without the mediation of Brahma, came humans, Gods and creation.

Unhappy with positing an indescribable void, another Vedic account posits the existence of a divine principle in the beginning. Thus, in a passage that closely resembles the biblical account of creation (Jn. 1:13), the *Rig Veda* views the origin of the One true divine principle which projects itself as *Vaak*, the divine word, and bringing forth the Cosmos that we know from the monistic *Hiranyagarbha* or Golden Womb. In this description it is not clear what *Hiranyagarbha* stands for. Since, it is the cause of the material World, it must be some material principle, dependent on the divine principle for its existence. Whatever be the exact nature of *Hiranyagarbha*, in this account of *sristi* the divine principle is the efficient cause. The efficient cause first creates *Vaak*, and then using it as the material cause creates the Universe.

Yet, another Vedic passage speaks of the existence of a cosmic egg or embryo in the beginning. From this cosmic egg, "the lord of creation" (later identified as Brahma) was born, as the great oceans heated up. The lord of creation, then, creates the Cosmos.

One of the advanced theories of creation and dissolution has been symbolically presented in the deeply mystical, poetical Nasadiya Sukta of the *Rig Veda* (*Rig Veda*, X, 129.1). Swami Vivekananda offers the following translation to the Rig Vedic Hymn of Creation:

> Existence was not then, nor non-existence,
> The World not was not, the sky beyond was neither.
> What covered the mist? Of whom was that?
> What was in the depths of darkness thick?
> Death was not then, nor immortality,
> But, motionless did That vibrate
> Alone, with Its own glory one-
> Beyond That nothing did exist.
>
> At first in darkness hidden darkness laid,
> Undistinguished as one, as of water,
> Than That which lay in void thus covered
> A glory did put forth by *Tapah*!

Once again the poetic, aphoristic style of the passage makes it difficult to grasp the meaning without the help of a learned interpreter. And interpretations vary depending on the school of Philosophy to which the interpreter belongs. Vivekananda, taking an Advaitic view, offers an interpretation, which sounds very similar to the vacuum fluctuation theory of the formation of the Universe proposed by Stephen Hawking. According to

Vivekananda, this hymn could be interpreted thus: In the beginning there was Reality which was beyond all sorts of differentiation, including the differentiation into being and non-being – these two, like any other pair of opposites belongs to *maya*. It was without motion or vibration (*anidavātam*). Then, when the *kalpa* (lifespan of the Cosmos) begins, the *anidavātam* commences to vibrate and the undifferentiated Reality differentialites into *prāna* (primal energy) and *ākāsa*. In the next outflow of energy from Reality, *prāna* is activated and it begins to blow on *ākāsa* (sky), causing condensation of atoms. Subsequent outflow of primal energy causes the formation of different elements, of which the Universe is composed. Therefore, everything that we see around us, feel, touch, taste, is simply a differentiated manifestation of this *ākāsa*.

Undoubtedly, these cosmologies are born of the speculations of people who, as part of their religious quest, mediated on the origin of the Cosmos. Though they did not present a unified picture, they shared an assumption that the origin of the Cosmos is knowable, and they all used symbolism to explain the origins. But later, hymns were increasingly skeptical of such symbolism; the tenth book of the *Rig Veda* includes this verse: "Who truly knows, who could here declare when was born, whence comes this creation?" According to this verse, the origin of the Universe is incomprehensible as it precedes not only humanity but also the Gods, and even being (*sat*) nor non-being (*asat*). In *Rig Veda* 10. 129, we find this passage:

Neither being (*sat*) nor non-being (*asat*) was as yet. What was concealed? And where? And in whose protection?..... Who really knows? Who can declare it? When was it born, and when came this creation? This *devas* were born later than this World's creation, so who knows from where it came into existence? None can know from where creation has arisen, and whether he has or has not produced it. He who surveys it in the highest heavens, he alone knows – or perhaps does not know.

This skepticism could not last for too long, for the human mind always seeks explanation. If the World exists, surely there must be a cause. If it cannot be known by empirical or Philosophical means, symbolism is the next option. So the Puranic views falls back on symbolism. In the Puranas it is Brahma who creates the Cosmos. Brahma, however, is not necessarily regarded as the creator God, this account, The Supreme God first brings forth Brahma, the creator God, who in turn brings forth the Cosmos. But, not all Puranic writers accept the idea of the Universe being created by Brahma. Jinesha, the author of Mahāpurana, a ninth century Hindu scripture, holds the view that the Universe is uncreated and eternal. He argues that the doctrine that the World was created is ill-advised, and should be rejected. In his own words:

Some foolish men declare that a creator made the World. The doctrine that the World was created is ill-advised, and should be rejected. If God created the World, where was he before creation?... How could God have made this first, and then the World, you are faced with an endless regression….. Know that the World is uncreated, as time itself is, without beginning and end. And it is based on principles.

The eternity of the World, however, is a minority view. According to the mainstream Puranic view, the Universe is brought forth, destroyed, and re-created in all eternally repetitive series of cycles.

The Puranic account of the Universe includes also an elaborate discussion on the life-cycle of the Cosmos. In its life-cycle, each Universe lasts for about 4,320,000,000 years (one day of Brahma) and at the end of it, it is destroyed by fire or water elements. After the destruction, Brahma rests for one night (which is as long as the day), before a new Universe is created. This process of *sristi* (creation) and *samhara* (cataclysm) repeats for 100 Brahma years (311 trillion human years) that represents Brahma's lifespan. This means that during the lifespan of a Brahma, 36525 Universes would come into and go out of existence.

The Puranic Cosmology locates the present Cosmos in the 51st year of the present Brahma. This means that about 155.5 trillion human years have elapsed since he was born. Since, the lifespan of a Brahma is 100 Brahma years, the present Brahma will die after another fifty Brahmas years (i.e., 155.5 trillion human years). After his "death" it is necessary that another 100 Brahma years pass before he is reborn and the whole creation begins anew. This process is repeated again and again forever.

Brahma's life is divided into one thousand cycles (*mahāyuga*, or "great year"). Each *mahāyuga*, during which life, including the human race, appears and then disappears, has 71 divisions, each made of 14 *manvantaras* (1000-year period). Each *mahāyuga* lasts for 4,320,000,000 years. *Manvantara* is Manu's cycle, the one who gives birth to and governs the human race.

Each *mahāyuga* consists of a series of four shorter *yugas* or ages. The *yuga*s get progressively worse from a moral point of view as one proceeds from one *yuga* to another. As a result each succeeding *yuga* is of a shorter duration than the age that preceded it. The current *Kali Yuga* (Iron Age) began at midnight 17th / 18th February in 3102 BC in the proleptic Julian calendar.

It must be noted that all these dates and time spans are products of pure speculation, having no Scientific data or Philosophical arguments to support them. Therefore, we must not take them literally to mean exactly what they state, but see them as symbolic statements which seek to convey two ideas – (1) long lifespan of the Universe – expressed by the symbolic number 4,320,000,000 and (2) a cyclic concept of history, which sees cosmic events as repetitive.

The Upanishads share with the Puranic and other Hindu cosmologies the cyclic concept of the Cosmos. In a story in the Upanishads, Brahma is conceived as the creative force behind a series of Universes. He is pictured as being seated on a lotus, the symbol of divine energy and divine grace. The lotus grows from the navel of Vishnu, the sleeping, whose dream is the Universe. Brahma opens his eyes and comes into being. Brahma closed his eyes, and a World goes out of being.

2.2.3 Cosmology in the Later Indian Thought

After the Vedic-Upaniṣadic period, Indian Philosophy develops in different directions, giving rise to various schools to various schools of thought. And to explain the diversity, we must look at the later developments. After the Vedic and Upaniṣadic period, we find efforts towards systematizing Philosophical speculation, giving rise to what is called *sūtra* literature. Sūtra, literally means "thread." In this context, it means "a brief mnemonic statement." As Philosophical discussion took place, orally, and as they were passed down through oral traditions, it was perhaps felt necessary to condense the insights into short aphorisms and link them up or thread them together, so that scholars could memorize them easily and transmit them to the next generation, giving explanations. A typical *sūtra* work consists of a collection of many *sūtras* or aphorisms of this kind arranged into different topics. Six *sūtra* works are considered authoritative and form the basis of the *ṣad darṣanas* (six schools of insights or Philosophy). They are the *Brahma Sūtras* of Badrayana, the *Mīmāmsa Sūtras* of Jaimini, the *Nyāya Sūtras* of Gautama, the *Vaiśeṣika Sūtra* of Kānada, the *Yoga Sūtras* of Patānjali, and the *Samkya Kairka* of *Isvara* Krishna. (According to tradition, there was a *Samkhya Sūtra* by Kapila, who is regarded as the founder of that system. But, the sūtras available are not recognized by all as the original sūtras. The earliest systematic work available now is *Samkhya Karika*).

While the sū*tras* were easy to memorize, being aphoristic and mnemonic, they were vague and nuclear to the uninitiated. This necessitated the creation of the *bhashya* literature which provided the much-needed explanation and interpretation of the *sūtras* through commentaries. In some cases, on the same *sūtra* work different authours wrote different major commentaries (*bhashyas*), intended to justify each one's respective standpoints. For example, we have various *bhashyas* on the Brahma *S*ūtras – *bhashyas* of Shaṅkara, Rāmanuja, Mādhava, Vallabha, Nimbarka, Baldeva among others – each of them written from a different perspective to justify a particular standpoint. The followers of each interpretation formed a school of Vedānta, and some of them wrote commentaries on the bhashyas themselves to justify, elaborate or criticize them.

This development gave rise to the six schools of Indian thought (called the ṣad darṣanas). They share a common ground in the Vedic system; but are different from each other due to the different Philosophical perspective each one assumed in Indian Philosophy is: Nyāya, Vaiśeṣika, Samkhya, Yoga, Karma or Pūrva Mimamsa and Uttara Mimamsa or Vedānta. They are called *āstikas* (from the Sanskrit word *asti*, "it is so"), because all of them to present a developed and comprehensive explanation of Vedic knowledge.

Parallel to this movement, there was another movement that rose by criticizing the Vedas. Since, the proponents of this movement rejected the authority of Vedas, they came to be known as *nastikas* (from the Sanskrit words *na asti*, "it is not so"). They include Charvaka, Buddhist and Jain Philosophers.

The diversity in perspectives often gives rise to conflicting view on various Philosophical issues. Yet, there is an underlying unity behind the diversity. The source of this unity can be traced to their common origin in the Vedas, the earliest available records of Indian Philosophy and literature. The Vedas form the background for later Philosophical speculation, exercising on it either a positive or negative influence. Hence, all Philosophical speculations in India share a common background, which provides them a source of unity.

One unusual feature of the history of Indian Philosophy is that the growth of the various schools of thought had not been successive, as in the case of Greek and Western Philosophy but simultaneous. Various systems of thought coexisted, without one super ceding the others. This parallel growth of systems of thought in India creates a peculiar problem for a scholar of Indian thought, who wants to have unified account of what Indians believed at a point in history. Any attempt to present a comprehensive, unified account is bound to highlight some common features while downplaying or even leaving out the variations. Acknowledging this limitation, we can still try to present an account of the post-Vedic and Puranic understanding of the Universe.

A. Cosmology in the Nyāya - Vaiśeṣika

i. Dissolution (Pralaya)

The doctrine of *pralaya* is accepted by all the Hindu Philosophical systems except the Mimamsa. The Nyāya – Vaiśeṣika gives an account of the *pralaya* that sound similar to the heat-death theory proposed by modern Scientific Cosmology, except for two major differences. First, the heat-death theory sees the dissolution of the Universe as a mechanical process, whereas in Nyāya – Vaiśeṣika, it is the work of *Isvara* (God). Second, the state of dissolution in Nyāya – Vaiśeṣika is a temporary state, intended to give rest to the weary souls; at an opportune time it is to be brought to an end with the commencement of a new act of creation. By contrast, the heat-death theory proposes a permanent collapse of the Universe as all the useful energy in the Cosmos gets dissipated.

If we set aside these differences, Nyāya – Vaiśeṣika description, *Isvara*, wishing to give some respite or rest to all living beings who had been subjected to repetitive birth and rebirth, desires to bring about dissolution (*samhareccho bhavati*) of the Universe. Simultaneously, the *adrsta* force (constructive force that helps the integration and unification of atoms for the creation of the World) residing in all the souls and forming bodies, senses, and the gross elements, ceases to act. As a result, no further bodies, senses, or other products come into being. Then for bringing about the dissolution of all existing things, by the desire of *Isvara*, the separation of the atoms commences. Gradually, all combinations are disintegrated. All *kshiti* (earth) is reduced to the disintegrated atomic state. This is followed by all *ap* (water), then all *tejas* (fire), and then all *vayu* (air).

In the state of *pralaya*, as the *adrsta* (constructive force) ceases to act, souls associated with dharma-adharma and past impressions (*samskara*) remain suspended in their own inanimate condition. They remain lifeless, knowledgeless, non-bodies that they possess knowledge through the activity of *manas* (mind). *Pralaya*, however, is not seen as a beneficial activity, since dissolution is believed to be brought about to give some rest to the sufferings of the living beings.

ii. Creation

After a period, when living beings are rested enough, *Isvara* wishes to create again; and this desire of *Isvara* works in all the souls as *adrsta*, and sets in motion the beginning of a new creation. The creative action follows the reverse order. The action of *adrsta* begins in the *vayu* (air) atoms which are in contact with the souls, in whom *adrsta* has become active. By the creative action of *adrsta*, air atoms come in contact with one another, forming *vayu*. After *vayu*, *ap* (water) is formed by the conglomeration of water atoms, and then the *tejas* (fire) atoms conglomerate and then the *kshiti* (earth) atoms. When the four elements are thus formed, *Isvara* creates Brahma, the creator God, and directs him to do the rest of the work. Acting as a deputy, Brahma then supervises the due disposal of the fruits of karma according to the merit or demerit of the souls. Thus, a new World is created. *Isvara* brings about this creation not for any selfish purpose but for the good of all beings. According to Prasastapada, "The Supreme Being decides to recreate the Cosmos so that we souls can experience Worlds of shapes and solidity."

Many Nyāya books do not speak of the appointment of Brahma as deputy, it is also held that in the process of creation *Isvara* does not act independently, but relies on other causes such as: (1) material causes like subtle atoms, *adrsta*, souls and *karma* (2) the time of fruition of *karma* (3) the appearance of auxiliary causes (4) the presence of beings related to what is to be created (5) the fruition of the karma of those related beings, and, finally (6) the removal of obstacles that prevent the fulfillment of the above conditions. One difficulty with this account is that it makes God the mechanical executor of an inexorable law, without the slightest room for freedom or spontaneity.

In many Nyāya – Vaiśeṣika books, there is also speculation on *Isvara*'s motive for creation and dissolution. Some suggest that *Isvara* creates and destroys to amuse himself (*kridartham*) or to manifest his powers (*vibhuti*). Vacaspati and Vatsyayana proposed mercy as the motive of creation and dissolution. God created the World, directs karma and reveals the Vedas for the sake of others.

Isvara creates the Cosmos "so that we souls can experience Worlds of shape and solidity," and after a time he dissolves it to give some rest to the sufferings of the living beings. He rejects both these views. He argues that God is not in need of amusement or of manifesting his powers. Uddyotakara conceived the law of karma and the action of *adrsta* as something too mechanical and too rigid to allow any freedom to *Isvara*. *Isvara* creates and dissolves the Universe because the activity belongs to his very nature (*pravrtti-svabhavikam*), just as it belongs to the nature of the earth to support, and to the nature of water to wet. Despite these disputes, there is agreement that the exterior World is in perfect harmony with people's actions. All the changes and modifications in the external World take place in accordance with the merits and demerits of the souls associated with them.

iii. The Composition and Nature of the World

Nyāya came to ally itself with the Vaiśeṣika and accepted the atomist view of the material Universe. The gross World we perceive is the outward aspect of the World of minute, indivisible, unchangeable, eternal atoms. There are four kinds of atoms, namely, earth, water, fire, and air atoms. Atoms are the objective substratum of the material Cosmos. In addition, there is a fifth element *ākasā* (space). It is merely the substratum or the medium of all sound; it is absolutely inert and structureless.

Each of these Five Elements has its own distinctive range of qualities: earth, for example, has tangibility, and colour, taste and smell as its distinctive characteristic; water has tangibility, colour and taste; fire has tangibility, and colour; air has tangibility and *ākāsa* has sound. Though sometimes water and air are seen to smell, it is not because they have those qualities, but due to the presence of minute particles of earth carried within the water particles or air particles.

During *pralaya* due to the non-activity of *adrsta*, atoms remain in an uncombined state but at the creation stage they cannot retain that state. At the time of creation, by the will of *Isvara* and the activity of *adrsta*, individual atoms come together to produce the Five elements – earth, air, water, fire and ether. Then, by their combination, all the material substances that constitute the World are produced.

There are two views regarding how the combination takes place. According to the generally accepted view, at the first stage of creation, by the will of *Isvara* and the activity of *adrsta*, atoms form combinations of two called *dvyanuka* (binary atoms). Then two, three, four or five *dvyanukas* form themselves into grosser molecules of *tryanuka*, *caturanuka*, etc. But, according to the second view, atoms are regarded to as having an incessant vibratory motion and also an inherent tendency to unite; and they are believed to unite in twos, threes or fours, either by the atoms falling into groups of twos, threes, etc. directly, or by the successive addition of one atom to each preceding aggregate.

Whatever be the exact process of combination of atoms, behind it there is the activity of *adrsta* and the will of *Isvara*, which give "the direction of all such unions in harmony with the principle of a 'moral government of the Universe,' so that only such things are produced as can be arranged for the due disposal of the effects of *karma*."

Nyāya – Vaiśeṣika, atoms are said to be eternal. They are not produced by the chemical operation of heat. An elementary substance produced by primary atomic combination may, however, suffer qualitative changes under the influence of heat (*pakajotpatti*). The impact of heat corpuscles decomposes a *dvyanuka* into the atoms and transforms the characters of the atoms determining them all in the same way. Heat particles then reunite the atoms so transformed to form binary or other molecules in different orders or arrangements. This accounts for the specific characters or qualities found in the final product. Vaiśeṣika holds that there is first disintegration into simple atoms, then change of atomic qualities, and then the final recombination under the influence of heat. This doctrine is called the doctrine of *pilupaka* (heating of atoms). Nyāya, on the other hand, thinks that no disintegration into atoms is necessary for change of qualities, but it is the molecules which assume new characteristics under the influence of heat.

For Nyāya – Vaiśeṣika, the World of things it thus created out of atoms with the help of karma and *adrsta* is real. The atomic theory does not imply in any way that the World of roses, cats, computers, hurricanes, rains and sunshine is unreal or illusory. For the atomic theory the World is also eternal. Drastic change can occur in the Universe especially at the time of *sristi* and pralaya. But, there is no absolute creation and no ultimate annihilation, because the atoms which constitute the substratum of each creation are eternal.

B. The Cosmology of the Vedānta

i. The Nature of the Universe

In the Vedānta school, often regarded as "flower of Indian Philosophy," there is speculation on the nature of the Universe. This speculation occurs in the context of the discussion on the nature, powers and activity of Brahman. Therefore, Vedantic Cosmology cannot be separated from this core concern.

In all forms of Vedānta Philosophy, the Universe is believed to have a life cycle of its own, spread over billions of years. In its cycle, it assumes two states – the unmanifested or undifferentiated form, which cannot be characterized as being or as non-being, the gross Universe originates, grows and expands and ultimately dissolves into its subtle causal form. After some period, the gross Universe resurfaces and the cosmic process continues ceaselessly. For Vedānta, creation, perpetuation and dissolution make one complete cyclical process that repeats itself eternally. In course of time, there come into existence many Universes, all of which follow the same rhythm, *sristi* and *pralaya*; and the whole process is said to recur at a period of 1,000 *mahāyugas* or 4.32 billion years or 4,320 million years.

Each *mahāyuga* is divided into a series of four shorter *yugas* or ages. They are *Krita Yuga*, *Treta Yuga*, *Dvapara Yuga* and *Kali Yuga*. As the *yugas* proceed from one to the next, they are said to get progressively worse from a moral point of view. As a result, each succeeding *yuga* is of shorter duration than the previous one.

Vedānta Cosmology includes elaborate description of *Yugas*. *Satya* or *Krita Yuga* is the first of a *mahāyuga*. *Satya* means "truth;" and *Krita*, means "action." This is the age in which people did unquestioningly what their benevolent elders told them. This is the age of virtue and moral perfection. It lasts for 1,728,000 years. It is a bright, golden age on earth. The great God, Vishnu, in his form of Brahma, the creator of the World, is the presiding deity. This is the age when *dharma* (ideal, the righteous behavior or moral duty) "walks steadily and securely upon all four feet." People are loyal to dharma and devoted to meditation, the highest virtue. Everyone is born good and lives a happy, contented, unselfish and beautiful life in this *Yuga*, sorrow does not exist.

Krita Yuga is followed by the *Treta Yuga*, the second age each *mahāyuga*. *Treta* means "three." It is the third *yuga*, counting backwards form the present *yuga*. It is an age in which people are specially "protected" by their elders. During this *yuga*, virtue and moral perfection still exist, but they are believed to have declined by one-fourth. Correspondingly, the duration of the age is believed to decline by one-fourth, so that its duration is reduced to 1,296,000 years.

Vishnu, the preserver of the Universe, is said to be the presiding deity during *Treta Yuga*. People are devoted to the pursuit of knowledge, which they consider the highest virtue. As in *Krita Yuga*, in *Treta Yuga*, too, benevolent trees and plants supply food and clothing to everyone in abundance. Because of the ideal weather, people need not construct houses for shelter. But, as greed begins to raise its head, some people become its devotees, and these greedy people try to make the fruit-bearing trees and plant their private property. When that happens, the benevolent trees disappear, and life on earth becomes difficult for the first time. Heavy rainfall creates rivers. The soil turns fertile for the growth of many new kinds of trees and plants. The new trees and plants, these are ordinary. People must work hard to acquire food and clothing from them. Because of the rain and severe changes in the weather, they also need to construct houses for shelter.

In the *Treta Yuga* people are said to be more passionate and greedy. They are no longer happy with what they have. Dissatisfaction, resentment, and anger replace satisfaction, peace, and contentment in their hearts. People of this *yuga* covet their neighbours' possessions. The strong take land by force from the weak in order to possess more food and greater wealth. Many men take the wives of others.

Treta Yuga is followed by *Dvapara Yuga*, the third age in each *mahāyuga*. As the prefix *dva* (which means "two") suggests, eternal dharma now has to balance on two of its four legs, creating an unsteady balance between good and evil. Virtue and moral perfection still exist, but they have declined to one-half of what they were in the *Krita Yuga*. As a result, the duration of this age is half of that of the *Krita Yuga* (i.e., 864,000 years). Vishnu, the preserver of life on earth, is still the presiding deity. People devote themselves to sacrifice, which they consider the highest virtue. In the *Dvapara Yuga*, disease, misfortune, suffering, and death are part of everyone's existence. People have become more passionate and greedy resulting in regular conflicts and periodic war. Religious doctrines are developed in an attempt to guide human behaviour towards dharma, but the gradual process of moral deterioration continues.

Dvapara Yuga is followed by the fourth age in each *mahāyuga*, namely, the *Kali Yuga*. *Kali* means discord, strife and war. This is the Dark Age in which virtue has almost vanished. In duration, this age is only one-fourth of the *Krita Yuga* (432,000 years). Vishnu in his form of Shiva-Rudra, the destroyer of life on earth, is the presiding God. In the *Kali Yuga*, people achieve noble rank in society based on the amount of money and property they own rather than their moral virtue. Greatness is measured only in terms of material wealth. Sexual passion alone binds husband and wife together in marriage. People become successful in life through a succession of lies, and their only source of enjoyment is sex. The only remaining virtue is charity. In the Kali *Yuga* only the poor are honest. They live under continuous fear of hunger, disease, and death. Harsh weather and primitive living conditions make them prey to devastating illness. One who attains the age of twenty-three is considered very old.

These four *yugas*, taken together, constitute one *mahāyuga*. Its total duration adds to 43,20,000 years. One thousand such *mahāyugas* constitute one day of Brahma called *kalpa*. So one day of Brahma will be 4,320 million years or 4.32 billion years. A similar expanse of time will make his one night, and that is another *kalpa*. Thus, Advaita teaches an expansive view of time that boggles our imagination.

ii. The Relation of the World to Brahman

In their conception of the Universe the Vedantins reject both materialism and dualism. They reject the materialist theory in both its pluralistic and monistic forms. Pluralistic materialism which explains the World as the product of material elements that by themselves combine together to form objects is as unacceptable to the Vedantins as monistic materialism which perceives the World as the transformation of an unconscious nature that spontaneously evolves all objects. The Vedantins are equally committed to reject dualism which sees the World as the product of two kinds of independent reality, such as matter and God, one of which is the material, the other the efficient cause which creates the World out of the first. The Vedantins argue that an unconscious cause cannot produce the World, and that even the dualistic conception of two ultimately independent realities, one conscious and another unconscious, producing the World by interaction, is unsatisfactory. They take their stand on the Upaniṣadic view that "all is Brahman" (*sarvam khaly idam Brahma*).

The commitment to the Upaniṣadic view that all is Brahman compels the Vedantins to accept that the Atman (or Brahman or Self) is both the efficient and the material cause of the World. So, they unanimously agree that the Atman, wishing to be many, desires to bring out the World. This conception raised two questions before the Vedantins: (1) if everything is Brahman - Is this material World, the World of our everyday experience, real? (2) How is this World of multiplicity produced? In answering these questions various views are expressed, of which three (i.e., that of Shaṅkara, Rāmanuja and Vivekananda) are influential.

Rāmanuja's View

Rāmanuja, taking the Upaniṣadic account of creation in a literal sense, holds that the omnipotent God creates the manifold World out of himself by a gracious act of will. At the same time, he acknowledges that the World is created out of matter. This is possible, because, within the all-inclusive Brahman there are both unconscious matter (*acit*) and finite spirits. Before the appearance of the phenomenal World, matter exits in Brahman in a latent, subtle (*sukshma*) and undifferentiated (*avibhakta*) form called *prakrti*. This *prakrti* is said to be an uncreated (*aja*) reality, existing within Brahman and is controlled by him, just as the human body is controlled from within by the human soul. At the time of creation, it serves as the material cause. In other words, at the time of creation, Brahman, using *prakrti* (which is nothing but the latent material aspect of Brahman) as the material cause, produces the World of diverse objects in accordance with the karma of the souls in the World of diverse objects in accordance with the karma of the souls in the World prior to the previous dissolution. This takes place in two stages. At the first stage, impelled by the omnipotent will of God, the undifferentiated subtle matter, *prakrti*, gradually becomes transformed into three kinds of subtle elements – fire, water and earth. These differentiated elements manifest also the three kinds of qualities (*gunas*) known as *sattva*, *rajas* and *tamas*. In the next stage, the three subtle elements become mixed up together and give rise to all gross objects which we perceive in the material World. During dissolution (*pralaya*) the material World goes back to its primal state and remains as *prakrti*, i.e., in a latent, subtle of the souls attached to the material reality matures for the next cycle of creation and dissolution to begin.

The understanding of how the World was produced forms the background of Rāmanuja's reflection on the nature of the World. For Rāmanuja the World, created out of the eternal *prakrti*, in accordance with the laws of karma, is real. What is denied is the independence of the eternal matter, *prakrti*. The Upaniṣadic texts which deny multiplicity of objects and assert the unity of all things, according to Rāmanuja, do not mean to deny the reality of the many objects, but only teach that in all of them there is the same Brahman on whom all are dependent for their existence, just as all gold articles are dependent on gold. What the Upaniṣads deny is the independence of objects, not their dependent existence. Even when the Upaniṣads speak of Brahman as the wielder of a magical power (*māya*), it does not mean that it is a trickster, which befools people by creating a grand illusion. It only means that the inscrutable power by which Brahman creates the World is as wonderful as that of a magician. For Rāmanuja the word *māya* stands for Brahman's power of creating wonderful objects or Brahman's wonderful power of real creation.

Shaṅkara's View

Shaṅkara's school called Advaita Vedānta takes a different view of how the World is created and about its reality. According to the Advaita Vedānta, Brahman alone is real. Brahman is pure *cit* (consciousness). Knowledge, will and action are inherent in Brahman, but not materiality. The action of Brahman consists in *sristi* and *samhara* (creation and annihilation). They presuppose power. When the Upaniṣads speak of prakrti or māya they refer to this power of Brahman. This means that in Advaita Vedānta prakrti does not denote a latent, subtle and undifferentiated form of matter, as it does in the Rāmanuja school of Vedānta. Similarly in Advaita Vedānta, *māya* does not mean the power of God for real creation as it does in Rāmanuja's thought. In Advaita Vedānta, *prakrti* and *māya* are synonyms and stand for the magical power of Brahman, with the help of which the "illusion" of a real World is produced, sustained and dissolved. *Māya*, as the power of Brahman, is not an independent reality, but is identical with him. Brahman projects the Universe and after a time dissolves it by animating his *prakrti* or his *māya*.

Since, *māya* is the power with the help of which Brahman creates the World of multiplicity (i.e., the phenomenal World), *māya* is, so to say, the instrumental cause. But, even this instrument does not have an independent existence, as it is merely the magical power of Brahman. Since, the *māya-shakti* – possessing Brahman is the only reality, in the act of creation; Brahman does not depend on anything outside him for his act of creation. This means Brahman in his act of creation has no material cause other than himself. In other words, in the act of creation, Brahman is both the efficient and material cause of the Universe.

To illustrate how Brahman can be both the efficient and material cause of the phenomenal World, Advaita Vedānta deploys the Upaniṣadic analogy the spider and its web. The spider weaves its web out of its own will, using its own silk. Therefore, the spider is both the efficient and material cause of the web. Similarly, Brahman who produces the Universe out of his own free will using his own māya-shakti (the power or energy of *māya*) is both the efficient and material cause of the Universe. Mundaka Upaniṣad puts it this way: "Just as a spider projects its own web and then re-absorbs it into its own body so also; That One Reality projects this variegated Universe and then absorbs it back into it."

Since, Brahman is both the efficient and the material cause in the production of the Universe, Advaita Vedānta regards the phenomenal World as a projection of Brahman on himself as the only substantial background. The *māya-shakti* of Brahman is, so to say, the instrumental cause of the Universe. In creation, the one God with the help of the power of *māya* appears as the manifold. This is *vivarta vāda*, or the theory of apparent modification in Advaita Vedānta.

Using this account of cosmogenesis as the background, Advaita Vedānta proceeds to elaborate the nature of the phenomenal World. It concludes that the World of multiplicity of objects, like the objects appearing in our dreams or illusion, is not real. In fact, the Universe is merely an illusion projected by Brahman on himself; it is a dream sustained by Brahman. It is by the power of ignorance that we perceive it as really real. This can explain its disappearance when the ignorance that envelops a person is overcome. The appearance of this World is taken as real by the ignorant, but the wise, who can see through it, find nothing but Brahman, the one reality behind the grand illusory show. Reality appears in many forms through the powers of creating illusion, *māya*. *Māya* as the power of Brahman is interpreted in Advaita Vedānta as God's will to create the World-appearance. It is by this power that Brahman, the great magician, conjures up the World-show with all its illusory objects. From the standpoint of ignorant people, who are deceived by it and see the multiplicity of objects instead of one Brahman, *māya* is illusion-producing ignorance. In this aspect *māya* is also called *ajñāna* or *avidyā* (synonyms of "ignorance") and is conceived as having the double function of concealing the real nature of Brahman, and making him appear as something else, namely, the World. That the World is unreal is established by the experience of one who realizes that Brahman is the only reality, argues Advaita Vedānta.

If we perceive the World as real, it is not because it is so, but due to wrong perception and it will vanish when the illusion arising out of ignorance is overcome. To explain how this illusion works, it is customary to use the example of ornaments made of gold. In the case of gold ornaments, gold is the only real substance and the different and forms (*nāma-rūpa*) which make them appear as many, are merely matters of verbal distinctions. Similarly, it is argued, in the plurality of objects there is the same Reality; the differences we perceive are merely verbal. Thus, in Advaita Vedānta, objects of the World and the World itself are denied separate, individual existence is dependent on Brahman.

Vivekananda's View

Vivekananda, the disciple of Advaitic mystic Rāmakrishna, gives an account of how the World is created, which would sound like repacking of modern Scientific Cosmology in the categories of Advaitic Philosophy. Similar to Scientific Cosmology's view that the basic building blocks of the Universe are energy and matter, Vivekananda proposes *prāna* (primal energy) and *ākāsa* (primal matter) as the "raw material" in the production of the Universe. In this conception *prāna* stands for all the various forms of power in the Universe, whether it manifests as attraction, repulsion, motion or heat, or even as it manifests as thought; and *ākāsa* for the formless, structureless, undifferentiated matter. Before the beginning of creation, *prāna* is without motion in it (*anidavātam*) and "sleeps" in the infinite ocean of *ākāsa*. Then, when creation begins, the motionless *prāna* commences to vibrate, and blow after blow is given to *ākāsa*. This results in the condensation of atoms; and as they are condensed, different elements are formed. Thus, Vivekananda sees everything in the phenomenal World as the product of the activity of *prāna* upon *ākāsa*. Everything that we see around us, feel, touch, taste, is a differentiated manifestation of this *ākāsa*.

Since, *prāna* and *ākāsa* are insentient and unintelligent, a question arises here: being insentient and unintelligent, how can they act to produce the elements? Vivekananda answers the question in a typically Vedantic fashion. He upholds the Upaniṣadic view of Reality. In the Upaniṣadic view, Reality is beyond even the distinction between being and non-being – since such distinctions are the effects of *māyā*. Following this line of thought, Vivekananda holds that before the creation of the Universe, Reality existed as undifferentiated reality without motion or vibration (*anidavātam*). Then, when the *kalpa* begins, the anidavātam commences to vibrate and the undifferentiated Reality differentiates into *prāna* and *ākāsa*.

Vivekananda holds that there are two distinct factors involved in the starting of creation. Firstly, divine will is the principal cause working behind evolution. Secondly, the inexorable law of *karma* determinates the time and the outcome of the new creation. The *karma* of living beings from the previous cycle lies in the causal state during the period of involution, waiting to bear fruit. When *karma* matures, the divine will becomes active and the process of creation gets into motion. Here, two important steps are involved. In the first step, the motionless Reality commences to vibrate, causing the undifferentiated Reality to differentiate into *prāna* and *ākāsa*. Then in the second stage of creation, under the influence of the divine will and of the matured karma, the motionless *prāna* commences to vibrate, giving blow after blow to formless, structureless and undifferentiated *ākāsa*. This results in the condensation of atoms; and the subsequent formation of elements and finally, the Universe itself. Because of the role played by *prāna* and *ākāsa* in bringing about the Universe, Vivekananda considers it inappropriate to call this process by the name creation. Instead, he speaks of the process of the production of the World as "projection from the latent to the manifest form" or "out-breathing of God."

Vivekananda goes on to describe the process of the formation of elements. *Ākāsa*, subjected to the repeated blows of *prāna*, first produces *vāyu* (air). *Vāyu* vibrates, and as the vibration grow more and more rapid, the resultant friction gives rise to *téjas* (heat). This heat, when subjected to the action of *prāna*, ends in liquefaction, producing *āp* (water). When water is further subjected to the blow of *prāna*, it becomes *kshiti* (earth or solid). Therefore, the order of creation is, first, *ākāsa*, then *vāyu*, *téjas*, then *āp*, and finally, *kshiti* or gross matter. Thus, *prāna* acting on *ākāsa* creates the whole Universe. Everything that we see around us, feel, touch, taste is simply a differentiated manifestation of this *ākāsa* and every manifestation of power, therefore, is *prāna*. The entire process is rooted in the one undifferentiated Reality and is initiated and sustained by the will of God and the matured karma of souls.

iii. The Disintegration of the Cosmos

When the cycle ends at the time of *pralaya*, a process of disintegration begins. Disintegration follows a reverse order. All that we call solid will melt into uniform heat vibrations, and then all that is in the form, and finally, all that is in the gaseous form will melt into the finer gaseous form, and finally all that is in the gaseous form will melt back in to original *ākāsa*. Likewise, at the time of *pralaya* all manifestations of power will slowly resolve into the original *anidavātam* (motionless state of *prāna*). In this dissolved state *prāna* is said to "sleep" in the infinite ocean of structureless, undifferentiated *ākāsa*. This state is believed to continue for a *kalpa* (a night of Brahma), before the beginning of the next cycle of creation and dissolution. Thus, the process of creation oscillates backwards and forwards. At one time it becomes potential, and at the next period it becomes active. This alteration, according to Vedānta has been going on through eternity.

C. The Cosmology of the Yoga School

i. Creation

Like all the other forms of Indian Philosophy, Yoga Philosophy, too, believes that the history of the Universe is cyclic, appearance of the Universe is followed by its disappearance and after a time its reappearance. The cycle is maintained by the indescribable Brahman who is described as *cit* (consciousness). Yoga describes the process of creation this way: wanting to create the Universe, Brahman (who is of the nature of cit, consciousness) first becomes *manas* (mind). *Manas* is the source of all creation and destruction. At the beginning of each so-called creation, the creative movement of *manas* energy is roused, which by its successive outflow gives rise to what is called *tanmātrās* (subtle states). Each successive outflow gives rise to a *tanmātrā*, the order of production being: first *ākāsa*, then *vāyu*, then *téjas*, then *āp* and finally *kshiti* (i.e., ether, air, fire, water and earth). This is followed by the creation of *ahamkāra* (ego) and *buddhi* (intelligence), thus bringing to completion the creation of the subtle body (*pury-astak*). Thereafter, the cosmic body of the Brahman is formed and developed in accordance with the root desire (*vāsana*) inherent in *manas*. Thus, we have the subtle body of Brahman made of eight constituents (five *tanmātrās*, *ahamkāra*, *buddhi* and the root *manas*). From this, develops the body of Brahmā and from the creative imagination of Brahmā we have the grosser materials and all the rest of the World-appearance. All these changes, however, are not real, but illusory; for during all the change, Brahman remains shut up within itself – changeless and unchangeable. That makes the changes in the World pure mental creation, and hence unreal. In Yoga, not only are changes unreal but all scriptures, Gods, Goddesses and all else that passes as real also are unreal.

ii. The Nature of the World

Yoga upholds the monistic view of reality. Brahman is the only reality. Ultimately, everything comes from Brahman. Existence, non-existence, unity, duality and multiplicity – all proceed from Brahman. *Ćit*, or mind, has evolved out of pure consciousness (*ćit*) or Brahman, and it is through the latter that all the power of action (*karma*), root desires (*vāsana*), and all mental modifications appear. Only in the eyes of a person who has not attained complete realization does this difference between the World appearance and Brahman seem to be so great. In magic (*indrajāla*), non-existent things are produced and existent things are destroyed, a jug is turned in to a cloth, and a cloth into a jug, and all sorts of wonderful sights are shown, though none of these appearances have the slightest essence of their own. Likewise, in the act of creation, the entire World-appearance is produced out of the imagination of the mind. There is no active agent (*kartr*) and no enjoyer (*bhoktr*) of the pleasures and sorrows of the World, and there is no creation or destruction whatsoever, impression to the contrary notwithstanding.

For Yoga Philosophy, Brahman is the sole reality. All objective appearance is nothing but manifestation of Brahman, and all that appears has simply no existence. In reality, they are all empty dream constructions of *manas* (mind). It is by the dream desires that physical objects gradually come to be considered as persistent objects existing outside of us. But, though during the dreams they appear to be real, they are in reality nothing but mere dream conceptions. In the dream conception a self-alienation of the pure consciousness takes place, whereby it posits itself as its other, determined by space, time, action and substance *désa- kāla-kriyā-dravyāth*. But, when the dream state is brought to an end through Yogic self-realization, it is claimed, all dream conceptions will vanish, leaving Brahman as the sole reality.

2.2.4 Cosmology Depicted by the Natarajan Icon

Throughout southern India, the God of destruction, Shiva, is depicted and worshipped in the form of Natarāja, the Lord of Dance.

The icon of the dancing Shiva is an artistic marvel. But, more than that, it is the summation of Hindu Philosophy and religion. Jawaharlal Nehru, the first prime minister of independent India regards it as "a well known example for the artistic, Scientific and Philosophical significance of Hinduism." It proclaims the Hindu view of the origin and end of the Universe and of "the ceaseless flow of energy going through an infinite variety of patterns that melt into one another." The dance of Natarāja called tānndava signifies the cycle of evolution and destruction of the Universe. Shiva dances, creating the World and destroying it. His large rhythms conjure up vast eons of time. The anonymous author of Hindu Cosmology explains the cosmological significance of Natarāja icon:

Shiva's dance is a symbol of the unity and rhythm of existence. The unending, dynamic process of creation and destruction is expressed in the energetic posture of Shiva. He dances in a ring of fire that refers to the life-death process of the Universe. Everything is subject to continual change, as energy constantly assumes new forms in the "play" (*līla*) of creation, except the God himself whose dance is immutable and absolute. The pictorial allegory of Natarāja indicates the so-called "five acts" of the deity: the creation of the Universe, its sustenance in space, its final dissolution at the end of the cycle of four World ages (*yugas*), the concealment of the nature of the godhead, and the bestowal of true knowledge.

Fig.1.1

The most noteworthy Natarāja image is the one found in the Shaivite temple in Chidambaram, the alleged site of Shiva's legendary dance in the presence of his consort, Pārvati. This magnificently modeled silver image, a superb example of Chola workmanship, is more than a graceful blending of details; it represents the constant process of creation, preservation and destruction of the Universe and invites the devotee to eliminate the illusion of ignorance to attain release from the eternal cycle of birth and death. Thus, the Natarāja image is the summation of Indian religion and Philosophy in artistic language, and should be read as pictorial allegories.

Shiva's dancing icon resides in the Golden Hall, a symbol of the nucleus of the atom and of the center (*bindu*) of the Universe. Natarāja has four hands. In his upper right hand he holds a small drum shaped as a clepsydra or hourglass, the symbol of the sound of creation. According to Zimmer, it is also the symbol of "the rhythms of sound, the vehicle of the World transmitting revelation, tradition and enchantment." The upper left hand, with fingers postured as half moon (*ardhanchandra mudra*), carries a flame, the element of destruction, representing the final destruction of the Universe. In the graceful balance of the hands, creation and destruction are shown as counterweights in the game of the cosmic dance. The quietness and serenity radiating from Shiva's face at the centre between the two hands, reemphasizes the Hindu view that creation and destruction are two inseparable sides of the one game of the cosmic dance.

Natarāja's lower right hand makes the *abhayamudra*, the gesture that offers peace and protection, by telling the devotee, "Fear not." His lower left hand, suspended at the height of the breast, points toward his raised left foot, the place of refuge and salvation. This is an invitation to the devotee to come to his feet seeking liberation from the enchantment of māya. His right foot is planted on the back of the dwarf, the demon Apasmāra Pursha, the personification of illusion, born of ignorance, over which Shiva's hairdo resides the river Goddess Ganga, whose waters bring divine grace and forgiveness. Finally, the dancing posture proclaims endless activity, the uninterrupted cosmic dance of energy that creates, sustains, destroys and recreates the Universe.

Thus, this magnificently modeled image, universally regarded as the quintessential image of Hindu art, Philosophy, religion and culture, is not merely a marvelous example of graceful Chola workmanship, but the summation of Indian wisdom depicted in the language of art. The image of Shiva dancing in joyous abandonment within a circle of flames graphically depicts his five cosmic acts of creation, preservation, destruction, unveiling of illusion, and liberation of the soul. The hourglass-shaped drum in the upper right hand, which reproduces the primordial sound of creation, symbolizes his creative aspect. Shiva's preservation of the Universe is suggested by his lower right hand held in the abhaya mudra (gesture of reassurance and safety). The flame in his upper left hand and that encircling the aureole represent the fire by which he destroys the Universe in order to recreate it. Natarāja lifts the veil of illusion through his engendering act of dancing. His act of liberating the soul is shown by his upraised left leg, which tramples on a prostrate dwarf signifying illusion.

2.3 Christian Cosmology

The chief Judeo-Christian religious text, the Bible, contains very little discussion on physical Cosmology by way of speculation on such themes as the origin, evolution and future of the Universe; or on its structure, physical arrangement, and composition. Even the rare references found in the Bible are couched most often in ambiguity, placed chiefly in the poetic exaggerations, not as literal expressions of the cosmological views of the authors.

The neglect of the need of developing a systematic cosmological view is understandable, because the Bible was not intended to be a treatise on Cosmology as much as the story of God's dealings with human beings, the story of salvation. Due to this focus on the story of salvation, cosmological issues received only a haphazard treatment, cosmological views finding expression only in those places where such views were required to take the narrative forward. In the absence of well developed cosmological views in its religious literature, what was often taught as Christian Cosmology, especially in the medieval period, was in the words of some scholars, "a bastardized mixture of Hebrew terminology and Greek Philosophy." Therefore, to get a picture of what Christianity has to say about the Universe, it is necessary to include in the narrative both what the Bible has to tell about it and what Christian tradition has added to is, borrowing from Greek Philosophy and modern Science. Accordingly, our discussion on Christian Cosmology will focus on both, what the Bible teaches and on what later Christians have added to it. To follow this development it might be useful to divide the discussion into three parts, the first part examines what the Bible teaches about the World. The second part studies how Christian view of the World got transformed under the impact of Greek Philosophy. In this section the views of two prominent Christian thinkers of the Medieval Period who ruled Christian thought till the last century – St. Augustine and St. Thomas Aquinas – are included. The third part examines how Christian Cosmology tried to accommodate itself to the findings of modern Science. In this section, the paleontologist – priest Teilhard de Chardin's views and the present scenarios are discussed.

2.3.1 Biblical Cosmology

A. The Biblical Account of the Origin of the World

Although, there is a wealth of reference to creation in the Psalms and prophetic literature, it is the opening chapters of the Book of Genesis which have dominated Judeo-Christian approaches to the doctrine of creation. As Gross notes, the first two chapters of Genesis develop in a majestic way the Christian view that God has created everything, and show how his work brought all creatures into existence, in a sort of pyramid, from chaos to humankind.

The creation story presented in these chapters is composed of two separate narratives coming from two different traditions. They have two different emphases which have been united in the final form of the canon. Biblical scholarship has attributed them to two different traditions referred to as J and P traditions.

To attempt to date and trace the development of these traditions within the canon is an interesting piece of scholarship. Yet from a cosmological perspective, it is less important than the question as to what the canon as a whole has to say about the Cosmos.

The most obvious cosmological statement in the text, a point on which both the traditions agree, is that the World was created by an effortless activity proper to God alone. This marks a radical departure from the Babylonian creation myth which narrates the story of Marduk, who creates the World after a monster, Tiamat. According to the Babylonian story, the World is created out of the dead body of Tiamat, whom Marduk had slained. There are hints of this theme in Isaiah 27, Psalm 74 and Job 26 and also in Genesis 1.2 with its reference to the formless void and the darkness over the face of the deep. In Genesis 1.2, the presence of a primeval chaos seems to menace the creative activity of God. Yet, these echoes of struggle with the forces of darkness notwithstanding, creation in both traditions are largely an effortless activity of God. In neither tradition, did God have to battle any evil force to assert His will in producing the Cosmos.

However, when the narrative moves to the details of the process of creation, differences crop up. In the first tradition called P, the World comes about from a void by a creative act of God. The first things to be created were the heaven and the earth. But, the narrative in its opening statement clarifies that in the beginning when God created the heaven and the earth, the earth was without form lacking order or any process of temporal succession. An important aspect of the creative activity was creating light and order by separation – the separation of light from darkness and land from sea. These tasks are accomplished through the word of God; they follow upon the command, "Let there be...." Creation, as one commentary puts it, takes place through a series of word-fulfillment events in which there is a stylistic connection between command and execution. The independence and sovereignty of God are embedded in this narrative. There is no struggle with the force of darkness. The supreme personal initiative and sovereignty of God are at work in creation.

In the P tradition, the production of the World is said to take place gradually taking, in all, six "days." The initial creation of the heaven and the earth is said to precede the first "day," raising difficulties for the interpreter. The creation of the formless heaven and earth should normally be regarded as the beginning of time. But, the biblical first day is the time when light is created and separated from darkness. The question in light is created and separated from darkness. The question in this regard is why was creation of the formless heaven and earth left out from the biblical calendar? Giving no hint of the reason for this omission, the narration moves to the details of the production of the phenomenal World with all its living beings in the first five "days." Then on the sixth "day" God turns to the creation of human beings, where his creative energy is most fully deployed. The first parents are said to be created in the image of God, to distinguish them from other creatures which were made 'according to their kind" (Genesis 1:11-12; 24-25).

The meaning of the word *day* in this narrative has been the cause of much ecclesiastical dispute, some insisting on a literal interpretation and others arguing for a liberal reading. But, in the light of the geological work of scholars like Charles Lyell, who suggested that the World must be much older and that it had reached its present form through long processes of gradual transformation, a literal interpretation of the Genesis account of the creation seemed untenable. To accommodate the geological insights within Christian Theology, many liberal Christian Theologians suggest that the "days' of Genesis were long intervals of indefinite length. This liberal spirit seems to attract more followers than the literalists. The consensus on the liberal spirit finds expression in the 1879 Declaratory Act of the United Presbyterian Synod, which in its final paragraph stated that in holding to the Westminster Confession of Faith "liberty of opinion is allowed on such points… not entering into the substance of the faith, as the interpretation of the 'six days" in the Mosaic account of the creation.

The liberal interpretation of the "days" of Genesis is not a new insight in the modern period. The irrational elements in the narrative had prompted St. Augustine to regard it as allegorical. St. Augustine noticed that Genesis opens with the statement that in the beginning when God created the heaven and earth, the earth was without form lacking order or any process of temporal succession. "The initial creation of heaven and earth, argued St. Augustine, precedes the first day and must be regarded as non-temporal." Again, he noticed that in the narrative day and night were created before the creation of the sun and the moon, the former taking place on the first "day" and the latter on the fourth "day." This seemingly irrational element prompted St. Augustine to conclude that the narrative is allegorical, calling for a liberal interpretation. In this liberal spirit, he interpreted the "days" of creation as standing for unknown periods of time. "What kind of days these are" wrote St. Augustine "is difficult or even impossible for us to imagine, to say nothing of describing them."

The liberal interpretation of the biblical account of creation shows in one respect a remarkable convergence with the views of contemporary Science. Current Scientific cosmogony based on the Big Bang Theory basically proposes that the Universe passes through three stages of development: (1) the initial explosion and subsequent expansion (2) an unsteady state of equilibrium when expansion stops for a period and (3) the expansion that marks the current phase of the Universe. According to the most widely held Scientific view, the Universe, starting exceedingly small (in cosmological terms) and expanding at an incredible speed, reached its massive dimensions. Then after a lull, in its current phase, it continues to expand because space itself stretches. The following passages in the Bible can be seen to prefigure this view:

God stretches out the heavens and treads on the waves of the sea (Job 9:8); He wraps himself in light as with a garment; He stretches out the heavens like a tent (Psalm 104:2); The Lord, lays the foundation of the earth and stretches out the heavens (Zechariah 12:1; Isaiah 31:13); He created the heavens and stretched them out; spread out the earth and all that comes out of it; and gave breath to its people, and life to those who walk on it (Isaiah 42:5); He founded the earth and stretches out the heavens like a canopy, and spreads them out like a tent to live in (Isaiah 40:21-22); He made all things, stretched out the heavens, and spread out the earth by Himself (Isaiah 44:24); He made the earth and created mankind upon it. His own hands stretched out the heavens; He marshaled their starry hosts (Isaiah 45:12); God made the earth by His power; He founded the World by His wisdom and stretched out the heavens by His understanding (Jeremiah 10:12; 51:15).

It is interesting to note that all these passages indicate two separate steps: first the heavens are created, and then they are stretched out. These stages correspond to the Scientific notions of the initial explosion, the subsequent expansion and the steady state of equilibrium. The Bible, however, has no conception corresponding to the Scientific notion of an expanding Universe. It seems to assume that in its current phase the Universe is in a state of steady equilibrium.

The second narrative called J uses a warmer, more picturesque style in its description of cosmogenesis. In this narrative, the details of the first five "days" are missing. The first act of God was to make the heavens and the earth. It was soon followed by the creation of human beings, who are made partly of earth and partly of a divine life-force, the two being linked in an essential unity. The narrative also stresses God's permanent care for human beings. They are created male and female to give company to each other and keep loneliness at bay; they are placed in the paradise, a symbol of profound harmony, a state of complete equilibrium; and the region they live in is provided with trees and plants.

Two characteristics of the combined narrative deserve to be highlighted. First, the biblical narrative of creation is not an answer to the question of the origin of the World and of evolution, as posed by Science. It developed in the context of a profound theological reflection on the significance of human existence and destiny. Creation is approached as the beginning of the story of salvation. Narrated in this context, the biblical account uses personal categories to express creation. It is the action of the personal God. As such divine purposiveness saturates and engulfs the whole of creation. Hence, as Hengstenberig notes, in the biblical narrative, the concept of authorship or responsibility is stressed more than that of causality. In the biblical account of creation theology takes precedence over Science. Creation is God's beneficent action towards human beings, not the working out of material causes and the laws that govern them. Creation is pure generosity, the act of loving and giving. Emphasizing authorship and responsibility over mechanical causality, creation is interpreted as the free act of God.

Secondly, though Genesis makes creation the beginning of all things, belief in creation is not reduced to a past event. Creation is an act of the present instant and continues till the hour of eschatological fulfillment. Creation is not a sort of stage for the drama of salvation. It is part of the salvific act since it founds and sustains the whole history of salvation. Human beings, and the entire creation has a role to play in this drama of salvation; for the World is given entirely to humans as a gift of God's goodness and as a task to be carried on to a fulfillment. To understand creation in its full significance, it will have to be placed, not as a stage for the drama of salvation, but as its first scene, as the beginning of a plot that gradually unfolds into a full story.

B. The Material Cause of the Universe

The question of the material cause of the Universe was not seriously addressed in the Bible. While the biblical author is certain that the World is produced by a free act of God, not involving any struggle with the forces of evil, he is ambiguous about the material cause of the Universe. Genesis 1 seems to presuppose a formless waste out of which the heavens and the earth are created. Other passages in the Bible hint at the notion of God created out of nothing (Romans 4:17; Hebrew 11:3). The verse often cited to support the doctrine of creation out of nothing is from the second book of Maccabees: "I beg you, my child, to look at the heaven and the earth and see everything that is in them, and recognize that God did not make them out of things that existed" (2 Maccabees 7:28). But, many commentators are doubtful whether this is a clear affirmation of creation out of nothing as it has traditionally been understood.

They argue that in speaking about nothing, this passage may not be referring literally to nothing. In the ancient World, that which is not may simply mean that which has no character, a formless waste. While this is clearly an expression of the sovereignty and power of God, they argue, it is not certain that this was in the mind of the writer of 2 Maccabees. In the absence of any other passage that clearly teaches creation out of nothing, many contend, it is better to assume that creation out of nothing is not an explicitly taught doctrine.

In the absence of any clear scriptural teaching on the matter, the early Christian thinkers, following Parmenides (c. 540-480 BCE), favoured the view that matter was eternal, and that God, in creating the World, and had imposed a shape upon the primordial substance. Parmenides had held that everything that exists had always existed. Nothing can come out of nothing. And nothing that exists can become nothing. Following Parmenides, the Greeks took it more or less for granted that everything that existed in the World was eternal.

The classical statement of this view is found in Plato's *Timaeus,* a highly significant Philosophical text for the theologians of the early Church, "God desires that all things should be good and nothing bad, so far as this was attainable. And so finding the whole visible sphere not at rest, but moving in an irregular and disorderly fashion out of disorder he brought order, considering that this was in every way better than the other." Justin, the Martyr, writing around the middle of the second century, was content to regard Plato as merely reproducing an idea found in Genesis, creation our of pre-existing matter. In his *First Apology,* Justin even claimed that Plato must have had access to the teaching of Moses in describing the fashioning of the World in the *Timaeus.* Thus, he thought he could detect the Bible in Plato, even if he was inadvertently doing the reverse. Perhaps, the most powerful consideration for not developing the doctrine of creation out of nothing in the earliest days was simply the Parmenidean view that "nothing comes from nothing." This principle was accepted by the Judeo-Christian tradition, working as an antidote against developing a doctrine of creation out of nothing the early period of Christianity. In this intellectual milieu, where scripture and prevailing Philosophy concurred against the notion of creation out of nothing, what is most surprising is that the doctrine of creation *ex nihilo* came so quickly and with so little controversy to be the accepted teaching of the church. The reasons for this affirmation were more Philosophical and Trinitarian, than scriptural.

Theophilus of Antioch and Irenaeus are regarded as the two key founders of the doctrine of creation out of nothing. This theory however was not original to Theophilus. His contribution to the theory is that he presents several arguments in favour of the doctrine that has already become settled at Antioch. If matter exists eternally alongside God, Theophilus argued, then God cannot be regarded as the creator of everything. Again, if like God matter is unoriginate, then to that extent it must be regarded as godlike. The sovereignty and power of God reside in God's having created the World out of nothing. Creation out of pre-existent matter would not reflect the greatness of God. This is reminiscent of St. Thomas Aquinas' later argument that a Universe without a beginning is a more fitting tribute to the goodness and power of its Maker. On the basis of these considerations about divine power, Theophilus affirms his conviction that the matter of Genesis 1.2, out of which God shaped the Cosmos, was itself brought into being by God from out nothing. Creation is thus a two-stage process in which formless matter is first created and then given form by God.

Irenaeus further develops the distinction between the unoriginate God and the originate World. This excludes any notion of the creation emanating from God. If we see the World or any intermediate agent as proceeding from God, then we introduce composition and change into the divine being. In describing the will of God as the sole ground of creation, Irenaeus defends the freedom and omnipotence of the biblical acceptable Christian alternative to pagan ideas of the eternity of matter and the emanation of the World from the being of God.

It is due to the works of Theophilus and Irenaeus that from the end of the second century the doctrine of *creatio ex nihilo* becomes the undisputed article of Christian faith. In the words of Gerhard May, "They developed the doctrine of *creatio ex nihilo* with such convincing stringency that from the end of the second century it becomes with astonishing speed the self-evident premise of Christian talk of the creation. We have to see in Theophilus and Irenaeus the specific founders of the church doctrine of *creatio ex nihilo.*

It might be noted that the word *nothing* used in the context of explaining creation, does not imply the existence of even shadowy realities from which the World emerges. The allusion here is, to works such as that of Jürgen Moltmann (1926 - ?). Moltmann, in his attempt to explain the existence of evil in the Cosmos, relies on Isaac Luria's cabalistic doctrine of *zimsum*. Zimsum signifies God's withdrawal into the divine being, as it were, and the consequent creation of a nothingness in which creation has its finite existence. The idea of making room is central to this notion. God, in withdrawing into the divine self by an act of self-retraction, creates the space within which other beings can have their existence and freedom. Thus, for Moltmann this nothing gains the characteristic of something with a negative character. As he writes, "The *nihil* in which God creates his creation is God forsakenness, hell, absolute death…." Though very imaginative and attractive, this idea would be unconvincing and unacceptable to the upholders of the doctrine of *creatio ex nihilo.* For them, to speak of creation out of nothing is simply to say that creation is not out of something, even if it means to speak of creation out of nothing is most neatly summarized by Tertullian. Since, the World does not proceed from the being of God and since the World has not existed eternally, God must have created it not out of something but out of nothing. The *nihil* refers primarily to the possibilities it excludes.

There were also strong Trinitarian reasons within Christian theology for affirming the doctrine of *creatio ex nihilo.* In his history of dogma, Jaroslav Pelikan points out that while the conflict with paganism had led to the doctrine of creation out of nothing this was made even more crucial by the subsequent conflict with

Arianism. The Arianistic assertion of the creaturehood of the Son led to a sharper distinction between the eternal origin of the Son and the creation of everything that was not God.

The doctrine of creation out of nothing enabled Christian theologians to distinguish the necessary God from the contingent creation. There could be no confusion of the different ontological statuses of these. In this respect, the doctrine can be construed as biblical even if not explicitly taught in scripture. Creation is the result of the divine will. It is a free act of God. The doctrine also has the function of avoiding any ultimate dualism in Christian theology. God and the World are not antithetical forces. The one is made to serve the other.

C. The Nature of the World

Though the Bible does not develop a systematic doctrine of the nature of the World, we find in it many passages that either make direct references to or imply certain characteristics of the Cosmos. Once obvious statement implied in the creation narrative is that the World is radically different from God. This is implied in the idea of creation as an effortless activity through the Word. Brevard Childs (1923-2007), in *Biblical Theology of the Old and New Testaments* (1992) emphasized this point by arguing that the Israelite Worldview draws a sharp distinction between God and the creation. The material World is freely created by God and is purged of all divine and demonic elements. Childs, in his study shows that there is a clear stress on the transcendence of God and the otherness of the World.

Secondly, the biblical author asserts the goodness of the World. Ancient cosmogonies have, as a rule, a markedly dualistic character. In these cosmologies the World, with its mingling of good and evil, comes from an encounter, a conflict, between a good principle of order and light, and an independent principle of disorder and evil. Even Genesis 1 uses images taken from such notion, but also stresses that everything God created was good. Since, from the start Israel knows God as its loving Lord, it was fundamentally impossible for its faith to see the World as a hostile power. Hence, the Old Testament views the World has a tranquility, a warmth and clarity. But, faith in the goodness of creation is no ground for naïve optimism. Israel was acutely aware that the created World can become corrupt.

Thirdly, the World is human oriented. It is created for the sake of humans who are the real object of God's love. The World is subject to human beings; it exists for their welfare; it is placed at their service. Therefore, they must not bow to the mysterious forces of nature. With this notion, the World looses fundamentally all divine status, though it can be recognized as a sign and a word given to humanity by God. It is a sort of covenant given to humans by God. The very existence of the World is to some degree a salvific work, since it is the theatre of the power and fidelity of God. This narrative also "affirms the unthinkable proximity of the creature to the creator." Creation is oriented to this intimacy.

Fourthly, the World is not a finished product. In the Bible, the World is not a stable cosmic order which was set up by creation once and for all. It is, in the words of Gerhard von Rad, "much less a being than a happening." Creation is, therefore, a promise ordained to a fulfillment. It is entirely caught up in the relationship between God and human beings. Hence, creation and redemption appear almost as one and the same act of God. God's creative action is not simply a thing of the past; it takes place here and now, and is yet to come. In the New Testament there are also hints suggesting that all things coming from God are moving towards him (1 Corinthians 8:6; Romans 11:36; Ephesians 4:6; Hebrew 2:10), though here the orientation to God is predicated particularly of the community, it is applied to the whole creation.

Fifthly, in spite of its original goodness, the World as it exists now is a "fallen" World. The present World is not the one that was originally planned and executed by God. It has undergone degeneration. Genesis 3:14-19 describes the degeneration: the right order is disturbed in people's relationship to God, to their neighbours and to the infra-human realm how long did the specially graced World last before the degeneration occurred is not mentioned, though the reason for the fall from grace is clearly stated. Human beings misused their gift of freedom, a boon in itself, but one that hides within it the temptation and the possibility of a wrong decision. The misuse of freedom takes place under the influence of the serpent, the embodiment of the evil principle, who attributes envious designs to God and promises the woman a neutral country from which she can pass judgment on God and his command. Thus, the urge to be like God and to be incomprehensible, and the fascinating desire to be master of secrets beyond the human horizon, so as to reach ultimately a region where they will be free of God, is awakened in the first parents. Thus, the cause of the fall from grace is the first parent's will "to be independent of God in a monstrous arrogance and content himself with creatures." This total absorption in the World produces a degenerated World. All creation participates in the drama of refusal (Romans 8:19-21).

Sixthly, due to the degeneration that has taken place, evil lurks in the World. The New Testament is very conscious of the power of evil present in the World. In St. Paul and St. John the Cosmos is defined by its hostility to God. It is true, of course, that this dualism is a moral one, and not strictly ontological. Though, God had created it good, by human rebellion, today it has become a home of evil, opposed to God, but capable of salvation. All things are from God, and look for his Lordship, when he will be all in all (1 Corinthians 15:28). The inadequacy and the brittleness of the present creation will be fulfilled in Christ. Thus, the permanent and fundamental optimism is replaced by hope.

Seventhly, probably under the influence of Egyptian and Hellenistic "wisdom," the World is seen as a matter of great significance for humans. In the book of Job the World is described as a spectacle (Job 36:25-26), and in the book of Wisdom, as the object of human research (Wisdom 7:17-20). It evokes astonishment and humility (Job 28:38-39) and hymns of praise (Psalm 8; 19; 24; 33; 93). It almost becomes proof of the existence of God (Wisdom 13:1-9). Here creation becomes the absolute foundation of faith. In the New Testament creation is chanted as one of the magnificent works of God (Acts 4:24; cf. Revelation 4:11; 10:6; 14:7).

Eighthly, in spite of its degeneration, this is a redeemed World. God reconciled everything to himself in and by Christ. Jesus made peace with everything in heaven and one earth by means of his blood on the cross. This includes even those who were once far away from God. Even God's enemies are brought back as his friends. Through his death on the cross Jesus has brought everyone into the very presence of God, and made each one holy and blameless without a single fault (Colossians 1:20-22). It is not human beings alone, but all creation participates in this drama of refusal and redemption (Romans 8:19-21).

Ninthly, the goal-oriented continuous creation is Christocentric. In the New Testament Christ is designated as the new Adam. In him creation is renewed. He is also presented as the image of the invisible God (Colossians 1:15; 2 Corinthians 4:4) in whom the ancient World of creation has been fully verified. In 1 Corinthians 8:6, Christ is recognized both as the Lord of creation and of salvation. It is through Christ that God created everything in heaven and earth, things we can see and the things we can't see – kings, kingdoms, rulers and authorities. Everything has been created through Him and for Him (Colossians 1:16). He is also said to be the first of all who will rises from the dead, and of everything (Colossians 1:18). God is said to have made peace with everything in heaven and on earth by means of Jesus' blood on the cross (Colossians 1:19-20).

Lastly, the history of this World is linear and unrepeatable. Creation and destruction are not repeated as conceived in Hinduism or Buddhism. The World we know has only one cycle of existence. It had a beginning and at an unspecified time it would end, never to repeat again.

D. The Structure of the World

The mainstream Christian doctrine recognizes four realms of the Universe: heaven, the physical Universe, purgatory and hell.

i. Heaven

In the Christian belief, heaven is the abode of God, where angels and God's elected ones, i.e., those who earned merit either by leading pure and holy lives on earth or after a course of purification in purgatory enjoy, in the company of Christ, the immediate, vision of God. In popular piety it is located in the sky, above the clouds. Jesus after his resurrection is said to have ascended into heaven, where, "he is seated at the right hand of God." Heaven is governed by laws different from the ones applied to life on earth. For example, in heaven there will be no marriage or death: "Marriage is for people here on earth. But, that is not the way it will be in the age to come for those worthy of being raised from the dead won't be married then. And they will never die again. In these respects they are like angels. They are children of God raised up to new life" (Luke 20:34-36). The meritorious ones who are admitted there receive, after the resurrection, glorified bodies and are supernaturally elevated to be capable of living in God's presence. There, all those redeemed are believed to be unspeakably happy in the eternal possession of God, though the degree of happiness may vary corresponding to degrees of merit. Entry into heaven is restricted to the perfectly pure and holy; but for those who have attained that state, either at death or after a course of purification in purgatory, entry into heaven is not deferred.

ii. Purgatory

The Bible contains no mention of purgatory and its existence is not universally accepted by all Christians. The Reformers, for example, deny the existence of purgatory, since it has no scriptural basis. Catholic thought, however postulates purgatory to answer the question regarding the future life of those who are not sinful enough to deserve eternal punishment or pure and holy enough to enter into eternal reward. Purgatory is conceived as an intermediate realm where those who die imperfect, but not in unrepented mortal sin undergo a course of penal purification to qualify for admission into heaven. Its physical location in relation to the physical Universe or its layout is not specified, though Christians believe that souls in purgatory benefit by the prayers and good works of the living.

iii. Hell

The Bible describes hell as a place of darkness, where "there will be weeping and gnashing of teeth" (Matthew 8:12). It is also described as a furnace to burn the evil doers (Matthew 13:42), a fireplace to throw the wicked (Matthew 13:50). Since, fire and darkness cannot co-exist, these descriptions must be taken to be symbolic expressions highlighting some sort of torture. But, taking biblical references literally, Christian piety conceives hell as a dark, slimy, burning place, located somewhere below the earth meant to torture forever, people who die in a state of unrepented mortal sin (and angels who disobey God). However, Christian doctrine generally conceives it not as a place of fire and worms but as state of the soul's being excluded forever from the beatific vision. Catholic doctrine is content with affirming the existence of such a state, with varying degrees of punishment corresponding to degrees of guilt and its eternal or unending duration, and refuses to enter into further speculation on its nature and structure. Rationalists, while acknowledging the existence hell, tend to deny the eternity of it, in spite of the authority of Christ. Professing Christians, who are unwilling to admit either the existence or its eternity, try to explain away Christ's words. But, the majority of Christians following the teachings of Christ and the apostles affirm the existence of hell, located somewhere below the earth, conceiving it either as a place or state of eternal torture of the wicked.

iv. The Physical Universe

In the Bible, it is the physical Universe that gets the most attention. The Bible contains references to its origin, structure and consummation. It is the physical realm, a proper object of human intelligence and Scientific enquiry. This realm alone falls within the purview of Cosmology, either mythical or speculative or Scientific, while the other three realms fall within the field of Christian eschatology.

In the biblical thought, in addition to the earth, the physical Universe consists of the sky, sun, moon, stars and waters. The sky, most frequently translated as "firmament," is the abode of the stars. In Hebrew, it is described as *raqiya* (*rakia*, Hebrew for a plate); but scholars differ on the exact definition of *raqiya*. Some say that it refers to a rigid, broad, solid plate possessing a certain thickness. Others claim that it refers to an empty space or one filled with atmosphere. Whatever is its exact nature, *raqiya* or the sky, according to Genesis, was set in the midst of the waters in such a way that it divided the water above from those beneath. Since, it is possible to see what is on the other side of the dividing wall (*raqiya*), it is quite possible that the author of Genesis regarded the sky as being composed of some sort of transparent material. The book of Ezekiel seems to suggest that the material of which *raqiya* is composed resembles ice (Ezekiel 1:22). It is quite likely that the author of Genesis, too, thought of *raqiya* as solidified, transparent water. Being solid it can't prevent the water above the vault from falling to the realm below, except at the time of rain; and being transparent, it would permit the stars, which are located above its vault, to be seen through it.

The sky is the abode of the sun, moon and stars which are either fixed in it or moved across it. While describing the nature of the heavenly bodies, the Bible seems to adopt an animistic view. Several biblical passages refer to the heavenly bodies as if they were living creatures. For example, they are born when God breathes the word (Psalm 33:6); they remain dark hoping in vain for light (Job 3:9); they rule the night (Psalm 136:9); they fight from their courses like warriors on the march (Judges 5:20); with the angels they sing together (Job 38:7) and praise God (Psalm 148:3); by a miracle, they are made to stand suddenly still (Joshua 10:12); the earth staggers like a drunkard (Isaiah 24:20); and in Jeremiah reverence is offered to the stars as living creatures (Jeremiah 8:2).

In later times the stars are spoken of as "the hosts of heaven." They stand in God's presence, to the right and the left of God's throne (I Kings 22:19; 2 Chronicles 18:18): they serve him (Nehemiah 9:6; Psalm 103:21), and praise him (Psalm 103:21, 148:2). Like the kings of earth, they may be consigned by God's judgment to the netherWorld (Isaiah 24:21) and God will in future execute judgment among them as among the nations of the earth (Isaiah 34:4). At the head of this starry host stands a "captain of the army" (Joshua 5:14); according to a passage in the Book of Daniel, he was the highest star in altitude (Daniel 8:11). This starry army belongs to God; hence the frequent expression "God of hosts' indicates that God is the actual leader of the heavenly array. If these passages may be regarded as other than poetical figures, then it would give credence to the accusation that the Bible contains animistic views.

E. The Consummation of the Present World

The most elaborate cosmological discussion in the Bible is regarding the consummation of history, variously referred to as the second coming of Christ, the end of the World, the day of the Lord, the end of times, the coming of new Jerusalem, the renewal of creation, and so on. Both the Old Testament and the New Testament it is most frequently referred to as the "end of times."

i. The Day of the Lord

Most frequently, the day of the Lord is conceived as a day of terror. The day of the Lord as prophet Joel foresaw, is a terrible day when destruction comes from the Almighty. He vividly describes the terrors of that day. On that day God will cause wonders in the heavens and on the earth-blood and fire and pillars of smoke. The sun will be turned into darkness, and the moon will turn blood-red (Joel 2:28-29). Joel is very graphic in his description of what to expect towards the end of history, prior to the day of the Lord: People will watch as their food disappears before their very eyes. There will be no joyful celebrations in the house of our God. Streams would dry up. The seeds will die in the parched ground, and the crops will fail. The barns and granaries will stand empty and abandoned. The animals will moan with hunger. Fire would have consumed the pastures and burned up all the trees. The cattle will wander about confused because there will be no pasture for them. The sheep will bleat in misery. Even the wild animals will cry out because they will have no water to drink (Joel 1:15-20).

Prophet Amos too, describes the day of the Lord as a terrible day. He warns the people who wished the Lord to come and rescue them from all their enemies: But, you have no idea what you are wishing for. That day will not bring light and prosperity, but darkness and disaster. In that day you will be like a man who runs from a lion – only to meet a bear. After escaping the bear, he leans his hand against a wall in his house – and is bitten by a snake. Yes the day of the Lord will be a dark and hopeless day, without a ray of joy or hope (Amos 5:18-20).

Prophets Zephaniah and Zechariah agree with Joel and Amos. According to them, the day of the Lord is a terrible day: "Swiftly it comes – a day when strong men will cry bitterly. It is a day when the Lord's anger will be poured out. It is a day of terrible distress and anguish, a day of ruin and desolation, a day of darkness and gloom, of clouds, blackness, trumpet calls and battle cries. Down go the walled cities and strongest battlements!" (Zephaniah 14:1-2).

Likewise, in Zechariah, we find this passage: "Watch, for the day of the Lord is coming when your possessions will be plundered right in front of you! On that day I will gather all the nations to fight against Jerusalem. The city will be taken, the houses plundered, and the women raped. Half the population will be taken away into captivity, and half will be left among the ruins of the city (Zechariah 14:1-2).

On the other hand, there are also passages in the Old Testament that describes the day of the day of the Lord as a desirable time. Prophet Isaiah draws a consoling picture of that day. According to him, that day is sure to come, and when it comes, people will want a proper relationship with God (Isaiah 2:12); and on that day will people praise God (Isaiah 26:1). Joel, too, agrees that on that day God will pour out his Spirit upon all people. Then people will prophesy. Old people will dream the dreams and young people will see visions. In those days, God will pour out his Spirit even on servants, men and women alike (Joel 2:28-29). Malachi, too, draws a consoling picture of the day of the Lord: "Before the terrible day is upon them, God will send the prophet Elijah and his preaching will turn the hearts of parents to their children, and the hearts of children to their parents" (Malachi 4:5).

The day of the Lord in the Hebrew thought is also God's appointed time to judge the nations, the time when God will separate and judge both evil and the good. According to Prophet Isaiah, on this day God will judge all unrighteousness and disobedience; on this day all accounts will be settled and the crooked made straight (Isaiah 2:12). For the unfaithful it will be a day of darkness and doom. On that day, God will search with lanterns in Jerusalem's darkest corners to find and punish those who sit contented in their sins, indifferent to the Lord, thinking he will do nothing at all to them. Their property will be plundered by the enemy, and their homes will be ransacked. They will never have a chance to live in the new homes they have built. They will never drink wine from the vineyards they have planted. Malachi describes the fate of the wicked, "the day of judgment is coming, burning like a furnace. The arrogant and the wicked will be burned up like straw on that day. They will be consumed like a tree – roots and all" (Malachi 4:1). But, Malachi predicts a glorious time for the righteous: "But, for you who fear my name, the Sun of Righteousness will rise with healing in his wings. And you will go free, leaping with joy like calves let out to pasture. On the day when I act, you will tread upon the wicked as if they were dust under your feet…" (Malachi 4:2-3). Joel too, agrees that for the faithful, the day of the Lord will be glorious, since anyone who calls on the name of the Lord will be saved (Joel 2:32).

One thing to be noted about the Hebrew concept of the day of the Lord is that it is conceived not in cosmic terms, but in terms of what would happen to the human race, and particularly to the Israelites. With the exception of a brief reference to God causing wonders in the heavens and on the earth by turning the sun into darkness, and the moon blood-red (Joel 2:28-29), none of the descriptions mention what would happen to the Cosmos. Presumably, what the Old Testament authors had in mind was a moment within earthly history when the imperfections of social and personal life will be vanquished by a decisive intervention of God, while the cosmic history for the most part remained unaffected. They are referring to the consummation, not of the Cosmos, not even of human race, but of the present-day society marked as it is by physical, moral and social imperfections. As such, these passages have little cosmological significance in the strict sense.

ii. The End of Times

In the place of the Old Testament phrase *the day of the Lord,* the New Testament uses the expression *end of times.* In the New Testament there are a number of passages that refer to the end of times. Unlike the day of the Lord in the Old Testament, the end of times in the New Testament is cosmic event, affecting the entire Universe. Luke mentions that towards the end of times "the stability of the very heavens will be broken up" (Luke 21:26). After describing a period of tribulation that precedes the end of times, Matthew describes cosmic events that accompany it:

> The sun will be darkened, the moon will not give light, the stars will fall from the sky, and the powers of heaven will be shaken. And then at last, the sign of the coming of the son of Man will appear in the heavens and there will be deep mourning among all the nations of the earth. And they will see the Son of Man arrive on the clouds of heaven with power and great glory (Matthew 24:29-30).

Based on this passage and a passage each from Isaiah, Paul's letter to the Romans, and the Book of Revelation, Christians believe that at the end of times the heavens above will melt away and disappear like a rolled-up scroll. The stars will fall from the sky, just as withered leaves and fruits fall from a tree (Isaiah 34:4). Creation itself will be set free from its bondage to decay and obtain the freedom of the glory of the children of God (Romans 8:21). At the end of times not only the old heaven and the old earth but the sea also will be gone forever (Revelation 21:1); and in the place of the old heaven and the old earth a new heaven and a new earth will emerge (Revelation 21:1-2). The physical characteristics of the new heaven and the new earth are not specified, but it will be the home of God among his people, where God will live with them and they will be his people. Living with them and being their God, he will remove all their sorrow, and there will be no more death, or sorrow or crying or pain (Revelation 21:3-4).

The Timing of the End of Times

Though the New Testament raises the question of the timing of the end of times, the answer given is ambiguous, indefinite and conflicting. Matthew 24:37-39; 24:44; and 25:36, Mark 13:32, Luke 21:34 and Acts 1:6 emphasize the unpredictability of the time when the end will take place, though its occurrence is certain. In Matthew 24:37-39 Jesus compares the unpredictability of the time of his return to what happened in Noah's day. People will be enjoying banquets and parties and wedding without realizing what is about to happen. And they will be caught unawares as it happened at the time of Noah. Matthew 24:44, Matthew 25:36 and Mark 13:32 are the most emphatic in forewarning the unpredictability of the second coming of Jesus. In Matthew 24:44 Jesus clearly states, "For the Son of Man will come when least expected." Matthew 25:36 and Mark 13:32 are parallel passages. Matthew 25:36 declares, "However, no one knows the day or the hour when these things will happen, not even the angels in heaven of the Son himself. Only the Father knows." When the disciples pushed for a more definite answer, Jesus emphasized the inevitability of the end and assured them that the end won't follow immediately (Matthew 24:6).

Nevertheless, there are reported words of Jesus which seemed to suggest that the day of the Lord will take place without much delay, during the lifetime of the hearers – Matthew 24:34, Luke 9:26, John 21:22, for example. Matthew's passage, which is the most vivid, reads thus: "I assure you, this generation will not pass from the scene before all these things take place." Luke too is clear that the end should come soon: "And I assure you that some of you standing here right now will not die before you see the kingdom of God." John wrote his passage at a time much after Jesus' death, a time when the expectation of the imminent end was dying out. So he interprets Jesus' words in such a way as to imply that Jesus in fact did not promise an immediate return.

Despite this ambiguity and inconclusiveness of Jesus' teaching on the timing of his return and he end of the World, Christians in the 1st century AD nurtured the hope that the end would come during their lifetime and lived under that certainty. When the converts of Paul in Thessalonica were persecuted by the Roman Empire, they believed the end was upon them. However, doubt regarding the imminent end rose as early as the 90s and by the 130s, Christian writers began to ask why the end had not come early as they had expected. Justin martyr declared that God was delaying the end of the World because he wished for Christianity to become a World religion. In the 250s, Cyprian once again assured Christians that the end was near and cited the sins of that time as a prelude to the end and proof that it is not far.

However, by the 3rd century most Christians believed that the end of times was not imminent. They recalled Jesus' teaching on the impossibility of speculating on the time of the end of times (for example, Matthew 24:44, Matthew 25:36, Mark 13:35, Luke 21:34), and then on discouraged attempts to divine the future. Yet some, relying on the Jewish description of the Six Ages of the World predicted the end of times to occur in AD 202. But, when that date passed, the date was changed to AD 500. When that date, too, passed, the importance of fixing a date to the end of times was marginalized till the third quarter of the last century, when it was revived, particularly among conservative Calvinist groups. Today, barring a few evangelical groups, no one engages in a speculation on the day when the end of times, will take place, though the expectation of it taking place at some unspecified future continues to dominate Christian doctrine, and influence Christian life and liturgy.

The Signals of the End of Times

Though, on the plea that speculation on the timing of the last things is futile Jesus refused to answer the disciple's query on the issue, he unhesitatingly told them what signals to look for. In response to a question from the disciples, whether there will be "any sign ahead of time to signal your return and the end of the World?" Jesus vividly describes the events to be expected before his return (Matthew 24:4-51). Before the end, said Jesus, many will come claiming to be the Messiah. They will lead many astray. And wars will break out near and far. The nations and kingdoms will proclaim war against each other, and there will be famines and earthquakes in many parts of the World. But, all this will be only the beginning of the horrors to come.

Then the disciples of Jesus will be arrested, persecuted and killed. They will be hated all over the World because of their allegiance to Jesus. And many will turn away from Jesus and betray and hate each other. Any many false prophets will appear and lead many people astray. Sin will be rampant everywhere, and the love of many will grow cold. In those days the prophecy of Daniel that predicts sacrilege and desecration of the holy places will be fulfilled. At that time false messiahs and false prophets will rise up and perform great miraculous signs and wonders, so as to deceive even God's chosen ones. But, the Good News about the Kingdom will be preached throughout the whole World, so that all nations will hear it; and then finally, the end will come. The sun will be darkened, the moon will not give light, the stars will fall from the sky, and the powers of heaven will be shaken, following this, the Son of man will appear in the heavens to judge the living and the dead and to bring history to its fulfillment.

The Events at the End of Times

Many passages in the Bible describe the last events following the period of suffering, turmoil, strife and war. They include the return of Jesus, the resurrection of the dead, the Last Judgment, the consummation of the present World and the renewal of creation. In the Bible these are called the last things. Despite the terrifying nature of the events towards the end of times, Christianity teaches that the consummation of the present age is not something to be feared, but to be sought with eager expectation, for it takes place in accordance with the will of God (Romans 8:20). Mk. 13:8 and Romans 8:22 compare it with a mother's birth pain. Though painful in itself, it brings fruits that rare desirable. According to Paul, the whole creation, in fact, waits with eager longing for the 'revealing of the sons of God" (Romans 8:22). And not only the creation, but Christians themselves, who are the first fruits of the Spirit, groan inwardly as they wait eagerly for the redemption of their bodies and adoption as God's children (Romans 8:23). Christians wait for the end of times with patience (Romans 8:25) and in their hope, they believe, they are saved (Romans 8:24).

The Order of Events at the End of Times

Though some, notably followers of Eastern Orthodoxy, regard most popular discussion of "the last things" to be fundamentally and dangerously false, there are a considerable number of Christians who are willing to speculate on the subject, particularly on the order of events prior to and during end of times. Their discussion has given rise to various controversial positions concerning the order of events leading to and following the return of Jesus. They arrange the last events in one of the following order:

The Preaching of the Good News throughout the Whole World

A question is generally raised regarding the status of Christianity prior to the beginning of "the last things." It is asked whether all people will be converted to Christianity prior to the end of times. In response to this question, some evangelical conservative groups assert that prior to the end of times all people will be converted to Christianity. Isaiah 60:3, Zachariah 8:20-22 are often quoted to support this view. The more liberal view is that Christianity will continue to be like yeast or leaven, which though little in quantity, permeates every part of a large measure of dough. The hope is that the World will be transformed by Christian values through the preaching of the gospel, though not all people will become members of the church. Jesus' own teaching is that "the Good News about the Kingdom will be preached throughout the whole World, so that all nations will hear it; and then, finally, the end will come" (Matthew 24:14). This passage and the parables relating the kingdom of God to yeast (Matthew 13:33), and the mustard seed (Matthew 13:31-32) are sufficiently vague and ambiguous enough to permit both these views.

The Elimination of Suffering

Likewise, another question is generally raised regarding the human condition immediately prior to the beginning of the last things. It is asked whether prior to the end of times all suffering out to be eliminated. Once again two views are expressed. The minority view holds that all suffering ought to be eliminated prior to Christ's return at the end of times. By contrast majority view, taking cue from Matthew 13:29; Mark 14:7 and Revelation 21:3 holds that suffering, disease, injustice and death will continue until the second coming of Christ; they will completely eliminated only when the Kingdom of God will be fully established. But, the Christian hope of the kingdom of God will not be realized in this lifetime. The relevant passages in the New Testament seem to support this view. According to Mark 14:4, Jesus told his disciples, "You will always have the poor among you, and you can help them whenever you want to." According to Matthew 13:29: God lets both weed and wheat grow together until the harvest. It is at the time of the harvest that the weeds are sorted out and burned and the wheat put in the barn. And according to Revelation, it is only when "the old World and its evils are gone forever" and when the new World is established that God himself will be with them and remove all of their sorrows, so that "there will be no more death or sorrow or crying or pain."

The Second Coming

Towards the end of this period of tribulation, Christians expect "the sign of the coming of the Son of man" to appear in the heavens. The central of Christian worship calls the Christian's attention toward the return of Jesus Christ and the renewal of the creation. Many biblical passages strengthen this expectation. For example, Paul tells the Corinthians, "For as often as you eat this bread and drink this cup, you proclaim the Lord's death until he comes" (1 Corinthians 11:26).

For Christians the return of Jesus Christ is the most important eschatological event. Matthew describes the manner of his appearance, "And they will see the Son of Man arrive on the clouds of heaven with power and great glory. And he will send forth his angels with the sound of a might trumpet blast, and they will gather together his chosen ones from the farthest ends of the earth and heaven" (Matthew 24:30-31).

The Resurrection of the Body

The visible coming (Greek: *parousia*) of Christ in power and glory will be the signal for the rising of the dead. According to the Catholic teaching, there is to be only general resurrection, in which all the dead who are to be judged will rise, the wicked as well as the just. They are believed to rise with bodies they had before their death, though their bodies have undergone transformation. It is not specified how the risen and transformed body is different from the previous one or how the resurrected bodies of the good are different from those of the evil. Regarding the qualities of the risen bodies, in the case of the just we have three biblical description (I Corinthians 15:12-14, Matthew 13:43, Philippians 3:21) to serve as a basis for theological speculation. Basing on these passages, Christians believe that it will be glorious like the risen body of Christ, shining in quality. But, Christian doctrine is not sure about the quality of the risen body of the wicked. Though not formally stated, it is sufficiently certain that they will have incorruptible bodies.

The General Judgment

After the resurrection of the dead, Christians anticipate the Final Judgment, when Christ will personally judge the living and the dead, to determine the eternal destiny of each according to whether their names are written in the Lam's Book of Life. Christians expect God to send forth his angels with the sound of a mighty trumpet blast to gather together his chosen ones from the farthest ends of the earth and heaven. Matthew 25:31-46 gives a graphic description of the Final Judgment. Matthew 25:31-35 describes the second coming of Jesus in glory and rewarding the good after separating them from the bad:

But, when the Son of Man comes in his glory, and all the angels with him, then he will sit upon his glorious throne. All the nations will be gathered in his presence, and he will separate them as a shepherd separates the sheep from the goats. He will place the sheep at his right hand and the goats at his left. Then the King will say to those on the right, "Come, you who are blessed by my Father, inherit the Kingdom prepared for you from the foundation of the World (Matthew 25:31-35).

The wicked, on the other hand, are punished. Their punishment consists in this: the King will turn to them and say, "Away with you, you cursed ones, into the eternal fire prepared for the Devil and his demons!" (Matthew 25:41). With these words they will be sent to eternal punishment. Their eternal punishment consists in a life of unimaginable sorrow and suffering, symbolized by the fire of hell, from which there is no release.

The Consummation of All Things

There is mention also of the physical Universe sharing in the general consummation (Peter 3:13, Romans 8:19-21, Revelation 21:1-3). The present heaven and earth will be destroyed, and a new heaven and earth will take their place. But, what, precisely, this process will involve, or what purpose the renovated World will serve is not specified. It is sometimes said to point to a period of history ruled by Christ. Christ's militant reign is to cease with the Final Judgment (1 Corinthians 15:24-26), but as king of the elect, whom he has saved, he will reign with them in glory forever. Once again, it is not clear what the reign of Christ would involve. Historically, it may refer to a time when the earth will produce what is needed for human welfare, when sin, injustice, violence and war will be conquered, and when people will begin to live in a just and human society, loving and caring for each other. However, the cosmological significance of the renewal of creation and the reign of Christ is not clear.

iii. The Order of Events in the Book of Revelation

Revelation 20:1-12 paints a different picture of the end of times. This passage speaks vaguely of a Messianic Age or a Millennium of Messiah, a 1,000-year reign of Christ. It suggests that the Millennium of Messiah will come about prior to the Final Judgment. The vagueness of the passage gives rise to three views on the order of events at the end of times. Some Christians think that the passage predicts Christ's second coming, which will inaugurate a literal 1,000-year earthly rule. The Final Judgment will take place at the conclusion of the Millennium of Messiah. Upon Christ's return there will be partial resurrection, only of the faithful, who will reign with Christ for one thousand years. During this time Satan will be imprisoned or restrained in the Abyss or Bottomless Pit. At the end of the thousand years, Satan will be released for a short period to deceive the godless people of God. The wicked will attempt to surround the Holy City once more during a millennial rebellion. Again, they will be defeated for all time and Satan will be cast into the lake of fire. The great judgment will follow. The devil will be condemned to hell for all eternity, together with those who have trusted in him rather than in God. This penultimate event is the Last Judgment, after which each person will be consigned to either hell or heaven. The end of all things is a new heaven and a new earth, a time when there will no longer be death and "God will be all in all" (1 Corinthians 15:28) this is that final moment of ultimate perfection and bliss toward which all orthodox Christians finally direct their hope.

The same passage from Revelation supports another view of the sequence of the last things. According to this view, the second coming will be in two stages separated by a seven-year period of tribulation. At the first stage, Christ will return in the air to rescue those who are Christians at the time. Then follows a seven-year period of suffering, in which the antichrist will conquer the World and kill those who refuse to worship him. At the end of the seven years, the final witness will go out, and Christ will return to the earth. He will defeat the antichrist and rescue the Jews and those who have converted to Christianity during the tribulation.

A third view, based on the passage from the book of Revelation, understands the "thousand years" as an idiomatic expression for the entire period following the resurrection of Christ until his return. The upholders of this view do not anticipate a physical throne set up in geographical Jerusalem on earth, where Christ will reign for one thousand years. They believe that Christ is reigning now, at the right hand of God, in fulfillment of the promises made to David that his throne would be without end. They are optimistic concerning the progress of the gospel and the increasing practical benefit of Christianity to all people. They anticipate that prior to Christ's return, the World will have gradually but entirely converted to Christianity, at least nominally, through the preaching of the gospel. The power of the Holy Spirit, working through the gospel, will eventually be pervasive. This, they believe, will ensure a future conversion of the Jewish people, en masse, to the Christian faith. Legal sanctions will ensure the punishment of the wicked and reward of the just. The Second Advent will be an event that continues the state of earthly affairs, rather than interposing a radical discontinuity to them. Some anticipate a final apostasy, immediately prior to the Final Judgment.

2.3.2 Developments under the Impact of Greek Philosophy

A. The Cosmology of St. Augustine

In early Christendom, the name of Augustine stands out as that of the greatest of the Fathers both from a literary and from a theological standpoint. His name dominated the Western thought until the thirteenth century and even now continues to retain its luster, notwithstanding the Aristotelianism of St. Thomas and his School.

As his thought was focused on the soul's relation to God, St. Augustine showed very little interest in the material World for its own sake. But, his general Philosophy involved a theory of the corporeal World, a theory consisting of elements taken from former thinkers and set in a Christian framework. Due to his primary interest in the soul's relation to God, while drawing from previous thinkers for his theories, he did not trouble himself with developing a comprehensive view of the Universe, but focused on those lines which seemed to him best calculated to underline nature's relation to and dependence on God.

i. The Origin of the World

To explain the origin of the World St. Augustine, in common with other Christian writers, held the view that the World came into existence out of nothing by God's free, creative act. In holding this theory St. Augustine differed from Plotinus, one of the pagan thinkers who had most probably been influenced by Christian teaching. Plotinus proposed an emanation theory which depicted the World as proceeding in some way from God without God becoming in any way diminished or altered thereby. Since, activity seemed to postulate change in God, Plotinus denied that God acts freely; rather God diffuses himself necessarily. However, St. Augustine rejected this view and held the doctrine of free creation out of nothing as a way of upholding and safeguarding the utter supremacy of God and the World's entire dependence on him. St. Augustine insisted that all things owe their being to God.

St. Augustine also rejects the biblical suggestion that the World is made out of some formless matter. Absolutely formless matter is for St. Augustine equivalent to nothingness. If formlessness is only in comparison with completely formed but which has inchoate form, in the sense of possessing the capacity to receive form, then such matter is not altogether nothing indeed. But, St. Augustine argues, such formless matter is something, and as nothing, it has what being it has only from God.

In the Confessions, St. Augustine shows an openness to the suggestion of the existence of some sort of formless matter before the creative act of God brought the World into existence, and identifies this matter with the mutability or potentially of bodies. But, at the same time, he indicates that if he could call it 'nothing' or assert that it does not exist, he would do so. If a pre-existing potentiality, or capacity of receiving forms, is admitted, it cannot be called absolutely nothing. Elsewhere, he argues that not only the possession of form but even the capacity to receive form is a good, and what is a good cannot be absolutely nothing. Yet this matter, which is not absolutely nothing, is itself the creation of God. "not preceding formed things in time but co created with form" St. Augustine identified the "unformed matter which God made out of nothing" with the heaven and earth mentioned in the first verse of the first chapter of Genesis as the primary creation of God. In other words, St. Augustine is saying that God created out of nothing not absolutely formless "prime matter," apart from all form, but form and matter together. In proposing this view, St. Augustine is not so concerned with developing a Philosophical doctrine of creation "for its own sake as with emphasizing the essential dependence of all creatures on God and the perishable nature of all corporeal creatures, even when once constituted in existence." In other words, St. Augustine is emphasizing that all creatures receive their being from God, and that their being is bound up with their mutability.

ii. St. Augustine's Theory of Seminal Reasons

Another cosmological theory which was dear to St. Augustine himself and to his followers was that of the "seminal reasons" (*rationes seminales*). This theory, which was calculated to exalt the divine agency at the expense of the causal activity of creatures, suggests that everything in the Universe was created in the seminal reasons, in a germinal form, which in the course of time develops into the objects of various species by their temporal unfolding. Thus, even man, as regards his body at least, was created in the seminal reasons. Copleston defines seminal reasons as "germs of things or invisible powers or potentialities, created by God in the beginning in the humid element and developing into the objects of various species by their temporal unfolding." They are invisible, potential things which are to be at a future time, but have not yet been made.

It is likely that in proposing the theory of seminal reasons, St. Augustine was influenced by the idea of the germinal potentialities in the Philosophy of Plotinus, which ultimately goes back to the seminal reasons of Stoicism. While proposing this theory, St. Augustine never supposed that seminal reasons were the object of experience, that they could be seen or touched; they are invisible, having inchoate form or a potentiality to the development of form according to the divine plan. The "seminal reasons" are not purely passive, but tend to self-development, though the absence of the requisite conditions and circumstances and of other external agencies may hinder or prevent their development. St. Bonaventure compared the seminal reasons to the rosebud, which is not yet actually the rose but will develop into the rose, given the presence of the necessary positive agencies and the absence of negative or preventive agencies.

Undoubtedly, seminal reasons is a vague idea of rather incomprehensible content. St. Augustine's assertion of it was on exegetical grounds, not on Philosophical or Scientific grounds. The idea originated in this way. According to the book of Ecclesiasticus, "He that liveth for ever created all things together" (18:1). On the other hand, according to the Genesis, the fishes and birds appeared only on the fifth "day" of creation, while the cattle and beasts of the earth appeared only on the sixth "day." The question before St. Augustine was, how these two statements can be reconciled. One biblical passage claimed that God created all things together, while the other held that some things were made after others, that is to say, that *not* all things were created together. St. Augustine's way of reconciling this incoherence was to say that God did indeed create all things together in the beginning, but he did not create them all in the same condition. In the beginning he created everything – all plants, fishes, birds, animals, and human beings themselves – invisibly, latently, potentially, in germ, in their seminal reasons. In this way God created in the beginning all the vegetation of the earth, for example, before it was actually growing on the earth. Later, prodded by God's plan and activity, they unfold on earth as actual at a time appointed by God. St. Augustine would thus solve the apparent contradiction between Ecclesiasticus and Genesis by making a distinction. Ecclesiasticus and Genesis are not speaking of the same thing. Ecclesiasticus is referring to germinal or seminal creation, which takes place all at once, whereas Genesis is speaking of actual formal completion, which takes place in course of history.

From what has been said it should be clear that St. Augustine was not considering primarily a Scientific problem but rather an exegetic problem, so that it is really beside the point to adduce him either as a protagonist or as an opponent of evolution in the Lamarckian or Darwinian sense.

B. The Cosmology of St. Thomas

St. Thomas is the greatest of the Schoolmen. From the thirteenth century until the second half of the 20th century his name dominated the Western thought and even now continues to retain its influence, notwithstanding the various Philosophical movements unleashed by Enlightenment. Like St. Augustine, St. Thomas showed very little interest in the material World for its own sake. But, his general Philosophy involved a theory of the corporeal World.

i. Cosmogenesis

St. Thomas regarded the Universe as composed of finite beings and argued that they must necessarily proceed from God, the First Cause, through creation. Moreover, this creation must be creation out of nothing. St. Thomas denied both the ideas of creation out of pre-existing matter (because God has to be absolutely prior) and creation through emanation (because God cannot change, or exteriorize himself in creation). Therefore, God must have created the World out of nothing, *ex nihilo*. When he used the word *nihil*, he meant "absolutely nothing." St. Thomas explains that in creation God is the efficient cause and there is no material cause whatsoever. For St. Thomas creation is thus not a movement or change in the proper sense; and since it is not a movement, there is no succession in the act of creation.

The Universe, by the very fact that it is created, has a real relation to God as creator, without God having a relationship to the World. If the statement that God as a creator has no real relation to creatures certainly sounds rather strange at first hearing, it is a strictly logical conclusion from St. Thomas' metaphysic and doctrine of the divine nature. By this he does not intend to deny that God has no care for his creatures.

St. Thomas rejected the suggestion that God creates by a necessity of nature and held that God created the World by an act of free will. He also rejected the idea of indirect creation suggested by Peter Lombard, who thought that the power of creation is communicable by God to a creature. St. Thomas argued that the power to create cannot be communicated to creatures, because the creature cannot accomplish the act of bridging the infinite gulf between not-being and being. Only a being with infinite power can do that.

St. Thomas also rejects both the suggestions that the act by which God created the World was a blind act or a necessary act. God's nature is not only infinite intelligence, but also infinite will, and that will is free. Such a being cannot act in any other way than according to wisdom, with full knowledge. This means God must act for a motive, in view of a purpose, a good. Therefore, St. Thomas argued, "The act of will by which God created was neither a blind act nor a necessary act, but an act which followed, to speak in human fashion, the apprehension of a good, apprehended as a good, though not as a good necessary to God." But, what was the good for which God created? St. Thomas argued that as infinite perfection, God could not have created in order to acquire anything for Himself. "He created, not in order to obtain, but to give, to diffuse His goodness." God could not have created in order to acquire anything for Himself because God's will cannot depend on anything apart from Himself. Therefore, he Himself as the infinite good must be the end of His infinite act of will. Hence, in the case of the act of creation the end is his own goodness. He acts to communicate his own goodness to beings outside Himself. Therefore, St. Thomas concludes, "Creatures attain their end; do the best for themselves, by manifesting the divine goodness."

St. Thomas was convinced that the Philosopher cannot settle the question whether the World was created in time or from eternity. He admitted that the acknowledgement that God created the World freely does not of itself show that he created the World from eternity. St. Thomas maintained that none of the Philosophical proofs adduced to prove that this creation took place in time, were conclusive. On the other hand, St. Thomas maintained, that it cannot be shown Philosophically that the World cannot have begun in time, that creation in time is an impossibility. In other words, St. Thomas was convinced that the question whether the World was created in time or from eternity cannot be settled by Philosophical means. Nevertheless, relying on the Bible, he maintained that the World was actually created in time and not from eternity.

ii. The Best of All Possible Worlds

St. Thomas considers the question whether God was restricted to willing the actual World he has willed, or whether he could have willed another order. He admits that God could not will another order, since the divine will cannot change. However, in order to safeguard God's freedom, he clarifies that God did not will this present order of things necessarily. He willed this Universe freely, but having willed it from eternity; he could not have willed any other Universe.

St. Thomas rejects the suggestion that the existing World must be the best possible and that God is bound, on account of his goodness, to produce the best possible Universe if he produces one at all. As God's power is infinite, there can always be a better Universe than the one God actually produces. It is then evident that St. Thomas would not agree with the Leibnizian "optimism" or maintain that this is the best of all possible Worlds. In view of the divine omnipotence, the phrase "the best of all possible Worlds" does not seem to have much meaning; for admitting that this is the best of the possible Worlds, would put limitation on

God's power. Thus, by its very nature, the Universe, as belonging to the created order, cannot be perfect.

iii. The Composition of the Material Universe

St. Thomas believed that the Universe is made up of corporeal substances. Reflection on the objects at once leads the mind to discover a distinction in the objects themselves. If I go to a garden, one month I see the plants as small saplings, newly planted. Later on, I see them as bigger plants. Their size has changed, but they remain what they were – roses, or marigold, for example. Reflection will show that the objects are composed of an unchanging substrata and changing qualities. St. Thomas called the former substance and the latter accidents. Here, St. Thomas is influenced by Aristotle's decision of the ten categories – substance and the nine categories of accidents.

Further reflection on change in material substances led St. Thomas to the idea that they are composed of an indeterminate substance and another principle which makes a thing what it is and places it in its specific class, like cat or grass. The first he called "prime matter and the latter "substantial form." Every material substance, St. Thomas concluded, is composed in this way of matter and form. St. Thomas thus accepts the Aristotelian doctrine of the hylomorphic composition of material substances.

2.3.3 Development under the Impact of Modern Science

A. Pierre Teilhard de Chardin

In the last century, Pierre Teilhard de Chardin (1881-1955) proposed an original and striking Worldview. Due to its originality, it failed to find acceptance among the conservative circles of the church hierarchy, but won the wide attention not only from readers belonging to different Christian traditions but also from people who profess no religious beliefs in the ordinary sense of the term. His views expressed in his writings which have appeared after his death, cannot be dealt with as an authoritative teaching of the church. Nevertheless, as the view of a prominent Christian who tried to interpret the World and the place of human beings in it in the light of the findings of modern Science and Christian faith, it deserves attention.

In his writings, Teilhard wishes to integrate his interpretation of cosmic evolution with his Christian beliefs. This he does by developing a Christocentric World-vision. His Christocentric World-vision comes out most clearly in his work *The Divine Milieu* (1926) which is a religious meditation on the Universe. Teilhard presents the World as a totality of which we are members. This totality is not simply a complex system of interrelated phenomena, a system which just happens to be there. In Teilhard's view, it has value and significance. To the Scientist the World presents itself as a complex composed of various types of phenomena. But, for Teilhard the World cannot be reduced to a collection or disconnected phenomena, for it forms a totality, one whole.

What gives unity and value to the Universe is the presence of life, consciousness and spirit. For Teilhard, the Universe cannot be reduced to its quantitative and measurable aspects alone, as the positivist Scientists do. Life, consciousness and spirit are essential components of the Universe, not as something over against the material World or as an epiphenomenon, but as an integral part. They were potentially there in matter from the beginning. There is nothing the Universe which does not possess a psychic aspect, an inner force, so as to speak. The World thus appears as a totality, a whole, which is developing towards an end, as increasing actualization of spirit. The Universe is an evolving organic whole, which possesses spiritual value and appears as a manifestation of the divine.

A mechanistic Science of matter is not excluded by the view that all elements of the Universe have their internal or vital aspect. Though consciousness was present in matter from the beginning, it is only with the emergence of the cell that the biosphere or sphere of life begins. The emergence of the cell marks a qualitative change, so that a distinction can be made between the biosphere and the earlier stage of "matter." This distinction legitimizes a mechanistic Science of matter.

The Teilhardian Universe is not a static system, but a dynamic system that evolves. For Teilhard, evolution is not simply a biological theory that explains the origin of the species. It is a theory that applies to the whole World. Evolution is the story of the development of the Universe as a whole, including the species.

The basic idea of evolution is that the Universe and the material realities within it did not come into existence as finished products. Rather, they appeared in the course of a gradual continuous and progressive process. Therefore, the World is to be evaluated not only by its origins, but also by its direction, inherent possibilities and the future trends. Teilhard holds that the early earth had latent germinal powers. Everything that was to appear, including humans was already there in the initial "stuff of the Universe." The evolutionary movement has a definite direction. Starting from the primordial atoms, it proceeds until the Universe arrives at the point he calls the omega point. It passes through the mammals, the primates and leads straight to humn. This process moves from the lithosphere (sphere of non-living beings) to the biosphere, from the biosphere to the noosphere (sphere of thought), and finally, from noosphere to the christosphere.

Teilhard holds that evolution is primarily psychic in nature. It is basically a development of the spiritual. This is one of the instances where he differs from most other evolutionists. The general opinion is that the inner instincts of the animal are developed, depending on its bodily structure. A beast of prey, for example, develops its instincts because its incisors have grown sharp and its feet have grown claws. But, according to Teilhard, an animal like the tiger sharpens its claws and lengthens its fangs because the "within" of its cosmic matter has developed it into a carnivorous animal. The living World is consciousness clothed in flesh. The axis on which evolution drives ahead is of the spiritual nature.

Evolution has not stopped with the arrival of the human being. Morphologically or anatomically it has come to an end. We cannot expect the human body to undergo any more major changes. But, the evolution of the spiritual still continues in humans; psychically, psychologically, intellectually, socially, and morally, the human being has been growing always. Because of the progress in civilization, humankind has acquired, in every thinking person, a fullness that is wholly new. Thus, though individual human beings may not have changed much, humankind has advanced tremendously. Thus, in humans evolution takes a unique turn. With the arrival of humans, evolution takes a path of conscious self-direction.

In Teilhardian thought not only physical adaptations of life forms, but modern inventions like the radio, television and means of transportation are stages in evolution. For, according to him, creative transformation of any kind which leads to better adaptation top the environment is evolution. Before the advancement of technology, adaptation was achieved by adapting the body of the organism. But, in human beings physical adaptation has reached its zenith, so that no more physical adaptation is possible. With the arrival of humans, technology takes the place of physical adaptation. Modern humans adapt to the environment, not by transforming their bodies, but by Scientific inventions. Therefore, technology is the continuation of evolution. In the creative transformation that is taking place in humankind, evolution continues its journey. In Teilhard's view, it can stop only when it reaches the ultimate goal – the omega point.

The technological transformation that is taking place in humans cannot be isolated from the Universe. When humans evolve, it is the Universe that evolves.

Teilhard recognizes three critical points in the journey of evolution: the transition from non-life to life, from animal to human and finally, from noosphere to christosphere. The critical point is a point at which continuous injection of energy produces alteration of an entirely discontinuous character. Or, more concretely, it is the stage where purely quantified additions produce of themselves a qualitative alteration. What happens at the critical point is not a matter of change of degrees, but a matter of a change of nature. After a critical point, properties of the evolving material undergo radical change. The critical point in evolution is change-over from one form of consciousness into another. Critical points are necessary because life, as an ascent of consciousness, could not continue to advance indefinitely along its line without transforming itself in depth.

Evolution, which is an ascent towards reflective consciousness, continues to advance in the direction of greater complexity and consciousness. The genesis of life on earth was a unique and once it had happened, an unrepeatable event. In other words, it is a moment in a process of evolution which is moving towards a goal. At the end of this process, Teilhard postulates a supreme consciousness, which is the converging point of all consciousness.

Positivist Science will deny a goal-oriented Universe. But, Teilhard is convinced that the Universe is moving through life towards first personalization and then towards a hyperpersonal focus of union which Teilhard calls omega point, the union of the personal and the collective on the planes of thought and love. In the increasing intellectual unification of humanity, as in Science, and in the pressures which contribute to social unification, he finds supporting evidence for his optimism.

The motive force for the evolutionary process comes from the upward striving consciousness, the "within" of cosmic matter. The upward swing is powered by Teilhard call radial energy, which is distinct from another form of energy – the tangential energy. The tangential energy links one element or particle with others to create complex organisms, whereas the radial energy plays the role of drawing the element or particle towards increasing complexity and consciousness. Other factors like the struggle for survival, natural selection mutation and sudden changes of hereditary factors also play a part. But, the development of life which clearly strives after increasingly complex forms can only be explained but the inner movement of the "within" under the influence of the radial energy. The radial energy that manifests as the upward striving of consciousness integrates and guides all the other factors.

According to Teilhard, the idea of the Universe evolving under the influence of the radial energy in no way undermines the supreme rolc of God in creation. At the basis of evolution Teilhard places a divine causality. This agency directs the process and supplies it with the creative energy needed. Rather than displacing God from the explanation of the World, the self-evolving Cosmos bears testimony to God's creative action.

In his interpretation of the World, Teilhard opposed dualism of any kind and sought unity of being. He was opposed not only to any sharp dualism between matter and mind or spirit but also to any bifurcation of reality into natural and supernatural spheres, independent of one another. He was enamored by the idea of the organic unity of the developing Universe, which converges through human consciousness and socialization on the omega point, which as a Christian he thought the risen Christ.

In a sense, Teilhard's World-vision renews the ancient idea of the "emanation" from God and the return to God. But, with him the return is not of the individual, nor is it a matter of the individual turning away from the World and seeking an ecstatic union with God. In Teilhard's view, the World is seeking an ecstatic union with God. The whole Universe, not merely human beings, returns to God, and this happens through the evolutionary process. The evolutionary process is itself the process of return, and individuals return as part of the whole Universe.

Teilhard does not hold the notion of a cyclic Universe which goes through emanation and return. For him evolution is a one-time process. With the return of the Universe to the omega point, the work of creation is complete. It is a stage when human beings and through them the Universe "through following the lines of evolution converges to the point of at which the person, while remaining a person, is united with all other persons in a whole which is greater than themselves" When this stage is attained, the history of the Universe finds its consummation.

This process, whereby the Universe, passing through the various stages of evolution, reaches its consummation in the transcendent unity of all things, can be looked at from two points of view – the natural and Christian. From the natural point of view, the Universe is seen as interiorizing itself, as taking more and more the form of self-reflection (through humans) in the noosphere. From the Point of view of Christian faith this process of cosmogenesis is seen as a process of christogenesis and its final outcome as christosphere.

Objections against Teilhard's World-vision are many, and it would take an ardent disciple to claim that such objections are completely groundless. But, as Copleston notes, "Teilhard's vision of reality has an indubitable sweep and grandeur which tend to make the objections appear as pedantic or irrelevant." And in the present context, as we are trying to take stock of one of the ways in which Christians have looked at the Universe from their faith perspective, it is valuable contribution. Teilhard's thought on the matter is indeed an original World-vision which extends, in the words of Copleston, 'the concept of evolution into a profoundly religious World-view, not by way of mere additions or superposition but rather through a process of broadening out so as to include distinguishable dimensions in an integrated and comprehensive vision." Undoubtedly, such an approach can provide to Christians an inspiring World-vision which is at once Scientific and in accordance with their faith, though it diverges from Christian orthodoxy.

B. The Present-Day Scenario

Once we leave the biblical accounts and medieval Christian Philosophy, and make an inquiry into what contemporary Christians and Jews about the Cosmos, we are on uncertain grounds, having different groups holding different cosmological views. We can identify three prominent views: the views of liberal tradition, young earth creationists and literalists.

The liberal traditions, both in Judaism and Christianity have held that the Bible is primarily a story of God's dealings with humans, not authoritative treatises on Scientific issues in general and on astronomic or cosmological issues in particular. Therefore, what the Bible teaches about the Universe is not about the Universe is not an essential part of religious faith. Rather it is a primitive form of Scientific Cosmology that got embedded in religious literature. As such, it is subject to change as Scientific Cosmology undergoes change.

So, for the liberals, there is no such thing as independent Judeo-Christian Cosmology; any well-substantiated and widely accepted Scientific Cosmology of any given time is acceptable to them. For reliable astronomical and cosmological data, they no more look at the Bible, but rely on the methods and conclusions of Science. Thus, the Catholic Church after having rejected Scientific cosmological endeavours during the Copernican revolution has, in the last century, been ever more increasingly involved with Scientific Cosmology. A Roman Catholic Priest working in the Pontifical Academy of Sciences, Georges Lemaitre was in fact, instrumental in the development of the big bang theory of the Universe. Like the Catholic Church, many other mainline Christian denominations and the Conservative and Reform traditions within Judaism also look towards modern Science for developing their cosmological view. Thus, the liberals in Judaism and Christianity have discarded the biblical Cosmology in favour of Scientific Cosmology, relying on the Bible only on areas where Science is silent, for example, the state of affairs before and after the existence of the physical Universe, life after death, etc. this view makes any discussion of modern-day Judeo-Christian Cosmology meaningless, since there is no such Cosmology distinct from the Scientific Cosmology of the time.

By contrast, the proponents of creationist cosmologies have tried to reconcile the observations that seem to suggest a Universe that is older than what the Bible suggests, with the story of creation found in the book of Genesis that suggests a relatively young Universe. They believe that the account of creation found in the book of Genesis is historically accurate, and argue that the observable physical evidence is more fully consistent with the account of Genesis than with generally accepted theories such as the big bang theory. They proceed to construct creationist cosmologies that explain modern-day astronomical observations in a way compatible with the story of creation found in the book of Genesis. To reconcile the biblical account and the big bang theory, they suggest that though the Universe as a whole is billions of years old, a significant portion of the observable Universe is a only a few thousands of years old. They appeal to the theory of continuous creation to support this view. Thus, they try to seamlessly fit the biblical account to the well-accepted theories of Science. In the reconciliation, they are willing to accommodate both biblical accounts to the well-accepted theories of Science.

The literalists are radical creationists. Insisting on a literal reading of the bible, they assert that geocentrism and a young, flat earth are the only acceptable account of the Universe. Unwilling to accommodate biblical passages, they interpret physical evidence within the framework of a literal and historical interpretation of creation according to Genesis and historical interpretation of creation according to Genesis and reject well-established Science that is at odds with their views. The numbers of those who hold this view are negligible and their arguments are routinely rejected by the majority of creationists who interpret the "six days" as a symbolic expression referring to an indefinite period of time, while insisting that the World, whether young or old is God's creation.

Chapter 3

Howness of Cosmos Origin: Creation and Emanation

The topic of this Chapter is being presented against the twofold background of St. Thomas Aquinas' teaching and Shaṅkara's Braham-jijñāsā. It hopefully traces their lines of convergency with regard to the origin of Creation and Emanatin. This chapter will elaborate the howness of Cosmos.

3.1 The Notion of Origin

For the Scientist the notion of origin designates the state of affairs which conditions the arising of a new phenomenon. It implies not only the general disposition of the Universe and its material energy at the initial moment of this arising but more properly the immediate antecedents, conditions, factors and the decisive instant of the change which initiates that phenomenon. The arising of the latter is an event – *eventus* – an observable novelty but within a basic continuity of matter and time and becoming, generally considered as evolutionary. Such an origination is specific not universal; and relative not absolute. Even if the Scientist seeks the origin of the whole Universe, he can only seek it through a mental journey backwards toward a primary state of matter – as extremely condensed energy, for instance – beyond which he can, nevertheless, assume a prior, though underminable state of the same matter.

The metaphysician, on the contrary, undertakes a more radical investigation concerning, the very being of the Universe and all its components including matter itself in any of its states. How is it that there exists a Universe rather than no Universe? This question is forced upon him by the general contingency of all the existents which through their connections make up the Universe. Whether our Universe has a first instant or is beginningless in its duration – alternatives which both boggle our imagination – it ever appears unable to account for its existence. Hence, we are presented with the question not of its temporal but of its ontological origin. This question is not to be answered through a backward journey in time but through an ecstasies (in the etymological sense of the term), a reaching of the mind beyond itself and the whole Universe towards a Reality which cannot be less than Being itself (*Esse*, *Sat*), Self-existent and Self-communicative. This is generally designated as God or the Absolute (the Brahman of Vedanta). Richard De Smet purpose was not to prove its existence but to speak correctly as possible of the origination of our Universe from this Absolute.

3.2 The Need for Lakshanā or Analogy

In all matters regarding the Absolute, language must be adapted and appropriated to a difficult task. Our everyday language is shaped by our experience of the relative which it normally endeavours to express. But, besides its power of expressing, it possesses various capacities of evoking, alluding to, indicating, conveying or even signifying indirectly yet correctly enough what it does not or cannot express directly. In India, its power of indirect signification or indication is called *lakshaṇā* (distinct from *lakshaṇā*: definition or characteristic mark). Of the three chief types of *lakshaṇā*, the one directly useful to the metaphysician is the *jahad-ajahad-lakshaṇā* which corresponds closely to the *intrinsic* analogy of the Christian Schoolmen which itself originates in Aristotle and Pseudo-Dionysius. It permits making sense of theological language or God-talk.

For instance, when Shaṅkara or some of his disciples explains that "*Satyam jñānam anantam*" (*Taittirīya Upanishad*, 1) is a valid definition of Brahman, they use that *lakshaṅā*, and display its process. The sentence means that the Absolute is Reality-Knowledge-Infinite. The pupil who naively understands the first term *Satyam* (Reality) in its primary and expressive meaning as 'concrete material substance' such as solid earth, is told that he must correct this misleading superimposition (*adhyāsa*) since the second term *Jñānam* (Knowledge) immediately negates it. Similarly his primary understanding of *Jñānam* (Knowledge) as a contingent activity or quality of the term *Anantam* (Infinite) debars such an understanding. *Jñānam*, says Shaṅkara, must be infinitised on the basis of the pure root *Jña* (know), not of any of its derivatives. The Absolute is not infinite Know-ledge. Knowing or Know-er; but pure Know in the most elevated sense of the verbal term. Here he uses the participle *sat* (be-ing) instead of the verbal root *as* because of an exigency of his Sanskrit language but his intention is similar to that of St. Thomas Aquinas when the latter says that God is eminently *Esse* (Be). Although two terms are used, their infinitisation implies that they merge in identity without, however, losing their *svārtha*, the positive meaning of their roots as Shaṅkara is careful to point out. Thus, their *lakshaṇā* is intrinsic analogy and the divine Absolute which they define as infinite Be and Know is yet simple (*akhaṇḍa* undivided, incomplex). This example shows how in all philosophic-theological topics our mind must and can transcend the anthropomorphism innate to language through *apavāda*, negation, removal of all limitations; and *paramārthāpatti*, assumption of the supreme sense which alone is consistent with absoluteness.

3.3 Application to the Notion of Creation

Let us now start from an '*adhyāsic'* assertion of divine creation, such as we find in the Upanishads or elsewhere. 'Brahman is the Root of the World' or 'Brahman is that omniscient, omnipotent Cause from which proceed the origin, subsistence and dissolution of this World' or 'God is the Creator of all things, visible and invisible' or 'Consider the heaven and the earth and all that they contain; know that God has made all that from nothing and that the race of men is born in the same manner.' All such formulations affirm that the one God, the Absolute, is the unique intelligent Source or Cause of the totality of entirety of all other beings. But, the terms they are made of are liable to many misinterpretations and a sifting of their anthropomorphism is be effected by the metaphysician. Hence, we come to negative definition of creation, such as the classical one formulated by Aquinas: Creation means a production of reality out of nothing itself or of any matter (*productio rei ex nihilo sui et materiae*). This will be elaborated and completed presently. Provided this purification is complete, the mind is ready to climb up to the level of eminence (the Dionysian *Hyperochē* or Shankarian *paramārthāpatti*) and to say, for instance, with Aquinas: Creation is the emanation of the whole Universe by and from the universal Cause (*emanatio totius universi universi a causa universali*).

3.4 The Step of Purification through Negation: Apavāda

All modes of production fail to give us an adequate support of representation for the idea of creation. Creation is unique and transcends them all. Like God Himself, it pertains to no genus. Hence, we have to ascend to it by way of negations (*apophasis*, *apavāda*). In order to reconcile the two ideas of 'divine' and 'production' with either pre-existing matter or pre-existing time, with necessity of want, with transformation and instruments of transformation, with mutability of the creator or his self-improvement, and with relationship that would be a reality in the Creator.

3.4.1 No Independent Pre-Existence of the Created

Let us first, eliminate the weak sense of 'production' as 'mere manifestation.' The created is not produced like the rabbit out of the magician's hat. It does not arise from a state of latency, dormancy, or concealedness, but from its own antecedent absence (*prāg-abhāvāt*). For it has no independent pre-existence but never exists except as divinely produced.

Virtually, however, or, to use Shaṅkara's terminology, as still undifferentiated, it pre-exists in the power of its Cause, just as it is eternally known by it independently of its production. "And so," writes Aquinas, "a creature as pre-existing in God is the divine Essence itself" (*Et sic creatura in Deo est ipsa Essentia divina: De Potntia*, III, 16, 24). This is an important application of the theory which the Indians call *sat-kārya-vāda*, namely, of the virtual pre-existence of an effect in the being of its cause. The statement of *Bhagavadgītā*, ii, 16: *Nāsato vidyate bhāvḥ* (Out of nothing, no thing can arise) is true for an Aquinas or a Bergson as much as for the Indian schoolmen.

3.4.2 No Pre-Existence of the Matter or of the Forms of the Created

Unlike any production of nature or man, creation neither needs nor pre-supposes any pre-existing matter or other constitutive element. This is due to its character of total origination. Neither is there a pool of pre-existing forms from which the creator would draw. What is created is the Universe of existence in which and with which their matter is co-created as well as any other possible constituent. Whether matter is energy or something else should not concern us here. What counts is the realization that the totality of the Universe derives immediately from the Creator.

The ontological origination of all finite existents *qua* beings does not preclude the temporal originations that take place within the becoming of the Universe. Matter is the permanent stuff of all transformations and generations. This prime matter is a ubiquitous component of the beings of the material Universe and never a distinct and complete existent apart from them. As a component it is not the term of any special creation but shares in the ontological origination of the material existents of the Universe.

A question raised in Vedānta Philosophy is whether the Absolute itself is not the 'material cause' of the Universe. The term used is *upādāna* which may be rendered etymologically as 'subdatum' (*upa +a +dāna*). It is indicated by the ablative case '*yatah*' and is thus the 'whence' is a material stuff, for instance, clay in jars or steel in scissors, etc. on the basis of such examples, some Indian systems have assumed the existence of an eternal stuff, the *Pradhāna* or *Prakṛti* of the Samkhya system or the primordial atoms (*paramāṇu*) of Vaiśeṣika, as the *upādāna* transcends such specific meanings. That which provides the substantial reality of effects need not be a material cause. In Vedānta, it is the Brahman-Ātman which is said to be *upādana* of the Universe and this Brahman is surely not material since it is Spirit (*Cit*) or pure 'Know' (*Jña*) as we have seen earlier. If it were the material cause or stuff of the Universe, it would have to produce it through self-mutation (*pariṇāma*) or atomic vibration (*spanda*) but any such process is excluded from the Absolute. Yet, as its total Source, Brahman is the immanent and reality-giving Cause, i.e., the *Upādāna* of the Universe.

Some quotations from Shaṅkara will throw further light on this problem. The causation of the World presupposes "no independent matter, unreducible to Ātman, such as the Pradhāna of the Sāṁkhyas or the primordial atoms of Kaṇāda" (*Aitareya Upanishad Bhāśya* 1, 1, 1). "What the *Shruti* calls *aja*, i.e., the causal matter of the four classes of beings, has itself sprung from the highest Lord" (*Vedānta Sūtra Bhāśya* 1, 4, 9). Brahman alone is "that from whence these beings are born," i.e., their *upādāna*, as denoted by the ablative *yaiaḥ*; "there is no other substance from which the World could originate" (*Ve. Sū. Bh.*, 1,4, 23). But, how can this divine *Upādāna* provide the reality of the Universe? Because, "in the beginning, before creation, when the differences of names-and –forms (*nāma-rūpa*, the specific essences) were not yet manifested, this World was but the one Ātman" (*Ait. Up. Bh.*, 1, 1, 1). These *nāma-rūpas* pre-existed only "in the manner of something future" *bhāvishyena rūpeṇa*), i.e., virtually, as effects pre-exist in the actual power of their cause. "These *nāma-rūpas*, which are identical with the Ātman in their unmanifested state, can become the causal elements (*upādāna-bhūte*) of the manifested Universe. Hence, it is not incongruous to say that the omniscient (Ātman) creates the Universe by virtue of his oneness with causal elements, namely, names-and-forms, which are identical with himself." Their manifestation, however, does not mean that the partless Ātman undergoes a process of diversification: "the case is rather like that of a clever magician who, independent of any materials, transforms himself, as it were (*iva*), into a second man seemingly climbing into space" (*Ait. Up. Bh.*, 1, 1, 2).

3.4.3 No Need of Instruments or of Demiurge

Considering that the creative power need not be applied upon a pre-existing material which it would brave to shape, Aquinas concludes that it needs no instruments. Similarly, Shaṅkara asserts that "the absolutely complete power of Brahman does not require to be supplemented by any extraneous help" (*Ved. S. Bh.*, 2, 1, 24).

The same reason rules out any demiurge. A demiurge might be required for the function of shaping up, structuring, ordaining and governing the Universe according to an intelligible pattern, in the same way as man in his works generally imposes his own plan upon the materials he uses. The Nyāya system which assumes the independent existence of the material of the World posits a divine Lord to fulfill universally this role of patterning agent or *nimittakārana*. It thus professes a dualism (*dvaita*), which accepts two distinct causes of the World, a material *upādāna* and lordly *nimittakārṇa*. But, Shaṅkara, who upholds a strict non-dualism (*advaita*), holds that the one Brahman which is the non-material *upādāna* of the World "is at the same time its *nimittakārṇa* because outside Brahman as substantial Cause there is no other ruling principle for the *Shruti* says that prior to creation Brahman was one only without a second" (*Ved. S. Bh.*, 1, 4, 23). It can pattern the World intelligently, being Intelligence itself; indeed, "its high Power is revealed as manifold, as inherent, acting as force and *knowledge*" (*Ved. S. Bh.*, 2, 1, 24).

3.4.4 No Need of a Temporal Beginning of Creation

Creation-talk is spontaneously mixed up with the notion of a first instant of the Universe. But, 'ontological origination' does not by itself imply 'temporal beginning' even if the reverse verse is true. Duration is a property of being; it denotes the 'unity of active existence' of a being. In God, it is eternity which is the strict unity of his perfect active existence. In mutable beings, it is time which is the relaxed unity of their imperfect and developing existence; every such being has its own concrete time or duration. Universal time is rather an abstraction which serves the mathematical purpose of measuring the concrete duration of mutable beings and the concrete duration of the Universe itself as the interrelated totality of such existents. It is this abstraction which seems to reign over and above creation and even to precede it but rather follows from its essential mobility and evolving changeability. Whether it starts from a first instant or is beginning less depends entirely on the Creator's free decision and cannot be settled by any deductive process. This is the conclusion of St. Thomas in *Summa Theologica*, 1, 46, 1.

3.4.5 The End of Creation Implies No Need or Despite in the Creator

Is it anthropomorphic to say that creation has an end, a purpose? Men's works are purposeful. Even a madman, Shaṅkara remarks, does not act without some purpose. But, can the Absolute have purposes? Would this not imply that it has desires and, hence, wants. But, then it would no longer be the perfect Brahman, which is Bliss (*Ānanda*) and Peace (*Śānti*) because "all its desires are eternally realized."

An Indian distinction comes here to our help. That between *artha*, goal, purpose, and *kāma-phala*, the fruit that accrues to the doer according to his desire (*kāma*) to satisfy a need which he feels. Creation is a *nishkāma-karma*, a work prompted by no desire to satisfy a need of the Creator. But, being an intelligent work, it is not devoid of *artha* or purpose. Obviously, this purpose can only be the good of the creatures. It is *loka-saṁgraha*, the maintenance of the cohesion of the World, and more precisely the welfare and the final salvation of man (*Bh. Gītā Bh.*, iii, 24).

This assertion raises a problem. For Shaṅkara, man's uppermost desire is to know the Brahman (*Brahma-jijñāsā*) not, however, through any inferior kind of knowledge for it is *avagati-*

paryanta, i.e., it aspires after a knowledge which "culminates in comprehension." And this most blissful realization (*vijñāna*) is "caused (*hetuka*) by the grace of the Lord since this is asserted by the infallible *Sruti*" (*Ved. S. Bh.*, 2, 3, 41). In the same way, a Christian like St. Thomas affirms that the deepest desire of man is for a blissful intuition of the divine essence itself and that this stands beyond the grasp of the natural power of his intellect through well within the reach of its desire and of its receptive capacity. It is at this point that St. Thomas articulates his teaching on divine grace and the possibility of a supernatural complementing of nature. His thesis of the natural desire of man's intellect for a beatific vision of God's every essence shows that the highest end of creation depends on the merciful liberality of the Creator. This gratuitous end will, even more than the lower but sufficient end which consists in *lok-saṁgraha*, bring about an extrinsic glory of God as the author of the final goodness of creation. But, this, being extrinsic, will not accrue to him as an accidental adornment or self-accomplishment. Nothing, indeed, can be added to the eternal perfection of the Absolute.

3.4.6 As Participated Being, the Creature is Non-Being

Creation is the production of finite existents in the whole measure in which they are be-ings. Obviously, the Absolute cannot produce other Absolutes but only finite participations of itself. But, what is the ontological weight and positivity of such be-ings? There are interpretations of Shaṅkara's Vedānta which view it as an acosmism and attribute only illusory being to all effects. What is the verdict of Shaṅkara himself?

Shaṅkara uses the terms 'being' and 'non-being' on different levels which we may clarify with a judicious use of capital and small letters. On the level of ordinary language, creaturely effects and their Cause are being (*sat*), are imbued with existence (*saitā*). "Should any effect originate from nothing, then, even though perceived, it would be imbued with unreality; but this is not the case, hence Brahman exists" (*Taittrīya Up. Bh.*, 2, 6, 1). Yet, Brahman transcends so immensely its effects that compared to them it must be said to be non-being (*a-sat*). This consideration is the root of apophatism. But, Brahman is not absolute Non-being (*atyanta Asat*) for it is non-being simply because it is absolute Being (*atyanta Sat*), i.e., Being in the supreme sense of the term (*paramārthataḥ Sat*). And now we have to say that compared to it creatures are non-Being (*a-Sat*) although they are not absolute Non-Being (*Asat*). They are, he says *Sad-Asad-vilakshaṇa*, unable to denoted by either *Sat* (Being) or *Asat* (Non-being) if these terms are taken in their supreme sense. This is the level of language on which Shaṅkara's teaching moves generally because his centre of reference is the Absolute rather that the relative existent. He is a radical valutionist who measures everything to the absolute Value, the Brahman, and declares its inequality to it rather than the degree of its participation of it. This manner of thinking and speaking is legitimate but it has misled many into acosmistic interpretations of his doctrine.

In the West, Aquinas generally prefers the language of participation. A participated being is in its own deficient way what the absolute *Esse* is without any restrictions. This *Esse* or Being is not a logical genus but the ontological Reality of God. And its participations are not parts of that partless Reality, not accidents, complements, explicitations or developments neither of it, nor in any way additive to it.

Shaṅkara too considers the effects of creation as mere *upādhis* (external affixes) of Brahman. An *upādhi* is an external adjunct, like the mask of an actor or the clothes of a man which only seem to characterize them; it has only the appearance of a *viśeshaṇa*, i.e., of a real attribute. Thus, all names-and-form as (*nāma-rūpa*) are but *upāhis* and in no way affections of their Cause. Not like any *upādhi* they need the support of this total Cause which pervades (*vyāpin*) them most intimately without any loss of its unalterable transcendence. This is why they are comparable to magical illusions which do not affect the magician but depend entirely on his power while the appearance of their independent subsistence is due to the spectator's ignorance. This comparison together with the concept of *upādhi* does away with pantheism and preserves nevertheless the central notion of the creatures' total dependence on their Creator.

3.4.7 Creative Activity is Not Additive to the Divine Essence

When man produces something he does it not only with the help of materials, instruments and so forth but also through an operation which is distinct from, and additive to, his substantial essence. This, however, is not due to the essential nature of causation but only to the weakness of his power which prevents him from ever being the total cause of his effects. Causing as such only demands to be an ontological communication of the cause to the effect so that what makes us say that this is an effect, whether it be its external form, its internal structure or its substantial reality, derives from the being of its cause. It does not demand necessarily that the cause lose what it gives or that it's causing be an operation additive to its own being. The higher the cause, the more immune to change and independent it is in the exercise of its power. The highest power is the power of intelligent volition which in its upmost degree can posit its term freely and without any self-alteration. Thus, no other novelty is consequent upon divine volition but the ontological novelty of its effect.

The supreme Ātman, says Shaṅkara, due to his "absolutely complete power" creates "like Gods, etc. who, without availing themselves of any extraneous means, produce palaces, etc. *by their mere intention* which is effective in consequence of those beings' peculiar power" (*Ved. Sūt. Bh.*, 2, 1, 25). His creative volitions are not additive to, but identical with, his essence. Indeed, "how are they found in Brahman? As essentially Reality-Knowledge, and as pure in virtue of being their own Ātman" (*Taitt. Up. Bh.*, 2, 6, 1). The distinction between creative volition and divine essence is not ontological but logical: it is by 'upādhic,' extrinsic, denomination in regard to its created term that this essence is to be thought of as creative volition.

3.5 The Positive and Adequate Definition of Creation

After reining the gross notion of creation with the help of negations meant to clear away all anthropomorphic misconceptions, we can now with St. Thomas define creation adequately and eminently (*paramārthataḥ*) as the intelligent and freely willed emanation of the whole reality or positivity of the Universe from the pure *Esse* (cf. *Summa Theol.*, 1, 45, 1).

The term 'emanation' comes from the Indo-European root *mad-*, to bubble, to flow; thus it means the flowing out as from a source. It is in this etymological sense that it is used here by Aquinas. From the time of Leibniz, however, 'emanation' became associated with the diverse brands of pantheism to express a necessary flowing of the Universe from an Absolute governed by an inner necessity of self-explication, self-development or self-realization. Whether this necessity is conceived as physical, 'vital,' or moral, pantheism destroys the simplicity of fullness and perfection of the subsistent Esse which it posits but anthropomorphically; its divine Principle lacks the perfect transcendence of the Brahman-Ātman or the absolute God; and its created emanations lack the radical contingency of true creatures. It is, therefore, in no pantheistic sense that the term 'emanation' is to be understood in the above definition.

What emanates from the Creator is the whole reality of positivity of the Universe. This includes the existence and essence of each of its beings, their preservation, their activities even of free will, their finalistic groping and development, the evolution from inorganic matter unto man, the achievements of his cultures, etc. It includes cosmic matter and spirits, time – whether beginningless or not, space – whether limited or unlimited, the necessary and the contingent, the regularities of law and the coincidences of hazard. Thus, creation does not concern only the origins of finite existence but as universal emanation it is also conservation, motion and activation (by the *pravṛtti-rahito-parvaraka*, the Mover devoid of motion of *Ved. Sūt. Bh.*, 2, 2, 2) providential governing and finalization.

But, what about the negativities in the Universe? These cannot be the proper effects of the power of the one who is pure Positivity but arise only consequentially from the natures of creatures: finiteness from their contingency; liability to physical evil such as harmful accidents, diseases, destruction or death from the competitiveness of the immense plurality of material existents within the one realm of matter where chance-encounters predominate; error from the imperfection of infinite intellects; and moral evils such as vices and sins from the imperfection of created free-wills. All these are tolerated rather than willed by the Creator who can nevertheless accomplish end of creation and thus overcome its inherent deficiencies.

From the side of the creatures, creation is total ontological dependence. This is a relation inherent in them and whose ground is their very positive reality as emanations from God. According to St. Thomas refined theory of relationship, this relation is not a logical not a real one because its ground is intrinsic to the related; its reality is co-created with the creature. As to Creatorship, its correlation, it is but logical relation because it is not grounded in anything pertaining to the Creator but in the same reality of his emanations which is extrinsic to him. Thus, these paired relationships are unreciprocal.

The name given by Shaṅkara to the relation of the Universe to Brahman is *tādātmya*, often translated as 'identity' but rendered more correctly as 'having that (*tat*) as one's *ātman*.' The term *ātman*, which is the reflexive pronoun, does not denote here what we normally call the self but the substantial cause (*upādāba*) as internal to the effect, as in the expression 'the jar is *mṛd-ātmaka*, i.e., is internally constituted of mud or clay.' In this expression, *ātman* does not connote intelligence but it generally does. The *tādātmya* of creatures is this their ontological dependence on That (Brahman) as on their innermost and transcendent Cause. "It is an accepted principle, even in the World, that an effect is intimately dependent (*anuvidhāyin*) on its (substantial) cause" (*Bṛhadaraṇuaka Up. Bh.*, 1, 5, 14). This dependence imparts no reality to the cause but only to its effects for "as long as an effect subsists, it is impossible to assume the dissolution of the latter the effect also cannot subsist. On the other hand, we may assume the continued existence of the cause although the effect is destroyed; for that is actually observed in the case of clay" (*Ved. Sūt. Bh.*, 2, 3, 14). Hence, that relation is not real in both terms. It is not reciprocal: "names-and-forms in all their states have Brahman alone as their Ātman, but Brahman has not its Ātman in them (i.e., *tādātmya* is not mutual). Since, without this (Brahman) they simply do not exist, they are said to have their Ātman in it (*tad-ātmaka*). And it is because of those who *upādhis* or external adjuncts (*names-and-forms*), that Brahman is related to all mundane activities" (*Taitt. Up. Bh.*, 2, 6, 1). This is another way of saying that the ground of 'creatorship' is found exclusively on the side of the creatures. This theory of *tādātmya* "does away with the independent (*svabhāvika*) existence of the embodied self … and of the World" (*Ved. Sūt. Bh.*, 2, 1, 14). These are not simply different (*anyat*) from the Absolute since in their whole being they depend on it. "The creature, says St. Thomas, is no part of the Essence of God but is essence is from God" (*non est ex essential Dei sed est ex Deo essentia*: *Summa Theol.*, I, 41, 3, 2). And Shaṅkara: "the effect is non-different (*an-anyat*) from the Cause, i.e. is essenceless and absent apart from it" (*vyatirekenā'bhāvah*: *Ved. Sūt. Bh.*, 2, 1, 14). Thus, explained, the non-difference implied by *tādātmya* does not eliminate distinction but stresses the ontological character of the creature's dependence as well as the Creator's transcendence. "If absolute equality were insisted on, the relation of cause and effect would be annihilated…, (a relation) which is abased on the presence in the cause of an excellence (with is absent in the effect)" (*Ved. Sūt. Bh.*, 2, 1, 6).

All these clarifications do not suppress the mystery of creation. Even on the level of eminence, theological language remains apophatic. It points correctly to the realities it deals with but is unable to express them (*lakshyate na tū-`cyate*: *Taitt. Up. Bh.*, 2, 1). Because our experience knows of no exact parallels of creation, our metaphysical thinking about it can never reach the level of experiential language. But, "all metaphysics worthy of the name tends to consume itself in the deep silence of mystical introversion" (Pierre Scheuer).

Chapter 4

The Problem of Creation

4.1 Theism versus Pantheism

How should one understand the relationship between God and the Universe? We have come to God as the ultimate cause of all finite realities and aspiration for the infinite. What do the concepts of cause and effect mean when they are used to describe the unique relationship between the absolute reality and the World? The specificity of the causal relationship between the Infinite and the finite is usually expressed by the term creation. It is not enough to affirm God's existence and dispose of atheism. A new problem arises of determining how God and the World are linked to each other and what is the meaning of the term, "divine creation." The theist is confronted by the problem of pantheism.

According to the Indian Philosophical tradition rooted in the Upanishads, the object of metaphysical reflection is not whether an absolute reality, Brahman, exists or not; it is evident that it exits. What needs to be clarified is the manner in which God and the World are related to each other. The metaphysics that derives from the Upanishads, called Vedānta , deals exclusively with this problem. In the course of centuries of Philosophical speculation, several forms of Vedānta systems took shape and proposed a number of interpretations and models, often in contradiction with each other, but all meant to explain the relationship between the infinite and the finite. The debate between theism and pantheism has much to gain from careful consideration of Vedantic metaphysics.

At the onset of our enquiry we realize the complexity of forming an adequate idea of the God-World relationship. As our knowledge of God is only analogical, we may not expect more than an 'analogical' grasp of the divine causality through the use of the most adequate model. Moreover, we must give our reasons for eliminating interpretations that do not tally with what we have come to know of God's essence and the nature of the created reality.

Several views regarding the cause-effect relationship have been advanced by Philosophers of East and West. Aristotle, for one, made the distinction of four causes: the material cause (the substance out of which something is made), the formal cause (the idea or the blueprint), the efficient cause (the agent and the instrument), the final cause (the purpose). In Indian Philosophy the three classical theories of causality are: *Vivarta-vāda* or the illusory transformation of the cause into effect (Shaṅkara), *Parināma-vāda* or *Sat-kārya-vāda* or the real transformation of the cause into its effect (Rāmanuja), *Arambha-vāda* or *Asat-kārya-vāda* the production by the cause of an effect understood as a totally new reality not contained in the cause. In modern times, some personalist Philosophers have made the distinction between: a) Mechanical causality that relates an object to another object, b) Fabricating causality that relates a subject to the object he makes, c) Personal causality that relates a subject to another subject in interpersonal relationships such as education, spiritual influence, etc. These distinctions can help to clear the ground on how to conceive – or not to conceive – of the God-World relationship. Thus, for instance, if we say that God is the material cause of the Universe (as most pantheists do) we implicitly deny his transcendence. If we opt for the *Vivarta-vāda* view of Shaṅkara we are bound, it seems to deny the reality of the finite World. If we follow the personalist understanding of the God-man relationship as an intersubjective I-Thou relationship, we expose ourselves to the hazard of a too anthropomorphic model.

We shall first expose and criticize a number of non-theistic (pantheistic and monistic) concepts of 'creation' and the models we derive from them to understand the God-World relationship. In conclusion of this first part we present a general criticism of pantheistic metaphysics. In the second part we identify and evaluate three theistic models of creation: the dualist, the transcendental and the dialectic.

4.1.1 The Non-Theistic Models of Creation

A. Absolutism: Parmenides and Shaṅkara

Metaphysical Synthesis: There is only ONE BEING (*SAT*), the ABSOLUTE. The finite contingent reality is non-being (*aSAT*) because it is not absolute. Only the absolute reality truly exists; this in non-dualism or, as Shaṅkara says, "Kevala Advaita.' It follows that "Jagan mithya", the World is false, unreal. Parmenides too asserted that the multiple and changing realities perceived by our sense were not the real World. Reason alone can be trusted to obtain right knowledge, and reason reveals that being is one and stable. We call this view 'absolutist' (or "Kevala-advaita-vedānta") because only the absolute reality is being.

The Concept of Creation: How can Absolutism understand the relationship of the Infinite and the finite, if the infinite absolute is Being and the finite is non-being? *Shaṅkara* proposes the theory of '*Vivarta-vāda*' to explain the paradoxical situation of a cause that is and an effect that is not. '*Vivarta*' means that what takes place is only an illusory transformation of the cause into the effect. The model he chooses is that of a magician who 'creates' illusory effects. Thus, Brahman produces an illusory World. But, a Cause of illusory effects is itself an illusory cause. Both cause and effect are illusory. There is no 'creation' properly speaking, but only the absolute reality.

Critical Remarks: Absolutism wrongly identifies being with absolute. In fact being is first a datum of experience identified in a multiplicity of limited beings. From the analysis of the empirical reality the mind derives the abstract notion of Being, the common denominator of all that exists. Further, on the basis of this discovery, it is led to infer the existence of an absolute reality. Such a metaphysics starts with the empirical to conclude in due course to a transempirical absolute. But, Absolutism is a metaphysics that begins with the wrong end, that is, with the conclusion rather than with the premises. It affirms the absolute reality at the start and this procedure renders it unable to recognize any other reality.

Vivartavāda is Shaṅkara's way of forming an adequate model to conceive of the God-World relationship, which, in this case, is the relationship of Being to non-being, *SAT* to *aSat*. Within the context of absolutist metaphysics the transformation of Brahman into the World can only be illusory. Creation is the magic or the '*Māyā*' of God. Shaṅkara's critics (almost all the Vedantic systems that came after him) will raise two major objections. First they reject the absolutist view that the finite World is not real. Second they wonder for whom the magic of illusion is produced. For there can be no illusion without people subjected to and victim of the illusion. The very notion of illusion contracts the monistic viewpoint of absolutist Advaita.

B. Static Pantheism: Spinoza and Vallabha

Metaphysical Synthesis: There is only one reality, the absolute Substance. But, the World too is real. Shaṅkara's view that the World is not real is rejected, replacing his '*Kevala-advaita-Vedānta* ' with '*Suddha-advaita-Vedānta* ' which sees the World not as illusion but as a part or a mode (Spinoza) or a manifestation (Vallabha) of the absolute reality. The substance of the World is identical with the divine substance. According to Vallabha, the divine substance is *sat-cit-ānandam* but when it manifests itself in material beings, it is *sat-cit-ānandam* in which the *cit-ānandam* aspect of the divine substance is concealed. When it manifests itself in spiritual souls, it is *sat-cit-ānandam* in which *ānandam* aspect of the divine substance is concealed. In one way or another every reality is *sat-cit-ānandam* and that is why Vallabha asserts that "everything is an Avatāra" (a divine manifestation).

The Concept of Creation: Creation is understood as the relationship between the whole and the part or the relationship between the manifested and the unmanifested. The duality of Creator and creatures becomes a duality of viewpoints. The same reality is perceived either partially, as finite, or in its totality, as infinite. "Not because he is husband that a man is dear to his wife but because in him the wife perceives Brahman Himself": this Upaniṣadic saying brings out the idea that there are two ways to look at the World: either in ignorance as a finite reality or in knowledge as the all-pervading divine substance.

Vallabha calls this concept of creation: "*Avikrita-Parināma-Vāda*", that is, the theory of change without transformation. While the cause does not undergo any real transformation, there occurs a change in the perception one has of the cause. In other words, there is a noetic change in the knower, but no substantial transformation affecting the cause. Creator and creatures are not two realities but two ways looking at the same reality.

Critical Remarks: Pantheism is a square denial of the radical antinomy that we have discovered between the finite and the absolute. We had reached that conclusion in taking earnestly our experience of finitude, imperfection and evil found in ourselves and the World around. Merleau-Ponty's view that "contingency and finitude are not small truths to which are given a small part to play in larger metaphysical synthesis" is a decisive refutation of pantheistic metaphysics. One cannot simply brush aside experience and regard finitude as an illusion. If the absolutist is wrong in denying the being and reality of the finite, the pantheist is wrong in turning a blind eye to the finitude of the finite World. Sound metaphysics must hold both the reality as well as the finitude of the created World.

The finite World and the infinite absolute cannot be regarded as the same reality. If an absolute reality exists it has to be transcendent to the finite World of human experience. Pantheistic monism affirms the immanence of the divine but denies its transcendence. Theistic metaphysics asserts both the transcendence and the immanence of God.

C. Dialetical Pantheism: Hegel

Metaphysical Synthesis: The absolute reality is not transcendent to the World. Nor is it immanent to the World in the sense of static pantheism. It is in the making in the World. "The World is the autobiography of the absolute Spirit", he writes. God is not yet, he will be at the consummation of history. The Absolute reality is not an already constituted, but a reality in the process of becoming itself. The finite World is evolving towards the realization of the absolute Spirit.

The Concept of Creation: How is the finite reality related to the infinite? While in static pantheism, the finite was a part or a manifestation of the infinite, in dialectical pantheism the finite is a moment of the infinite in the making. The 'spatial' model of static pantheism is substituted by the 'temporal' model of dialectical pantheism. In static pantheism the finite reality is lifted up to the infinite, in dialectical pantheism the infinite is brought down to the finite. Creation in dialectical pantheism is the self-evolving process of the finite to the realization of the finite Spirit.

Critical Remark: Hegel's intention was to denounce the estrangement – according to him – of finite and infinite brought about by theistic metaphysics and to find a new paradigm to reconcile them. However, the concepts of a 'historical absolute' and of a finite reality in the process of becoming infinite are contradictory. There is nothing in experience or reason to support such a thesis. How can the finite World become the infinite unless this infinite reality is already present in it from the beginning? If the finite is able to become the infinite the reason must be that the finite precontains the infinite. Moreover how can one conceive of an absolute reality that is not yet but will be? The concept of an absolute reality in the making is preposterous. Hegel's successors perceived the contradiction and evolved a metaphysics of a finite historical World without the infinite. Hegel's pantheistic idealism of the absolute Spirit was supplanted by atheistic humanism.

D. Emanationist Monism: Rāmanuja

Metaphysical Synthesis: In static pantheism there is no transformation of cause into effect but according to Rāmanuja's brand of Vedānta metaphysics, the effect emanates from the cause; Brahman undergoes a real transformation. Reality is one (non-dualism or *advaita*) but it is a complex or differentiated (*Visiṣta-advaita*) form of unity. The complex inner structure of Brahman includes the individual souls which all pre-exist in him in a subtle form. Brahman is, as it were, pregnant with what will become, at creation, the souls of the World.

The Concept of Creation: is emanation of the souls from Brahman. Rāmanuja conceives of the divine creation on the pattern of human procreation: the World (the human souls) issues from Brahman like the new born babe from his mother's womb. He uses the *Brhama-Parināma-vāda* view of the cause-effect relationship or *Sat-kārya-vāda* in which the effect is precontained in the cause. This amounts to saying that Brahman is the material cause of the human souls which emanate from the divine substance.

Critical Remarks: Rāmanuja's metaphysics of *Visiṣta-advaita-vedānta* is a peculiar from of semi-pantheism. It looks pantheistic on account of its inclusion of the souls within Brahman. However it is not pantheistic for two reasons. On the one hand the souls exist from all eternity as distinct individualities within Brahman. They are parts of Brahman's "body" but not identical with Brahman's "soul." On the other hand, the material World – unlike the spiritual souls – does not emanate from the divine substance because an imperfect effect cannot be produced by a perfect cause. But, then how to explain the existence of matter? Rāmanuja is not clear on this point. Should one say that matter arises 'out of nothing' while the souls arise out of God?

It is difficult to agree with Rāmanuja's complex idea of the divine substance. Moreover his concept of creation amounts to admitting that Brahman (his 'body', at least) is the material cause of the individual; souls. This is a denial that God is transcendent to the finite World.

E. Processionist Monism: Plotinus

Metaphysical Synthesis: Plotinus calls the absolute reality the one, which is not 'Being' because the absolute transcends the finite beings. The One holds nothing in common with the beings that proceed from it (hence 'processionist monism'). The finite realities do not emanate from the One, they proceed from the One. In the case of emanation, the effect is precontained in the cause: *Sat-kārya-vāda* theory of causality. But, in the case of 'procession' the effect is not precontainted in the cause: this is the *Asat-kārya-vāda* theory of causality. The effect is totally dissimilar to the cause that produces it. Nothing can be known of the cause through the effect. That is why Plotinus does not call the absolute 'Being', but the unknowable and attributeless (*nirguna*) ONE. There is no analogy, no resemblance between the infinite and the finite.

The Concept of Creation: is procession. The created finite World does not emanate from the divine substance (which, therefore, is not the material cause of World). It proceeds from the One, without being out of the substance of the One. Plotinus adds that the finite World necessarily proceeds from the one. It seems that for him the infinite needs the finite as much as the finite needs the infinite. There is no free creation. His metaphysics is thus monistic without being pantheistic. The finite World, though being real and totally other that the One, is a necessary constitutive component of the absolute One. The infinite would not be what it is without the procession of the finite.

Critical Remarks: Plotinus and Shaṅkara (as well as Parmenides) uphold the transcendence of the absolute reality, which theistic metaphysics upholds as an essential requisite to arrive at an adequate concept of the God-World relationship. In no way can the divine cause be taken as the material cause of the Universe. The *Vivarta-vāda* theory of causality (of pantheism) is substituted by Shaṅkara with the *Vivarta-vāda* theory, while Plotinus adopts the causal relationship of the *Asat-kārya-vāda theory.* In both cases the transcendence of the absolute reality is affirmed. Still both have a price to pay for the kind of explanation they offer to safeguard the transcendence of the absolute. In the case of Shaṅkara, the 'distance' he introduces between infinite and finite induces him to deny the being and reality of the finite World. In the case of Plotinus the transcendence of the absolute leads him to conclude that the absolute is not being. One has to choose, it seems either the non-being of the absolute. Theistic metaphysics offers a different solution by upholding the analogy of being which Plotinus and Shaṅkara overlooked. It brings out the applicability of being to both the infinite and the finite, though in different manners. Even though the infinite cause transcends the finite effects. The cause 'communicates' and the effects 'participate.' While pantheism maintains the univocal identity in being of infinite and finite. Plotinus and Shaṅkara uphold the equivocal dissimilarity of infinite and finite. Theistic metaphysics takes a middle course through the doctrine of analogy in which infinite and finite are shown to be both similar and dissimilar.

In other words what is defective in Plotinus' (and Shaṅkara's) metaphysics is an exclusive stress on the TRANSCENDENCE of the absolute with no regard for its immanence. Pantheism, on the contrary, stresses only the immanence of the divine. Sound theistic metaphysics avoids both 'transcendentalism' and 'immanentism.'

For Plotinus 'creation' is necessary. But, how can one say that the infinite is in need of the finite without destroying the autonomy of the absolute One? If God is in need of his creatures, does it not follow that the created World is a 'part' of the divine substance? Transcendental theism (see below) holds that the God-World relationship is unilateral: the World needs God but God does not need the World.

Criticism of Pantheistic Metaphysics

In the course of history, pantheistic metaphysics has attracted thinkers of either a mystical frame of mind (in the East) or a rationalist approach (in the West). The pantheistic outlook flows within from an inflated religious interpretation of reality (everything is divine) on from a one-sided understanding of being through unifying reason alone (everything is one). However a critical evaluation of the pantheistic model shows that it cannot be reconciled with some essential requirements imposed by the way in which we have been led to the affirmation of God.

Failure to Explain the Metaphysical Problem

Pantheism rejects the real distinction between the absolute reality and the finite World. But, in doing so it causes the affirmation of God to be useless. God identified with the World does not explain the World any longer. The World lacks the character of 'absolute' existence, so if an absolute reality exists; it has to be different from the World. When a state of affairs cannot be explained by itself, the recourse to ANOTHER reality is needed to explain it. But, the pantheist does not use inferential reason to interpret the data of experience: he would simply claim that he has a direct intuition of the divine.

False Dilemma: Either Monism or Dualism

The pantheist censures the theist for being a dualist in accepting two kinds of realities: the infinite and the finite. There can be no reality other than the absolute reality. Therefore, everything exists within that one reality which cannot have a rival in existence. Monism is compulsory.

There is a point in this criticism raised by the pantheist: metaphysical dualism (two types of realities 'facing' each other, so to say) is untenable. Still the pantheist is wrong in narrowing the option between monism and dualism. There is a third viewpoint situated between monism and dualism: the metaphysics of non-dualism (Advaita) in which God and the World are neither identified nor counted as two rivaling realities in virtue of the transcendence of the absolute.

Non-dualistic theism maintains the distinction of infinite and finite (unlike monism which fuses them). At the same time, it is not dualistic because the absolute is transcendent and does not exist on a par with the finite reality. The infinite and the finite, belonging to different levels of existence, do not rival each other. On the one hand they are not ONE reality, on the other hand they are not TWO either, all the more because the finite exists in total dependence on the infinite. 'Non-dualism' is an appropriate term to describe this unique relationship, inconceivable to the pantheist who rejects the transcendence of the absolute reality. Undoubtedly 'transcendence' is the key-concept in support of non-dualistic metaphysics, on account of which the faulty dilemma between monism and dualism is exposed.

Finitude and Evil Underrated

We quoted Merleau-Ponty (1908-1961) above as stating that contingency and finitude are not small truths in a metaphysical synthesis. For the "metaphysics of contingency" which he supports, contingency is the whole truth. While we disagreed with that view, we also disagree with the pantheist for whom finitude and contingency are no truths at all. The pantheist underestimates the data of human experience, the 'facts of life,' dismissing them as ultimately illusory. He holds that for the person with right perception and true knowledge, everything is divine, everything is and "*avatāra*." Though pantheism and theism converge in their affirmation of God against atheism, pantheism unlike theism is the affirmation of God at the cost of finite existence. Its metaphysics of 'God alone' is untenable to those who regard experience as an invaluable instrument of knowledge.

Consequently the pantheistic approach encounters serious difficulties when confronted with the problem of evil. It links evil with finitude but just as finitude is illusion, so is evil, caused by the ignorance of subjective experience. For the pantheist, everything is good because God is good and there can be nothing 'outside' the divine goodness. Evil and suffering exist only for the ignorant ego. They disappear when the illusions of individual existence are overcome.

4.2.1 The Theistic Models of Creation

Of all the models of creation analyzed so far Shaṅkara's absolutism and Plotinus' processionism offer the most valuable contribution for an understanding of the God-World relationship. Unlike the pantheistic models they stress the transcendence of the absolute reality. However, theistic metaphysics raises objections to the absolutist reduction of the finite World to the status of '*asat*' (non-being) as well as the processionist's view of necessary creation.

A. Dualistic Theism: Aristotle and Mādhva

Metaphysical Synthesis: The absolute reality is a 'prime mover' (Aristotle) or the "ruler and Lord" of the Universe (Mādhva). In both cases the absolute is not the cause of finite existence, but only the cause of the material and spiritual processes at play in the finite World. The God of Aristotle is the great 'magnet' that acts as final cause. The God of Mādhva gives direction to a Universe which subsists distinctly from Him. The infinite and the finite coexist from all eternity in a master-servant relationship; they constitute two realities (Mādhva's dvaita-Vedānta) even though the finite reality is 'ruled' and directed by the infinite in being, but only in acting, moving and evolving, etc, Thus, the divine creation is nothing more than 'moderating,' ruling, directing. The creator is the 'shepherd' of the finite World and the cause of its existence.

Critical Remark: This metaphysical dualism has little to offer in explanation of the existence of the finite reality. It admits the existence of two absolutes even if one absolute is subordinated to the other. Metaphysics must explain not only how the World functions and moves but also how and why it exists. An absolute reality that is not the explanation of the being of the finite World is no longer an absolute reality but some sort of 'demiurge' or architect who interferes in World matters without causing them to be. For metaphysical dualism God is not the 'Creator' of the World but an outsider who rules from afar. There is a point in the pantheist's objection to this brand of theism: how can there be anything 'outside' the one absolute reality? The dualism of the infinite and the finite is not more acceptable than pantheistic monism.

B. Transcendental Theism: Thomas Aquinas

This is the classical theism expounded by Thomas Aquinas and many others. It attempts to give a model of creation that agrees with the requirements issuing from the nature of the absolute reality reached by rational inference and from the finite condition of existence given in human experience.

Three compulsory statements determine the position of classical theism regarding the relationship between the infinite and the finite.

i. Creation is the Unilateral Relationship of Ontological Dependence Between the Absolute Reality and the Finite World.

1) Relationship: Creation is not 'action' but a pure relationship. A human action usually involves four constitutive elements: a) an agent, b) some pre-existing matter on which the agent will act, c) the transformation of that matter according to the agent's plan, d) the effect obtained by the agent's activity. In the case of creation stages b) and c) are irrelevant for there is no pre-existing matter and no transformation taking place. There is only the agent and its effect with nothing between them. Creation is no production but the relationship of cause to effect.

Some popular models of creation depict it as a divine action that begins and produces novelty. This imagery does not help us to grasp what theistic metaphysics intends to convey by the concept of creation. It is not a question of the 'coming to be' of the World from the Creator but the actual, timeless presence of a finite reality in a relationship of total dependence on the absolute presence of God.

2) Ontological: Creation implies the total dependence of the finite on the infinite at the deepest level of being. The finite World owes its existence to the absolute reality which is more than a ruler or a moderator (dualism). The effect depends on the cause for its very existence.

3) Unilateral: In creation the relationship of dependence is unilateral and not reciprocal. The infinite does not depend on the finite, the absolute reality does not need the World; it is the other way around. Therefore, classical theism disagrees with Plotinus' view that creation is necessary. By definition the absolute reality is self-sufficient. It is contradictory to state that infinite and finite are inter-dependent.

Still the question arises for classical theism to explain why the absolute reality is the cause of an effect that it need not have created. If creation is 'free,' is there a reason for it or is it arbitrary?

ii. Creation is "Out of Nothing"

The expression 'out of nothing' does not convey anything positive. But, it is meant to clarity the notion of creation by eliminating misconceptions. It is useful to know what should NOT be said.

'Out of nothing' here means two things: not out of the divine substance and not out of any pre-existing substance. In saying that creation is out of nothing, we reject that God is the material cause of the Universe and on the other hand the idea that He is only a demiurge or architect that orders and rules an already pre-existing World.

The expression 'out of nothing' serves to bring out the transcendence of the absolute reality, which creates the World not from its substance but 'out of nothing.' Rāmanuja' *Brahma-Parināma-Vāda* or the *Sat-Kārya-Vāda* theory of causality according to which the effect is precontained in the cause is thereby ruled out.

The expression 'out of nothing' seems to agree with the *Asat-kārya-Vāda* theory of causality which states that the effect is not precontained in the cause. Thus, the theistic concept of creation has much in common with Plotinus' notion of procession; the finite World 'proceeds' from God, is caused by God though not from his substance, and therefore, so to say, 'out of nothing.'

However, there seems to be a contradiction between the two statements: 'the World is out of nothing' and 'the World is created by God.' If the World comes from God, how can we say that it is 'out of nothing?' This difficulty is solved if we make a distinction between 'by God' and 'out of God' or, in Latin, 'a deo' and 'ex deo.' The finite World exists by God and not out of God, that is, by the power of the divine causality but not from the divine substance. In other words, God is not the material cause of the finite reality but its supreme efficient cause.

To sum up let us say that if the finite World is 'out of nothing,' it is 'by the power of God.' Perhaps the best model is provided by Shaṅkara's magician: an agent who produces illusory objects out of nothing. If we substitute a real finite World for the illusory objects, we obtain the model of 'a supreme magician who creates a real World out of nothing.'

iii. Creation as 'Communication' and 'Participation'

The concept of 'participation – of the finite in the infinite – and its correlate of 'communication' – of the finite to the finite are – used by Aquinas to stress two important features of transcendental theism.

Firstly in using this terminology, one avoids the faulty pantheistic model according to which the finite World is a part of the infinite. 'Participation' which preserves the distinction of infinite and finite is quite different from 'being a part' which, in not preserving it, disposes of the transcendence of the absolute reality.

Secondly and more importantly Aquinas' metaphysics of participation dissociates itself from the non-participationist transcendentalist views of Plotinus as Shaṅkara. For absolutism as well as processionism, the disparity between infinite and finite is such that what one *is*, the other *is not*. The transcendence of the absolute is amplified to the point of rendering participation and communication unthinkable. Thus, the metaphysics of participation provides a balanced approach to avoid the extremes of pantheism and 'transcendentalism' in offering another option rather than identification or estrangement between infinite and finite.

The metaphysics of 'participation-communication' is rooted in the doctrine of the analogy of being. While the univocal understanding of being leads to pantheism and its equivocal use produces non-participationist transcendentalism, the analogy of being is the foundation of the theistic metaphysics of participation. For the pantheist the divine substance is immanent in the finite, for the transcendentalist the absolute reality is radically other than the finite, but for the participationist theist God is both immanent and transcendent.

C. Dialectical Theism: J. Robinson, J. Macquarrie

Some Philosopher-theologians of our time who reject atheism as well as pantheism are not satisfied with the classical theism of the thomistic tradition, a few of them have coined the new term of "Pan-en-Theism." Others have vehemently rejected the new terminology as too close to "Pantheism" and preferred to call the new approach "dialectical theism." We shall first expose the difficulties and objections that these thinkers raise against classical theism, then examine what they have to offer in exchange and finally give our own assessment of their ideas.

Criticism of Classical Theism

Classical Theism presents a 'monarchical' view of God, that is, a view in which God is regarded as "one-sidedly transcendent, separate from and over or above the World" (Macquarrie). It does not sufficiently recognize God's immanence. God is thought of as an 'object apart from the World', an entity in 'addition' to those we meet in the World. He is seen as "an 'outside' creator, so far and distant as to be virtually non-existent" (Wijngaards). The way classical theism presents the transcendence of God cuts him off from the World and human life. J. Robinson, in his famous book "Honest to God," accuses traditional theism of 'transcendentalism,' a term we have used to describe Plotinus' non-participationist metaphysics. A God who is totally other, a God who is no longer the 'God of the World and man' does not interest anybody. In fact it justifies the modern phenomenon of atheism and secularization. (Robinson).

Creation 'out of nothing' as understood by classical theism places the World outside God. It stresses the total otherness of the creator, the complete externality of creation, a view that may lead to either dualism or even atheism (Macquarrie).

Classical theism asserts that creation is 'free,' that creation is a 'unilateral' relationship: God acts on the World but the World does not act on God. But, then what is the point in creation at all? Is it just "part of the divine sport, a capricious act with no further significance"? (Macquarrie)

Pan-entheism and Dialectical Theism

To remedy the deficiencies of classical theism the reality of God must be "re-mapped", writes J. Robinson. One should no longer place God "up there" but "in the midst", in the World. This does not mean that God is identified with the World. He is definitely other than the World. The best expression, according to Robinson, is that God is the beyond in the midst. The transcendent is immanent. God is within us (Wijngaards). The World itself is 'the divine milieu' (Teilhard de Chardin). The absolute reality is the ground of the possibility of an evolving finite World (K. Rahner).

The error of pantheism is to ignore the divine transcendence, the error of classical theism is to ignore the divine immanence. Both are over-simplifications on account of their one-sidedness. 'Immanentism' as well as 'transcendentalism' are corrected, synthesized and harmonized by pan-en-theism which holds that God penetrates the whole Universe, that every part of the Cosmos exists in God who nonetheless transcends it. To picture the relationship between finite and infinite pantheism would use the model of the sea and the waves, but Pan-en-theism would rather adopt the model of fish encompassed by the ocean. The finite is distinct from the infinite but it subsists within it, it is not 'external' to it.

Still the tern 'pan-en-theism' is not favoured by several proponents of a revision of classical theism, for it is too close in its formation to the word 'pantheism.' So a better term to describe the new idea is 'dialectical theism.' It stresses that it is a kind of theism - not pantheism - called 'dialectical' to make clear that the one-sidedness of classical theism is avoided (Macquarrie).

Dialectical Theism discovers within God several dialectical oppositions. "These oppositions are not destructive contradictions… in every opposition, each side has its own right and each side can and must be asserted" (Macquarrie). The most important of these dialectical contrasting features are: being and nothing, the one and the many, knowability and incomprehensibility, transcendence and immanence, impassibility and possibility, eternity and temporality. Thus, for instance, the affirmation that God is 'He who IS' must be completed by the contrasting assertion that God is 'He who is more than being' to emphasize that He is not so much 'being' as 'letting be.'

Assessment of Dialectical Theism

The 'new' theism is a useful reminder to classical theism that the immanence of the absolute reality must not be belittled in order to give full weight to the affirmation of its transcendence. Too much has been said to foster a certain image of God as an impassible supreme being 'up there,' an 'outside' creator, a 'supernatural' divinity. It is against this trend that pan-en-theism and dialectical theism react by suggesting the new image of a 'God within us.'

Still Classical Theism properly understood as a non-dualist (advaita) metaphysics of participation and communication grounded on the doctrine of the analogy of being contains in itself all the requirements set forth by the 'new' theism. The modern language offers images and models emphasizing some aspects of the God-World relationship but the metaphysics that sustains them does not differ substantially from Classical Theism. Thus, the so-called dialectical oppositions in God correspond to the affirmative and negative ways of the analogical knowledge of God.

The major point of contention turns around the notion of creation understood by Classical Theism as a unilateral relationship between infinite and finite. Dialectical Theism discards the idea of a purely asymmetrical relation to espouse the view that God is not impassible; he is 'affected' by everything that goes on in the World. In particular he does not remain "untouched by the sufferings of his creatures" (Macquarrie).

However, if we recognize the utility and value of these new approaches, let us keep in mind too that they issue forth from thinkers more concerned with (Christian) theological and spiritual intentions than with Philosophical speculations. That explains why the 'new' theism does not hesitate to adopt the anthropomorphic language of the personalist approach. But, then everything we have said above in criticism of this approach is equally relevant to a proper evaluation of the so-called 'new' theism.

Chapter 5

Whatness of Cosmos Understanding the Universe: Philosophical Cosmology

5.1 Characteristics of the Universe

We notice four chief characteristics of the bodily World and of individual bodies in the World, viz., *composition, mutability or changeability, contingency,* and *limitation or finiteness.* We must say a special word on each of these.

5.1.1 Composition

All bodies are *composed* or *compounded.* The Latin verb *componere*, from which our words "compose" and "compound" derives, means literally "to put together." This root-meaning serves us well. For, when we say that a body is composed or compounded, or that it is "a composition" ("a synthesis," if one prefers a Greek word), we truly mean that it is "put together;" that it is a conjoined or assembled reality; that it is a thing made of elements, principles, parts and members. There are five notable types of composition.

In ontology (the Science of fundamental metaphysics) we learn that every existing creature (and hence every existing body) is the union of essence and existence. Such a creature is constituted in its own basic reality or make-up as just such a thing, just that kind of thing (essence); and is it actually set out, and holds place among realities that are here (existence). Only of God, the infinite and wholly self-sufficing Actuality, can it be known with certainty that His essence and His existence are perfectly identified in His altogether simple or non-composed Being. Now, the union or composition of essence and existence in actual creature (that is, in an *existing* creature) is called *Entiative Composition*; that is, it is the composition by which a creature is constituted in its actuality of being. This type of composition is not of immediate concern for the student of Cosmology; it is of importance for ontology. But, even here it affords an instance of the truth or our assertion that all bodies are compounded or composed; for each existing body is a composite essence and existence.

The second type of composition is *Essential Composition.* This is the union of principles, members, elements, or parts which come together to make up an *essence.* The essence of a thing is its inmost fundamental constitution; it is what makes the thing, in its ultimate being, the kind of thing it is. The essence of a tree, for example, is not its size, not its botanical classification, not its location, nor its age, not its fruitfulness. All these the tree, *has,* but these things do not *make the tree* a *tree.* What makes the tree a tree is its *essence.* And this essence is itself a compounded or composed thing. It is composed of *prime matter* (or primary matter) and *substantial form*; that is, it is a *material* thing cast in a definite kind of mould or *form* which gives it actuality as such a specific bodily being. It is a union or composition of matter and form, and this is an *essential composition* since it constitutes an essence. Take another example: that of a human being. A man is not his age, not his sex, nor his nationality, nor his strength, nor his culture; a man is a man because he has the *essence* of man, and this *essence*, physically considered, is a composite of *body and soul.* – essential composition is often call substantial composition. The terms are not strictly synonymous, since even accident has its essence, and a composed essence. But, any discussion of essences and notably such a discussion as we here undertake as a prelude to cosmological Science, is concerned, first and foremost, with substantial essences. This fact justifies the somewhat loose use of terms which make practical synonyms of *essential composition* and substantial composition. Essential composition is of two kinds, *physical* and *metaphysical*. The physical composition of an essence is the sum or union of those physical parts of elements which come together to constitute the essence as a *physic*, that is, a being in nature, a thing among things. The metaphysical composition of an essence is the sum or union of those realities in it which explain it to the understanding mind, even though these realities be not distinct *things* in the order of nature outside the mind. Thus, the essence man (that is, *human being*) is physically composed of body and soul; these are elements which come together to constitute or compose man, as a thing in nature, independently of the understanding (creatural) mind. So we say that, physically considered, "man is a creature composed of body and soul;" we say that body and soul make a man's *physical essence*. The essence of man is metaphysically composed of animality and rationality; these are realities which the mind lays hold of in knowing what man *means*; for the mind knows man as an animal with understanding and free-will. Animality and rationality are not parts of man in the physical sense (as body and soul are), but they are realities which the mind discerns in man, and they are said to be metaphysical elements or "parts." So we say that, metaphysically considered, "man is a rational animal;" we say that animality and rationality make man's *metaphysical essence*. It is manifest that natural bodies are metaphysically compounded or composed, for each of them is *a thing* of certain essential *kind,* and the mind, in knowing such a reality naturally compounds the ideas or notes of "thing" and "of this kind." But, it is no less apparent that natural bodies are physically compounded. For we apprehend them as distinct realties and (as epistemology proves for us) our knowledge is trans-subjective or in accordance with fact; there are distinct, and essentially distinct, realities in the World of bodies around us. But, all bodies are at one in the point of being bodily;

they are all material; in this they are not distinguished either in themselves or in the view of the investigating mind. Therefore, a natural body must be a composite of *that which is has in common* with other bodies, and *that which it has in special* to make it the actual and precise kind of body that it is. Consider the fundamental, the essential difference between a lifeless body and a living body. As *bodies*, that is, as material things, these do not differ; but they emphatically do differ in the *essential kind* of body that each is. We see at once that a natural body is compounded; it is compounded of a fundamental and common material the essential difference between a lifeless body and a living body. As bodies, that is, as material things, these do not differ; but they emphatically do differ in the essential kind of body that each is. We see at once that a natural body is compounded; it is compounded of a fundamental and common material or materiality and that which gives to this materiality an actual existence in a determinate specific kind. In other words, we see that a natural body is essentially (and physically) compounded of prime matter and substantial form.

c) Contrasted with Essential Composition is *Accidental Composition*. This is the union of accidents among themselves (as of whiteness and sweetness in sugar) or the union of accidents with their substance (as of whiteness and sweetness with the substance called sugar). It is the function of ontology to prove that there are in the World physical accidents which are really distinct from the substances which they mark of qualify. But, there is no need here to formulate an elaborately Scientific proof of the fact. It is the common experience of all that what we know substances are not their accidents. Substances have accidents, but they are not constituted by their accidents, and hence their accidents are not to be identified with them. Water, for instance is not to be identified with its temperature; it has, at any given moment, a certain temperature; but it does not change in its essence or substance when the temperature is changed; it does not cease to be water when it loses coldness and acquires heat. Now, this non-essential, non-substantial, union or composition which conjoins a substance with its accidents is accidental composition. So is the collection of accidents which converge in any substance, considered merely as a collection, without reference to the substance which they qualify. Examples of both types of accidental composition are readily conceived: a man with his age, knowledge, degree of grace; a tree with its size, location, number of leaves; the hardness, size, flavor, temperature, of an apple. All natural bodies are composed of substance and accidents. Abstractly, it may be possible to conceive of a finite substance (that is, a creatural substance) with no accidents whatever; but it is not possible to conceive of such a substance existing as a body in the World around us. Some accidents a natural body will certainly have, yet it is not to be identified with these. Therefore, a natural body evidences in itself an accidental composition of substance and accidents.

d) Another type of composition is that known as *Integral Composition*. The term integral is derived from Latin *integralis* (a non-classical form of integer) which means "untouched; unhurt; having lost nothing; not defective," and hence the World connotes "rounded perfection." The parts or elements (chiefly quantitative, and, so far as Cosmology is concerned, always quantitative) which belong to the rounded completeness of a reality, but do not constitute that reality in its essence, are called integral parts, and are said to be united with the reality which they perfect or complement by integral union or integral composition. We are all aware, by common experience, of the fact that a reality may be constituted in his essence, he may be a man, and a complete man, and yet lack some bodily member or power that normally and naturally he should possess. For the human essence requires a certain minimum in quantity and bodily equipment, but is normally and naturally fitted with more than this minimum; and the members and powers which are thus naturally superadded to the absolute requisites for essence are things that lend perfection, completeness, beauty, grace, to the essence in its being and its operation. A man who has lost hand or foot, or whose hair has unhappily disappeared or whose teeth are gone ("in whole or in part," as the legal phrase has it), or who is short-sighted or hard of hearing, is still a man, still a complete human essence, despite such deprivation. He has lost certain members of powers which normally and naturally belong to his essence, and which bring to that essence a certain rounded perfection when they are joined or compounded with it. When present, such perfections are joined or compounded with the man's essence by integral composition. It will be noticed at once that integral composition is a variety of accidental composition. In one sense, integral composition may, at least occasionally, be called substantial composition (as, for instance, in the union of hands or feet with the undivided substance of the human body), but it is never essential composition. Here we see, for the second time, that the terms essential composition and substantial composition are not truly synonymous. Essential composition is the union of elements necessary for the constitution of an essence, whether that essence be the essence of a substance or the essence of an accident. Substantial composition, in a wide sense, is the union of elements or members that do, as a fact, enter into the unbroken structure of a substance, whether they are necessary to that substance or not. It is manifest that natural bodies are marked by integral composition. For natural bodies are marked by quantity; they have parts extended in space; and such parts (quantitative parts) are regularly capable of being changed or reduced without destruction of the bodily substance itself. A stone has a certain size; break off a part, and the stone is still a stone, but it is not so much as it was, nor is it held in the same unbroken hulk; and in so far it has lost something which actualized or perfected it in an accidental way. Now, what a body can lose, in quantitative parts, without loss of its essential or substantial character, is conjoined with it by integral composition. A tree has many leaves and branches; take off some of these and the tree is the loser, but it does not cease to be a tree; it has lost a certain "perfection" which was conjoined with it by integral composition, that is, joined with it as an actual perfecting part, member, or element, but not joined with it as something essentially requisite.

e) A fifth type of composition is *Numerical Composition*. This is the union or assembling of items or elements (which, taken singly, are complete in themselves) to constitute a sum, or a totality, or a collective unity. Thus, we speak of crowd as "composed" of persons; we speak of a wall as "composed" bricks or stones. We all know, with R.L.S. that the World is a vast *collection* of kinds and varieties of objects, and of individuals of each variety. Now, each individual, and indeed each part (complete *as such*) of each individual, can be *numbered,* or *counted* as a single item in its group and individual groups can be numbered or counted as items or members of larger groups, and so on. The five peas in a pod can be *numbered* (1,2,3,4,5), and they can be taken collectively as *one podful*, that is, they can be joined or "composed" by *numerical composition* to constitute a single group or collection. And the pods can be numbered as items of a totality called a peck of peas. And so on. It is manifest to the most inattentive observers that the bodily World is characterized by *numerical composition.* In itself, numerical composition is a variety of accidental composition. For, although the numbered items or parts of a totality may be necessary for the constitution of an essence or of a substance, the special aspect they present *as distinct items that have come together to make a total* does not include anything further or other; it does not include their possible effect upon one another, such as their possible effect upon one another, such as their affinities, their substantial fusion, their integral of essential union. It includes only association or collection of numerable items, elements, members, parts; nothing more. And such association or collection is in self an accidental composition.

It is manifest, then, that the bodily World which is the material object of Cosmology is, in every respect, a *thing composed or compounded.* For we have been at pains to point out the fact that any natural body (even the World of bodies taken as a collective unity or numerical composite) is compounded in essence and substance and is inevitably marked by accidental composition. It is certain; therefore, that one constant and ever-present characteristic of the bodily World is its *composition* or *compositeness.*

5.1.2 Mutability or Changeability

All bodies are mutable, that is to say, all natural bodies are subject to *change*. Now, change (or mutation) may be defined as the passing from one state or condition to another. In the technical language of Philosophy, change is "transit from potentiality to actuality." *Potentiality* is the state of a reality with respect to what it may become: thus, the infant is in potentiality with respect to adulthood, and we say that the baby is *potentially* a grown-up. *Actuality* is the state of a reality taken statically *as it is*: thus, the infant is *actually* an infant, while *potentially* it is an adult. In other words, a reality is actually *what it is;* it is potentially *what it may become*, whether the new and unactualized state is a matter of substance or of accidents. A change, therefore, or a transit from potentiality to actuality, is the fact and process of passing from the present state (*actuality*) to another which is to come or to be acquired (*potentiality*). Thus, change is the fact and process of *becoming*; and things subject to *becoming* (as all natural bodies are) are said to be *mutable* or *changeable*, or to be marked and characterized by *mutability* or *changeability.*

There are two chief classifications of change, viz., *Substantial Change* and *Accidental Change.* Accidental change is of three notable types: *quantitative change, qualitative change,* and *local change.* Of these we must say a brief word.

Substantial Change is the transformation of a substance (or substances) into a different substantial reality. The change of food into flesh, or a living body into a lifeless body, of hydrogen and oxygen into water, and of water into hydrogen and oxygen, are examples of substantial change. Substantial change is (in the language of Philosophy, which must not be interpreted in the manner of everyday speech nor even in that of laboratory Science) *generation* and *corruption.* These are but two aspects of the one substantial change. The generation of a new substance is the corruption of the old. This is expressed in a famous Latin axiom, *generatio unius est corruption alterius et vice versa,* "the generation of one thing is the corruption of another, and vice versa." When, for example, hydrogen and oxygen become water, the gases undergo *corruption* and the water is *generated.* When a man dies, the human substance is *corrupted* (that is, broken up, not rotted or crumbled slowly away) and the same process is the *generation* of the inorganic substances which compose the corpse. Generation and corruption are two aspects of one *instantaneous* change which removes a substantial form by supplanting it (with absolutely no time interval) by another substantial form or other substantial forms by supplanting it (with absolutely no time-interval) by another substantial form or other substantial forms. Those natural bodies are all subject to substantial change is manifest to any attentive observer. For we see about us, in this World of bodies, no item or individual substance that has not been generated and that is not to be subjected to corruption. Plants, animals, and men, are brought into being, and they die; food is digested, coal is burned up; solid rock is subjected to chemical forces which, in time, transform its substance. There is nothing in the bodily World which (after a first creation) did not come here by generation; nor is there anything here so wholly indestructible that it must keep its substantial being eternally unchanged. In a word, all natural bodies are subjected to substantial change; substantial mutability is their constant mark or characteristic.

Accidental change is, as the very term indicates, a change or transformation of non-substantial realities. When a quart of milk is half consumed, the remaining pint is still the substance in the mild; there has been no change of substance in the mild that remains; only no so much remains; there has been a change of amount or *quantity*. This is *quantitative* change or amount or *quantity.* This is *quantitative* change, a type of accidental change. When a baby grows into a youth, the human substance is not changed; the baby and the youth into whom the baby grows are one and the same essence and substance; the change that has taken place is (in point of size or bodily bulk) a quantitative change. Again, when hot water becomes cold, there is a change; a change in *quality*, or a *qualitative* change. Of course, there is quantitative change too, for some of the water (however small the amount) evaporates during the time required to affect the change in temperature; but the change in temperature, considered in itself, is a qualitative change. The baby changes in qualities as well as in quantity as it grows larger; such qualities as its appearance, complexion, agility, alertness, are changed as the baby grows up, and these changes are, considered solely in themselves, qualitative. Qualitative change is, like quantitative change, a type of things in which qualitative or quantitative change occurs are no *thereby* changed: the milk is still milk, though it quantity is diminished; the water is still the same person (human substance) though it undergoes quantitative and qualitative changes. The third type of accidental change is *local change* or change of place; it is perhaps the most manifest of all types of change in the World where everything is "on the move," everything is subjected to motion. The movement of the heavenly bodies, of the earth, of leaving in a breeze, of hands swinging by one's sides, of walking feet, of twitching eyelids, of revolving wheel, of a growing weed, is, inasmuch as it involves a change of place or position, a local movement or local change. It is certainly manifest that the World of bodies is subject to constant accidental change. It is a World full of movement or local change, from the coursing spheres to the whirling parts of an atom; it is a World of quantitative change, for it has temperature, and lights, and shadows. We cannot doubt the truth of the statement that accidental change is a constant phenomenon in the World of natural bodies, and that; in consequence, accidental mutability is a constant mark or characteristic of such bodies. In passing, the student will do well to notice that substantial change is never gradual or effected by successive steps; it is always *instantaneous*. Though a lump of coal may take long while burning up, and it is not consumed by the substantial change, but by the accidental changes which prepare each grain of coal for that final and instantaneous transformation which destroys it as coal (*corrupts* it) and produces or *generates* ashes and smoke. Accidental change is never instantaneous, but gradual or *successive*, even though it consumes a very small period of time.

From this detailed study it is clear that the bodily World is, in every respect, a thing subject to change, *a reality marked by mutability or changeability*. Mutability is a constant and ever-present characteristic of natural bodies, in their substantial as well as their accidental being. Rightly are they called *entia mobilia*, or *mobile beings*.

5.1.3 Contingency

A contingent reality is one that has in itself no absolute necessity or requirement for existing, but is dependent upon (or contingent upon) that causes that produce and sustain it. There are only two conceivable kinds of reality from the viewpoint of necessity in existence; for a reality either *has got* to exist or it *hasn't*. If it *must* exist, by its own nature and essence, it is called a *necessary being;* if it involves in itself no necessity for existing, it is called a *contingent being*. A necessary being is *uncaused*; it is wholly self-sufficing; it is itself the perfect explanation and reason for its existence. Now, such a being (as the Science of ontology proves in abundant detail) is *infinite, non-material, eternal, non-composed.* And, since an infinite being is necessarily *one,* not a plurality, it is manifest that there can be only one necessary being. This Being we call God, and it is part of theodicy (the Philosophy of deity) to prove beyond question that God actually exists. Now, if God is the one and only Necessary Being, and if there are only two kinds of being (*necessary,* and non-necessary or *contingent*), it follows inevitably that all reality other than God is *contingent being.* We shall show presently that the bodily World cannot be identified with God. For the present, it suffices to point out that *necessary being* is non-material and non-composed, whereas natural bodies are material and, as we have shown above, are marked by constant and ever-present characteristic of *composition.* Contingent *reality* or being is *caused* reality. And the World around us is a tissue of causation. Even the mistaken persons, who deny causality, are forced to admit some sort continuous succession and contingency as the explanation or reason of the things confronting them in daily life. A foolish man may deny, in theory, that there is any such thing as cause and effect; but he does not fail to put the tea-kettle on the fire when he wants hot water; not does he depend upon his own Philosophy of denial when some careless motorist has barged into him and done him a hurt. Normal reason recognizes causality in the World, and all Science and Philosophy are built upon this recognition. And contingency accompanies causality as a shadow accompanies a man walking in sunlight. For what is caused (that is, an *effect*) depends upon or *is contingent upon* its cause. Caused being or contingent being is, as we have said, being that does not *require* existence, does not, by its own nature, *demand* existence; it is a thing that *can* exist, and its capacity for existing is met by the cause or causes that confer actuality upon it by bringing it into existence and holding it here. Thus, contingent being is rightly called *ens ab alio,* that is, being or reality which depends on something other than itself necessary being, on the other hand, is *ens a se,* that is, being which exist of itself, not depending at all upon anything other than itself. Now, in this World we find substantial change (*generation and corruption*) which continually brings new substances into existence and takes other substances out of it. Substances have "their exits and their entrances." In the face of this obvious fact, it would be merely nonsensical to say or to think that bodily substances have no dependency or contingency upon their producing and sustaining agencies. Contingency in the bodily World is inescapably obtruded upon our notice; it is a certain and universal fact. There is not one bodily being in the World that has not *come* here; there is not one such being that is *unproduced;* in other words, there is not one natural body that is not *contingent.* Consider the point in a somewhat larger or more abstract way; there is not in the World a single natural body that can be called *necessary,* for what is necessary cannot be clearly conceived of, or accurately imagined, as *non-existent.* And we can easily conceive of any natural body as non-existent, for the complete and adequate concept of any such being does not involve the point of actual existence. What bodies we behold around us are here; but we know, and with certainty, that they *might not* be here. Now, any reality; that is, it *is* here by reason of something other than itself which has produced it, which sustains it, and which therefore accounts for its being here. Any reality that *might not* be here *would not* be here if existence had not been bestowed upon it by something other than itself. Thus, we state that any such reality is *contingent* reality. Therefore, we are completely justified in the statement that all natural bodies, without exception, are marked and characterized by *contingency.*

5.1.4 Limitation or Finiteness

A *finite* reality is one that has limits or boundaries. It is a reality that can (in one way or another) be *measured* as to content, place, power, or activity. An *infinite* reality has no limits or limitations no boundaries or borders; it is boundless in all perfection, non-material, non-composed, necessary. There is only one infinite Being (and ontology proves to demonstration the absolute impossibility of a plurality of infinities or infinite beings); this Being we call God. And, since God is not identified with the World (as we shall shortly prove), it is certain that the World, and Worldly bodies, are not infinite; in other words, they are *finite*; they are marked with the characteristic of *limitation* or *finiteness.*

Sometimes we use the word "infinite," and the word "infinity," in a figurative manner. When, for example, we are told that focusing our camera in a certain way will give us a field for photography "from 100 feet to infinity," we understand that the phrase means merely "100 feet or over." When a mathematician speaks of infinity or even of an "infinite number," he means a number *indefinitely* large. For a distance or a number, to be *actually* infinite, would be such that it could not, even in thought or imagination, be made larger or smaller. And there is no distance and no number that cannot be instantly imagined as cut in half, or as multiplied by two. Distance or number (or size, in general) can be called *potentially* infinite (or *indefinite*), inasmuch as there is no point at which one must stop in imagining its extent; one can go on multiplying a number by itself without ever reaching a point where further multiplication is impossible; but, at *any* point in the process of multiplication, the number (whether it be abstract number, or square yards, or cubic miles) is actually *finite.* Hence, the use of the term "infinity" in mathematics, or in the art of photography, or in the Science of astronomy, is figurative or metaphorical use; the term means "indefinitely large."

We assert that all natural bodies are *finite*. Of the *finiteness* of the material Universe itself we shall speak again in another place, but even here we may notice that since the material Universe is made up of limited bodies, it is itself limited; for finite added to finite can never equal actual infinity. However, our immediate purpose here is to indicate the fact that any and all of the natural bodies observable in the World are limited of finite. It may seem unnecessary to stress so obvious a fact, yet it is important for us to pause upon the point for a moment and to conceive it with the greatest clarity.

The World is filled with many *individual* things, one of which is not another, and each of which is manifestly bounded and limited within the extent of its own quantity. Now, when two things are so really distinct that one is not the other in any sense, then there must be limitation *on the part of at least one* of the two things concerned. And, unless there be question of marking the distinction between a contingent being and the Necessary Being, there will be limitation *on the part of both* beings concerned. But, we have already seen that natural bodies are contingent, and hence, each individual of them is distinct from every other individual, and, by that distinction, is strictly *limited*; all natural bodies are, therefore, finite realities. In other words, finiteness or limitation is a universal characteristic of natural bodies.

In the World of bodies, we notice more than individual differences among single bodily beings; we notice differences of *kind*, differences among species and genera of natural bodies. A person is not likely to confuse a lifeless cold and living body, or a plant like a vine with an animal like a dog or cat; these are not only bodily things that differ as individuals, but they differ in essential constitution so that they are known as different *kinds* of bodies. These bodies are different in kind because of each of the kinds (class, genus, species) is contained, so to speak, within its own definitely determined character; each is *limited* to its class or kind. Again, we notice limitation or finiteness as a characteristic of natural bodies.

Again, the World is, as we have seen, marked and characterized by *composition.* Natural bodies are made up of distinct elements, parts, member, one of which is not another. Each element or part is of a certain kind, scope, power, character; further, each element or part is one part. In other words, each element or part is a finite or limited thing, and a body made up of limited parts is itself limited. Once more we conclude inevitable that limitation or finiteness is a characteristic of the bodily World.

There have been Philosophers and Scientists who held that the World is not limited. Such, for instance, were Friedrich Büchner (1824-1899) and Ernst Haeckel (1834-1919), German materialists. We shall deal with the error of such teachers when we come to the consideration of the actual extent of *space.* Here it must suffice to repeat what we have already noticed, to wit, that a World made up of natural bodies which are limited must be itself limited.

One final proof of the limitation of natural bodies: in every contingent reality we mark a clean distinction between existence and that which has existence, that is, between the actual *existence* and physical *essence* of the existing thing. We say that a contingent reality *receives* existence, and every receiver limits what it receives, just as a cup limits the liquid poured into it, or the hand encloses with limitation the object that lies within its grasp. Existence in a contingent reality is limited to *this thing which exists,* and this received and limited existence is what accounts for the thing being actually here. Further, that which exists, the existing *essence,* is a thing of definite scope, power, or kind. On the score, then, of both existence and essence, a contingent reality is a limited reality. Now, all natural bodies are contingent realities. It follows inevitably that all natural bodes are limited or finite bodies, and that *finiteness or limitation is a universal characteristic of the bodily World.*

To sum up: All natural bodies are composed, made up, compounded; all are subject to change or mutation; all are contingent or dependent upon causes; all are finite or limited. We have here the four outstanding and unmistakable characteristics or the World of bodies, that is, of each and every natural body. And from these characteristics or natural bodies we are able to proceed to a better understanding of what such bodies are in their inmost being, their nature and essence.

Even now, without further study, we are in position to discuss that interesting doctrine called cosmological *optimism* which asserts that this World is the best of all possible Worlds. The Philosopher Wilhelm Leibniz (1646-1716) was one of the many who proposed such a doctrine. Now, we have seen that the World is marked by certain university present characteristics, each one of which indicates a kind of lack, a want of self-sufficiency, an imperfection. But, the best of all possible Worlds would be a *perfect* World. Manifestly, then, the World is not the best of all possible Worlds. But, we must not leave the point with such a blunt assertion. We must make a distinction in the meaning of the word *perfect.* When is a reality to be called *perfect*? It is to be called *absolutely perfect* (that is, unconditionally, unlimitedly perfect) when no further perfection can even be imagined as added to it; when it is boundlessly perfect so that it involves in itself the actual fullness of being. Obviously, only the one infinite Being is absolutely perfect. But, a reality may be *relatively perfect,* that is, perfect in *relation* to, or *relative* to, the purpose it serves or the nature it bears. Thus, we say (relatively speaking) that the new cot is "a perfect fit," or that a work of art is perfect, or that we are in perfect health. Similarly, we may say that this World is *perfect,* meaning that it is marvelously well suited for the purpose it serves; that it is wondrously beautiful in the structure of its bodies, in the harmony and balance of its parts, and so on. In this sense, it is *the best World,* but only in this sense. For God's power is boundless, and is therefore not exhausted in the creating and preserving of the World as we find it; and, on the other hand, we have seen that the World is made of bodies that have manifest and characteristic imperfections. Therefore, *absolutely speaking*, this World is not to be called "the best" or "the best possible;" *relatively speaking,* it may be called so.

An objection is sometimes posed in this form: Is not God forced by His boundless goodness to give to every creature of His hands all the perfection that it could possibly have? The answer is that God is not forced at all. God (whose power and goodness are one in infinite identity with the divine essence itself) freely chooses to create, and creates most wisely, that is, creates things so that they will serve their purpose in a marvelously perfect way. Indeed, one might go to the extent of saying that God's creatures are always such as serve their purpose in the best way possible. But, this is not at all the same thing as saying that creatures, in themselves, have all perfection possible. Indeed, the imperfection of one creature may be a help to the perfection or the perfective action of others. Thus, the World, which was physically hurt and rendered imperfect by the Fall (consider the points of harsh climate, unfriendly animals, noxious plants, destructive storms), serves the needs of fallen man far better that an unspoiled Eden could do. For were man (dull, and stupid, and inclined to evil, since the Fall) free of the hardships inflicted upon him by the imperfections of the bodily World, he would inevitably make his heaven upon earth and fail to work out his eternal destiny.

If we cannot accept *cosmological optimism,* neither can we subscribe to *cosmological pessimism* which asserts that the World is wholly evil, and that no perfection whatever is to be found in it. The doctrine is absurd upon the face of it. For the imperfections or Worldly or natural bodies (and we are not concerned to deny them; quite the contrary) are truly *im*perfections, that is, they are deficiencies *in existing perfection.* They are, so to speak, points where existing perfection breaks off, or breaks down, or falls short. Evil or badness is always a negative thing; it is a *lack*; it is an *absence* of reality that should be present. Now, in the face of a real World, an actual World, a World that is *here*, the assertion of pessimism is as silly as the denial of the existence of the World, and indeed that is what the assertion amounts to.

5.1.5 The World Not Divine

The doctrine that World is *divine,* that is, that the bodily Universe is somehow identified with God, is called *pantheism*, a word which derives from the Greek *pan* "all; everything," and *theos* "God." There are two fundamental forms of pantheism, viz., *real* pantheism and *idealistic* pantheism. Idealistic pantheism holds that the bodily World is only a skein of images or ideas in the mind of God and has no real existence of its own. Such pantheism is latent in the teachings of Immanuel Kant (1734-1804) and was developed openly in the doctrines of Kant's followers, Fichte (1726-1814), von Schelling (1775-1854), and Hegel (1770-1831). The error of this form of pantheism is shown in the Science of criteriology (the Philosophy of true and certain knowledge), and need not concern us here; Cosmology necessarily accepts the bodily Universe s trans-subjective and real. The second form of pantheism, that is, *real pantheism*, is of two distinct types: the first of these asserts that the bodily World is *an actual part* of the substance of God, that it is an extension or an "outpouring" of God's real being and substance; the second type of real pantheism asserts that the World is a *real manifestation* (rather than a real *part*) of God, as, for example, a smile is a real manifestation of benignity or amusement, rather than a real *part* of the face on which it appears. The first type of real pantheism is called *emanationism*, from the Latin *emanare,* "to pour out;" the second type is called simply *pantheism,* or sometimes, *phenomenalism,* from the Greek *phaino*, "to show; to manifest."

Emanationism and *Phenomenalism*, inasmuch as they identify all things in God, teach that there exists *one single substance,* viz., the divine substance. Hence, these types of pantheism are *monistic,* or forms of *monism,* a term which derives from the Greek *monos*, "single; one; only."

Emanationism cannot be true. In ontology (or fundamental metaphysics) and also in theodicy (or natural theology) we have the clear proof that God is the all-perfect, necessary, non-composed, changeless, infinite Being. But, as we have already seen, this bodily Universe is indelibly and universally marked with the characteristics of imperfection, contingency, composition, mutability, and finiteness. Hence, to identify God and the material World is a contradiction in thought and in terms. It is absolutely impossible for such a contradiction to have existence as an actual fact; one might as easily conceive a thing as simultaneously *existing* and *not existing*.

The same argument avails when we come to consider *phenomenalism*. For the one infinite substance which the phenomenalists admit is said to manifest itself in the bodily World, to show itself in what we mistakenly call bodily being, but which is really a series of divine modes, or moments, or determinations, or aspects. But, such a series is manifestly a limited thing (whereas the one substance is unlimited or infinite); it is changeable (whereas the one substance is necessarily immutable); it is a complexity of various things (whereas he one substance is simple or uncomposed). Further, the pantheism of manifestation conflicts with the findings of consciousness which are the elements and basis of all knowledge. If one cannot know that I am myself, not some other person or all other persons and all other things; if one cannot know one's actions of breathing, eating, walking, thinking, choosing, then one's knowledge is wholly untrustworthy, and one can know nothing with certainty. For there is no clearer certitude than that which makes me certain of my own individual being and function. But, if one can know nothing with certainty, one can surely not know with certainty that phenomenalism is true. One can only lapse into the silence and self-contradiction of absolute skepticism. Reason bars the way to such an evil laps. Phenomenalism is therefore in conflict with reason. And what is in conflict with reason must be rejected s false by all men, and first of all by the Scientist and the Philosopher. Again, pantheism (emanationism or phenomenalism) would lead to impossible consequences. For if the World is God, then all activities in the World are divine; all are therefore equally good. Thus, sin and virtue are made one; responsibility is wiped out; morality ceases to be; crime is impossibility. Now, normal human reason is unprepared to accept such blasphemous, such chaotic consequences. On the principle of causality, which may here be expressed as "by their fruits you shall know them," we must conclude that a doctrine productive of such impossible "fruits" is itself impossible.

Closely approximating pantheism is the vague doctrine (or complexus of many doctrines, variously propounded) known as *theosophy.* Theosophy acknowledges the existence of real finite Worldly realties, but makes them *immanently divine*; it holds that God is indwelling in every creature in such a way as to make all creatural activity the directly exercised activity of God Himself. Manifestly, this sort of doctrine is pantheistic, if it may not be reduced to plain pantheism, and it is to be rejected for the same reasons that compel the mind to reject pantheism in it's more open and defiant forms.

5.2 The Constitution of the Universe

The second page of the first chapter discusses the *essential* constitution of bodies. It asks what makes any natural body *a body*, and what makes it an actual or *existing* body of its definite *specific kind.* Theories on the ultimate constitution of matter, that is, of bodies and of the material Universe, may be listed under the headings, viz., *Monism, Atomism, Dynamism,* and *Hylomorphism.*

5.2.1 Monism

A. Meaning of Monism

Monism is a term derived from the Greek adjective *monos*, which means "single" or "alone." By its etymology, therefore, monism means a theory of a World which is "all of a piece," a single substance or a single cloud of unsubstantility; it stands opposed to diversity, real plurality, and real variety.

In this World of bodies, we are aware of *multitude* or *number;* that is, we see that there are many bodily objects round about. And we are aware of diversity *in kind* or specific nature, and of *variety.* That is, we see that bodies are not only numerous, but that they are of different fundamental kinds, and that there are many differences in externals among bodies of the same fundamental kind. We agree that all bodies are at one in point of *bodiliness,* but we do not find in bodliliness alone a complete or existible essence; a body cannot exist merely as a body and nothing else; it must be a body of a definite specific or essential kind, and, indeed, it must, to exist, be an individual body of that kind. Men and brutes and trees and stones are different, not only in point of individuality or number, but of essential kind; and within the limits of each kind we find great variety in size, color, shape, and so on; and we notice that variety extends into the most trivial of accidental differences among distinct individuals of each kind. Now, monism will not admit the actuality of fundamental diversity; it admits no *kinds* of matter, but only matter which is *one kind.* It explains the World we live in, either as illusory, or as presenting only an apparent diversity; at most, it will never concede that diversity is fundamental that is, *specific* or *essential.*

B. Tenets of Monism

There exists only one actuality, one existing kind of reality. What this reality is, is variously explained by monists. The materialists call it *matter*, and the cruder materialists understand by *matter.* The bodily World of our experience. They say that the World is one great lump of stuff out of which various things are shaped; this stuff is "all there is;" there is nothing non-material in existence, nothing but a matter-World accidentally differentiated. In a word, the World is one pan of dough; the different things in the World are merely differently-shaped biscuits, but all are of the same dough. More: there is no cooker or baker. The dough is self-shaping. In last analysis, then, the solely existing matter must be the Necessary Being or God. Thus, *materialistic* monism is always *pantheism*. Indeed, all types of monism are more or less perfectly *pantheistic*.

Monism has a great variety of expressions, even though it is in itself the foe of real variety. The one actuality is called *substance* by Baruch Spinoza (1632-1677), and it is endowed with infinity of *extension* and of *thought.* Fichte (1762-1814), said that the one existing reality is the "Absolute Ego," or universal I-*ness,* which becomes aware of its dreams or thoughts or mental images (and these are out bodily World) and then realizes that, after all, these are not different or distinct from itself. Following upon this vague (and pantheistic) doctrine, von Schelling (1775-1854) made the one actuality a *universal reason,* and Hegel (1770-1831) made it an indeterminate universal *idea.* Schopenhauer (1788-1860) explains the Universe as "Will" unfolding and manifesting itself in individual things. Von Hartmann (1842-1906) says the one reality is "The Unconscious" which gradually comes to awareness by "will" and "idea," and projects the image-individuals which we call the various Worlds. Bergson (1859-1941) says the only reality is "becoming" or "duration" and this is brought into actuality by an inner "vital impulse" (*élan vital*). Spencer (1820-1903) holds that the one reality is "The Absolute" which is also "The Unknowable," and reduces the fields of Science and Philosophy to apparent happenings (*phenomena*) which reveal themselves as subject to a universal law of evolution.

C. Estimate of Monism

It is manifest that the monistic theories mentioned above are, with the exception of crude materialism, theories of unreality. They explain the World by explaining it away. Only the materialists come to grips with a bodily World which is "on its own," which is actually here in something of the manner in which normal consciousness apprehends it. Of course, materialism cannot stand, for, as we have seen, a bodily reality cannot be self-exercising or necessary; it demands its causes; it is *ens ab alio,* not *ens a se*. And the First Being is necessarily infinite, whereas matter is necessarily finite. For the rest, Spinoza makes matter infinite, and adds to this absurdity a second one, viz., the existence of *thought* in matter. Fichte, Schelling, Hegel, and the others, deny the actuality of the World they attempt to explain. They are like the man who should say, "What you see doesn't exist, but I'll tell you what it is."

Monism is an unjustified over-simplification of the problem of reality. It does not come to grips with the problem; it makes solution impossible by denying the terms of the problem. It does not explain; it explains away. Thus, it is unreasonable, and therefore unacceptable to Scientist or Philosopher.

Monism is not only in conflict with reason, but with the data of direct experience which are the foundation of all our knowledge. Any theory that denies the trustworthiness of consciousness and sensation, in their direct and simple findings, cuts all basis from human certitude and leaves us to the insane silence of skepticism.

Summary of the Article

In this brief article we have defined the term *monism* and have learned what monists hold to be true about the bodily World which is the material object of Cosmology, and the first field of all our knowledge actual division would affect the very nature of the material handled and change it into another specific kind of bodily substance. When the term *atom* was first applied to the minimum-particle of a chemically simple substance, it was thought that the word was just and properly descriptive; it was thought that the atom could not be divided; that it was really something uncut and uncuttable. But, modern Science has "cut the uncuttable," so to speak, and the atom now has its own "building stones," as we have noticed in another place. However, the term has been retained even if its original literal meaning is now no longer justified. This comment refers, of course, to the atom as handled in physical Science. In the Philosophy of matter here considered (that is, in atomism) the atom still means an uncut and uncuttable minimum of matter which, in one way or another, the cause and the explanation of the bodily World.

5.2.2 Atomism

A. Meaning of Atomism

Atomism is a doctrine which proposes to explain the bodily Universe by pointing out the fact that bodies are made of smaller bodies. And, while we acknowledge the manifest fact, we are not satisfied with the inadequate explanation.

It must be clearly understood that we are not now discussing *the atomic theory* which is the currently accepted *Science* of matter. We are discussing the theory of *atomism* which is an exploded *Philosophy* of matter. We recognize the value of the atomic theory. We are quite ready to acknowledge that chemically compounded substances are made up of minimum-particles called molecules, and that molecules are made up of chemically simple particles called atoms, and that atoms are made of protons and electrons and imponderable matter. This, after all, is plain Science fresh from the laboratory, and has nothing to do with Philosophy but atomism proposes itself as a Philosophy, and with this Philosophy we are immediately concerned.

The atomic theory may be illustrated as *the description* of a house by an enumeration of its parts, down to the smallest items used in the building. Atomism is illustrated in *the explanation* of the house in terms of its parts, without reference to architect or builder, and without reference to forest or lumberyard or quarry or brick-works. Very naturally, we may accept the description of the house as true and valuable, and at the same time we may reject the explanation of the house as nonsensical and inadequate. In a word, we accept atoms (and the atomic theory); but we reject atomism.

Atomism and *Atom* are words taken from the Greek *atomos* which means "uncut" and even "indivisible." The indivisibility here indicated is structural indivisibility or, in a very precise sense, physical indivisibility. For when one has divided and subdivided a bodily substance until available instruments can make no further partition, one has come to a minimum-particle of the substance. This minimum-particle is, as a quantity, still further divisible, and indefinitely so, for it has halves and quarters and hundredths and millionths, and so on endlessly. Hence, when we call a particle of bodily substance *indivisible* we mean one of two things: we mean either that we have no means of making a further actual division of matter, or we mean that further actual division would affect the very nature of the material handled and change it into another specific kind of bodily substance.

When the term *atom* was first applied to the minimum-particle of a chemically simple substance, it was thought that the word was just and properly descriptive; it was really something uncut and uncuttable. But, modern Science has "cut the uncuttable," so to speak, and the atom now has its own place. However, the term has been retained even if its original literal meaning is no longer justified. This comment refers, of course, to the atom as handled in physical Science. In the Philosophy of matter here considered (that is, in atomism) that atom still means an uncut and uncuttable minimum of matter which is, in one way or another, the cause and the explanation of the bodily World.

B. Tenets of Atomism

There are two types of Philosophical atomism, *Mechanistic Atomism* and *Dynamism Atomism*. Both hold that matter is to be explained ultimately in the fact that the bodily substance is made up of minimum-bodies, called atoms, which coalesce to form the World and all the bodily things in the World, lifeless and living. Both hold that the atoms are all of the same specific *kind*; that is, both types of atomism teach the *homogeneity of matter*, which means that there is no *essential* difference between clod and plant, between plant and animal, between brute and man; he World is "all of a piece." But, after agreeing that matter is made of *atoms* which are of the *same specific kind,* the two schools of atomists part company. We shall speak of their tenets in separate paragraphs:

Mechanistic Atomism (also called *Pure Atomism*) hold that the atoms or minimum-amounts of bodily substance differ only in size and in motion; they have no indwelling power, force, or faculty, by which they act; they are guided by no tendency, purpose, or finality, in the unions which, as a fact, they effect; they do not lose their identity or undergo substantial change when they coalesce to form natural bodies, for in all their movements their own being is invariable and constant. The movements of atoms is an external or extrinsic movement, a thing *undergone,* thing *communicated* to the atoms from something outside themselves. Since, the atoms have no force or power of their own, they cannot exercise any positive activity, and therefore all their movement is a matter of applied outside force. Hence, pure atomism postulates *a mover* or *a motor-force* outside the atoms; and ultimately this must be the First Mover of God. Pure atomism is, therefore, necessarily *theistic; it presupposes God. Atheists,* indeed, like the Roman poet-Philosopher Lucretius, have held by the theory of atomism, but they do so only by ignoring the *cause* of motion and focusing upon the *fact* of motion as an explanation of the Universe. But, acting thus, they deify matter itself (at least equivalently), and become *pantheistis.* Some Christians, like Descartes and Secchi, have professed pure atomism as the Philosophy of the bodily World, but these do not attempt to explain man's spiritual activities (intellection and volition) in terms of atoms and local motion; indeed, Secchi limits his atomism to the inorganic or non-living World.

Notable names associated with the history of pure or mechanistic atomism are, among the ancients, Heraclitus and Anaxagoras of the 6 century B.C.; Democritus of the 5 century B.C.; Epicurus of the late 4 and early 3 century B.C.; Lucretius of the first century B.C. In Christian times, Gassendi (1592-1656) and Descartes (1597-1650) were proponents of atomism.

Dynamism Atomism teaches that the atoms or minimum-particles of bodily substance are endowed with an indwelling force or power of motion. Some atomists of this type say that the motion of atoms is due to a twofold power of attraction and repulsion; others find a sufficient explanation of motion in the repulsive power alone. Some say that the atoms come into immediate contact to form bodies; others declare that the atoms are always separated, even in the most solid of bodies, by vacuum-intervals or vacuoles, -and thus these latter atomists teach the actuality of *action in distance* which we have already noticed as a physical, if not an absolute, impossibility. Dynamistic atomism, like pure atomism, holds that atoms are changeless and non-corruptible; they keep their being, constant and invariable, in all combinations.

Many atomists of the dynamistic school admit that force-endowed atoms will not explain the phenomena or life, at least of human life. These affirm the existence of an entelechy or soul which unites with certain atom-formed bodies to communicate activities of a superior nature. But, apart from a few Christians, these Philosophers seem to make the life-principle an adjunct joined *accidentally* to the living body. We, on the contrary, hold that the life-principle, in every living body (plant, brute, man), is a *substantial form* which joins matter to constitute the living body as a single if compound substance.

C. Estimate of Atomism

To say that natural bodies are made up of smaller bodies may be perfectly true, and may have a Scientific value. But, such a statement does not even start the Philosopher upon his quest. The Philosopher wants to know what a body is, and the small body sets him the same problem as the larger body of which it is a part. Hence, no theory of atoms can be a Philosophy. It still leaves unanswered the penetrating Philosophical question, *what makes a body a body?* Thus, without going further, we may reject at once both types of atomism described above, and presented as an ultimate explanation of the Universe.

In special, we may point out the following facts which render atomism inadmissible as a Philosophy of the bodily World:

1. If all atoms are of the same nature (as atomists declare) it is impossible to explain a various Universe. The World presents to our knowledge a great number of bodies that differ *essentially*, and these manifest properties and activities that are *different* and often *opposite*. Yet atoms which are all of one essential kind, and which retain their nature unimpaired in every collection, would constitute a World in which *essential difference* would be utterly impossible. Hence, we say that atomism is to be rejected because it fails to account for the existence of essentially different bodies, and of bodies with essentially different properties.

2. Pure atomism holds that motion, externally applied, gathers atoms into collections that make up all the various bodies of the World. There is, however, much to contradict this simple statement. Take the one instance of *chemical affinity,* which every

Scientist, even the tyro, recognizes as a palpable fact. By force of this affinity certain bodies are drawn into combination with certain other bodies; and this in a constant manner, and according to fixed and definite proportions of the bodies in question. But, if pure atomism were true, anybody would combine with any other, and we could not observe any special affinities or note their precise requirements. Further, pure atomism contradicts itself in saying that bodies have no forces or powers of their own, for it teaches that atoms cannot be divided, that they are indestructible. Now, this is only saying that atoms resist division, and such resistance is a force or power. It cannot be retorted that this is no special power, but only a phase of being, since being stands opposed to non-being by that fact of actuality or existence. No, for there is here no question of being, but only of the quantity of atoms. Quantity does not perish when it is divided; the total quantity is the same in the undivided and in the sum of its divided parts. To say that atoms resist division of their quantity is to say much more than that they hold on to their being. It is to assert a force or power in atoms, which, by the terms of pure atomism, can have no force or power. In a word, it is a neat self-contradiction. Now, a self-contradictory system cannot be accepted as a sound Philosophy.

3. Dynamistic atomism, admitting some indwelling force or power in atoms, keeps this a definitely mechanical power, that is, the power of local movement. But, there are many things in the World (apart from the activities of living things) which mere local movement is powerless to explain. Light, electricity, radioactivity, affinities, are things which involve mechanical action or local movement, but which have, over above, characteristics which are altogether unexplained when local motion has had its full hearing.

Summary of the Article

In this Article we have defined *atomism,* and have made clear distinction between the Scientific theory of atoms, or *the atomic theory,* and atomism or *the atomistic Philosophy.* We have distinguished two types of atomism, *pure* or *mechanistic* atomism and *dynamistic* atomism. We have found both types in admissible because they leave the Philosophical problem of the bodily World not only unsolved but unattacked. Moreover, we have found in both types of atomism inadequacies of explanation and self-contradiction of doctrine.

5.2.3 Dynamism

A. Meaning of Dynamism

The term *dynamism* is taken from the Greek word *dynamis* which means "force" or "power." We have several words in English which derive from this source; for instance, dynamic, dynamo, and dynasty. Thus, *dynamism,* by reason of its etymology, suggests some theory of power or force as the explanation of the material World.

B. Tenets of Dynamism

Dynamism is not a clear-cut system, but has various forms, and perhaps its most notable effects are found in the influence it brings to bear on Scientific and Philosophical systems which are not purely dynamistic. However, it is possible to select out a few points of doctrine which all dynamists (pure or mixed) defend. Thus, dynamism holds: (a) that bodies are made up of non-extended, non-quantified elements; (b) that these elements are *points of force or power*; (c) that these points attract one another up to a certain stage or distance, and then hold one another off; thus they act upon one another across a vacuum or void (*action in distance*); (d) that the points of power are changeless, undergoing no transformation of nature when they combine to form bodies.

Notable names associated with the history of dynamism are, among the ancients, the Pythagoreans of the 6 century B.C.; Zeno of Elea of the 5 century B.C.; and, in a very limited way, the great Plato of the 5 and 4 centuries B.C. In modern times, Giordano Bruno (1514-1600), Wilhelm Gottfried Leibnitz (1646-1716), Christian Wolff (1679-1754), Giuseppe Boscovich (1711-1787), Immanuel Kant (1724-1804), Eduard von Hartmann (1842-1906) are listed as dynamists in their interpretation of the nature of bodies.

C. Estimate of Dynamism

Dynamism contradicts the definition of *substance* and turns the World into a non-substantial reality. For it defines bodies in terms of their *accidents*, and thus makes the Universe a great mass of accidents without anything substantial in which to inhere. A power of force is in itself *a quality*, and leads on to function or *action;* and Philosophy lists both *qualities* and *actions* as accidents, that is, as realities which are not regularly suited for existence *themselves* (that is, *alone*), but for existence as the marks, limitations, characterizations, or modifications of something else.

Again, dynamists either admit the real extension of the Universe, and of bodies in the World, or they call the extension merely apparent. (a) If they admit real extension, they are wholly illogical, for extension cannot be the product of inextended elements: zero added to zero will still be zero. Nor can they affirm that the inextended points of power (which are the constituents of all bodies) are actually held at a distance from one another and thus effect a truly extended body; for inextended points *with nothing whatever between and among them* still results in an inextended totality. (b) If the dynamists call the World a mere apparent World, they have still to explain the apparition, and this they cannot do in terms of their own Philosophy. They say, some of them, that we get the impression of continuity in bodies form the fact that the point-forces are in perpetual motion, just as we get the impression of a continuous ring of fire from a torch that is whirled rapidly in a circle. The illustration is objectionable on two counts: First, the flame of the torch is actually extended; there is no illusion about that to start with; whereas, according to dynamism, the whirling point-forces are inextended and thus invisible in themselves, and they are certainly not rendered visible by being moved rapidly about. Secondly, an illusion is due to a misapplication of actual experience of what actual continuity or solidity is; but dynamism renders this prerequisite experience impossible, and hence destroys the possibility of illusion.

Dynamism openly professes the activity of point-forces on one another *across a void*. This *action in distance* means activity without a channel to convey the activity. We have already considered this action-theory, and have found it inadmissible.

Finally, dynamism cannot explain the unity of organic parts in a living body; it cannot explain the unity of constituting parts in molecule or atom in lifeless matter. It cannot explain unity at all. For points of force, inextended and always invariable in nature, cannot really enter upon unity without compenetration. To avoid this, *action in distance* has to be admitted, and *action in distance* (could it exist) is certainly fatal to organic or inorganic unity.

The extreme type of the modern "electrical theory of matter" is neither more nor less than dynamism. Most modern physicists accept the theory of electrically-charged particles of matter, and this is quite intelligible and does not come into conflict with reason.

But, the extremist do not say that the particles of matter (protons and electrons) are electrically charged; they say that these particles are no true particles of matter at all but only points of electric power. This, as we have said, is dynamism pure and simple, and is to be rejected for the reasons alleged above.

Summary of the Article

In this Article we have defined *dynamism* literally or *nominally*, and we have also given its *real* definition which attempts to explain the World of bodies in terms of non-extended, non-quantified, points of force or power acting and reacting among themselves across a void. We have found this Philosophy deficient and unacceptable for many reasons: it conflicts with findings of sense and or reason; it denies, at least equivalently, the substantial character of bodies and of the World; it involves in itself the self-contradictions of "extension born of inextension" and of "phenomena without any stage of which to appear;" it teaches the impossible doctrine of *action in distance*; it fails utterly to explain continuity or unity in the bodily being and function. We have noticed that the extreme form of the modern "electrical theory of matter" is a dynamistic system, and is, for this reason, inadmissible.

5.2.4 Hylomorphism

A. Meaning of Hylomorphism

The term *hylomorphism* is a combination of two Greek nouns, *hyle* "matter," and *morphe* "form." It is, therefore, a "matter and form" theory. It is the Philosophy which seeks to explain the essential constitution of a natural body in terms of a twofold principle, one material and indeterminate, the other formal and determining.

It is supremely important that we understand the name *hylomorphism*, and the doctrine which it indicates, with full thoroughness. We must carefully avoid taking terms *matter* and *form* in a loose, casual, or colloquial sense. These terms are highly technical, and, in their present use, they must be understood in strictest Philosophical meaning. For this reason, it may be allowed us to approach the study of hylomorphism by making a journey of investigation through the wide and intricate domains of those much used and much abused words, *matter* and *form*. Perhaps no other words in the English language are more commonly used, more various in meaning, more loosely understood.

1. *Matter* is a word capable of the widest variety of meanings. Let us look at just a few of these: (a) *Matter* is often used as synonym for *body*; thus we speak of ponderable and imponderable matter, of solid and liquid matter. (b) The word *matter* sometimes means any object of thought, discussion, study, or experience. Thus, a person says, "I have no opinion on the matter;" "We shall take up the matter with the authorities;" "This is a matter of importance;" "Spiritual experience is not a matter for laboratory experiment." (c) Sometimes *matter* indicates *importance,* as in the sentence, "It matters very greatly what a man believes;""It is no mater whether you be rich or poor;" "The point you raise is not material to the discussion." (d) Often the term *matter* which is literally the opposite of things *spiritual,* and in contrast with *form,* is used in close combination with these terms, as in the expressions, "We are

interested in spiritual matters;" "This is a matter of the spirit, not the body;" "This is a matter of form;" "These formal matters do not concern me." Of course, this employment of the term *matter* is only another instance of its use in the sense explained above under *b*, but the manner in which careless colloquial usage thus tangles and confuses the term with its opposites seems to call for special notice. (e) Often *matter* is used to indicate *meaning* or *information* or *data* as contrasted with the manner or style of expression. Thus, one may say of a treatise, "Many fine words, but little matter;" "Your matter is satisfactory, but your style is very crude;" "The matter is all here, but where is the logic that should mark its presentation?"

Now, in our present study *matter* (and its adjective *material*) can have but one fundamental meaning, although that meaning has a *primary* and a *secondary* implication. Matter, in primary sense, is the basic stuff out of which a bodily being is made. Matter, in a secondary sense, is an actual existing body. Thus, we have *primary matter* and *secondary matter,* or, in the ancient Latin terminology, *material prima* and *materia secunda. Materia prima* or *primary matter* is usually (and less elegantly) called *prime matter.* In the system of hylomorphism, the matter considered is *prime* matter.

Prime matter is the substrate common to all bodily being. A man, a dog, a tree, a molecule of coal, an atom of hydrogen, are all *bodily.* Each of these realities is a body. Each is an *actual existing* body. That is, each is *material secunda* or secondary matter. But, all the bodies mentioned are *bodies.* They have something *in common,* although, as finished realities, they have essential differences. In other words, as *secondary matter* (that is, individual bodies) they are distinct and different; in point, however, *prime* matter they are not distinct at all—one is *body* as truly and completely as any of the others or as all of the others together. It is only because some *determining* element (different in each case) *has combined with prime matter in a substantial way* that we have the different bodily substances, viz., the substances of man, of dog, of tree, of coal, of hydrogen. The *prime matter* which is the determinateness, nothing to make it *actual,* nothing to make it this or that *kind of body*, but waits, so to speak, for the coming of the substantial determinant which will give it actuality as *materia secunda*, a finished body of definite type actually existing. Prime matter is thus *the subject* of the determining element which gives it existence as a substance. Thus, we may define prime matter as follows: "A passive and indeterminate substantial principle which is the subject of all substantial determinations and substantial changes, and which remains changeless *in itself* under such changes." The molecule of coal (a secondary substance, that is, an existing body) is made up of prime matter and the determining element or principle which makes it *coal* and no other substance. Now, burn up the coal, and the secondary substance is changed; it is reduce to ash and smoke. But, the prime matter *in itself* is not changed at all. It *supports* the change, so to speak; it is the same amount of prime matter which *was* determined or set in the substantial character of coal; and now it *is* set or determined as other substances; but *it is the same prime matter* throughout.

2. *Form* is a term which, like *matter,* has a great variety of meanings, of meanings that are different and sometimes even opposite. Hence, we must carefully determine the sense in which the word is to be used in our present study. To illustrate the various senses in which the term *form* may be employed, consider these few instances of its use: (a) *Form* is frequently used as a synonym for outline or shape, and we speak of the ovular form of a race-course, or of the symmetrical form of a drawing. (b) Sometimes *form* means a plan or program, a record, or a questionnaire. Thus, a performer is said to go according to form, a race-horse is judged by the form-sheet, an applicant for a position is requested to fill up a form. (c) The word *form* is often used for *good condition,* and a golfer is said to be "in form" or "at the top of his form." (d) Frequently the term *form* suggests something unimportant, or something easily done, a requisite but facile unwinding of "red tape." Thus, certain procedures are called "questions of form" or (confusion worse confounded) "mere matters of form." (e) The adjective of *form* that is, *formal,* is often employed to indicate a certain dignity, or a certain decorum involving precise details of

dress or conduct. Thus, we speak of "formal dress," of "a formal occasion," of "a formal introduction."

To Philosophers, *form* is a word of tremendous meaning; far from meaning *unimportant* (as in the phrase, "a mere question of form") it means the exact opposite. It means something thunderlingly important. It means that which *determines* a thing, sets it in its being, in its essence, in its accidents, in its actuality. Any *determining* element in a reality is a *form*. And (as in the present study) when we speak of bodily substances, the term *form* means *substantial form*, that which makes a bodily substances an existing reality (that is, an *actuality*) of the precise essence and nature that we find it. A man, a dog, a tree, a molecule of coal, an atom of hydrogen are all *material*; they are all *bodily*, and this fact is due, fundamentally, to their common element or *prime matter*. But, these bodily things *exist,* they are *actual,* they have each their own essential or specific *kind* of being; each is essentially and substantially distinct and different from all the others. Now, it is the *substantial form* of man which makes the one bodily being a human being; it is the substantial form of animal which makes this other body an animal; it is the substantial form of plant which makes the third body a plant; it is the substantial form of coal which makes this molecule a molecule of coal and not of any longer substance; it is the substantial form of hydrogen which makes this atom an atom of hydrogen and not, for instance, an atom of calcium. That, which sets and determines a substance of this precise kind or essential nature, is its *substantial form*. Of course, man, dog, tree, coal, hydrogen, have *accidental* forms too. The human being will be of a certain age, sex, size, nationality, condition of health, temperature, location, and so on; at any given moment, he is marked and determined by many points of fact or actuality. But, these many and variable forms do not constitute his substance as *this kind of actual body.* They are *accidental* forms, not *substantial* forms. Similarly, the tree will be of a certain size, age, botanical class, location; the molecule of coal will be in a certain place, at a certain time, it will have its certain temperature at any given moment; so too with the atom of hydrogen. But, these determinants (that is, forms) do not make the tree, or the coal, or the hydrogen, the *substance* that each is; they are *accidental* forms, not *substantial* forms. It is the commoner doctrine of scholastic Philosophers that each individual body has only one substantial form, and a plurality of accidental forms. We must be careful to understand the meaning of the phrase "each individual body." For what we mean by the phrase is *a continuous body*. Now, any living body is continuous throughout its living structure; and a lifeless body is strictly continuous at least in its minimum-particles.

We may define *Substantial Form* (with which alone we are concerned in our present study of forms) as "An active and determining substantial principle which is the term (that is the goal, the end, the completed being) of all substantial changes in bodies, and which constitutes each individual continuum in its essential actuality."

Hylomorphism is the doctrine of Aristotle (4 century B.C.), of St. Thomas Aquinas (1225- 1274), and of Scholastic Philosophers generally.

B. Tenets of Hylomorphism

Hylomorphism is the Philosophical doctrine which explains the essential constitution of bodies in terms of a twofold substantial principle, the one principle passive and indeterminate (*prime matter*), and the other principle active and determining (*substantial form*).

Hylomorphism teaches that *prime matter* has, in itself, no determinateness of any kind. It cannot exist *alone*, for existence is a determinate state of being, and hence *a form*, whereas prime matter is, in itself, wholly without form, and is contrasted with form. Prime matter is, therefore, *pure potentiality*, that is, it is an unmixed readiness or capacity for being actualized by on-coming *form* which fuses with it to bring to existence an actual body of a definite essential kind. But, prime matter is not an abstraction of the mind; it belongs to the order of substance, indeed the most imperfect substance. For an imperfect substance is one that regularly requires substantial union with some other substance to give it existence in a specific kind of actuality. We may find a homely, and somewhat unworthy, illustration of prime matter in the picture of a citizen who, by reason of sickness or other cause, cannot stand upright; but when supported by a kindly companion, he is quite able to assume an erect posture. The illustration is indeed only a weak analogy drawn from accidentals, but it may be profitably suggestive; it may help in the understanding of the statement that prime matter is not mere nothingness, nor mere abstract possibility, but is a most imperfect substantial reality which requires form to bring it to actuality, that is, to existence in a definite kind of bodily being. Prime matter is, in bodies, the principle of their passivity (that is, their capacity for receiving accidental forms, and also for receiving new substantial form and induces substantial transformation, as illustrated, for instance, in the burning of coal). Prime matter is thus the principle of what of the inertness or inertia of bodies, and of what Philosopher of an older day called their "indifference" to the forms that might possibly actuate bodies, changing them accidentally or transforming them substantially. Further, prime matter is the principle of the quantity or extension of bodies. For while every substantial form requires a definite minimum of matter for its subject (that is, for constituting a body), and while this minimum quantity of matter will be various kinds of bodies, it remains the fact that quantity *as such* affects the matter rather than the form; this may be illustrated in the fact that a small baby which presently becomes a large man or woman is not changed substantially by the change in quantity, but retains the identical substantial form throughout growth. Rightly, then, do we assert that prime matter of a body is *the proper subject of quantity* in the body, and that quantity is the *proper accident* of the matter rather that an accident of the form. Of course, since prime matter cannot exist alone, but only in an *in-formed* condition, it is true that it has no quantity on its own account; but the point we make is that *in existing bodies* (or, if the phrase be preferred, in *in-formed matter*) quantity is attributable to the matter and not to the form as such, even though the form brings to the matter its *actual* capacity for quantification, and enables that capacity to be realized in fact.

Hylomorphism teaches that *the substantial form,* in each individual (that is, continuous) existing body its *essential or specific kind.* It is the substantial form which makes this body a human being; it is the substantial form which makes that body a plant; it is the substantial form which makes that other body a molecule of coal and not some other substance. Further, it is *Substantial Form* of a body which determines its *nature* or its operating capacity and its active character. For, while it is the compound of matter and form, the *substantial composite* which we call *a body* or *material secunda,* which exercises the operations or activities proper to such a being, it is the substantial form which is the root-principle of these activities. It is the whole man that walks and digests; it is the complete tree that grows. But, the man does not walk and digest because he is material, but because he is *an actual bodily being of this essential kind* and it is the substantial form of man which makes him so. The tree does not grow because it is material; indeed, many material things (that is, bodies) do not grow; the tree grows because it is constituted *as this kind of bodily substance,* and it is the substantial form of tree which makes it so. Again, it is the substantial form which gives direction, tendency, finality in bodily being and activity, but it is manifest here that, granted such finality exists, it is the form and not the matter of bodies which is its root-principle. Form is the root-principle of the activities themselves, and, in consequence, it is the root-principle of all involved in the activities, such as direction and tendency. Matter in itself is indeterminate and "indifferent," and hence has not, *of itself,* any direct influence upon activities or their drive or direction.

About prime matter and substantial form, the following points are to be carefully noted:

1. Prime matter has not in itself any determinateness, and therefore we cannot speak of it as of *kinds*, or even say, with precision, that it is *of one kind.* Still, the limitations of language impose upon us the necessity of saying that prime matter is *uniformly the same* in its nature throughout the various Universe.

In other words, prime matter, considered alone (although it must be remembered that it cannot *exist* alone) is a single sort of reality.

2. Prime matter is *dependent* on substantial form for existence and for specific determination.

In other words, prime matter cannot exist unless substantial form combine substantially with it to give it actuality in this or that essential kind of reality in this or that definite individual. For this reason the substantial form is called *the principle of specification.* It is that which *specifies* a body; that is, it is the substantial reality which determines the *species* or *essential kind* of the body. Now, bodies cannot exist *in universal*; there is no such thing in nature as an existing *body-in-general*; for bodies to have existence *individuality* is required; bodies can exist only as these and those concrete individual actualities. Of course, the mind understands what *body* means (*a* body, *any* body, *every* possible body) and can define *body* with a single definition which expresses the essence of all individual bodies, actual and possible. For the mind understands *in universal*. But, as we have said, concrete existence cannot be *in universal*, but must be *in individual*. Therefore, when we say that the substantial form constitutes a body in its specific or essential kind, we say at the same time that the substantial form constitutes a body of that kind *as an existing individual body.* Still, the fact that this individual body (say, this tree) is *this* body and not some other individual body *of this kind*, is due to the fact that the substantial form is united substantially *with precisely this matter* to which it gives *actual* quantity, and not with some other "portion" of matter to which it would give actual quantity. In other words, if the substantial form of this tree has actualized prime matter in joining substantially with it to constitute *this* tree, the same substantial form, in joining with some other "portion" of prime matter, would have constituted *another* individual tree of this kind, but not precisely *this* tree. Therefore, although all the actuality of the tree is referable to the substantial form, and even the actual individuality of the tree is so referable, the passive matter has played a part inasmuch as it was precisely *this* matter which the form actualized. And, being actualized, the prime matter took on quantity, and exists as *this precise quantified matter* (not necessarily this precise quantity or amount of matter – for the tree grows and does not lose individuality by added size, quantity, or amount). Now, it is as *this precise quantified matter* that the tree is *this individual tree*. For this reason we say that *quantified matter* is *the principle of individuation*. The old Latin phrase is *material signata quantitate* or simply *material signata*; that is, "matter marked by quantity," or "quantified matter," is the principle of individuation in a body.

3. Substantial form depends, in its own way, upon prime matter. If the substantial form be incapable of existence *alone*, it requires union with matter to give it existence. Of course, what *exists* is then "in-formed matter," that is, the composite called *a body* but the matter exists in the body, and the form exists in the body, and neither exists (or, in the present case, neither *can* exist) alone. A substantial form which thus depends upon union with prime matter for its existence is called *a material form*, not because it has matter in its own make-up, for it has not, but because of its *dependence* upon matter for existence in an existing body. All substantial forms in the bodily World, with the single exception of the human substantial form, are *material* forms. For sake of illustrating the interdependence of prime matter and material form, consider again the ignraoble picture of the citizen mysteriously incapable of standing alone. Now, suppose that his charitable friend is in the same regrettable condition. Neither can stand alone. But, shoulder to shoulder, they *both* can manage it, and can make their way along the street. An interesting case of "united we stand," similarly, prime matter and substantial form are each powerless to "stand alone;" neither is a complete substance; neither is capable of independent or individual existence. But, "together they stand;" together they constitute an actual and complete substantial composite, that is, an actual body. The human substantial form is, as Philosophical psychology proves, the spiritual soul. As a substance it is *complete*; as a man it is *incomplete,* for the soul is not the whole human being, but only the noblest *part* of a human being. The soul is not *generated*, that is,

substantially produced by a transformation of existing substances; it is, in each instance, directly created by God. This point is amply proved in psychology; here we cannot enter upon a proof. And, the moment of the soul's creation is the identical moment of its substantial joining with the matter which it makes a human body; technically we say, "the moment of the soul's *creation* is the moment of its *infusion*." Therefore, the soul does not pre-exist to its body. But, the soul endures after leaving its body. Since, the soul is spiritual, it is naturally deathless or immortal. It does not depend upon matter for existence since it is not a *material* form, but a *non-material* or *spiritual* form. Hence, the human soul (that is, the human substantial form) does not depend upon matter for its own existence as a soul or for its own proper spiritual operations, but only for existence and function as the actuating form of an existing human being; its dependence on matter is thus extrinsic, not intrinsic. It is manifest from the foregoing considerations that, whereas prime matter is not diversified as of different kinds, substantial forms are diversified. There are material substantial forms and non-material substantial forms. In this World, the only non-material substantial forms are human souls. In the celestial World the angelic beings are *pure forms*; they are pure spirits, with nothing material about them in structure or dependency. And, since matter is the principle of individuation, and angelic beings lack all matter, angels are not, strictly speaking, individuated; they are not *individuals*, but each angel is a *species*, that is, a distinct essential kind of spiritual substance. The angels are *complete* substances, both as form and as essences. Human souls which have been severed by death form their respective bodies are individuated by the *real relation* which each bears to the quantified matter which it "in-formed" in earthly life. Material forms are diversified as sentient forms, vegetal forms, and mineral forms. The term *mineral* is applied to the substantial form of any non-living bodily substance.

4. In any actual body, the substantial form is *one* in itself or actually. Some of the minor substantial forms (sentient, vegetal, mineral) are *potentially* multiple. That is, the individual body,

which is a single continuous quantity, is actuated by only one substantial form, but *it may be divided* into a plurality of individual bodies of the same species, and each of the bodies so resulting has then its own substantial form. Thus, a rose-bush may be cut and divided into one substantial form *actually*; but, in the plant in question, the bodily substance is capable of division in such wise that life may be preserved in each of the parts; therefore, the plant has a potentiality or capacity for such division, and its substantial form is said to have a parallel potentiality or capacity by reason of its dependence upon the matter of the plant. Thus, we say that the rose-bush is actually one, potentially many; similarly we say that *the substantial form of the rose-bush* is actually one, potentially many. Substantial forms of the higher type (human souls, and the substantial forms of most animals) are never multiple, either actually or potentially; each of such forms is necessarily *one* substantial form, having no capacity for division according to division of the body-structure (or matter) on which it, intrinsically or extrinsically, depends.

5. In every living body, the life-principle (*soul, entelechy, bathmic force, plasmic energy*) is the substantial form. When this form is driven out by the death of the living body, the remaining structure is substantially different from the living body. The corpse of a man is not a man; it is a package of various inorganic (non-living) substances, and naturally tends to break up into these, and so the body decomposes. Hence, a corpse is not a single substance but a mixture of many substances, whereas the living man, actualized by the spiritual substantial form called the soul, is a single, if compound, human substance.

6. Substantial change involves the incoming of a new substantial form and the simultaneous outgoing of the old substantial form, the prime matter remaining. Substances manifest their character by their properties, and when these are wholly changed we know that the substance has changed. When, for example a living body (whose properties are vital functions, heterogeneity of organically united and interdependent parts) is changed to a dead body (whose properties are non-vital activities,

unrelated groupings of homogenous parts, equilibrium and rest) we know that substantial change has occurred: the living body has changed into a plurality of lifeless bodies. Again, when hydrogen and oxygen are brought together in due proportions under a proper agency, the gases are changed into water. The properties of water are not the same as those of the gases, and therefore we know that the change is a change of substance; the two substances (hydrogen and oxygen) have become a single compound substance called water. Substantial change is *instantaneous*. Inasmuch as it is the production of a new substance (or substances) it is *generation*; the same change, inasmuch as it is the reduction or removal of the old substance (or substances) is *corruption*. The corruption of one substance *is* the generation of another, and vice versa.

7. When a compound substance (such as water) is generated by fusion or substantial union of other substances, we have what is called *a compound*. A compound is to be carefully distinguished form *an accidental mixture*, which is the commingling of various substances, each of which retains its identity; such for instance is the mixture of sand and slat. *A compound* is a substantial unity. The substantial forms or the elements which are joined together in compound are said to endure in the compound *in a virtual manner*, but they do not endure there *actually*. The substantial form of water is a true substantial form, distinct and different form the form of hydrogen and the form of oxygen. But, since water really owes its being and activities to the substantial union of these gases; and since their forms can be readily generated again from the water, it seems that their forces are somehow latently present (that is, *potentially* present) but not *actually* present in the water itself. And this potential presence is not a purely passive thing, for the water is capable of being reduced to the gases and, indeed, may be said to have a kind of tendency to such reduction; the potential presence of the elements is a kind of *active* potentiality. We call this sort of potentiality *virtual*. Thus, we say that the elements in a compound are present in the compound, not *actually* (for actually the compound is a true substance distinct from the elements) but *virtually*. More precisely, we say that *the substantial forms*

of the elements are virtually present in the substantial chemical compound.

8. When a new substance is *generated*, a new substantial form or forms *are educed form the potentiality of matter*, and simultaneously another form or other forms *are reduced to the potentiality of matter*. No question here of non-material forms, for such forms are never generated or corrupted. But, what is meant by generation as an *educing* from, and by corruption as a *reducing* to, the potentiality, a capacity for the receiving of substantial forms. Prime matter is altogether passive, wholly inert, entirely "indifferent," as to which form, in any instance, is to be joined with it to constitute a complete body. Yet, under certain conditions, wrought by existing substances (and fundamentally by existing substantial forms) prime matter is rendered *proximately apt* for the receiving of a certain form, and under the action of existing forms, it actually receives such form. Thus, the new substantial form is said to be *educed* form the potentially of matter. The new substantial form is, so to speak, *drawn out* from prime matter by the activity of existing forms. Thus, under the activities (mechanical, physical, chemical) of hydrogen and oxygen, prime matter (which is actually in-formed by the substantial forms of these gases) is rendered ready for the receiving of the new form of water, and, under the same agencies, actually receives it. At the same instant, the forms of hydrogen and oxygen are *reduced* to the potentiality of matter, inasmuch as these forms are, so to speak, thrown back into the capacity of matter to have such forms. Yet, since our example concerns a compound which is resolvable again into its elements, the reduction of the forms of the gases to the potentiality of matter is not a complete reduction to pure passivity, but to a state of virtual potentiality. When an animal dies, to take a further example, the life-principle (which is the substantial form of the animal) is reduced to the potentiality of matter in the sense that mater which was once a sentient organism, and now is so no longer, *can* have the substantial form of such a substance, as is proved by the fact that it *did* have such a form. But, the life-principle does not endure virtually in the corpse of the

animal nor in the various substances that are gathered together in the "package" we call the dead body; no, the educing of a sentient life-principle from matter will require the conjoining of new elements (male and female) in a vital process which has nothing to do with this dead body. The life-principle of the animal is wholly removed. Yet it is not accurate to say that it is annihilated, for it is not; the accurate phrase is "reduced to the potentiality of matter." In the potentiality of matter, of course, there is no *actuality* of the reduced form; potentiality and actuality stand opposed; therefore, the life-principle of an animal which is so reduced, does not *exist* (for existence is a synonym for actuality), but is purely *potential.*

9. Matter and form (that is, prime matter and substantial form) are to be conceived of as two co-principles, imperfectly substantial, which are naturally ordinate for substantial union together to constitute a complete bodily substance. Matter and form are not to be thought of as two *existing* things, each ready for union (as, for instance, hydrogen and oxygen are) with the other. For forms do not pre-exist to the matter which they in-form, nor has prime matter any existence of its own; existence comes with the actual union of the matter and form, and is actively referable to the form.

10. Since, bodies come from other bodies by generation and corruption, it is manifest that to have new bodily substance, we must have old bodily substance; there must be a bodily source for bodily being. But, it is equally manifest that the process of generation cannot proceed in an infinite series of bodies from other bodies, and these from other bodies, and there from still other bodies, and so on forever. For an actual infinity in anything limited (like a series or chain of creatures) is a contradiction in thought and in terms. *Processus in infinitum non datur,* says the Philosopher St. Thomas Aquinas; that is, "There cannot be a chain–of things or events—that is actually infinite." Hence, the *first* bodily beings cannot have come into existence by way of generation, that is to say, by way in which infinite actuality can come into *first* existence except by an *absolute* production, under the action of Boundless Power, no materials or prerequisites

or material sources being required. Such a production is called *creation*. Thus, we see the inevitable truth of the terse statement of the Scholastic Philosopher, "Bodily substance has its *first* origin in *creation*; thereafter, bodies come from bides by way of substantial change."

C. Estimate of Hylomorphism

Hylomorphism appears to be the only Philosophy of bodies that succeeds in presenting a satisfactory account of bodily substance *in all respect*. That there are points of obscurity in its application to certain phenomena is readily admitted; but that there are points of contradiction in the system itself, or in its certain application to thoroughly known data, or in its tentative explanation of data which are still obscure, is flatly denied. For more than two thousand years, this system (acclaimed and despised by turns) has remained the only consistent system of all the theories that attempt to account fundamentally or Philosophically for the bodily Universe. On its record alone, its endurance, its consistency, it merits the deepest respect of Scientific and Philosophical minds. Indeed, it can lay claim to actual *proof*, a negative proof, of course, in the fact that it alone has maintained itself in integrity, while all other systems (atomism, dynamism, and monism) have twisted and changed, and cast off elements and taken them on, and contracted here and expanded there to meet momentary difficulties, and have failed in the end. Argue the point very mildly thus: if all systems of the Philosophy of bodies may be reduced to four, monism, atomism, dynamism, hylomorphism, and it the first three of these four are found to be patently inadequate and even self-contradictory, while the fourth appears to meet all requirements, and is not, at any point, in conflict with itself or with data it attempts to explain, then, manifestly, the fourth system is the true one.

Summary of the Article

In this Article we have defined *hylomorphism* as the *matter-and-form* Philosophy of bodies. We have indicated the precise meaning of the terms *prime matter* and *substantial form*. We have set forth the tenets of hylomorphism, incidentally defining important related matters such as the *principle of individuation*, the *principle of specification*, the meaning of *complete* and *incomplete* substances, the distinction between *material* and *non-material* substantial forms, the *unity* of substantial forms and the *potential multiciplicity* of inferior substantial forms, the nature of *substantial change,* the manner in which the *forms of elements* endure in a compound, the mode of *bodily substance*. We have set forth the case for hylomorphism as the one true Philosophy of bodies, offering first a *negative* proof, and then a twofold *positive* proof, the latter drawn from the respective facts of *substantial change* and the *extension and activity* of bodies. Incidentally, we have indicated the startling misstatements about *hylomorphism* made by eminent modern Philosophers, and we have taken warning, lest prevalent ignorance about this most valuable system, and falsifications of its doctrines which are currently broadcast, should cause us to underestimate its value or importance.

Chapter 6

Finiteness of the Cosmos Reflections on Cosmology

There was a time not so many years ago when many of the popular prophets would have said "Yes" to this question. Scientists who would have called themselves atheists or agnostics preached the gospel of what they called "Scientific humanism." By applying the principles of Science some of them even thought they could develop ethical systems to guide human conduct. Now, as will become clear, I think they were mistaken. But, in our day, I believe the pendulum has swung to the other extreme, and with a violence which I fear is equally misguided.

6.1 Can Science Provide an Answer to the Quest for Meaning?

Criticisms of the Scientific Approach

But, first let us see what is true in the highly emotive case argued by the anti-scientist. I have a number of headings here, and I think that what we should perhaps do is pick up under each heading a feature of the Scientific approach, see why it causes offense to these sensitive defenders of the human spirit and then see how we ourselves should react to the threat that they point out.

Science does adopt and insist on strict criteria for what counts as valid Scientific evidence and valid inference. For the Scientist, mere opinion is not enough. He has to go further and show that if what he is claiming were not the case, then some facts of experience would not be as indeed as they are. This emphasis on fact, then, is very down to earth and understandably threatening to someone whose life revolves around the World of the imagination. And it is possible to teach Science in such a way as to devalue the role of the human imagination and to desiccate the aspiring Scientist before he ever gets into the practice of Science. But, we have only to read the writings of the leading Scientists, those who have made great discoveries, to recognize that the practice of Science at its best is a cooperative exercise in which imagination plays just a vital a part as respect for facts.

What the Scientist does is expose his whole being, particularly his imagination, to the challenge of what he has tried in every way to identify as solid facts. He presents himself with these facts, knowing that there will be no routine way of grinding out valid conclusions. His aim, rather, is to have his imagination stimulated so that, with luck, he might hit on a hypothesis worth testing, one that might account for what produces the fact that intrigue him. And any good Science teacher will treasure any gifts that his pupils have for imagination just as much as he will treasure their ability to reason logically. The teaching of Science is above all a human enterprise. It is the passing on, not merely of facts or technique, but of a craft, an attitude, a spirit in which the interactions of the Scientist with his data can spur the imagination on to make a new discoveries about the principles on which the natural World is organized. The hallmark here, I suggest, is obedience.

Now this is a long way from the image of the Scientists as essentially a dominating manipulator of nature. But, what the early founders of modern Science had to discover – and they were stimulated to do this, as you will find if you read Bacon, by their reading of the Bible – is that anyone who wants to have dominion over nature must begin by listening, observing, respecting, and obeying the implications of the facts; by not bringing preconceived ideas, as the medieval predecessors of modern Science did, to the natural World and insisting that nature should dance, as it were, to their tune composed beforehand. Such a person must be ready to have his imagination disciplined by the data.

Rationality vs Rationalism

This brings out a vital distinction which is often neglected in the anti-Scientific propaganda of our day: the distinction between rationality, which is an attempt to be obedient with one's mind to the implications of the data one has, and rational*ism*, which is an attitude that sits in judgment on what ought to be, on the grounds that my predilections make *this* attractive to my reason and *that* not.

Now, I'm not denying that there are stages, perhaps particularly in a subject like theoretical Physics, when purely aesthetic considerations have guided Scientists; they have discovered principles (as they tell you in their autobiographies) simply by playing a hunch that was attractive to them. What I am suggesting, though, is that if a Scientist goes through his daily life, in effect putting nature on the Procrustean bed of his own preferences and ignoring whatever does not fit in with his predilections, and then he is moving in the opposite direction of healthy Science. And this rationalistic attitude, which says, "I can't believe that electrons would be composed of such-and-such," this authoritarian attitude which has occasionally cropped up in the history of Science, is always a barrier.

When we read attacks on Science, then, based on the grounds that it is rationalistic, I think we have to bear this distinction particularly in mind. Science indeed ought to be rational, as any honest man ought, in order to follow out the implications of what he knows or believes to be fact. But, rationality is not the same as rationalism. I'm going to argue, in fact, that in this strictness about what follows from what, and what counts as valid criteria of evidence and so forth, the Scientist is far from being an enemy to meaningfulness generally; in fact, he is expressing the most open attitude possible for the discovery of meaning, an attitude that is essentially, though not exclusively, Christian.

The Spectator Standpoint

Now, secondly, Science is much berated because it adopts and recommends what we might call a spectator's standpoint. The Scientist tries to describe the World as it would be even if he weren't there. At least that is classically the Scientific effort, the emphasis being on withdrawal and detachment from the situation described. And you'll find many people condemning even this approach on the grounds that it's unnatural to partition the World into "that out there" and "me here" when, if we think about it, all of our experience is participation between us and our environment. These critics accuse Science of distorting reality.

But, if we think about it, we realize that the Scientist doesn't adopt the spectator's standpoint because he wants, as it were, a particularly distorted but convenient version of reality to play with. He adopts it for essentially communal purposes. The Scientist sees himself as the "mapmaker" of his community, and he has other mapmakers to cooperate with. It is vital that the mapmakers be able to compare data, and therefore it is vital that they be able to express their picture of the World from a standpoint that is shareable by others – a spectator's standpoint in the sense that one Scientist can bow out and another take his place. So to attack the Scientist on the grounds that he praises detachment, as if this meant the same thing as adopting a lofty and disdainful attitude toward the real World is totally to misrepresent and misunderstood what Science is all about.

Having said that, though, let me again, let me again say that Science badly taught and I wish I could believe that it weren't often badly taught can inculcate this kind of lofty disdain for the muddy untidiness of the real World. The Scientist can become a kind of intellectual snob who won't bother with a problem that can't be parceled up neatly and observed for the sake of prediction. So that it's not altogether wide of the mark to warn Scientists against this as a danger; and indeed it can take the form of a sort of paralysis of commitment, a paralysis of the natural human capacity for committing oneself when the data are rather scanty. Professionally, of course, the Scientist is prohibited from publishing a finding unless the data are strong enough to make the odds, let us say, more than twenty-to-one against the possibility that he's been deceived by chance. That's just a standard routine for keeping a lot of shabby claims from cluttering up the literature that future generations have to read. And in that sense, commitment on the basis of inadequate evidence is professional suicide. A Scientist must try to make statements about the physical World that are reliable enough for his fellow mapmakers to build on.

But, this attitude toward publishable data, this reluctance to commit oneself on the basis of inadequate evidence, need not and must not be allowed to extend to the affairs of everyday life. A Scientist, if he sows seed in his garden, doesn't not refuse to do so unless he is guaranteed that nineteen out of twenty seeds will germinate, or anything of that sort. Scientists are capable of preserving their attitude of caution and their reluctance to commit themselves in their professional lives without losing the common touch. True, if Science is badly taught, then the generation listening to the badly taught Scientists can get the wrong idea. They may think that exercising this caution is a fine way to prevent them from being let down by life, and end up being the sort who are never taken in, never able to commit themselves unless they've got good solid guarantees.

On this point J.H. Oldham (1874-1969), makes a significant remark in a little book called *Life is Commitment,* which is very well worth reading. "To refuse to choose," he says, "is to choose to drift. It is a refusal of responsibility and consequently of life in its full human meaning." And Oldham is right; if this attitude of cautious detachment is allowed to overtake the whole of the Scientist's life, then to some extent he loses his life, loses some of its full human meaning. But, again, this is a totally unnecessary consequence of being a good Scientist.

The "Impersonal"

A third criticism of Science is that it has changed our vague, woolly, and perhaps superstitious attitude toward natural events into a belief that nature is a theatre of purely impersonal forces. Science in its modern form began with a strong emphasis on what has been called the "de-deification" of nature. The Greek tradition saw nature as quasi divine, almost a living being. It was sensible to attribute to nature purposes, desires, tendencies, and so on. The mechanistic Science that became popular at the time of the founding of the Royal Society took the deity out of nature; it insisted, on biblical grounds (e.g., Genesis 1), that nature was a created entity, like man himself, but a non-divine entity, given to us by God for responsible development.

Science had a biblical emphasis, then, the sort of thing which I would suggest Christians have nothing to be ashamed of. But, there have been critics and they have a point – Toynbee (1889-1975) is one example who have taken offense at the removal of the divine element from nature. Toynbee would say that man, having de-deified nature, has felt free to rape the natural World, to dominate it in a selfish manner, behavior that is now causing his own destruction. I myself think that Toynbee exaggerates, and perhaps he meant to provoke us. But, it is a fair point that if we lose the attitude of stewardship which the Bible also inculcates, if we forget that our biblical notion of dominion over nature includes the responsibility of answering to a Creator who has given us that dominion, then very easily our command over a secularized nature can become something self-centered and, in the end, self-destructive.

The other accusation by Keats, that the de-deification of nature destroys wonder which is a little more difficult to defend. It is perfectly true that when we understand the colors of the rainbow as a Scientist would explain them, in terms of the refraction of light, then at a certain level we say, "Now we see how the trick is done," and we may even discover how to do the same sort of trick ourselves with a garden hose and a spotlight. So that kind of wonder, about how it is done, is removed at a certain level. But, any Scientist will tell you that the more he discovers about the field in which he is doing research, the more, when he thinks about it, it strikes him with awe. The sheer marvel of the complexity of the interacting pattern of activity that he studies leads any Scientist worth his salt to an attitude close to worship, whether he's religious or not. You can look at the writings of any of the great Scientists and find this kind of awe expressed. In principle at least, then it is simply false to say that the de-deification of nature automatically brings with it any reduction of the wonder which the Scientist feels on contemplating the natural World.

Chance

Now I want to move to another level of Science, for which, it has to be admitted, some Scientists have done what might be called a bad public relations job. I am talking about the field of chance, which, incidentally, was a field to which Pascal made one of the first theoretical contributions. He was one of those who worked out some of the simpler mathematics of probability, for the benefit, I believe, of some of his friends interested in gambling.

In Science today chance is not only an index of our ignorance. True, the chance of drawing a black ball out of a bag full of black and white balls is something we calculate on the assumption that *we don't know* where the balls are in the bag, rather than an indicating that the actual behavior of the balls in indeterminate. But, chance in Physics has in this century come to bear a deeper significance. It has been found experimentally that when subatomic particles such as electrons interact, or are blown apart in the disintegration of an atom, then the way they rebound is not determined exactly by any of the laws known to Physics. Instead, there is a fuzz of uncertainty about the predicted paths of the particles. By speaking of an element of "chance" in such encounters, then, the physicist means not only that we *don't* know exactly how they will work out, but that we *can't* know. The equations we use in Physics, the theoretical models we use, and the methods we use to get our data are such that when one gets down to the level of microparticles, there isn't in the whole of Physics an equation that fully determines the behavior of any of those particles.

There have been those who have argued from this fact that our World must be looked at as a much less meaningful place than we originally thought it was. One of the most notable of these is the biologist Jacques Monod (1910-1976), who in 1971 published *Chance and Necessity*, a book essentially about the role of chance in biology. In it, he says:

Chance alone is at the source of every innovation, of all creation in the biosphere: pure chance, absolutely free but blind, at the very root of the stupendous edifice of evolution. This central concept of biology is today the sole conceivable hypothesis, the only one compatible with observed and tested facts. The biosphere looks like the product of a unique even those chances of occurring were almost nil. The Universe was not pregnant with life. Our number came up in the Monte Carlo game.

And on these grounds Monod claims that "man at last knows that he is alone in the unfeeling immensity of the Universe out of which he emerged only by chance." He claims further that these discoveries make it impossible to believe in any concept of a Creator.

Now, any anti-Scientist who wants ammunition and who has some sympathy for a religious view of life doesn't need much more than this sort of utterance to justify his vigor. But, I contend that, for all Monod's eminence as a Scientist, he is here perpetrating a Philosophical blunder, confusing two fundamentally different notions of chance. Chance as a Scientific concept is essentially an indicator of our uncertainty about what is likely to follow from given circumstances. We speak about the chance of drawing out the black ball from the bag, because we are uncertain where the balls are lying in the bag. We speak about the chances of an electron rebounding in a given direction, not only because we don't know where it is, but because even if we did know, the laws of Physics wouldn't allow us to predict with any precision in what direction it would rebound. But, in either case, chance is not a name for an entity "out there" that does things. It is simply a name for our own ignorance of what's going to happen. It is a quantitative measure, but it is not in any sense an entity, so it makes no sense to credit it with initiative in the way that Monod does when he talks about it as "absolutely free but blind," and so forth.

The other notion of chance, with which Monod confuses the Scientific notion, is a pagan mythological concept: Chance (with a capital C) as a kind of deity – the deity of *chaos*. Though he professes to speak as a Scientist, what Monod says makes sense only as a reference to some kind of capricious agent – an alternative to the God of order. Talk about such a crazy deity is indeed a rival alternative to Christian talk of a rational and coherent Creator. But, what is quite clear, once you look at it, is that nothing in Monod's *Science* justifies this way of talking. So it is not his Science, but his metaphysics, which lies at the back of his atheistic interpretation of the theory of the random origin of living molecules from which he starts.

If you go back to the biblical view of the natural World, just, as it were, looking at the alternative view to see what would follow from it, then nothing is clearer in the biblical theology of nature than that the Bible regards all events in our World – whether or not they are random or "chance" in a Scientific sense – as attributable to the agency of God. Even when people draw lots (according to the book of Proverbs), "the whole disposing thereof is of the Lord." In other words, the Creator of whom the Bible speaks is one who gives being to the whole space time in which we find ourselves, every event in it – just as, to use Dorothy Sayers' analogy, a novelist has to give being to all the events that occur in her novel, whether or not some of these are chance occurrences in the World of the participants.

Thus, it is a mistake to suggest that, from the standpoint of biblical theism, a theory of the origin of biological molecules that traces the chain of events back to one labeled "random" or "chance" is an exclusive *alternative* to the biblical doctrine of the origin of all things in God as Creator. The truth is the opposite. Monod's *Scientific* hypothesis, for what it is worth, fits as peaceably in the biblical view of things as any other, because the only question at issue is the factual one of what kind of a story our Creator has in fact written. Chance in its Scientific sense, then, is not the name of an agent; and therefore any suggestion that the Scientist's admission of chance is anti-theistic is based on confusion.

Reductionism

But, now we come to an idea that is more general and in some ways more difficult to cope with because it comes up in so many different forms. It is what is often called "reductionism," or, as I like to call it, "nothing-but-ery." It is typified by saying, "Once you look into it scientifically, what you think is A is nothing but B." And if the Scientist has done his sums correctly he can usually justify the second part of the statement, which has a demoralizing effect on the layman particularly: he feels that he is being robbed.

There are a good many popular writers of Science who, I'm afraid, lend credence to this. Take, for example, Desmond Morris's (1928-?) book, *The Naked Ape* (1967). His thesis is that man can be regarded for Scientific purposes as nothing more than, nothing but, one of the apes. The jacket of Morris's book says, "Since, he first became intellectually aware, man has indulged in lofty and exhaustive inquiries into his own nature. Now this ethological analysis by an eminent zoologist puts him firmly in his place alongside the 192 other species of apes and monkeys, among which man is most easily distinguished by the nakedness of his skin." So you see that there is some justification for the complaint of those who say that Science is out to destroy the human image. Or take Richard Dawkins' (1941- ?) book, *The Selfish Gene* (1976), which has a great many ingenious and entertaining things to say. But, the jacket copy again declares that "Richard Dawkins introduces us to ourselves as we really are" (note the word "really"), telling us we are "throwaway survival machines for our immortal genes. Man is a gene machine, blindly programmed to preserve its selfish genes."

It is hardly surprising if those who value human nature react to such claims by saying, "If this is Science I don't want it, it's nasty." And it's very easy to be tempted to respond in a manner that virtually gives away the game to these clever blurb writers. Because if you take away the question-begging words "merely" and "really" and ask what it is that is being said as a matter of Scientific fact, then in each case I suggest that the facts are neutral and not in the least damaging to human dignity. Take a human pelt and put it alongside other pelts of other species and you will identify the human one by its nakedness. So what? That's what you would expect. Man from that standpoint belongs to the classification of the apes, and the fact that he is naked is just the easy way of identifying which skin is his.

Similarly, it may well be true – a very ingenious point by Dawkins - that from a certain point of view the entity which is preserved through reproduction is the genetic specification, rather than the species, or whatever. If you fasten on the genetic specification and say, "that's the thing that's really out to preserve itself," then you can make very interesting and illuminating new appraisals of the process that you're studying. But, again, this is a neutral fact. Why shouldn't it be so?

The fallacy in both of these cases, I suggest, is the fallacy of reductionism or "nothing-but-ery," which is suggesting that once you have a complete story, you leave no room for any other story of the meaning or significance of the situation at another level. And I suggest that it's important not to respond to this kind of "nothing-but-ery" by attacking the Science. If we do spot a flaw in the Scientific argument, then as an act of charity to a fellow Scientist we ought to get on with pointing it out. But, to hunt for flaws in the Scientific description in the hope of rescuing the significance of the other level would be to give the game away completely. The key to this sort of situation is to recognize that completeness of description at one level doesn't necessarily rule out the need for description at others.

Think of looking through a microscope at a newspaper page at varying degrees of magnification. When you examine it very closely, you can't see much more than a lot of inky blobs. If you reduce the magnification, though, pulling back a little from what is being presented, you see now what you might believe to be a part of a letter of the alphabet. What you discover eventually is that it is a letter *e*. here we have a situation in which the initial description, in terms of ink blob, could have been complete, but it would have missed the point that what we have here is a letter *e*. Describing this as "a letter *e* and nothing but a letter *e*" would be just as accurate as describing it as "ink blobs on paper, and nothing but ink blobs in paper." It's a question of choice of level, and the completeness of the one description doesn't in the least prove that you don't need the other or that it isn't valid.

Now imagine what might happen if you reduced magnification still further, steadily increasing you viewing distance. You find that what you've been looking at is the letter *e* in the word "independence," and that word in turn is in the middle of an inflammatory article about politics; here is a new level of significance, not at all a *rival* of the others, but systematically ignored by them.

Nor can the higher level of meaning be down-graded as a mere "optional extra," as if the lower-level account was somehow more "realistic." The motorist, who drives past a "NO ENTRY" sign, dismissing it as nothing but enamel on metal, may be scientifically accurate; but the arm of the law could soon disabuse him of the idea that this was the most "realistic" view of the sign!

So you see the point is a very simple one. It is false to suggest that if you can completely describe man as nothing but a mass of molecules, or nothing but a population of nerve cells acting according to physical laws, or nothing but a carrier of selfish genes, then you has invalidated other levels of significance in man. It is a Philosophical blunder of the worst sort, a disgrace to Science; and one has at this point some sympathy with people who are taken in by these claims and as a result attack Science. But, it is not Science that should be the target; Science doesn't of itself deserves any of the blame that falls deservedly on the heads of those who try to degrade human dignity in the name of these descriptions.

The Bogey of Determinism

We've been skirting round or leading up to what many people see as the biggest threat of Science to the meaningfulness of life: determinism. Determinism, as I've already mentioned, is not part of the apparatus of theoretical Physics anymore. The theoretical physicist calculates probabilities, and has given up the hope of using his present system to calculate outcomes absolutely, precisely, in a determinate way. But, I think we would be very mistaken to imagine that this affects in principle the deterministic character of Science itself. It would be just tomfoolery, for example, for me to pretend that the result of flipping a light switch isn't, for all practical purposes, "physically determined." In this sense Science still, by and large, works with the concept of determination.

This is true particularly in human Science, an area in which we might feel and I think the enemies of Science do feel that determinism is least welcome. We might feel that we'd like the Scientist to keep his detached and predictive hands off our bodies. But, of course when we put ourselves in the hands of the doctor for medical treatment, our attitude suddenly changes, and we long for him to know more of what determines what, in order that he can do his best to ensure that we will be healthy. What I'm suggesting is that, if you look into it, it is false to claim that determinism at a physical level destroys human dignity; this accusation exhibits the same kind of fallacy as the idea that Scientific descriptions of man damage his dignity. We all know the story of the little girl who said to the judge, "it ain't my fault, judge, it's my glands." And Dickens' story of Gradgrind illustrates the same Philosophical principle through an interesting twist – Gradgrind's son commits a crime, and is found out: "If a thunderbolt had fallen on me," said the father, "It would have shocked me less than this." "I don't see why," grumbled the son. "So many people are employed in situations of trust. So many people out of so many will be dishonest. I've heard you talk of it a hundred times, its being a law. How can I help laws? You've comforted others with such things, father, and comfort yourself."

This notion – that physical determinism relieves individuals of responsibility for their actions has quite an ancient pedigree. Indeed, it can be traced back to the Greeks. But, is it in fact rational? Does it follow that if you had a completely determinate physical story about the going-on in a man's brain when he decided to do something, then the outcome would not be determined by his choosing? I suggest that it would be quite fallacious to infer this; that we've got to recognize that determination at one level doesn't exclude determination at another. Now you may say this sounds very abstruse, an example of begging the question, but as a matter of fact there is today a very common illustration which we all accept – they way in which people use computers. Not all of us use them, but we all suffer the consequences of their being used on our electricity bills and our income-tax accounts.

If you were to ask the tax man who has produced your bill just what has determined the behavior of the computer, he would take great pains to show you that its calculations were determined by certain laws of income-tax arithmetic, plus certain conditions pertaining to your particular income bracket. But, if you were to ask an electronics engineer what determined the behavior of that computer and allow him to lift the lid and look inside, he would tell you a physical story, not a mathematical one: he'd say the behavior of that mass of transistors was determined by the laws of Physics as applied to the copper and whatnot in its components. His determination of behavior at that level is more complete in terms of the laws of Physics – but nobody with any sense would suggest that this rules out the claims of the income-tax inspector.

The same logical point applies, I suggest, to our choosing as determining our behavior, *vis-à-vis* the physical story that a physicist or a physiologist might be able to tell about the determination of the processes inside our heads. Just as it is illogical to conclude that the two different descriptions of the computer couldn't both be true, it is illogical to conclude that if there were a complete physical explanation of what determined the processes inside my head, then I couldn't be held to have determined my behavior by my choices. It simply doesn't follow.

Assume, for the sake of argument, that all that you believe and know and feel and think is represented in some sense by the physical configuration of your brain. I have shown elsewhere (for example, in *Brains, Machines and Persons*) that even if that configuration were fully mechanistic in its workings, no complete specification of your brain would exist that you would be bound to accept as inevitable, unless the specification were of its past. In particular, no complete specification of your immediate future of your brain could have an unconditional claim to your assent, even if your brain as mechanical as the workings of a clock.

The reason for this, of course, is that if all your mental processes are represented in your brain, then no change can take place in any mental state of yours without a change also taking place in the physical state of your brain. And therefore, the validity of any completer specification of your brain depends on whether or not you believe it. So it doesn't have an unconditional claim to your assent. No matter how clever I might be in preparing the specification, it can't be equally correct whether or not you believe it. If I accurately describe the makeup of your brain at the moment you read or hear my description, it will be incorrect by the time you've accepted its truth, because the simple act of acquiescence will have changed your brain's make up. Alternatively, if I can allow for the effects of your believing the description, so as to produce one that you would be correct to believe, then its correctness will *depend* on your believing it – so you would not be mistaken to disbelieve it!

In that sense, then, the immediate future of your brain is open to *you*, undetermined for *you*, and would remain so even if the physical elements making up your brain were as determinate as the solar system. There isn't time to say more about this, but I think it is an important point to recognize: that in order to defend the responsibility of ourselves and our fellow men for our choices, we don't even have to argue – let alone prove – that there must be some gap in the chains of cause and effect in our brains that the Scientist might look for.

Let me emphasize that although we've talked about "deterministic" Science and we've imagined powers of prediction to the nth degree, the fact is that human Science, being a limited enterprise, is always tentative. But, what I have been arguing is that there is no need for people (particularly Christians) who cherish the gaps that do exist in the explanatory structure of natural Science. In particular there is no need for us to oppose the Scientific approach to the study of man. There is, I think, some truth in Nietzsche's remark that Science dethrones man, but I suggest that the thrones that Science can remove him from are those which he had no business occupying in the first place.

Here we make contact with a main strand in the thinking of Pascal himself. His greatest concern was that we should give up all our bogus claims to greatness as human beings so that we could reckon realistically with our true greatness as creatures of God, called to know and love our Creator and to become members of His family. He made it clear how little greatness we can claim for ourselves: "What a chimera then is man; what a novelty; what a chaos; what a compound of inconsistencies; a judge of all things, yet a feeble earthworm; a depository of truth, yet a heap of uncertainty; the glory and the outcast of the Universe. If He magnifies Himself I abase Him; If He abases Himself I magnify Him; and persist in contradicting Him till he admit that He is an incomprehensible monster."

Actually, however, Pascal is not as harsh and grim as he sounds here. Let me quote from another of his thoughts on religion and Philosophy:

> In blame equally those who make it their sole business to extol man, and those who take it on them to blame him and those also who attempt to amuse him. I can approve none but those who examine his nature with sorrow and compassion. It is dangerous to show man in how many respects he resembles the lower animals, without pointing out his grandeur. It is also dangerous to direct his attention to his grandeur

without keeping him aware of his degradation. It is still more dangerous to leave him ignorant of both; but to exhibit both to him will be most beneficial.

Science: No Enemy of Meaning

What I've been arguing, then, is that although a few individual Scientists and their followers may have sparked the notion that Science is out to destroy meaning, this notion has in fact been based on confusion. For its limited purposes Science may systematically ignore the meaning of what it studies, but it has no grounds whatsoever for denying that meaning. The Scientist tries, in principle, to make his descriptions exhaustive in their own terms on their own level. But, this doesn't in the least mean that he is trying to exclude or invalidate descriptions at other levels whose meaning may in fact be even more important.

It follows that those who rightly want to defend the meaningfulness of human life have no rational incentive to denigrate Science as such. This applies particularly, I suggest, to the defense of the Christian faith and the particular claims made by it. Ours is declared to be a created World. I've already indicated that believing this declaration doesn't involve us in any need to fight Scientific theories of its created past, whatever their form. The question is simply one of fact: What past has God created? But, whatever is true about it, whether discovered by Scientific method or any other method, is, from the biblical point of view, one of God's facts. It is to Him above all that we owe the duty to do full justice to the way He has made things.

This includes doing full justice to the uncertainties as well as the certainties. But, Christians in particular should beware of over-stressing these uncertainties and giving the impression that it is the uncertainty of Science that allows religion to survive. On the other hand, I've suggested that we have to beware of what has been called "scientism" - the illicit imposing of an imported meaning on Science, a meaning which then pretends to the prestige of Science itself. "Evolutionism" is a case in point. The biological theory of evolution, I've been suggesting, is theologically neutral, but to personify Evolution with a capital "E," as a kind of idol which can act, is to commit a solecism from a Scientific point of view. It is to go out on a limb with no Scientific backing whatsoever.

Science as an Expression of Religious Obedience

So finally, our question: Can Science and technology provide an answer to the quest for meaning? My answer, as you can see, is ultimately "No." I don't, on the other hand, think they do anything to destroy the meaning or the mystery of our World when properly understood; and they do, I suggest, enlarge our understanding. They give fresh material for our wonder and, the Christian would say, for our worship of the Creator. On ultimate questions of the meaning of the whole show, however, they are systematically silent, because these are not Scientific questions. But,– and this is the point – the fact that they are not Scientific questions doesn't mean that they are improper questions for the Scientist or anyone else to ask as a human being. It means only that if they are to be answered, the answers will have to come from outside the system within which the game of Science is defined. It's like chess-playing. If someone says, "Let's play chess," and someone else asks, "Why?" a question has arisen that the rules of chess are not framed to answer.

What I've tried to show, in particular, is that Christian theism is far from being an enemy of Science: it actually offers the most rational basis for the practice of Science as but one aspect of the obedience that the Creator requires of us and our World. There is no question of having to isolate Christianity from Science in order to maintain peace between them. Rather, I suggest, they belong together as naturally as root and fruit: there is in principle an organic unity between biblical Christian faith and natural Science.

The Meaning of Science

In summary, then, what have we been suggesting that Science means? First and foremost, it means an increase in our accountability; an increase in opportunities for compassionate action and the exercise of responsible foresight for the benefit of our fellow men. For example, disease is on the one hand something that may be checked by antibiotics and things of that sort, or it may be something which statistically can be checked by forms of genetic control. Energy supply is something which no doubt we can derive from solar devices and other convenient means in some locations. But, countries which get less than a rich supply of solar energy, look rather dimly on the suggestion that we should turn in the future to solar energy as the replacement of, let us say, nuclear energy. Disease, energy, food supply, too – these are all examples of areas in which the mere suggestion that we should downgrade Scientific investigation and turn our backs on technology would seem grossly uncompassionate and irresponsible.

Secondly, I think Science means unlimited growth of our wonder and awe at the mysterious Universe in which we find ourselves. I referred to this before, but I think the point is worth underscoring. Just as in the seventeenth century when this point was often emphasized, it's true today – and perhaps increasingly true – that each discovery which explains something that puzzled us also reveals something more marvelous and intricate in the structure of our Universe.

Thirdly, Science means the steady growth of our confidence that precedent can be a reliable guide to expectations, as a Christian theist would say, our confidence in the trustworthiness of the Creator who holds in being the natural World. Today we probably take this too much for granted. But, we need only look back to the period before natural Science developed in its modern form to see that this idea was by no means obvious then. Precedent was only a very limited guide because at that time Scientists hadn't developed the procedures for so classifying precedent that they could single out one factor and say, "This is the thing that is the same in A as it was in B." So many uncontrolled factors entered in that it just didn't occur to people, even in areas that we now think we understand, that there would be a precedent worth observing.

Of course, there were some precedents they were aware of. As the book of Proverbs quaintly puts it, "Does not the ringing of the nose bring forth blood?" recognized sequences of cause and effect were not confined to those discovered scientifically. What is new about our modern Science is its technique for so isolating individual factors in a complicated situation that we're now able to identify very subtly defined precedents and say, "Given this subtle combination of circumstances, then a rather precise outcome can be expected." The increasing confidence that this is a valid way of organizing our lives is something that, from the standpoint of Christian theism, increases our reasons for thanking God for His trustworthiness.

In this sense it's clear that Science can lead us to truth. But, we have to remember the personal aspect of this concept of truth emphasized by the biblical writer. "I *am* the Truth" was the claim of Christ. R. Hooykaas (1906-1994), puts it this way: It is evident that Truth in the biblical sense is not an abstract truth but a Person, Christ, or the Spirit of Christ. So taking into account both kinds of truth, we could perhaps better say that [to the early founders of the Royal Society] it was truth [with a capital "T"] which led to the freedom necessary to find truth [with a small "t"].

Then, paraphrasing Pascal, he concludes: "We cannot be radically free until, tired and exhausted from the vain search after truth; we have stretched our arms to the Liberator."

The Sciences of inert matter have made immense progress, while those of living beings remain in a rudimentary state. The slow advance of biology is due to the conditions of human existence, to the intricacy of the phenomena of life, and to the form of our intelligence, which delights in mechanical constructions and mathematical abstractions. The applications of Scientific discoveries have transformed the material and mental Worlds. These transformations exert on us a profound influence. Their unfortunate eject comes from the fact that they have been made without consideration for our nature. Our ignorance of ourselves has given to mechanics, Physics and chemistry the power to modify at random the ancestral forms of life.

Man should be the measure of all. On the contrary, he is a strange in the World that he has created. He has been incapables of organizing this World for himself, because he did not possess a practical knowledge of his own nature. Thus, the enormous advance gained by the Sciences of inanimate matter over those of living things is one of the greatest catastrophes ever suffered by humanity. The environment born of our intelligence and our inventions is adjusted neither to our stature nor to our shape. We are unhappy. We degenerate morally and mentally. The groups and the nations in which industrial civilization has attained its highest development are precisely those which are becoming weaker. And whose return to barbarism is the most rapid. But, they do not realize it. They are without protection against the hostile surroundings that Science has built about them. In truth, our civilization, like those preceding it, has created certain conditions of existence which, for reasons still obscure, render life itself impossible. The anxiety and the woes of the inhabitants of the modern city arise from their own weakness. We are the victims of the backwardness of the Sciences of life over those of matter.

The only possible remedy for this evil is a much more profound knowledge of ourselves. Such knowledge will enable us to understand by what mechanisms modern existence affects our consciousness and our body. We shall thus learn how to adapt ourselves to our surroundings, and how to change them, should a revolution become indispensable. In bringing to light our true nature, our potentialities, and the way to actualize them, this Science will give us the explanation of our physiological weakening, and of our moral and intellectual diseases. We have no other means of learning the inexorable rules of our organic and spiritual activities, of distinguishing the prohibited from the lawful, of realizing that we are not free to modify, according to our fancy, our environment, and ourselves. Since, the natural conditions of existence have been destroyed by modern civilization, the Science of man has become the most necessary of all Sciences.

The critical review of the data concerning man yields a large amount of positive information. We are thus enabled to make a complete inventory of human activities. Such an inventory will lead to the building up of new schemata, richer than the classical ones. But, our knowledge will not, in this manner, progress very strikingly. We shall have to go farther and build up a real Science of man. A Science capable of undertaking, with the help of all known techniques, a more exhaustive examination of our inner World, and also of realizing that each part should be considered as a function of the whole. In order to develop such a Science, we must, for some time, turn our attention away from mechanical inventions and even, in a certain measure, from classical hygiene and medicine, from the purely material aspect of our existence. Everybody is interested in things that increase wealth and comfort. But, no one understands that the structural, functional, and mental quality of each individual has to be improved. The health of the intelligence and of the affective sense, moral discipline, and spiritual development are just as necessary as the health of the body and the prevention of infectious diseases.

No advantage is to be gained by increasing the number of mechanical inventions. It would perhaps be as well not to accord so much importance to discoveries of Physics, astronomy, and chemistry. In truth, pure Science never directly brings us any harm. But, when its fascination beauty dominates our mind and enslaves our thoughts in the realm of inanimate matter, it becomes dangerous. Man must now turn his attention to himself, and to the cause of his moral and intellectual disability. What is the good of increasing the comfort, the luxury, the beauty, the size, and the complications of our civilization, if our weakness prevents us from guiding it to our best advantage? It is really not worth while to go on elaboration a way of living that is bringing about the demoralization and the disappearance of the noblest elements of the great races. It would be far better to pay more attention to ourselves than to construct faster steamers, more comfortable automobiles, cheaper radios, or telescopes for examining the structure of remote nebulas. What real progress will be accomplished when aircraft take us to Europe or to China in a few hours? Is it necessary to increase production unceasingly, so that men may consume larger and larger quantities of useless things? There is not the shadow of a doubt that mechanical, physical, and chemical Sciences are incapable of giving us intelligence, moral discipline, health, nervous equilibrium, security and peace.

Our curiosity must turn aside from its present path, and take another direction. It must leave the physical and physiological in order to follow the mental and the spiritual. So far, Sciences concerning themselves with human beings have confined their activities to certain aspects of their subject. They have not succeeded in escaping from Cartesian dualism. They have been dominated by mechanism. In physiology, hygiene, and medicine, as well as in the study of education and of political and social economy, Scientists have been chiefly absorbed by organic, humoral, and intellectual aspects of man. They have not paid any great attention to his affective and moral form, his inner life, his character, his esthetic and religious needs, and the common substratum of organic and psychological activities, the intimate relations of the individual and of his mental and spiritual environment. A radical change is indispensable. This change requires both the work of specialists devotion their efforts to the particular knowledge related to our body and our mind, and of Scientists capable of integration the discoveries of the specialists in function of man as a whole. The new Science must progress, by a double effort of analysis and synthesis, toward a conception of the human individual at once sufficiently complete and sufficiently simple to serve as a basis for our action.

Individuality is not merely an aspect of the organism. It also constitutes an essential characteristic of each component part of this organism. It remains virtual in the fertilized ovum, and progressively unfolds its characteristics as the new being extends into time. The ancestral tendencies of this being are forced to actualize by his conflict with the environment. They incline his adaptive activities in a certain direction. In fact, the mode of utilization of its surroundings by the body is determined by its innate properties. Each individual responds to these surroundings in his own way. He chooses among the things of the outer World those which increase his individualization. He is a focus of specific activities. These activities are distinct but indivisible.

The soul cannot be separated from the body, the structure from the function, the cell from its medium, the multiplicity from the unity, or the determining from the determined. We are beginning to realize that our surface is not our real frontier that it merely sets up between us and the cosmic Universe a plane of cleavage indispensable to our action. We are constructed like the castles of the Middle Ages, whose dungeons were surrounded by several lines of fortifications. Our inner defenses are numerous and entangled one with another. The skin is the barrier that our microscopic enemies must not traverse. But, we extend much farther beyond it. Beyond space and time. We know the individual's centre, yet ignore where his outer limits are located. These limits, in fact, are hypothetical. Perhaps they do not exist. Each man is bound to those who precede and follow him. He fuses in some manner into them. Humanity does not appear to be composed of separated particles, as gas is of molecules. It resembles an intricate network of long threads extending in space-time and consisting of series of individuals. Individuality is doubtless real. But, it is much less definite than we believe. And the independence of each individual from the others and from the Cosmos is an illusion.

Our body is made up of the chemical substances of the environment. These substances enter it and become modified according to its individuality. They are built up into temporary edifices, tissues, humour, and organs, which ceaselessly disintegrate and are reconstructed during our whole life. After our death, they return to the World of inert matter. Certain chemical compounds assume our racial and individual peculiarities. They become truly ourselves. Others only pass through the body. They participate in the existence of our tissues without taking any of their characteristics, just as wax does not modify its chemical composition when made into statues of different shapes. They flow through the organism like a large river, from which cells draw the substances required for their growth, their maintenance, and their expenditure of energy. According to Christian mystics, we receive from the outer World certain spiritual elements. The grace of God permeates soul and body, just as atmospheric oxygen, or nitrogen from the food, diffuses in our tissues.

Individual specificity persists during the entire life, although tissues and humours continually change. The organs and their medium move at the rhythm of physiological time, that is, at the rhythm of irreversible processes, towards definitive transformations and death. But, they always keep their inherent qualities. They are not modified by the stream of matter in which they are immersed, any more than the spruce trees on the mountains by the clouds passing through their branches. However, individuality grows stronger or weaker according to environmental conditions. When these conditions are particularly unfavourable, it dissolves. Sometimes, mental personality is less marked than organic personality. One may rightly ask whether it still exists in modern men. Some observers doubt its reality. Theodore Dreiser (1871-1945), considers it a myth. It is certain that the inhabitants of the new city show great uniformity in their mental and moral weakness. Most of the individuals belong to the same type. There is a mixture of nervousness and apathy, of vanity and lack of confidence in them, of muscular strength and tendency to fatigue, of genetic impulses, irresistible and not strong, sometimes homosexual. Such a state is due to profound disorders in the formation of personality. It does not consist only in an attitude of mind, a fashion which could easily change. It expresses either a degeneration of the race, or a defective development of the individual, or both these phenomena.

This debasement is, in a certain measure, of hereditary origin. The sup-pression of natural selection, as already mentioned, has caused the survival of children whose tissues and consciousness are defective. The race has been weakened by the preservation of such reproducers. The relative importance of this factor of degeneration is not yet known. As we have already mentioned, the influence of heredity cannot be distinguished clearly from that of environment. Feeble-mindedness and insanity surely have had ancestral cause. The intellectual weakness observed in schools and universities, and in the population in general, comes from development disorders, and not from hereditary defects. When these flabby, silly young people are removed from their customary environment and placed in more primitive conditions of life, they sometimes change for the better and recover their virility. The atrophic character of the products of our civilization, therefore, is not incurable. It is far from being always the expression of a racial degeneration.

Among the multitude of weak and defective there are, however, some completely developed men. These men, when closely observed, appear to be superior to the classical schemata. In fact, the individual whose potentialities are all actualized does not resemble the human being pictured by the specialists. He is not the fragments of consciousness which psychologists attempt to measure. He is not of to be found in the chemical reactions, the functional processes, and the organs which physicians have divided between themselves. Neither is he the abstraction whose concrete manifestations the educators try to guide. He is almost completely wanting in the rudimentary being manufactured by social workers, prison wardens, economists, sociologists, and politicians. In fact, he never appears to a specialist unless this specialist is willing to look at him as a whole. He is much more than the sum of all the facts accumulated by the particular Sciences. We never apprehend him in his entirety. He contains vast, unknown regions. His potentialities are almost inexhaustible. Like the great natural phenomena, he is still unintelligible. When one contemplates him in the harmony of all his organic and spiritual activities, one experiences a profound esthetic emotion. Such an individual is truly the creator and the centre of the Universe.

The restoration of man to the harmony of his physiological and mental self will transform his Universe. We should not forget that the Universe modifies its aspects according to the conditions of our body. That it is nothing but the response of our nervous system, our sensory organs, and our techniques to an unknown and probably unknowable reality. That all our states of consciousness, all our dreams, those of the mathematicians as well as those of the lovers, are equally true. The electromagnetic waves, which express a sunsets to the physicist, are no more objective than the brilliant colours perceived by the painter. The aesthetic feeling engendered by those colours, and the measurement of the length of their component light-waves, are two aspects of ourselves and have the same right to existence. Joy and sorrow are as important as planets and suns. But, the World of Dante, Emerson, Bergson, or G. E. Hale is larger than that of Mr. Babbitt. The beauty of the Universe will necessarily grow with the strength of our organic and psychological activities.

We must liberate man from the Cosmos created by the genius of physicists and Astronomers, that Cosmos in which, since the Renaissance, he has been imprisoned. Despite its stupendous immensity, the World of matter is too narrow for him. Like his economic and social environment, it does not fit him. We cannot adhere to the faith in its exclusive reality. We know that we are not altogether comprised within its dimensions, that we extend somewhere else, outside the physical continuum. Man is simultaneously a material object, a living being, a focus of mental activities. His presence in the prodigious void of the intersidereal spaces is totally negligible. But, he is not a stranger in the realm of inanimate matter. With the aid of mathematical abstractions his mind apprehends the electrons as well as the stars. He is made on the scale of the terrestrial mountains, oceans, and rivers. He appertains to the surface of the earth, exactly as tress, plants, and animals do. He feels at ease in their company. He is more intimately bound to the works of the art, the monuments, the mechanical marvels of the new city, and the small group of his friends, those whom he loves. But, he also belongs to another World. A World which, although enclosed within himself, stretches beyond space and time. And of this World, if his will is indomitable, he may travel over the infinite cycles. The cycle of Beauty, contemplated by Scientists, artists, and poets, the cycle of Love, that inspires heroism and renunciation. The cycle of Grace, ultimate reward of those who passionately seek the principle of all things. Such is our Universe.

The day has come to begin the work of our renovation. We will not establish any programme. For a programme would stifle living reality in a rigid armour. It would prevent the bursting forth of the unpredictable, and imprison the future within the limits of our minds. We must rise and move on. We must liberate ourselves from blind technology and grasp the complexity and the wealth of our own nature. The Sciences of life have shown to humanity its goal and placed at its disposal the means of reaching it. But, we are still immersed in the World created by the Sciences of inert matter without any respect for the laws of our development. In a World that is not made for us, because it is born from an error of our reason and from the ignorance of our true self. To such a World we cannot become adapted. We will, then, revolt against it. We will transform its values and organize it with reference to our true needs. Today the Science of man gives us the power to develop all the potentialities of our body. We know the secret mechanisms of our physiological and mental activities and the causes of our weakness. We know how we have transgressed natural laws. We know why we are punished, why we are lost in darkness. Nevertheless, we faintly perceive through the mists of dawn a path which may lead to our salvation. For the first time in the history of humanity a crumbling civilization is capable of discerning the causes of this decay. For the first time, it has at its disposal, the gigantic strength of Science. Will we utilize this knowledge and this power? It is our only hope of escaping the fate common to all great civilization of the past. Our destiny is in our hands. On the new road, we must now go forward.

Does the Universe have any purpose? Is the emergence of life anything more than a cosmic accident? Was there any intelligence operative in the Universe prior to the appearance of man? Is life anything more than atoms and molecules? Is mind anything else than the result of complex movements of the physical and chemical components of the brain? Is there any divine influence present in nature? Is evolution moving in any meaningful direction? Do our individual lives have any ultimate significance in the unfathomable depths of cosmic time and space?

These are a few of the questions that modern Science has raised for those of us who believe or hope that there is indeed some final meaning to our lives in the Universe. These are not new questions. They have been with us for some time, and they have inspired a number of responses. But, many of these responses have been reactionary repudiations of Science itself. Others have been intellectually shallow. And still others have been intellectually inaccessible to sincere and able inquirers.

The present work is intended for any intelligent reader who by some acquaintance with the exciting discoveries of modern Science may have asked some of the questions raised above. I shall attempt to make presentable to such a questioner the view that our Universe is not without purpose and that there is absolutely nothing in the Scientific approach that contradicts the essence of a religious interpretation of reality. Instead there is much in Scientific discovery and speculation that may help us to understand religion in a new and adventurous way. But, in my exposition I have sought only to explain it Philosophically. Therefore, we need to have a close look at the theory of creation and the criticism of contemporary Science.

6.2 Philosophical Implications of Modern Scientific Cosmologies

The big bang theory, the steady state theory and Stephen Hawking's (1942-?) no-boundary proposal are modern Scientific answers to the question of the origin of the World. The big bang theory postulates a 'beginning' of the Universe. Does the theory lend support to the traditional Christian belief in creation? Does it amount to a Scientific support for the creation of the Universe in time by an extra-Scientific agent, and as such can it be used as religious apologetic? The steady state theory and Hawking's no-boundary proposal instead propagate an eternal Universe. Does this imply that the Universe was uncreated? What support do such theories lend to anti-religious propaganda? These are the questions that we can deal here in the second part of this chapter.

6.2.1 The Big Bang Theory

A. Historical Development

We begin with the two rival systems of the Universe, namely, the Ptolemaic and the Copernican. Commonly known as the geocentric and the heliocentric theories, these systems have played a significant role in shaping modern cosmological thinking. In the *Ptolemaic system* the earth is placed immovably at the center of the Universe. The sun, moon and the planets move around the earth in complex orbits. Planetary motion was explained with imaginary circles called deferent's and epicycles. This system remained the last word in astronomy until Copernicus. The *Copernican system* is a description of the planetary system in heliocentric terms. Nicholas Copernicus rightly pointed out that planetary motion was sun-centered. The sun was assigned a central position, the earth and other planets moved around it. This theory therefore gave a true picture of the World and the study of Cosmology was liberated for fresh discoveries and perspectives. *Great Astronomers and Philosophers* like Nicolas of Cusa (1401-1464), Tycho Brahe (1546-1601), Galileo Galilei (1564-1642), Johannes Kepler (1571-1630) and Isaac Newton (1643-1727) helped refine cosmological thinking. Scientific development gave humanity a new perception of reality. Besides, technological advancement gave us the needed instruments to peer deeply into the sky. Thus, theories were backed by empirical observation and we moved further in our understanding of the Universe. *Einstein's Theory of Relativity* gave us a better understanding of space, time and motion. With the advent of *Quantum Mechanics* more light was shed on the internal structure of matter. Matter was now explained in terms of particles which defied even the most powerful microscopes. Both The Theory of Relativity and Quantum Mechanics revolutionized Science. They radically questioned certain concepts such as Newton's absolute motion, absolute space, absolute time, absolute mass, the wave nature of particles, and the certainty of experimental results. *The discovery of the expanding Universe* is Edwin Hubble's (1889-1953) discovery of the expanding Universe in the late 1920s that marks the beginning of a new era of cosmological discoveries. Earlier, Albert Einstein (1879-1955) himself had come to this discovery but he went against his own findings and postulated a 'closed' Universe. We should also mention the Russian mathematician Aleksandr Friedmann (1888-1925) who had made place for expansion in his model. When he read Einstein's paper he saw that the relativistic description of reality necessarily pointed to an expansion. But, Friedmann's papers published in 1922 and 1924 in the acclaimed German journal, *Zeitschrift für Physik* (The Physical Journal), failed to be taken as something real about the Universe. Yet, Friedmann's work was the harbinger of the big bang theory.

The expanding Universe proposal of Hubble can be plainly understood as the expansion of space. To explain it with the help of an analogy, we may imagine the whole of space to be a large rubber sheet on which the solar system, the galaxies and stars are placed. If we stretch the rubber sheet from all the sides we realize that the space between the various objects we have placed on it expands. The expansion does not involve our sun, our solar system, or even our galaxy: none of them is expanding. It is the space between the galaxies that is expanding. The billions of galactic systems that dot the Universe beyond the Milky Way are rushing away from us. A closer examination reveals that they are not just racing away from us but are actually racing away from one another. By means of his careful distance measurements, using the Cepheid and M.L. Humason's extension of Slipher's redshift work, Hubble was able to clearly demonstrate that the more distant the galaxy, the proportionately faster its recession velocity. This relation was known as *Hubble's Law.* The expansion is uniform: no matter which galaxy one happens to be in, all the others are moving away from it; there is no privileged location. Again, the galaxies are not moving in space; rather they move with space. Space itself expands like a rubber sheet. Hubble's Law lent great credibility to the earlier speculation of Astronomers and Cosmologists that the space of the Universe was indeed expanding. It suggested that the Universe must have had a definite beginning in time. Now

Astronomers were firmly set on the trail of the big bang. For if the Universe is expanding, it is quite reasonable to think of a time when everything was together. It is justifiable even to think of a 'beginning' to this whole process

Let us now examine the contribution of Georges Lemaitre (1894-1966), the 'father' of the big bang theory. Lemaitre, a Belgian astronomer, was working with the equations of Einstein's General Relativity, and quite independently he too reached the same conclusions as Aleksandr Friedmann. He emphasized that Einstein's equations implied that the Universe must have begun in a very dense state. Perhaps because of his religious beliefs, Lemaitre preferred a beginning to the Universe. He explained the beginning in terms of a big bang, a radioactive disintegration of an atom. He suggested that if one extrapolated the expanding Universe backward in time, the galaxies would converge at some point into an atom. Lemaitre called this atom the *primeval atom* or the super-atom. The primeval atom was in a state of extremely hot and highly compressed matter. The entire content of the Universe was packed into a sphere about thirty times bigger than our sun. Today it is assumed that the primeval atom was infinitely dense, and that it had no dimensions. Such an object is called a singularity. Now the primeval atom, being a state of extremely hot and highly compressed matter, was unstable and so it exploded. The explosion of this primeval atom accounts for all that exists at present in the Universe.

Lemaitre's theory was based on Hubble's discovery, but this alone was not enough evidence for the establishment of his theory. Before it could be accepted as the standard model of creation, some more evidence would have to be found. The required evidence came with the discovery of universal microwave radiation. To understand this discovery let us first familiarize ourselves with radiation. James Trefil (1938-?), author of *The Moment of Creation* (1983), gives us a very practical example. When we watch the colour of the heating element of an electric stove turn from dull red to bright orange our eyes are sensitive to that particular type of visible radiation we call light. But, when we have turned the stove off and the colour of the heating element has returned to normal we can still feel the heat. In other words the stove is still radiating. This can be explained thus: the heating element experiences a drop in the temperature and so the radiation which is given out moves from the range of visibility to another range. Our eyes are insensitive to this radiation which can only be detected by instruments and special photographic films. This radiation is called infrared. Though unperceived by our naked eyes, infrared radiation can be detected by the sense of touch.

6.2.2 The Steady State Theory

As the big bang theory gathered evidence a rival theory was making waves. In 1948, the steady state theory was proposed by Herman Bondi (1919-2005), Thomas Gold (1920-2004) and Fred Hoyle (1915-2001). This theory is a deductive theory and as such it begins with a methodological postulate known as the Perfect Cosmological Principle, which is a development of the Cosmological Principle. The Cosmological Principle "assumes that the Universe is approximately isotropic about any point in space. Since, our Universe appears isotropic from any point it follows that it is uniform and homogeneous in space." The Perfect Cosmological Principle on the other hand "postulates that the large scale aspects of the Universe must be independent not only of the position of the observer but also of the time at which the observation is made." In other words, the Universe looks the same when viewed not only from any point in space but at any time as well.

Basing themselves on this principle the steady staters argued that the Universe is eternally unchanging, and that it maintains a steady state. But, then, what about the observed expansion of the Universe? Hoyle tried to account for this fact by proposing the theory of *continuous creation*. He suggested that as the Universe expands, new matter is continuously and spontaneously created in the space opening up between the galaxies. Thus, even though the Universe is expanding and the galaxies are moving apart from each other, the Universe essentially remains unchanged. The continuous creation of matter ensures that there is no decrease in the density of the Universe due to expansion over a period of time. Consequently, there is no need to assume that the Universe has a beginning. Hence, the name 'steady state.'

The steady state theory, therefore, comes up with a new and different notion of creation. It does not speak of creation in terms of temporal beginning. Creation in this theory is a continuous process and not an event which takes place at a definite moment. Creation occurs everywhere, at all places and at all times. Secondly, this theory insists that the matter is not created out of radiation or anything else but out of *nothing*. The expounders of the steady state theory maintain that this is a spontaneous process and must be accepted as a basic property of the Universe

6.2.3 The No Boundary Proposal of Stephen Hawking

There are theorists/Scientists other than the steady-staters who argue that the Universe has no beginning. One of them is Stephen Hawking. In his best seller, *A Brief History of Time: From the Big Bang to Black Holes* (1991), Hawking takes up the proposal he had made at a conference held by the Vatican Academy of Sciences in 1981. He discusses on a popular level the 'no boundary' proposal for the quantum state of the Universe. At the Vatican conference he had supported the big bang theory, that the space-time Universe had a real beginning in a physical state of infinite compression, known to mathematicians as a singularity. In the above mentioned book he instead maintains that space-time may be finite in extent but without boundary. Such a Universe would be like the surface of the earth which is limited in area but has no boundaries or edges. There would be therefore no moment of creation, just as the surface of the earth has no beginning or end. The Universe would simply 'be' and would be determined by the laws of Science.

According to Hawking, such a theory has profound implications for the role of God as creator. In his own words:

> "The idea that space and time may form a closed surface without boundary also has profound implications for the role of God in the affairs of the Universe .... So long as the Universe had a beginning, we could suppose it had a creator. But, if the Universe is really completely self-contained, having no boundary or edge, it would have neither beginning nor end: it would simply be. What place, then for a creator?"

Hawking seems to think of God as an explanatory principle for the edge of the Universe, i.e., he sees God as the one who begins the process of creation. Such a proposal can raise serious questions. We may ask, is it correct to take the beginning of the Universe as proof or disproof of God's existence? But, first, let us outline our understanding of creation.

6.2.4 The Thomist Notion of Creation

Some of St. Thomas' insights about creation belong in my opinion to the permanently valid achievements of the human mind.

A. Creation as Divine Causation

St. Thomas reserves the term creation to designate the divine causation of the World. Creation is a divine production. But, production here is not an ordinary change or event, something brought forth from a state of latency, dormancy or concealedness. It is not a transformation of some pre-existing matter. "When we say that the Universe was created we do not mean that something became something else, but that something began to exist." Therefore, St. Thomas' answer to the question, whether to create is to make something from nothing? Is an emphatic yes. God created the World out of nothing, *ex nihilo*. God creates from absolutely nothing. If the World were made out of some pre-existing material then this material would be either God Himself or something other than God. But, God is the first cause and is prior to anything else in the World. There is no second to him. Secondly, God is simple, spiritual and unchangeable; and since

He cannot change, He cannot exteriorize Himself in creation. Obviously then, He cannot be the material cause of the Universe. Accordingly, St. Thomas maintains that God is the efficient cause of the Universe and creates the World out of nothing, *ex nihilo*. Further, since there is neither any pre-existing object nor pre-existing matter, God does not need any instrument or demiurge by which He brings about change.

B. Temporal Beginning

Creation-talk is spontaneously mixed up with the notion of a first instant of creation. St. Thomas however has a different approach. When he tackles the question, whether the Universe of creatures always existed? He answers that nothing except God is eternal, and that God creates by his most powerful will. Since, the will of God is the cause of things, and since this will is absolutely free, we are not in a position to answer the above question with absolute certainty. God could will it any way He thought best. Therefore, in St. Thomas' view "whether the World-duration is without beginning or starts from a first instant depends entirely on the Creator's free decision and cannot be settled by any deductive process." Neither the eternity nor the temporality of the Universe can be demonstrated on the basis of reason alone. It is by revelation alone that we know that the World had a temporal beginning. The implication is that for St. Thomas the idea of creation does not necessarily involve temporal beginning.

C. Time Co-Created with the Material World

The idea of 'temporal beginning' needs to be further purified. St. Thomas holds that time was co-created with the material World. Discussing the issue of time in the *Summa Theologiae* (1265-1274), he explains the words of Genesis, "in the beginning," as meaning "in the beginning of time." Properties of things are co-created with things; they do not exist prior to the things created. Since, time is a property of the Universe it is co-created with the Universe. Thus, the beginning of time cannot be taken as a measure of creation. "For time itself is contained in the Universe, and therefore when we speak about creation we should not inquire at what time it happened."

D. What is Creation?

Negatively speaking, creation may be defined as "the production by God of a reality that did not exist before either in itself or in its materials or any of its elements." Positively, it may be defined as "the free emanation of the whole reality of the Universe from the pure Esse." The term 'emanation' here is understood as 'flowing out.' It is the flowing out of the whole Universe, including matter, from pure Esse (Being). It is production of reality, in the sense of ontological (and not necessarily temporal) origination. Significantly, St. Thomas says that this "act of creation is not located in the category of action or passion but in that of relation." This relation of the Universe to its Source is a relation of total ontological dependence:

> "Creation is not to be considered as some 'big bang' that happened in the past, or a push that God gave the Universe to get it going. God does not create necessary beings and then dissociate himself from them, leaving them self-sufficient. In fact, he cannot, since every creature has existence (esse) only inasmuch as it participates in divine existence."

In simple words we can say that the contingent Universe is necessarily and in every condition relative to and inseparable from its immanent though transcendent Cause.

Let us summarize the Thomist notion of creation. Firstly, for St. Thomas, creation is not the transformation or change of some pre-existing matter. It presupposes and employs no previously existing matter. In this sense the Universe is created *from nothing*. Secondly, creation does not necessarily imply a temporal beginning. Even if the World had no beginning it would still have been created because according to St. Thomas, creation is a relation of total ontological dependence of the Universe, at every moment of its existence, on God.

6.2.5 Critiques of Modern Scientific Cosmologies

In the light of the Thomist notion of creation, we will evaluate the three competing Scientific theories regarding the origin of the Universe examined earlier.

A. The Big Bang Theory

The big bang theory does not hesitate to speak in terms of a moment of creation. But, we might ask, does this theory really speak of an absolute beginning? For we do not know what existed before the primeval atom. Lemaitre does not tell us anything about the origin of the primeval atom itself. From where did this primeval atom come, and all the superdense matter which was packed in it? Besides, how long was this primeval atom in existence before it underwent transformation? Science falls short of an explanation of the primeval atom, though it assures us of its existence. "Science can best say when the primeval atom exploded or when the hydrogen cloud started contracting." Beyond that point, we do not know.

It is quite possible, as Gamow suggests that the primeval atom is the result of a collapse of a previously existing World. Or again, the Universe could be an infinitely oscillating Universe. We do not know. More radically, since Science is based upon observation and verification, can Scientists answer questions with regard to the absolute origin of the Universe? Is Science capable of formulating a coherent idea of the temporal origin of the Universe? We suggest that it is not. The method of Science does not permit it. Scientists cannot claim to know the absolute beginning of the World because they would be unable to verify it scientifically and be absolutely sure that there was nothing prior to it. Besides, because Science is a spatio-temporal discipline, it can only study events which are located in time. But, if, as we have been saying, creation is an extra-temporal relationship, it cannot be placed in a time-stream. Accordingly, empirical Science is not competent to discuss the question of the absolute origin of the Universe. We can conclude with the following quote:

> "The theory of the primeval atom does not, in as much as it is a strictly Scientific theory, postulate a 'beginning' of the Universe in the strict sense of the word. All that it asserts is that certain asymmetrical, physical processes now observed, cannot be extrapolated indefinitely into the past. Extrapolation leads to a zero point. This zero point is, if you will, the beginning of our present state of the Universe, constituted as it is by these asymmetrical processes. But, Science is not competent to pronounce whether the beginning is an absolute beginning or no."

Or as M.A.H. MacCallum says, "the Big Bang idea remains ultimately an assumption of characteristics of the Universe (in the form of the properties 'at', or just after, the initial singularity) rather than a full explanation of them, and so leads us on to metaphysics or religion, and beyond Science."

B. The Steady State Theory

When we come to the steady state theory, the first question to be asked is what is meant by 'creation out of nothing.' Is their understanding of 'nothing' similar to that of a Philosopher like St. Thomas, for example? Or is this 'nothing' some type of emptiness, what we would commonly call a vacuum? We must note that, for Scientists, though the vacuum does not have ordinary matter, it is not absolutely empty. They hold that a system is in a state of vacuum if it is in a zero energy state. But, does zero energy imply the complete absence of energy? No, because Scientists tell us that the "vacuous state refers not to absence of things but to a specific distribution of things. It is not absence of 'being' but of certain effects. One should say that 'nothing' in Science does not mean no-thing, but no-net-effect." Therefore, we need to be careful about the Scientists' use of the word 'nothing.' In Philosophy the word 'nothing' means absolute nothingness. Hence, what Scientists understand by nothing may not be exactly what Philosophers understand by nothing.

Next, we may question the steady staters' use of the word 'creation.' It appears that the steady staters confuse between the Scientific use of the word 'creation' and 'creation' in the Philosophical sense that we have outlined earlier. The steady state theory places a lot of emphasis on the continuous creation of matter. Matter simply appears, it does not come from anywhere. All that the steady state theory tells us is that the amount of matter in the Universe, in some way yet unknown to us, increases. Are the steady staters justified in calling such a process 'creation' (even creation out of nothing)? It would seem not. "What the proponents of the steady state theory postulated most gratuitously was not the emergence of hydrogen atoms from radiation, a perfectly legitimate process, but their coming into being out of nothing and without a Creator." It is fallacious to claim gratuitously that the hydrogen atoms come into existence at a steady rate out of *nothing*.

Going by what we have discussed about the Thomist notion of creation we can say that to give the name creation to a process which merely speaks about an unexplained increase of matter, appears to be a misnomer. When the steady staters claim "to explain creation of matter, all that they do is to describe the specific properties of the matter which has appeared and is alleged to have been created." But, we know that it is not enough just to describe the matter which has been allegedly created; it is important to explain its creation as well. The theory must tell us from where this newly created matter comes. Though in recent times efforts have been made to explain such a process through the quantum mechanical phenomenon called quantum fluctuation,[1] the steady state theory fails in this regard. Since, it does not know how this matter comes into being, it simply regards it as 'created.' The creation of matter is thought to be a spontaneous

1 Quantum fluctuation involves minor fluctuations in the energy of a system considered to be in a state of vacuum. The fluctuation is a slight tilt towards the negative or positive sides of zero and lasts for a brief moment. The result of such a fluctuation is the spontaneous creation and annihilation of pairs of particles like an electron and a positron.

process which cannot be treated causally. Thus, we can conclude that "as a strictly Scientific hypothesis the steady state theory has nothing to do with 'creation' in the proper, Philosophical sense of the word." It borrows this metaphysical term and uses it without any apparent awareness of its semantical difficulties.

Another area where the steady state theory comes under fire is when it asserts that the Universe is unchanging (by way of density), and therefore has neither a beginning nor end. It would therefore regard the Universe as uncreated. But, we must remember that even an eternal Universe would raise the question of creation, because the question of creation is quite distinct from the question temporal beginning. Confronted with an eternal Universe, we would still have to ask: Why is there something rather than nothing? Besides, it seems very illegitimate to assume the spontaneous arising of matter, and then draw the conclusion that the World has no beginning. Can we say that such matter has no material antecedent at all? "However, uncaused it may appear to me now; there is no guarantee that I may not discover a whole series of causes tomorrow." Science is never omniscient and hence when it reaches a dead-end it cannot make such absolute claims and rule out causes of things.

C. The No-Boundary Proposal of Stephen Hawking

How do we react to Stephen Hawking's no-boundary proposal which holds that there is no moment of creation? Hawking maintains that the Universe is self-contained. Physical laws, he feels, can sufficiently explain our physical Universe. Now it is quite possible that there is no edge to space-time, no moment of creation, and Hawking could be right in his no-boundary proposal. Perhaps he could even prove it to us one day. But, can it be claimed that the Universe is therefore uncreated? For even if our Universe was a self-operating being, we could still ask: "Why is it self-operating? Who made it so? Just because something is self-functioning, it does not become self-made." This is the real question of creation. It is a question that arises upon recognition of the contingency of the Universe. Each element in our Universe is contingent, and even an infinite number of contingent beings does not amount to one necessary being. It is the contingency of our World rather than the question of its temporal origin that points to a ground external to itself. Thus, it is misleading to take the beginning of the Universe as a proof or disproof of God's existence. Hawking seems to think of God as an explanatory principle for the edge of the Universe, i.e., he sees God as the one who begins the process of creation. This is not only a rather simplified but also an inaccurate version of creation. Creation, we have said, is a relationship of total dependence on God, and it does not necessarily involve a temporal beginning. Hence, it is incorrect to take the beginning of the Universe as proof or disproof of God's existence. As Don Page rightly remarks: "whether or not the Universe has a beginning has no relevance to the question of its creation, just as whether an artists' line has a beginning and end, or instead forms a circle with no end, has no relevance to the question of its being drawn."

6.2.6 The Philosophical Significance of Modern Cosmologies

Each theory that we have examined says something about the origin of the Universe, in so far as it speaks of either a moment of creation or an eternal Universe. Very often these theories create waves of great excitement when they appear on dailies and weeklies with catchy headlines, used either as religious apologetic or as anti-religious propaganda. How do we feel when we are told that Scientific investigation backs up Revelation? Do we heave a sigh of relief? And what is our reaction when we come across a theory which stresses that the World is eternal and therefore has no moment of creation, and hence no Creator too?

If our understanding of creation and Creator hangs in the air, we will surely panic. But, if we understand creation in its metaphysical sense, as a relation of total ontological (and not necessarily temporal) dependence of the creature on its Cause, then we will regard claims like, "no creation, no Creator (God)" as just hot air. Because "a relation of dependence would be compatible with either temporal arrangement: creator and creature coextensive, or creatures beginning with time." Thus, the point that George Soares makes is still quite valid: "the theological theses of God's existence and His creative activity are completely unaffected in any essential point whether we regard the Universe as evolving according to Lemaitre, or unchanging according to Hoyle."

We cannot therefore make a facile connection between the big bang theory and creation and use it as support for our religious beliefs. On the other hand, there is no need to be perturbed by claims that Universe is eternal, or that there is no initial moment of creation. The existence of God is not dependent on the beginning or eternity of the Universe. Modern cosmologies which speak about the origin of the Universe have no theistic implications, if we understand creation in its proper theological and Philosophical sense.

6.2.7 The Limits of Science

Science and Philosophy are quite distinct in their methodologies. Science studies quantitative correlations and not causes in the Philosophical sense. Studying the absolute cause of the Universe is beyond the scope of Science due to the self-imposed limitation of its method. Science cannot steep itself in metaphysical considerations such as the creation, contingency and purpose of the Universe. Scientists should hand over such considerations to Philosophy and thus avoid the vice of shifting terrains. "The Universe needed by Science is done a great injustice when it is mystified by Scientists who confuse questions of mathematical Physics with questions of metaphysics as if the tools of the former were appropriate for the latter." The method of Science precludes its raising questions about the *absolute* origin of the Universe. Empirical Science can neither raise nor answer the question, why is there something rather than nothing. Besides, "Science is absolutely powerless to show that any stage of material interaction is not reducible to a previous state, however hypothetical." This is a serious limitation because it brings to light the inability of Science to explain a direct creative act. It is beyond the power of Science to explain how something comes into being out of *nothing*. It is with utmost care therefore that we have to study questions which regard the Philosophical and theological implications of Scientific theories.

Chapter 7

Proposed Solution for Cosmology Conclusion

Does the Universe have any purpose? Is the emergence of life anything more than a cosmic accident? Was there any intelligence operative in the Universe prior to the appearance of man? Is life anything more than atoms and molecules? Is mind anything else than the result of complex movements of the physical and chemical components of the brain? Is there any divine influence present in nature? Is evolution moving in any meaningful direction? Do our individual lives have any ultimate significance in the unfathomable depths of cosmic time and space?

These are a few of the questions that modern Science has raised for those of us who believe or hope that there is indeed some final meaning to our lives in the Universe. These are not new questions. They have been with us for some time, and they have inspired a number of responses. But, many of these responses have been reactionary repudiations of Science itself. Others have been intellectually shallow. And still others have been intellectually inaccessible to sincere and able inquirers.

The present work is intended for any intelligent reader who by some acquaintance with the exciting discoveries of modern Science may have asked some of the questions raised above. I shall attempt to make presentable to such a questioner the view that our Universe is not without purpose and that there is absolutely nothing in the Scientific approach that contradicts the essence of a religious interpretation of reality. Instead there is much in Scientific discovery and speculation that may help us to understand religion in a new and adventurous way.

Let me confess at the very outset that I think it is possible to reconcile the human hope of some cosmic purpose with what modern Science has told us about nature. In a broad sense at least, religion is not opposed to Science. The essence of "religion" is a basic confidence that the "ultimate environment" of our lives is trustworthy and fulfilling rather than indifferent or hostile toward us. What I mean more specifically by this "ultimate environment" as an encompassing, transcendent sphere of redemptive care will have to await discussion at a later point. However, I think it is important to state clearly at the outset the direction in which I am moving. I am going to argue that there is nothing in evolutionary theory, molecular biology or recent Physics, or any of the natural Sciences for that matter, that rules out a religious interpretation of the Universe in the sense that I have just described "religion." Furthermore, I think that the Sciences are completely congruous with religious symbolism and that we can restate the religious vision in a fresh manner by a study of the Universe of modern Science. In supporting these statements I do not think I will have to manipulate any of the commonly accepted ideas presented by the Sciences. I am deeply respectful toward, indeed in awe of, what Science has produced especially in the decades since Darwin's *Origin of Species* was published (1859). And I have no intention of trying to force Scientific discoveries to conform to the religious hypothesis. I cannot, nor can anyone else, give a Scientific demonstration of the validity of the religious hypothesis.

It must be acknowledged that religious assertions are not verifiable or falsifiable, at least in the same manner as Scientific propositions are. The religious conviction that the Universe is at heart, in its transcendent depths, a graceful, caring, enlivening environment is in a different order of discourse from Scientific hypothesis concerning, for example, how species evolved or how matter is converted into energy. So, regardless of how one would assess the truth-status of religious ideas, they do not fall neatly within the realm of propositions that we associate with Science.

However, we are forced to ask earnestly today: is this intuition of cosmic care consistent with the findings of modern Science? And if so, how? If our Universe is influenced by any cosmic purpose, how would we know it and what shape would it take in nature and history? These are the questions we must address.

If indeed there is a transcendent ground of cosmic purpose we must humbly admit that we could not get our minds around it in any secure or final fashion, it would "comprehend" us, but we would not be able to comprehend it. And yet, in some mode of consciousness or other, our minds would have to make contact with this encompassing purpose, or it with us, if we are to talk about it at all. What would this mode of consciousness be, and what would be its relation to Scientific knowledge?

In spite of the spurious connotations the term will probably have for many readers, I shall use the word "faith" to refer to this non-comprehending intuition of ultimate meaning. I shall attempt to show that the word "faith" may be understood as the mode of consciousness whereby we open ourselves to being grasped by a more comprehensive dimension of reality than the mind itself can objectively master. It is a mode of consciousness which will inevitably arouse the suspicion of those who adhere to what has been called "the epistemology of control" according to which nothing may be called real unless it can be grasped objectively by the methods of Science. "Faith" requires the renunciation of the epistemology of control. And such asceticism is not very appealing within the contemporary academic setting. Therefore, I shall not be surprised if my reference to faith should evoke feelings of uneasiness in some readers even at this very early phase of our inquiry.

Still I cannot divorce my discussion of the Cosmos from considerations of the possible role of faith in opening up levels of reality otherwise inaccessible. Especially if our Universe is evolutionary and hierarchical, as I shall argue, the role of faith in making us aware of further possible emergent dimensions cannot be disregarded. Through "faith" our human consciousness acknowledges its limitedness and at the same time allows itself to be taken up into a higher or deeper dimension of reality wherein it is give its ultimate purpose in the scheme of things. Accordingly, if purpose is indeed a reality in our Universe, it lies beyond the control of both our ordinary and our ordinary and our Scientific modes of cognition. This would explain its elusiveness, its inaccessibility, its unobtrusiveness. There is, therefore, a certain wager or risk involved in our entrusting ourselves to a teleological (purposeful) vision of things. For we may never hope to lay out the nature of this vision, be it with the same degree of clarity and certitude, which we set forth our Scientific judgments about nature. We simply cannot "master" any supposed teleological dimension into Cosmos, and so we may be tempted to turn away altogether from consideration of this possibility. I think Science is correct in its methodical exclusion of teleological hypotheses from its own rendition of the Universe. For if a teleological dimension does exist it would lie beyond the objectifying, controlling technique of Scientific knowing.

Let us therefore take a look at the Christian Philosophers who have paved the path to understand Cosmos in a unique and important way.

7.1 Whiteheadian Aesthetical Approach of the Cosmos

The vital question is whether Scientific knowing is the only legitimate mode of knowing. Or is there room for faith? John Haught proposes that a hierarchical view of the Universe will allow us to clarify how faith and Scientific knowledge can coexist and complement each other in our Universe. But, he makes no pretense of exposing clearly and distinctly what nature's purpose may be. In the final analysis, as Alfred North Whitehead (1861-1947), teaches us, clarity and distinctness do not necessarily give us reality in its fundamental and concrete aspects. Perhaps we need symbols and myths to put us in touch with reality in its deeper dimensions. This is the wager he proposes that we take.

The central issue in Science and religion today is whether nature in its evolution has no purpose or ultimate meaning. All the other questions that cluster around the topic of Science and religion converge on that of nature and purpose. Questions such as whether the language of "faith" has any authority in a Scientific age, or whether mind and life are reducible to atoms and molecules, whether only the tangible is real, whether the human person is anything more than a complex physico-chemical mechanism, whether we are free or determined, whether there is no "objective" truth to the symbols and myths of religion-all of these questions are asked at all only because what is fundamentally at issue is whether there is an ultimate context that gives meaning to cosmic process and significance to our lives in this process. It is questionable whether our own lives can be seriously taken as deeply meaningful unless the cosmic context of these lives is itself imbued with purpose. Thus, the problem of nature and purpose is not merely an academic one; it flows from our deepest and most personal concerns as to whether we really belong to the Universe, or rather must awaken to our utter solitude, our "fundamental isolation."

Several decades ago, the American Philosopher, W.T. Stace (1886-1967), wrote that religion, "...can get on with any sort of astronomy, geology, biology, and Physics. But, it cannot get on with a purposeless and senseless World. If the scheme of things is purposeless and meaningless, then the life of man is purposeless and meaningless too. Everything is futile; all effort is in the end worthless."

For some time, however, influential Scientific thinkers have insisted that the findings of astronomy, geology, and biology and Physics rule out the hypothesis of cosmic purpose, or at least render it very dubious. If they are correct, then religion, no matter how lyrical or comforting, has no basis in reality and should be abandoned by all honest, truth-loving persons. Science seems to have made questionable any religious affirmation of ultimate meaning.

Haught agrees with Stace that the central issue is that of cosmic purpose. Unless there is some purpose to the "scheme of things" it seems doubtful whether the individual can consistently and coherently attribute meaning to his or her own existence either. The Universe must somehow support us if our own will to meaning is to find any satisfaction. I find it difficult to understand those Philosophers who hold that the individual's life can have meaning even if the Universe as a whole is void of purpose. If our environing context is indifferent or hostile to us, I do not see how we have a chance of salvaging any ultimately satisfying meaning for ourselves. We are so intricately connected with our Universe that any "simple location" of our own existence, any setting it apart from the totality in which we are embedded, will surely skew our self-understanding. And if the Universe to which Science says we are organically tied is pervasively purposeless, how can our individual lives avoid being infected by the insignificance that runs through the whole?

7.1.1 Klemke's Meaning of a Purposeful Cosmology

And yet there are some Philosophers who hold that our chances for personal meaning are not jeopardized, but are even enhanced, by our living in a purposeless Universe. E.D. Klemke, just to give one recent but representative example, clearly illustrates this point of view. He begins by observing that there is no "evidence" for any purpose in the Universe:

From the standpoint of present evidence, evaluational components such as meaning or purpose are not to be found in the Universe as objective aspects of it. Such values are the result of human evaluation. With respect to them, we must say that the Universe is valueless: it is we who evaluate, upon the basis of our subjective preferences. Hence, we do not discover values such as meaning to be inherent within the Universe. Rather, we "impose" such values upon the Universe.

And in a spirit of honesty Klemke gives us the epistemology (that is, the view of what constitutes true knowledge) which undergirds his skepticism about meaning in the Universe:

> "...I here maintain what I hold throughout the rest of my existence, both Philosophically and simply as a living person. I can accept only what is comprehensible to me; i.e., that which is within the province of actual or possible experience, or that for which I find some sound reasons or evidence. Upon these grounds, I must reject any notion of meaning which is bound with the necessity of faith in some mysterious, utterly unknowable entity. If my life should turn out to be less happy thereby, then I shall have to endure it as such."

As Shaw once said: The fact that a believer is happier than a skeptic is no more to the point than the fact that a drunken man is happier than a sober one. The happiness of credulity is a cheap and dangerous quality.

I admire this statement for its clarity and the intellectual honesty that underlies it. If indeed it is true that there is no ultimate purpose to things, then we should face up to this fact, no matter how much it hurts. (Here I shall not pursue the question as to why we should do so.) But, then Klemke goes on, with his usual pointedness, to express the view which I would like the reader to ponder: "An objective meaning – that is, one which is inherent within the Universe or dependent upon external agencies – would, frankly, leave me cold. It would not be mine. It would be an outer, neutral thing, rather than an inner, dynamic achievement."

Klemke is an adequate representative of those who argue for the meaningfulness of the individual's life even thought the Universe may be empty of meaning itself. Therefore, any attempt to construct a vision of the Universe (a Cosmology) in which there is some over-arching meaning (teleology) must address itself to the kinds of claims Klemke is making. Haught briefly isolates three of these claims and their deeper implications of which I shall pose it as in the remainder of this chapter.

First there is an epistemological assumption that we should give our assent to no proposition unless there is adequate experiential (empirical and Scientific) evidence for it or unless it is capable of being "comprehended." Ofcourse, the proposition that the Universe is meaningful is indeed unreceptive to experiential verification and falsification. Therefore, Klemke discards teleology as unacceptable. In this hierarchical view we shall acknowledge that a higher level may comprehend a lower, but a lower, but a lower cannot comprehend a higher. If purpose is intrinsic to a hierarchical Universe, then it would, be located at a higher level than that of human consciousness. Thus, it would by nature be beyond our conscious comprehension. The obvious question, then, is whether Klemke's epistemological assumption that all of reality must be accessible to our human faculties of comprehension is necessarily appropriate to the nature of the Universe. Should there in fact exist a teleological dimension to the Cosmos, comprehension (in the sense of getting our minds around something) could not occur. Instead what I earlier called "faith" would be the appropriate stance of consciousness with respect to ultimate meaning. Faith is an attitude of acknowledging the limits of comprehension and of opening ourselves to being comprehended by that which transcends us. To make our own intellectual possessiveness the criterion of all that is real is an example of the "epistemology of control." And as Huston Smith has stated: "An epistemology that aims relentlessly at control rules out the possibility of transcendence in principle."

Klemke holds that ultimate meaning is beyond comprehension (beyond verification or falsification). Thus, far I would not care to argue, though what precisely is meant by "ultimate meaning" or by "verification" could be more carefully pondered. What I am most concerned with is the inference Klemke draws from his observations on the elusiveness of any hypothetical ultimate meaning: if it cannot be comprehended, then its reality is in question. Behind this proposition there lies the assumption that the human mind is the highest level in the cosmic hierarchy. By a "hierarchical Cosmos" I mean a Universe in which there is a multiplicity of systems, levels, dimensions or fields so arranged that the higher or greater exercise an integrating and organizing influence over the components that constitute the subordinate levels. For example, the living cell organizes and integrates the subsidiary molecules in what is an obviously "hierarchical" fashion. The human mind exercises a hierarchically integrating influence over the biological, neurological, and chemical processes in the brain and body. Klemke, like many modern Philosophers, assumes that there are no higher organizing and integrating fields of influence more comprehensive than the human mind. And it is to this point of view that much of the speculation and reflection in the present book will be addressed. How do we know that our own minds are not superseded by, transcended by and comprehended by a still higher level (or by higher levels)? How do we know that we do not live in a hierarchical Universe in which our consciousness is not the supreme organizational field?

It makes all the difference in the World, as we speculate on the issue of nature and purpose, where we locate our human highest level or is it perhaps relatively low on a cosmic scale of gradations of comprehending dimensions? Because of its bearing on the question of purpose, therefore, much of this paper will focus on the feasibility and legitimacy of hierarchical thinking. Consequently, I shall repeatedly make reference to what I shall call the "hierarchical principle" as the axiom to guide our reflections. This principle is formulated as follows: a higher level can comprehend a lower, but the lower cannot comprehend the higher.

A striking aspect of Klemke's position is his assertion that the Universe is inherently valueless. Klemke is consistent when he claims; therefore, the Universe is purposeless. For what renders a process purposeful is its orientation toward value. And where there are no value-oriented occurrences there can be no ultimate meaning. What is interesting about the claim that the Universe is intrinsically valueless is that this view is usually rooted in speculation influenced by modern Science. It is true that ancient Greek atomists excluded any final cause (any ultimate goal or good) in their explanation of the Cosmos, and ancient tragedy also questioned whether the Universe is purposeful. But, with the exception of a few skeptics, prior to the seventeenth century most Philosophy as well as religion treated the Universe as inherently value-laden. What rendered it valuable was the commonly accepted view that it was permeated by Mind, Intelligence, Reason, Logos, Torah, God, Spirit, and Presence. The Cosmos, as Jacob Needleman (1934-?) puts it, was perceived as a teaching. And the proper response to this instructive Cosmos, itself seen as the embodiment of Wisdom, was a reverential obedience. The individual's mind was seen as a microcosmic version of the Cosmic Mind, and so the authentic life for the individual required his or her attunement to the intelligence of the cosmic totality. The idea that the Universe is intrinsically valueless was the last thought that could have occurred to traditional minds.

Whatever happened that makes it possible now for Philosophers like Klemke to state with such ingenuousness that the Cosmos is intrinsically devoid of value, and therefore of purpose? Clearly it is the expulsion of mind from the cosmic totality and its relegation to our individual craniums. It has been pointed out that prior to the Enlightenment; the human mind was seen as a mirror of the Cosmos. That is, its function was to reflect the intelligibility and value that are intrinsic to the Universe. After the Enlightenment, however, it is perhaps best envisaged as a lamp. The human mind is the source of, rather than a reflection of, whatever meaning exists. If mind exists at all today (and some question whether it has any intrinsic reality because of its intangibility) it resides locally and tenuously only in our brains. According to some modern Scientific thinkers there was no mind in the Cosmos at all prior to the emergence of man in evolution. G.G Simpson (1902-1984), the famous biologist of evolution, for example, starkly implies this conclusion: "Man is the result of a purposeless and natural process that did not have him in mind. He was not planned. Man plans and has purposes. Plan, purpose, goal, all absent in evolution to this point, enter with the coming of man and are inherent in the new evolution which is confined to him."

Discovery that the Universe apart from man or before his coming lacks and lacked any purpose or plan has the inevitable corollary that the workings of the Universe cannot provide any automatic, universal, eternal, or absolute ethical criteria of right and wrong. If the Universe is itself mindless, then it cannot provide a basis for our valuations. Our own minds are left isolated, stranded in a strange and hostile environment which offers no support in our own quest for meaning. Our minds, unaided and alone, have to illuminate the Cosmos which itself is void of light.

What happened that brought about this sense that mind and Cosmos are alien to one another? Was it simply the rise of Science in the last three centuries? Certainly Science has given us pictures of vast tracts of lifeless and unconscious space. Physics, astronomy, chemistry and geology as well as biology have considerably altered our cosmographies. Science has methodically excluded consideration of value and purpose from the field of its inquiry. Moreover, it deals with the quantitative more than the qualitative aspects of thins. It abstracts altogether from those questions which interest us "existentially," such as what, if any, is the meaning of our lives. For these reasons we may legitimately suspect that Science has been a major factor in the turn away from teleology. Stace, whom I quoted earlier, even goes so far as to put the whole burden of modernity's turn away from belief in cosmic purpose on the seventeenth century's preoccupation with "how" questions to the exclusion of 'why" questions:

> The real turning point between the medieval age of faith and the modern age of unfaith came when the Scientists of the seventeenth century turned their backs upon what used to be called "final causes." The final cause of a thing or event meant the purpose which it was supposed to serve in the Universe, its cosmic purpose. What lay back of this was the presupposition that there is a cosmic order or plan, and that everything that exists could in the last analysis be explained in

terms of its place in this cosmic plan, that is, in terms of its purpose.

Though Galileo, Kepler and Newton did not personally deny the reality of purpose, Stace insists that they made this notion useless in terms of what Science aims at, "namely prediction and control." Science turned exclusively to the search for material and mechanical causes and turned its back on final causes. Hence, increasingly modern thought, affected by the methods of Scientific inquiry, has issued us a picture of the Universe in which purpose plays no part. Stace continues: "You can draw a sharp line across the history of Europe dividing it into two epochs of very unequal length. The line passes through the life time of Galileo. European man before Galileo-whether ancient pagan or more recent Christian thought of the World as controlled by plan and purpose. After Galileo European man thinks of it as utterly purposeless."

Even allowing for some rhetorical exaggeration by Stace, Haught thinks we must dig much deeper than he has to find the fundamental causes of the picture of a Universe void of value, mind and purpose. Prior to the emergence of modern Science, the roots of its disengagement of nature from mind and value were already present in our Western cultural heritage. These roots go deep down into ancient mythologies that have for centuries nurtured our philosophies and spiritualities. It is not surprising that what we call "modern Science" should also have failed to escape their nourishing influence. Haught refers especially to the myth of dualism. And I think some understanding of dualistic mythology, Philosophy and psychology may help explain the case of which Stace is speaking and the divorce of mind from nature that gives Klemke's ideas their essential structure.

Dualism is the mythic, religious or Philosophical view that separates spirit from matter and mind from body. A mythical version of dualistic thinking may be found in what Paul Ricoeur calls the 'myth of the exiled soul." This myth, like most important myths, is a theodicy. It is an attempt to explain where evil comes from and how we may escape from it. It came to expression in ancient Orphism, Manichaeism, Gnostism, and Zoroastrianism and has persisted down through the centuries in religious and Philosophical forms of expression. It tells of how the soul, having its origin in the World of the spirit, strays here below into the (evil) realm of matter. The soul takes up a temporary dwelling in a "body" which functions as a prison and as the source of evil desires and suffering. Recognizing its distinct status, the soul ideally resists being absorbed into the bodily casing derived from inferior matter. Through various forms of ascetism, renunciation of instinct, contemplation of the spiritual and ideal, and eventually through death, the soul migrates back to its original home.

This is a powerful and touching myth, not least because it gives a rather tidy answer to the perennial human problem of suffering and evil. It is also appealing because it preserves the sense of our special significance over against the material World. It is not remarkable, therefore, that his myth has been so durable throughout our history, including the history of ideas. In antiquity, Plato, and, at the beginning of the modern age, Descartes, stand out as the best known figures in the history of Philosophical dualism. Numerous thinkers have been shaped by this Platonic-Cartesian tradition. Recently, for example, one of its most outspoken contemporary apologists, Hywel D. Lewis (1910-1992), has recapitulated the argument on behalf of dualism. Lewis states that there is a radical difference between mental states and physical states and that the essence of dualism consists in this distinction. Dualism explains why we spontaneously value sentient and conscious beings more than inanimate objects, namely, because there is an added higher component in the former that does not exist in the latter: "...we seem compelled to recognize some reality which cannot be itself described in strictly physical terms, however close the involvement may be with material conditions. It is for these reasons that we speak of cruelty to animals but not to pieces of wood or stone...This is the obvious divide from which dualism takes its course." Furthermore, dualism gives legitimacy to what we call "inner" experience. It provides a basis for the sense of freedom and dignity without which a genuine humanism would collapse. So numerous are its advantages that Lewis wonders why anyone would challenge dualism. Gilbert Ryles' (1900-1976), famous critique of dualism, for example, is unsatisfactory since in the final analysis it differs little from the old-fashioned materialism of behaviorists like J.B. Watson (1878-1958), for whom distinct "inner" states of awareness do not exist. In general, it is "irritating" to Lewis that so many distinguished Philosophers fail to recognize the appropriateness of "the Platonic-Cartesian way." Our own experience of our sentience and consciousness should be enough to vindicate the dualistic position.

Yet I must emphasize that while dualism seeks to preserve the core of our humanness from being lost in matter, ironically it prepares the way for the materialist interpretation of the World it seeks to avoid in the first place. For by placing the soul or mind in a sphere radically different from that of physical reality, dualism abandons the physical Universe to the realm of the spiritless and mindless. And it is fundamentally the mindlessness of nature that renders it incapable of sustaining purpose.

Ofcourse, one may imagine, as did the natural theologians of the eighteenth centuries, that a divine mechanic situated outside of the mindless World-machine could manipulatively direct it in a "purposive" way. But, this view itself collapsed eventually because it was not a truly teleological one. If the World of nature is radically purposeful it is not sufficient that its purpose be extrinsic to it. Instead any teleological influence must be felt intimately by all aspects of the World. This means that the fundamental constituents of nature must have built into them a quality of receptivity to transcendent meaning that would allow them to be brought into the sphere of influence of any supposed universal teleological principle. The name Haught gives to this hypothesized quality of receptivity to meaning is "mentality." We can ask whether it is scientifically and Philosophically legitimate to attribute "mentality" to every aspect of the Universe. Haught's position is that unless the Universe is pervasively "mental" there would be no possibility of nay global meaning taking up residence within it. For this reason a critique of the dualism which separates mentality from the physical Universe by exiling it to the sphere of human consciousness must be the first step in any effort to present a teleological picture of the Universe.

The consequences of the dualistic siphoning of mind from nature are not terribly dramatic until the age of Science. For in archaic and ancient settings reality seemed to be almost completely permeated with a spirit of vitality. Rivers, plants, the earth, humanity, the climate – the entire environment – gave the impression of being saturated with life. Panvitalism according to Hans Jonas (1903-1993), was the common view; where there was an apparent absence of vitality, as in a corpse there was a tendency to deny the reality of any dead matter and to look upon death itself as an illusion. But, once Science uncovered the pervasive lifelessness of the physical Universe, and pointed out how precariously infinitesimal is the quantity of life and mind, then more dramatic consequences began to flow from our dualistic heritage. Mind and life are now experienced as strangers, as anomalies, as accidents, that have erupted on a landscape of deadness and mindlessness that is unsympathetic with or at the most neutral toward them. Having segregated mind from matter, spirit from the body, and life from the inert, dualism bequeaths to us a new problematic that has given contemporary Science its characteristic methodological ideal. Instead of being confronted with the ancient problem of how to explain death if everything around us exudes life, we now have to apologize for the precarious fact of life (and consciousness) if everything around us in our Universe is intrinsically dead and mindless. Jonas elaborates on this ironic twist of problematics:

> "Death is the natural thing, life the problem. From the physical Science there spread over the conception of all existence an ontology whose model entity is pure matter, stripped of all features of life. What at the animistic stage was not even discovered has in the meantime conquered the vision of reality, entirely ousting its counterpart. The tremendously enlarged Universe of modern Cosmology is conceived a field of

> inanimate masses and forces which operate according to the laws of inertia and of quantitative distribution in space. This denuded substratum of all reality could only be arrived at through a progressive expurgation of vital features from the physical record and through strict abstention from projecting into its image our own felt aliveness."

This means that the lifeless has become the knowable par excellence and is for that reason also considered the true and only foundation of reality. It is the "natural" as well as the original state of things. Not only in terms of relative quantity but also in terms of ontological genuineness, nonlife is the rule, life the puzzling exception in physical existence. As a result of this inverted theoretical situation, Jonas concludes "...it is the existence of life within a mechanical Universe which now calls for an explanation, and explanation has to be in terms of the lifeless."

The explanation of the "living" in terms of non-living stuff has become the ideal of much modern Scientific inquiry. It is obvious to many, for example, that biology is reducible to Physics and chemistry, and, therefore, that life is reducible to inanimate matter. The amazing advances in molecular biology blur the traditional hierarchical distinctions between man, animal, plant and mineral; and the neurophysiological "explanation" of human consciousness in terms of the components and machinations of the brain even more dramatically illustrates how pure "matter' has assumed dominance in any attempt to make sense of our Universe and its manifestations.

It is the dualism of soul anybody, spirit and nature, mind and matter that has made possible the shift of problematics from that of how to explain death if everything is alive, to that of how to explain life if everything is dead. Dualism is the pivotal mythic and Philosophical construct on which this inversion has turned. While dualism may have been an important factor in our coming to vivid awareness of the faculty of mentality which makes us aware of our special status into World, it has simultaneously purged nature outside of ourselves of the qualities of mind and aliveness that we experience in the subtlety of our own conscious activity. It has therefore exorcised the Cosmos for the mentality without which it would remain imperious to any deep incarnation of transcendent meaning. It has given rise to what Paul Tillich (1886-1965), has called an "ontology of death." Anything that is not part of our subjective experience is relegated to a World "out there" and is denuded of the vitality associated with thought and experience. This World outside of our own minds is then envisaged as inhabited only by dead, inert and passive material objects.

The bifurcation of reality into two such disparate regions culminated in Descartes' noted distinction of *res cogitans* (minds) and *res extensa* (matter). The influence of the dualistic myth and metaphysics on the birth and growth of modern Science has been amply documented. It is enough only to point out that the inertness bequeathed to matter by dualism has become the basis upon which the quantification of physical reality and motion in Newtonian and Cartesian Physics has been constructed. And perhaps we may even say that without the dualistic premise modern Science as we know it could not have developed as rapidly as it has.

It is also true, though, that dualism still lurks behind the dominant contemporary philosophies of nature in which matter remains essentially mindless and lifeless. It is dualism that, in the final analysis, provides the background for the present day attempts to specify or explain biotic and conscious operations in terms of the Sciences (Physics and chemistry) the deal with the allegedly inanimate. Without the sphere of unconscious and lifeless chunks of matter delineated by dualism such a methodological ideal (which animates current efforts especially in biology to find the physico-chemical "secret" of life) could hardly have taken hold in modern Scientific thought. In a curious way we owe a great deal to what is perhaps a serious mistake in Cosmology.

Standing at the end of the history of this dualism it is easy for us to see why any attribution of "mentality" (and therefore of purposefulness) to nature will be dismissed as romantic anthropomorphism by Philosophers like Klemke. By expelling anything that resembles feeling, experience or perceptivity from the fundamental "building-blocks" of nature, modern thought has also eliminated the possibility of attributing purpose to the Universe. It has rightly recognized that without a vein of "mentality" in the Universe there can be no purpose either. And so, by rejecting the alliance of nature and mind, it has removed to that extent the feasibility of our searching for purpose in the World of nature. For where there is no dimension of "mind" there can be no implantation of aim or purpose either.

In turn, the rejection of a teleological Universe has led in many cases to doubt about any human purpose whatsoever. Needless to say, there has been a close connection all along between the modern experience of meaninglessness and the development of the picture of an impersonal Universe that gives no backing to our projects. The same dualistic myths that have made us feel exceptional have also led to our sense of alienation from nature and purpose.

It is possible in theory to anticipate, therefore, the enormous implications that a new alliance of nature and mind might have for the contemporary crisis of meaning. Nothing less imposing than the significance of our lives is bound up with the quest for a union of mind and nature established on solid grounds compatible with reason, common sense and Science. If we could grasp somehow that our subjectivity is a blossoming forth of nature itself, and not some enigmatic "nothingness" or separate substance over against nature, we would have at least the context in which to discuss once again the question of nature and purpose.

The basis for a synthetic vision of mind and nature is worked out most comprehensively by Whitehead, and we shall investigate his ideas in an introductory fashion.

There is yet a third element in Klemke's proposal. It is his optimism that we can tolerate and accommodate ourselves to a purposeless Universe. It is his bold post-Enlightenment assertion that teaches of us as individuals is capable of suffusing our lives with whatever meaning we need. In fact, Klemke holds, the more naked the Universe is of purpose the less interference we would have from it in forging our own meanings. Whatever meaning traditional myth, Philosophy and religion saw in the Cosmos, we now recognize as the creations or projections of the people hat inhabited it. We should now, in the spirit of modernity, fully acknowledge and accept our own creative role in such projections. We should give credit where credit is due – to ourselves. The individual is radically responsible for his or her own life's meaning since the Universe has no help to offer on this score.

Again, the way toward this kind of thinking was paved by dualism. It is the irrepressible presence of dualism that allows us to think that our mental activity is not really a part of or continuous with nature. Dualistic mythology is the cultural backdrop for Klemke's Cartesian-Sartrean sense of his mind's being in a separate ontological category from mindless nature. And like Sartre, Camus, Russell and other cosmic pessimists before him, Klemke seems unaware of the tenacious hold that the dualistic way of organizing the World may have over his consciousness. In the pages that follow I shall give considerable attention to the way in which the dualistic separation of value from the Universe has structured the whole repeatedly question whether we are required to adapt ourselves to the dualistic mythology that has been such a powerful influence in the history of culture and thought.

In order to entertain the hypothesis that there is cosmic purpose one must assume that nature and mind are somehow interwoven. If the Universe of nature were completely void of what we shall call "mentality," it would not be capable of receiving or sustaining any intelligible orientation toward value, that is, any purpose. Once physical reality has been pictured as impermeable to mind, the stage is already set for estranging the individual from the Universe, for divorcing purpose from nature. On such a stage there appears the modern Philosophy of Scientific materialism.

7.1.2 Rejection of Scientific Materialism in Purposeful Cosmology

We are left, therefore, with three parallel sets of questions:

- Is life reducible to atoms and molecules?

- Is mind reducible to brain, which in turn is composed of atoms and molecules?
- Is the Universe as a whole reducible to mindless matter?

Scientific materialism is the Philosophy of nature which answers "yes" to all three questions. As defined by one of its contemporary defenders, Harvard's Edward O. Wilson (1929-?), Scientific materialism is "...the view that all phenomena in the Universe, including the human mind, have a material basis, are subject to the same physical laws, and can be most deeply understood by Scientific analysis." Obviously any teleological interpretation is thereby excluded in principle. Scientific materialism holds that any true and meaningful knowledge that we may gain about life, mind and Universe can be gotten only through the analytical methods of Science. Everything else is where speculation if not wishful thinking. Oparin's ten-volume history of the World is a chronicle of the reshuffling of atoms and molecules rather than the story of a World's struggle toward the realization of value or purpose.

Scientific materialists look upon life and mind as "epiphenomena," that is, as secondary and derivative rather than "really real" in themselves. The only real "phenomena" are the "physical" components that make up all tings. Even those organisms that act as though they are "alive" or as though they are "thinking" are purely material. Aliveness and thought have no intrinsic reality themselves. They owe their flimsy and precarious "existence" to the combinations of atoms, molecules and cells that make up living and thinking organisms. Living and thinking are simply ways in which pure "matter" acts in certain complex combinations. The fundamental components of living and thinking entities, however, are themselves inanimate and unconscious. Reality, in the fundamental sense, is utterly void of life and mind. And if that is so, then it is also without purpose.

In Science and the modern World, Alfred North Whitehead wrote of the Scientific materialism stemming from the seventeenth century: It has held its own as the guiding principle of Scientific studies ever since. It is still reigning. Every university in the World organizes itself in accordance with it. No alternative system or organizing the pursuit of Scientific truth has been suggested. It is not only reigning, but it is without a rival. And yet-it is quite unbelievable. This conception of the Universe is surely framed in terms of high abstractions and the paradox only arises because we have mistaken our abstractions for concrete realities.

Scientific materialism, according to Whitehead, is a misrepresentation of the Cosmos because it is based on the "fallacy of misplaced concreteness." This fallacy of misplaced concreteness is simply the confusion of abstractions with concrete reality. It is the tendency to take our mental constructs and imaginative models of the World, such as those of the machine, wave or particle, as though they corresponded exactly to the World itself. This is an understandable temptation since we have to simplify things in order even to begin to understand them. But, we do not always heed Whitehead's exhortation first to seek simplicity and then to mistrust it. We easily do the first, but tend to balk at the second. I would suggest that we fail to mistrust our over-simplifications for the same reasons that we are inclined toward the epistemology of control. Somehow and for some reason we fear giving up our sense of mastery over the Universe. But, we do so at great peril to our Cosmology and to our general vision of things.

Whitehead's critique of Scientific materialism is that it is too abstract. This indictment perhaps sounds strange, since if anything seems concrete it is the collection of allegedly irreducible particles of matter out of which nature is composed according to the materialist's Philosophy. What could be more concrete than atoms in the void? The elegant simplicity of the atomist Philosophy, or contemporary equivalents in an updated particle Physics or molecular biology, may easily seduce us into the assumption that bits of matter or indivisible mechanisms are the bedrock foundation of reality. And yet, on more careful analysis, they turn out to be "high abstractions."

Why do mindless chunks of matter not qualify for being the ultimate "concrete" constituents of nature? Simply because they are the product of the Scientific method's prescinding from certain aspects of the Universe with which it is incapable of dealing. These aspects that are left behind (by the use of the machine model and the still dominant particle model) are part of the concrete fabric of the Universe, and so any adequate Cosmology should advert to them as well. The neglected elements I am referring to are the "qualitative" aspects of things, aspects which escape the net of mechanistic and quantitative modes of understanding. More specifically they are the aspects of beauty, value and importance, none of which fall within the realm of ordinary Scientific discussion.

Of course, these aspects of the Universe that are left out of Scientific discussion will be looked upon by the materialist as epiphenomenal, as our own subjective desires projected onto the blank neutrality of the Universe. Value seems to fall within the same arena as the so-called "secondary qualitative" isolated by classical Physics and the Philosophy of John Locke (1632-1704). Secondary qualities are those aspects of things which seem to depend for their existence upon the perceiver. Colour, taste, smell, sound and touch all require an experiencing subject in which to reside, and so they apparently do not have any "objective" reality to them. They are derived only from the perceiver who cloaks the objects with secondary qualities. Meanwhile the object itself onto which the secondary qualities are projected is said to be made up of "primary qualities." Primary qualities are those features of objects allegedly exist independently of any experiencing subject. The object's mass, position and momentum, for example, do not seem to depend upon my being present to perceive them. They exist independently of my experience; they endure throughout the process of accidental changes, and, therefore, they seem to be more real, more concrete than the secondary qualities. Scientific materialism usually holds that primary qualities are the concretely real foundation of things and that secondary qualities are the frothy result of our projecting elements of unreliable subjectivity onto them.

The important implication of this distinction of primary from secondary qualities (itself rooted in the mind/matter dualism which we looked at earlier) is that it provides the cosmological basis for a denial that there is any intrinsic meaning in the Universe independent of meaning – creating individuals. It has become very easy after the seventeenth century to situate the whole notion of meaning or value in the same context as secondary qualities. The values that we cherish and that give our lives whatever meaning they may have seem to depend for their precarious existence upon the sensitivity of evaluators. Our sense of the importance of things, events, persons, and of the Universe itself, seems to share with secondary qualities the characteristic of being totally subjective and arbitrary. Accordingly meaning does not appear to be intrinsic to the Universe. The Cosmos seems inherently vacant of purpose, and teleology is apparently the mere product of our own valuations.

The restriction of value to the realm of subjectivity depends upon a prior separation of our consciousness from the Cosmos. This separation has recently been challenged not only by Philosophy but also by developments in Science itself. Hence, our discussion of the issue of purpose in the Universe must inquire about the possibility of some other assessment of the relation of mind to nature.

Whitehead has emphasized the continuity between our own becoming and that of physical reality. We are in utter continuity with the processive Universe. If we take this continuity seriously then we must abolish the dualistic tendency to read our mental activity as though it were not also part of the inner essence of nature. Scientific thought, under the impact of dualism, has simply assumed that mental occurrences are not part of the cosmic arena, that mentality and nature belong to completely different realms.

Haught suspects that most of us have been so influenced by dualism that we find it quite difficult to think of our mental activity as part of the occurrences that make up nature. We somehow feel that our minds are outside of nature. And this feeling of mental exile is understandable as long as we conceive of nature itself as mindlessness of nature that Whitehead asks us to question. Any absolutely clear line of demarcation that segregates our mental functioning from its cosmic matrix is purely arbitrary-indeed an illusion, a vestige of dualistic mythology.

Scientific materialism itself denies that there are no arbitrary breaks in nature. Everything is not a continuum with everything else. Everything that exists is explicable in terms of the mass-energy plenum. Our mental processes are also in principle fully explicable in terms of matter and energy. Seemingly, therefore, materialists are monists, since for them reality is reducible to the one realm of the physical. They apparently reject any dualism that would give to mind a separate ontological status. However, although they are monists metaphysically speaking, in that they reduce reality to only one kind of stuff, they remain dualists in the epistemology, that is, in their view of knowledge. They demand that we be objective in our understanding of nature, and this objectivity requires that we keep our subjectivity detached from the object, nature. The Scientist's own mind must remain at a distance from the object being investigated in order that an "objective" [perspective become possible]. This divorce of the Scientific subject's mind from the object being examined amounts to an epistemological dualism.

Furthermore, materialism's epistemological dualism leaves open the door for the existential alienation of the subject from its cosmic context. It establishes a way of thinking that eventuates in the sense, expressed earlier by Klemke, that I am a stranger in an indifferent and hostile Universe. The epistemological dualism implicit Scientific materialism inevitably leads to the feeling that nature is without purpose and that my own conscious life lacks any grounding in the Universe.

The consensus of much recent thought, however, a great deal of it coming from physicists themselves, is that mind is intrinsic rather than extrinsic to nature. The Universe permeated not only with process but also with mentality. As in the ancient mythic visions, our own minds actually belong in the context of the Cosmos.

Physicist David Bohm (1917-1992), who dares to speculate on what he considers to be the Philosophical implications of modern Physics, asks whether thought itself might not be part of reality as a whole. He challenges us to ask: "...how are we to think coherently of a single, unbroken, flowing actuality of existence as a whole, containing both thought (consciousness) and external reality as we experience it?" To meet the challenge before us our notions of Cosmology and of the general nature of reality must have room in them to permit a consistent account of consciousness. Vice verse, our notions of consciousness must have room in them to understand what it means for its content to be "reality as a whole." The two sets of notions together should then be such as to allow for an understanding of how reality and consciousness are related.

Relativity theory and quantum Physics in the present century have given rise to a great deal of speculation like that of Bohm's much of this speculation has concluded that the Scientific observer is not a detached spectator dualistically split off from nature. Rather the observer is really a participant whose mental activity cannot be separated from, and indeed inevitably intersects with, the objects being investigated. Physics itself seems to have blurred the line drawn by dualism between subject and object.

A more Philosophical way to vanquish the dualism of mind and nature to see them both as aspects of a unified cosmic process in which all the components of becoming are "mental." According to Whitehead something analogous to what we experience as mentality, something like "feeling" or "perception," is present throughout the natural World, not just in man, animals and plants, but also in the most fundamental constituents of the physical World. There is a "subjective" aspect to all "actual entities." If we place matter and man on a continuum, one very fruitful way to understand ourselves is to do as far as possible by specifying our material make-up. But, it is also possible to understand a great deal about the nature of physical reality by beginning from the other end of the continuum. Since, matter and mind are, after all, on the same unbroken spectrum, we may understand each partially in terms of the other. For this reason an understanding of mentality and its activity is not superfluous to our understanding of the whole Universe. It is possible to understand a great deal about mind by analyzing it in terms of its molecular basis. It is also possible to reach a more concrete understanding of physical reality by recognizing its mental aspects. But, how can we maintain something so apparently anthropomorphic? For the very least mentality is by nature an experiential occurrence. And experience begins with feeling. When we say that the Universe is mental, that it is composed of moments of feeling, it obviously appears as though we are projecting our own human experience onto something which is non-experiential. Is this not an instance of the "pathetic fallacy"?

In response, we must first re-emphasize that we are using the terms mentality, feeling, experience, and perceptivity in an analogous sense. Something like what we call feeling, perceiving, remembering, desiring, anticipating, liking and disliking must characterize every constituent aspect of reality. This does not necessarily mean that rocks have feelings. Rather it means that all objects, including inanimate ones, are composed of moments or occasions which have feeling as a constituent aspect of their actuality. The World of process is made up of units of becoming whose very essence is feeling. As Charles Hartshorne (1897-2000), has suggested, it may be that feeling of feeling is a "...ultimate principle, applicable to deity and every other singular actuality."

Science, of course, is unable by itself to penetrate the inner privacy or "subjectivity" of the moments of feeling that makeup reality. Science always remains outside in its abstracting from the interiority of nature's constituent occasions of experience. And for that reason our terminology will inevitably sound foreign to those attuned to a Scientific idiom. Therefore, it will strain our credulity at first to be told that the most concrete things in nature are not dead, inert, mindless. But, how else would our World hang together as a Universe unless things have a feeling for one another? To posit a subjective capacity to feel at heart of all the moments that make up the cosmic process goes beyond the limits of Scientific ways of thinking, but it is not a position that in any way conflicts with a coherent Cosmology. Science, after all, usually deals with aggregates rather than with the fundamental units of reality of which I am speaking. And it is true, of course, that aggregates made up of concrete moments of feeling exhibit macroscopically inert qualities. A rock for example may legitimately be called inanimate and mindless. But, the ultimate components of rocks or grains of sand or molecules and atoms are series of occurrence bound together by a feeling for one another. These series of occasions of experience (as Whitehead calls them) build up into patterns which give the outward appearance to our dull senses of firmness and immobility. With our sense we are not able to perceive directly the dynamic dance of mutual feeling that constitutes the foundation of the apparent stability of things. But, it is reasonable to infer from the fact of nature's intrinsic continuity with our own mental experience that there must be at least a rudimentary type of feeling that binds all things to one another. What better word than "feeling" can we employ to indicate the power of attraction that binds the multiplicity of occasion into the organic unity of a Universe?

One of the most immediately obvious aspects of our experience is the sense of becoming. In fact it is so obvious that we seldom explicitly advert to it. But, if we reflect upon it now, and at the same time remember our continuity with the cosmic process, we will be able to clarify not only our own experience, but also essential aspects of the Cosmos itself.

Each moment of our lives is made up of becoming and perishing. Each moment is a "throb of experience" that comes into being, experiences a certain type of "enjoyment," and then perishes. Our personal lives are made up of a series of such becomings, enjoyments and perishings. Thus, each moment of "feeling" has a polar quality to it. One pole of memory reaches out and pulls in the past in a selectively qualifying manner. The other pole of anticipation reaches out into the realm of possibilities and selectively qualifies the present moment's mode of feeling. Each perishable occasion of our experience, therefore, is composed of memory-enjoyment-anticipation.

All of this may seem quite obvious to anyone who pauses to reflect on our humanly "mental" existence. What may not seem so obvious, however, is our suggestion that cosmic reality *is* in general composed of analogous types of occasions of experience. But, once we eschew dualism and accept the continuity of nature and mentality such a conclusion is not out of order.

The Scientific materialist usually attempts an explanation of phenomena exclusively in atomistic, molecular, macromolecular or genetic terms. Physico-chemical elements possess an empirical quality that can be expressed by way of pictures, models or mathematics. Its recondite nature, however, renders the idea of morphogenetic causation highly suspect. It appears simply too elusive to be given serious consideration by Science as such. Morphogenetic[2] fields have neither mass nor energy. And so to the materialist they do not seem to be part of the "real" World.

The absence of any direct empirical evidence of cosmic purpose is intricately linked with the lack of no immediately tangible evidence of morphogenetic fields that would exercise a causative influence on the formation of discrete systems in the natural World. It is nearly impossible for the mechanist to

---

2 "Morphogenesis" (from the Greek morphe=form, and genesis-birth, origin) means simply the process of something's coming-to-be according to a specific form. What, though, is meant by a morphogenetic "field"? The metaphor "field" is suggested by the effect that magnets or electromagnetic systems have on iron filings or on the entities that are non-contiguous with the magnetic source. And the notion of gravitational "fields" exercising influence across space has long been a major aspect of modern Science. In fact today the notion of "field" is often considered primary, while that of physical "body" is secondary to and derivative of field. After Einstein phenomena can no longer be explained in terms of energy alone: "...although energy can be regarded as the cause of change, the ordering of change depends on the spatial structure of the fields." So there is a well-established precedent for use of the term "field" in Scientific discourse. A morphogenetic field, then, would be the non-energetic context of causation that accounts for the origin and development of physical and biological forms.

conceive, let alone imagine, how something which is energetically passive and void of mass can be nonetheless real and influential. Yet I would suggest that cosmic teleology (whatever its specific nature), as well as morphogenetic causation in general, would share this trait of concealment.

7.1.3 Acceptance of Beauty in Purposeful Cosmology

Whitehead's Philosophy has to provide yet another way of thinking of our Universe in teleological terms. In both instances the kind of teleology being proposed is what must be called a "loose" teleology. Haught uses this expression, which has been taken over from Polanyi, in order to distance my approach from the restrictive opinion that the Universe has built into it some rigidly pre-determined destiny.

Haught think the best way of understanding cosmic purpose in our loose sense is to propose that it consists essentially in the aim toward beauty. Perhaps from the limitedness of our own perspective we can say no more, but at least we can say this much. An aesthetic notion of cosmic purpose is capable of embracing the mythic and religious representations of human aspiration as well as accommodating the modern Scientific understanding of the Universe. An aesthetic rendition of cosmic teleology allows us to speak of a pervasive cosmic aim without having to be too restrictive in specifying the exact goal toward which cosmic process may be oriented.

Within this very broad scheme centering on the notion of beauty it is still possible to entertain more specific proposals as to the ultimate meaning of things. For example, a number of teleological theories attempt to understand the cosmic process as one that aims toward the enhancement of consciousness. I have no objection to this teleological perspective. And there is increasing evidence from the Sciences that our Universe has evolved from rudimentary toward more intensely conscious structures. However, in Haught's writings he attempts to show that an aesthetic reading of cosmic purpose is more comprehensive than consciousness-oriented teleologies (such as that of Teilhard de Chardin). It is more comprehensive since it takes into account more caringly those segments of cosmic process that appear to us to be regressive, to move away from further enhancement of consciousness and away from the ideals we set up for our human existence. The Universe is not in every way directional in the manner we would perhaps like it to be. Thus, if we are to speak of cosmic purpose in a plausible way we must remain fully cognizant of the meandering and confusing nature of its evolutionary trajectory. Haught thinks an aesthetic perspective is comprehensive enough to accommodate and salvage all the waywardness of this evolutionary complexity.

The purpose of the Cosmos, then, is its aim toward beauty. How could such an aim render the cosmic process purposeful? In response to this question we must point out first of all that beauty is a value. And it is the struggle to realize value that makes any process purposeful. Thus, if the cosmic process is dominated by an urge toward realization of beauty, it may be called purposeful. The question though is whether and how we can understand value in aesthetic terms. We are so conditioned to think of value in moral or ethical terms that we may be bewildered by any attempt to express ultimate value in terms of criteria of beauty.

When critics of teleology reject the idea of purpose in the Universe their suspicions are almost always framed according to ethical criteria. For these critics the Universe is condemned for not corresponding in its behaviour to that of the ethical person: therefore, it is not good. If it is not ordered toward the ethical good, then it is not purposeful. In its evolution it displays a marked disregard for life, allowing all living beings and species eventually to pass into oblivion; and in its relentless laws of inertia and natural selection it exhibits crude indifference toward the dignity of persons. Nature seems to operate more by caprice, indifference or malice than by concern for its children. It is cruel experimenting with various forms of life in order eventually to discard them certainly makes it less than an adequate model for our won conduct. This is why Bertrand Russell (1872-1970), says that the Universe is unworthy of us. Our own goodness far outshines that of the Universe in which we live. How can such a Universe be purposeful?

If we were to evaluate the Universe purely in terms of ethical criteria of value we might be tempted toward cosmic pessimism. Even according to such ethical criteria, however, I think in all fairness we have to acknowledge the extent to which the Universe also manifests what we may call "care." For the most part the Universe sustains us instead of crushing us. Although the evidence is not unambiguous there is an aura of sustenance throughout nature. There are catastrophes of course, resulting from the varying degrees of hierarchical independence of one level from another. But, more remarkable than these episodes of chaos is the overall environing affirmation given to species and individuals. We cannot overlook this fact nor fail in gratitude toward it.

Even after making this qualification, however, Haught thinks that it is a mistake to argue for cosmic purpose on the grounds that the Cosmos conforms to our ethical ideal of care. For the fact is that this care is not all-pervasive. There are no guarantees for our safety. There is tragedy, suffering and death. There are logical and ethical contradictions in our Worldly experience. There are the absurd oppositions existing between life and death, growth and decay, pleasure and pain, ecstasy and sorrow, light and darkness, good and evil, order and chaos. It would be naïve to build a cosmological perspective without acknowledging these tragic conflicts.

The problem with the ethical perspective is that it cannot deal with these contradictions as such. It measures everything in terms of moral order and remains baffled by the chaotic. On the other hand an aesthetic perspective is quite at home in the realm of contradictions, for its very nature allows it to transform them into a harmony of contrasts. And Haught proposes that the caring aspect of the cosmic process can be better expressed in aesthetic than in ethical terms. Although, no doubt, an aesthetic understanding of cosmic order is less than adequate also, I think that it is superior to and broader than the ethical model as an approach to understanding what may be meant by cosmic order or purpose.

7.1.4 Appreciation of the Aesthetical Value in Understanding the Purposeful Cosmology

When we use the term "aesthetic" we are talking about beauty. Is it possible to put into words why things strike us as beautiful and why some things strike as more beautiful than others? Whitehead's thought provides the concepts for just such a clarification. First of all, beauty entails a synthesis of contrasts. Without contrasting elements there is sheer monotony, and monotony is not beautiful. At the same time beauty implies a resolution of contradiction or conflict, which requires harmoniousness or order that overrules chaos. When elements in pointing, poem or musical composition clash so as to destroy overall harmoniousness then the aesthetic quality of the work of art is diminished or lost. Therefore, we call beautiful any expression, entity or experience that transforms or resolves contradictions into contrasts. In order for such a resolution to take place, however, the conflicting elements must be situated within a framework of harmony that transcends and, therefore, softens the local clash of contradictory aspects. Within such a wider framework the localized disharmony can become a nuance that enriches the whole instead of a clash that destroys it.

Beauty, we have said, requires a harmony of contrasts. But, at times the harmony may tend to overrule the contrast and melt it down to homogeneity. When this occurs beauty has given way to monotony. The beautiful is threatened on two sides, by chaos on one side and no monotony or triviality on the other. Beauty is a balancing act between the extremes of chaos and banality. It is precarious, and therefore is precious. Beauty is a synthesis of harmony and complexity, order and novelty, stability and motion, form and dynamics.

Beauty is harmony of contrasts. Haught illustrates this point beginning with a very simple example. "When I simultaneously strike two adjacent keys on a piano the half-note interval between them causes a rather disharmonious, even unpleasant and unsatisfying sound to emerge. The sound amounts more to "noise" than to harmony, and so I would refrain from calling it beautiful. However, if in the course of playing a musical composition I strike the same two keys again simultaneously, then their local dissonance may actually contribute to the overall aesthetic intensity of the whole piece. The orderly patterning of sounds that makes up the whole musical composition resolves the local contradiction (dissonance) into an aesthetically satisfying contrast. This resolution of contradiction into contrast is of the essence of beauty."

A second example may be taken from *the art of painting*. "If I were to isolate a small segment of a great painting (say a few square inches) and prescind momentarily from the whole canvas, I would find in the fragment shades of color, texture and theme that added up to chaos or to monotony. In its isolation I would not find the fragment aesthetically satisfying. But, when I resituate this isolated segment back onto the whole painting I find that its formerly chaotic or monotonous qualities are resolved by the overall harmony and nuance into factors that contribute to the aesthetic value of the whole. A wider perspective can transform locally unaesthetic elements into aesthetic ones. There is no reason for us to reject the possibility that in a similar way the chaotic and monotonous episodes of all experience, ours as well as nature's in general, may also contribute to the value of the whole when viewed from a cosmic perspective (to which of course we do not ourselves have access)."

A third example may be derived from *literature*. "In reading a novel I may find that several episodes are independently developed early in the novel in such a way that they seem to have nothing to do with each other. Taken in themselves these fragments may appear either boring or unintelligible. I may find it a torture to go through them and may even be tempted to overlook them altogether. Yet by the time I reach the end of the novel I am glad I took the time to explore them. For in the final analysis the episodes which in themselves seemed monotonous our unintelligibly complex now enhance my appreciation of the novel as a whole. They have as significance and a connectedness when viewed from a wider perspective that they do not appear to have when I am too close to them."

Now from the Whiteheadian point of view the Cosmos is such an aesthetic reality. Both in its constituent occasions and in its overall reality the Universe a process of synthesizing and unifying its composite aspects into novel moments of present aesthetic "enjoyment." As each occasion feels its past it "orders" the diversity entering into it from the past into a novel feeling of aesthetic harmony and contrast. And as the creative advance of the Universe brings more and more novelty into the picture, the events of the past are continually given a new and unanticipated significance. As the sea of events that make up the Cosmos broadens and deepens, the meaning of each individual happening is itself intensified and widened. Its final meaning, therefore, cannot be determined form its own limited perspective any more than we can determine the meaning of the early episodes of a novel without reading it to the end.

The purpose of the Universe, therefore, cannot be adequately stated from within our own situatedness. We are ourselves part of the canvas. We are characters in the story. We do not have the perspective whereby to give a final assessment of our own significance, or that of any phase of evolution, in the total scheme of things. We may in part understand the idea of God, however, as the cosmic artist or story-teller by whom the significance of every event and every life is guaranteed, though we cannot articulate exactly in what this significance consists.

Thus, an aesthetic understanding of the Universe is able to express the religious sense that all things are "cared for" in an ultimate though hidden way. And it can do so more plausibly than can any ethical vision of things. The ethical vision is governed by the concern that justice be done, if possible here and how. And, of course, such concern is absolutely essential in the maintenance of civilization and the quality of life. Yet, as most great religious visionaries have themselves taught, the ethical vision is not ultimate. It must be transcended. Our ethical standards are not the final judge of the significance of things, neither of human lives nor of history, nor of the Universe. In placing the Cosmos in an aesthetic perspective we are following the impulse of a religious vision which acknowledges the inadequacy of our ethical criteria of good and evil. We must revision "good" and "evil" in an aesthetic manner and evaluate the Universe according to a deeper understanding of these usually ethically biased terms.

From an aesthetic perspective the goodness or value of an entity or event is measured by the degree to which contrasting elements are harmonized. The intensity of anything's value is determined by the extent to which its polar components are unified in an orderly pattern. Aesthetically understood, value entails a synthesis of complexity with order, novelty with continuity, nuance with harmony, richness with stability. An aesthetic pattern transforms these apparent contradictions into pleasing contrasts. And we spontaneously tend to value things that combine these contrasts more than we do things that are homogeneous and monotonous in their make-up. We appreciate the human brain more than we do a lump of clay because the brain integrates into an intense unity an incredible complexity, nuance, richness and novelty. Similarly we value art, literature and music in proportion to the intensity of their balancing nuance into satisfying contrasts. Somehow we sense that the complexity of a great work of art could easily have gotten out of control and undermined any efforts toward harmonizing its many facets into an intense unity. And so we inwardly applaud the precious achievement of balance and order when there are so many ingredients that could have led to imbalance and disorder. The more intense the aesthetic achievement, the more we value it.

The hero or genius arouses our admiration for essentially the same reasons as a work of art. Heroism, for example, is beautiful because it is the result of integrating a multiplicity of contrasting experiences (strength and frustration, joy and tragedy, rebellion and resignation, life and death) into the unity of a single person's story. Genius is beautiful because it requires the integration into a creative unity of a multiplicity of ideas, feelings and experiences that could lead to madness in a narrower personality. Because of the precarious nature of heroism and genius we esteem them more than the everyday modes of human existence. Similarly we might value a Universe in which contradictions are constantly being unified into an aesthetic whole: entropy and evolution; order and chaos; novelty and continuity; permanence and perishing.

7.1.5 Conclusion

The beauty toward which the Universe strives is enough to imbue it with purpose. Yet from the limited vantage point that I occupy in this evolving World it often seems that discord is more prominent than harmony. Much of my immediate environment is unintelligible. And as I extend my imagination and questioning beyond my situation outward toward the Universe I become even more bewildered by what it is all about. I may be tempted to take my own confusion and project it onto the Universe. I may read my own intellectual, moral, and especially aesthetic insensitivity into the Cosmos as a whole. I may see the Cosmos as lacking purpose.

However, the aesthetic model of cosmic purpose suggests that my own experience may be lacking in perspective. Perhaps, there is a vantage point on the Universe that I do not have, given the confines of my own extremely limited situation. I cannot exclude the possibility that my own experience is only an infinitesimal segment of a universal canvas, only a fragmentary movement in a cosmic composition, a brief episode in nature's narrative. For perhaps there is a wider angle of vision on the Universe to which I do not myself have access. Perhaps, this wider perspective, lying hierarchically above my own level of comprehension, is able to unify into an aesthetic whole those contradictions, monotonies and absurdities that deem most insurmountable. Perhaps, from this perspective my life has significance, a purpose, a meaning which I cannot grasp hold of in controlling manner. Perhaps, though, if I risk the surrender to such a possibility I may feel, even here and now, a portion of the peace that comes with the resolution of contradictions into contrasts. I may feel perhaps only briefly and episodically the beauty toward which the Universe tends, the beauty of which I am only a small but significant part.

7.2 Teilhardian Christological Approach of the Cosmos

7.2.1 The Universe as Ordered Unity

Precisely because the cosmic Body model is so central an element in Teilhard's thought, it is profoundly interrelated with other key elements. Indeed, it draws these other elements together and assimilates them so that they become substantive for the model itself. One such element is the theme that the Cosmos is a "unity," a "totum," an "organized whole," a "kind of gigantic 'atom,'" a "great organism." Whole, organism, and Body so clearly interrelate and converge, that Teilhard uses the categories interchangeably – and cosmological vision of organic unity merges with Christological experience.

A. Teilhard's Vision of Cosmic Unity

Teilhard was "an enthusiast of Unity," a man "driven by the passion for unity … to create unity where pluralistic fragmentation appears to reign supreme." But, if Teilhard was always in quest of unity, it was because he had, at the level of religious experience, already found it. We have already discussed the mystical ground of Teilhard's theology of the Universe (Christosphere – in the historical background), but it is well to recall here the intuitional character specifically of his theme of the organic unity of the Universe. Wildiers notes this deep origin of Teilhard's speculation:

> Undoubtedly, a salient feature of the picture which Teilhard… presented of the World is its closely knit internal coherence. What apparently gave it birth was a single initial intuition, which came to him at an early stage and attained greater depth and outreach as the years passed and as Teilhard tested it against his experience. He detected in the Cosmos as a whole an awe-inspiring and thorough going coherence, a profound organizational unity in which everything is bound up with everything and takes its *raison d'être* from its place within the whole.

In treating of the organic unity of the Cosmos Teilhard rarely resorts to speculative demonstration; he tries rather to evoke a certain religious insight or intuition, and he seems to know in advance that he will succeed in some cases and fail in others. He insists that he himself "can glimpse, or sense, a global Reality whose condition is that of being more necessary, more consistent, richer and more certain in its ways, than any of the particular things it embraces." But, "there are basically two types of mind, and only two: those who do not go beyond ...perception of the multiple ... and those for whom perception of this same, multiple is necessarily completed in some unity." "Those who do not see and those who do, Teilhard goes on to call these two groups. Seeing is, in fact, the key source for his theology of the Universe. What he writes of *The Phenomenon of Man* applies to all his writings: "This work may be summed up as an attempt *to see* and *to make others see*... Seeing. We might say that the whole of life lies in that verb – if not ultimately, at least essentially." What of those who reject the radical unity of the World, who opt for pluralism, ho do not *see?* For Teilhard such an option is not just a subjective disposition; rather, he sees pluralism as negative and non-productive, whereas monism *affirms,* opens the way for action. Monism, moreover, is grounded objectively in the actual organic unity of the World and sustained subjectively by an illumination, an intuition of this unity.

"It is precisely the value of this primordial intuition" which he feels sustains "the whole edifice of my belief." Surely this sort of affirmation raises the whole thorny issue of the nature-grace relationship. In this context, however, we want only to stress how fundamental for Teilhard is his commitment to the organic totality of the Universe, and how directly this commitment carries him toward his basic theological-spiritual model of the cosmic Body of Christ. Although Teilhard never provides a systematic treatment of his "cosmic sense" or intuition, he does offer some powerful and suggestive reflections regarding its parallel with the intuition of love, and he insists that all men are endowed with this "faculty" or "sense:"

> There is nothing astonishing, after all, in the existence of this "cosmic sense." Because he is endowed with sex, man undoubtedly has intuitions of love. Because he is an element, surely he must in some obscure way feel the attraction of the Universe. In fact, nothing in the vast and polymorphous domain of mysticism (religious, poetical, social, and Scientific) can be explained without the hypothesis of such a faculty.

If, as Teilhard goes on to maintain, one is monist by the very fact of being a man; if the "cosmic sense" is an "essential temperament" and a natural faculty, one may wonder why Teilhard invokes the need for *faith* and *conversion* for its exercise. It could be said, in reply, that the "faith" he demands is of a wholly subordinate and natural kind, but such and interpretation (though it would obviate some thorny problems) would seem to be ruled out by the famous opening lines of *Comment je crois* (How I Think):

> If, as a result of some interior revolution, I were to lose in succession my faith in Christ, my faith in a personal God, and my faith in Spirit, I feel that I should continue *to believe* invincibly *in the World*. The World (its value, its infallibility and its goodness) – that, when all is said and done, is the first, the last, and the only things in which I believe. It is by this faith that I live. And it is to this faith, I feel, that at the moment of death, rising above all doubts, I shall surrender myself.

Needless to say, a great deal of ink has been expended upon the explanation of this passage. Published attacks against the work began in Teilhard's own lifetime, and he himself addressed himself to its defense. For present purposes, two points seem to emerge from a consideration of the text which concerns us.

First, whatever else may be expressed or implied, the passage reveals how important the category of "Universe" is for Teilhard – how profoundly rich, seminal, and organic is his cosmological conception. De Lubac (1896-1991), whose emphasis is always on the primacy of the supernatural and the Christological in Teilhard, acknowledges the prominence and breadth of the Universe concept as revealed specifically by its organic character.

To appreciate Teilhard's thought at this stage, it is not enough to state that the World, in which the apologist expresses his faith, is incomparably richer and greater than that accepted by the unbeliever when both apologist and unbeliever set out on their common search. Nor is it sufficient to say that this World is richer and greater than the ordinary Universe of Science; or that this Universe of personal beings is something quite different from what most men generally understand by "Cosmos." The Teilhardian Universe... is richer and greater than that which the Christian himself generally envisages, when by a habitual methodical abstraction, he thinks only of the first result of the creation, adopting only the "natural" point of view of a Philosophy of the spirit.

The second point is that if such eulogies to faith in the Universe are to be given the orthodox Christian interpretation Teilhard insists they deserve, then the faith involved must be both open to and joined to a specifically "supernatural" faith in Christ's transforming action on the Universe. But, this is simply to repeat that Teilhard's concept of the Universe's organic unity directly implies his model of the Universe as Christ's cosmic Body. The latter model does not, then, stands alone; but neither does the former. The unity of the Universe is ultimately the Pleroma of Christ. As de Lubac astutely observes, the "primordial intuition" Teilhard speaks of is literally "primordial" – i.e., a starting point and not the whole picture. The faith he tries to evoke is faith "in its most wrapped-up form," and not a fully explicit Christian faith. What Teilhard is trying to do is evoke in us a very fundamental intuition of the Universe as Whole; only as we go on, with him, on the further steps to the completion of his vision, will this important starting point unfold and find its needed fulfillment in the vision of the Universe as Christ's cosmic Body.

B. The Great Option for the Whole

Every man has a deep, mysterious sense of the Whole. But, Teilhard sees this intuition as requiring an active response or commitment on man's part. We have seen him call this response "faith," but we must take care not to understand the "faith" in question in too intellectualist a way. Like Blondel, Teilhard stresses that it is a full, personal choice, of the sort that reorients one's whole life not only of thought but also of action.

This option is doubly vital in the context of Teilhard's evolutionary vision because man is seen not only as opting for a pre-existent unity, but also as summoned to achieve it – to carry cosmic unity forward towards its future consummation. This option therefore has crucial implications for every dimension (social and political, religious and economic) of human and thus cosmic existence:

> Pluralism or…Monism? This is the ultimate choice, by way of which mankind must finally be divided, knowing its own mind. In the view of the "pluralist" the World is moving in the direction of dispersal and therefore of growing autonomy of its separate elements. For each individual, the business, the duty and the interest of life consists in achieving, *in opposition to others*, his own utmost uniqueness and personal freedom….But, to the eyes of the "monist" the precise opposite is the case: nothing exists or finally matters except the Whole. For the elements of the World to become absorbed within themselves by separation from others, by isolation, is a fundamental error…. So the question can finally be posed… to fulfil ourselves individually by egotistically segregating ourselves from the mass; or to plunge resolutely into the stream of the whole in order to be incorporated therein.

Notice how Teilhard assigns an anthropological dimension to the Universe: man and World are not juxtaposed, but the latter finds its fulfillment in the former. At a still deeper level, the Universe is Christic, however, and not merely anthropological. Man commits himself to the unity of the Universe because the Universe is man's and man himself must be one; but beyond that, the Universe is Christ's, and Christ has made it one.

The profoundly religious ground of Teilhard's thought is clearly in evidence even here, at what seems to be its most "natural" level. Otto might be describing Teilhard when he writes of the mysticism of "unifying vision" which "looks upon the World of things in its multiplicity, and in contrast to this leaps to an 'intuition' or a 'knowledge' [wherein] the One itself becomes the object of intuition as that which is superior and prior to the many…."

As Ramsey notes, the language used to recount this sort of religious experience is geared to evoking a cosmic insight and dedication: So we see religious commitment as a total commitment to a whole Universe; something in relation to which argument has only a very odd function; its purpose being to tell such a tale as evokes the "insight," the "discernment" from which commitment follows as a response.

Certainly Teilhard wishes ultimately to speak to the deeper religious level in man, but this is not to say that his assertion of a fundamental unity of the Universe has meaning only on an ethereal level for an elite circle of illuminati. Teilhard's apostolate undoubtedly included a more empirical, concrete type of thinker, and he thus sought to vindicate in a great variety of ways the profound unity of the Universe.

C. Unity as Scientific-Philosophical Presupposition

Teilhard suggests that the underlying unity of the Universe may be not only a terminal insight of the matured thinker, but also a necessary starting point for the most elementary forms of reasoning. When a housewife, confronted by a puzzling quirk in her vacuum cleaner, spontaneously assumes that there is a natural cause – the cord poorly plugged in, or the nozzle clogged – she is but implicitly assuming that one phenomenon is decidedly related to another, that things don't just spontaneously "happen" in isolation. All of Science is based upon the same "presupposition." Teilhard is emphatic: On the pain of being irreducible to Scientific thought, everything must plunge its empirical roots into an indefinite past and into the entire area of its own present: this is the postulate which we find at the basis of all modern Scientific research. And elsewhere, for the fundamental unity of the Universe and the inexorable interconnection and interaction of the cosmic elements…preclude any new being from emerging into our experience otherwise than in function of all the present and past states of the empirical World.

Thus, there is built into modern man's very thought processes a "demand for the unity of knowledge and being," a demand which requires and presupposes the internal nexus of all phenomena of the Universe. But, does this requirement pertain to the very structure of man's knowing process, or does it simply emerge in modern times with the advent, e.g., of evolutionism? Teilhard's primary concern is never with speculative epistemological issues, but he does at times suggest that the latter is the correct explanation: Formerly we were not too surprised by the sudden addition of atom to the cosmic mass, or by its sudden displacement across space. Today we no longer doubt that the existence of a molecule of hydrogen, for example, and its localization at a given point in the Universe has required the immensity of a whole astral evolution.

Wildiers vividly contrasts the newer organic conception with the former, more mechanistic one. "Science," he concludes, "has gradually made it more and more clear that all entities are interconnected, so that we can now see the World as mighty, organic whole, in which every single thing is related to everything else." This shift from mechanical to organic model is crucial, of course, for Teilhard's insight into the Universe as cosmic Body of Christ. Were the Universe a mere machine, Christ's redemptive role might more easily be conceived as a liberation of Christian souls *from* such a mechanism (or, more positively, as a "lordship" of proprietorship over the machine viewed as a sort of stage-setting for man's spiritual drama) But, if the Universe includes man and is understood in the light of the organism model, then the Incarnation must relate Christ to all things, and his redemptive recapitulation must encompass the whole Cosmos. If man is to be integrally saved, then a Universe must be saved. And if the Universe is conceived of more as organism than as mechanism, Teilhard's cosmic Body model will appear not as theologically bizarre but rather as most relevant, appropriate, and fulfilling. It is clear, in any case, that for Teilhard the organic unity of the Universe appears as a necessary "presupposition" of modern Science. But, is it *only* a "presupposition"?

D. Unity as Verified by Science

Teilhard argues that this organic unity we have been talking about seems in our day to be "definitely accepted by the human mind." But, what is the justification of this acceptance? Is it merely a matter of positing an arbitrary "presupposition" or hypothesis which somehow finds broad consensus? Teilhard is convinced rather that this outlook has been justified by the findings of Science - and also by the coherence it brings to human knowledge: We shall never abandon these concepts again, but explore them, on the contrary, to increasing depth because we have been both drawn and driven to them by the full force of human thought for many centuries: and also because, once they are accepted, reality is found to grow clearer and more orderly so far as the eye can see.

Similarly, writing of evolution as "revealing the *irreversible coherence* of all that exists," Teilhard considered the problem of those who still rejected the concept: One might well become impatient or lose heart at the sight of so many minds (and not mediocre ones either) remaining today still closed to the idea of evolution, if the whole of history were not there to pledge to us that a truth once seen, even by a single mind, always ends up by imposing itself on the totality of human consciousness. Teilhard, then, regards the radical unity of the Universe as not only hypothesis but strongly verified by the physical and biological Sciences. We cannot, of course, embark on a technical investigation of these areas; but they are so essential to Teilhard's argument that we must at least advert to some major aspects here.

The data of Science verifies his unified vision, Teilhard insists, in terms of both the "spatial vector" and the "temporal vector" of the Universe. Indeed, these two factors themselves become conjoined in cosmic evolution: "Time and space are organically joined again so as to weave, together, the Stuff of the Universe." Regarding the "spatial vector," the realm of particular interest to the physicist, Teilhard stresses the physical interaction of the various elements of the Universe and the homogeneity of its structure. He speaks of a *fundamental* unity which matter proclaims the more insistently as we try to split and pulverize it artificially: of a unity of *similarity* unveiled by chemical and physical descriptions of its particles; and of a unity of *homogeneity* in virtue of which any particle can be explained only in terms of all the others. Because of this unity of homogeneity and the interaction of all the elements, Teilhard treats of the sum of the matter in the Universe as *one* reality - "Total Matter:" Consider in its physical, concrete reality, the Stuff of the Universe cannot divide itself but, as a kind of gigantic "atom," it forms in its totality ... the only real indivisible... the Cosmos in which man finds himself caught up constitutes, by reason of the unimpeachable wholeness of its whole, a *system,* a *totum* and a *quantum.*

Under the rubric of "system," Teilhard considers the Universe in its aspect of a number of elements marvelously ordered, thoroughly interdependent in a hierarchical, structured whole. He insists that this "systematic" quality of the Universe is attested by the "facts" of Science: "The existence of 'System' in the World is at once obvious to every observer of nature", he asserts, and then he goes on to describe that "System" in some detail. "It is impossible to cut into the network," he concludes, "to isolate a portion without it becoming frayed and unraveled at all its edges." The only way we can take it is "as a whole, in one piece." But, Teilhard stresses, the Universe is not constituted by the mere repetition of a single basic pattern on varying scales, such as

Pascal had suggested. There is, on the contrary, but one Universe in which there obtains a continuously varied interrelation; the only key unit of the Whole is the Whole. He explicitly rejects the conception of matter by analogy with the crystal, observing that matter never repeats its different combinations. Such vivid and emphatic reflections, well worth reading in full, are not without implication for anthropology (and thus for Christology); clearly even man's most spiritual functions are deeply rooted in the material, for "thought itself has need of a certain organic support, which is a function of certain physico-chemical conditions." Thus, Teilhard wishes to substantiate his cosmological vision, at least in part, by recourse to the data of Physics and chemistry. Competent judgment on this endeavor rests, of course, with thoroughly trained Scientists who are also steeped in the rich complexities of Teilhard's unified vision. Many followers of Teilhard will insist with Coffy, that the unity disclosed by Science is "not a matter of imaginary vision or poetic dreams," but "a physical reality," and indeed Scientific progress seems all the more clearly to vindicate such a position, as a few examples serve to indicate.

Consider, first, the recently discovered "quasar" phenomena. Quasars are quasi-stellar radio sources so distant that their light and radio waves seem to have taken billions of years to reach us. Thus, in viewing them we may be looking back in time perhaps to the infancy of the Universe, studying phenomena at a very remote distance in the Cosmos. Teilhard argues, in the second place, that the same basic physical elements and forces obtain throughout the Universe. The prominent physicist Robert Jastrow (1925-2008), corroborates this claim, observing that it is remarkable that all objects in the Universe from the smallest nucleus to the largest galaxy, are held together by only three fundamental forces – a nuclear force, the force of electromagnetism, and the force of gravity.

"All objects in the Universe hold together", he continues, according to certain constant forces; and they are built up by the same elements. And since "each atom exerts a small gravitational attraction on its neighbor," the Universe is a web of interaction and influence at the fundamental level of its elements. Even though a Scientist might be puzzled by some of Teilhard's more poetic phrases, therefore, he would certainly agree that the Universe is best conceived as woven together into a single extraordinary whole. Perhaps most of us in our day-to-day lives tend to look upon the various objects of our experience as thoroughly individual and juxtaposed. The World of Physics, as well as the thought of Teilhard, invites us to a deeper view.

E. Unity as Evolution

From the foregoing discussion of the "spatial" dimension, let us turn to Teilhard's much more emphatic insistence on the temporal, evolutive dimension. This is, as Crespy observes, the "first of the great Teilhardian insights," that *"Time is the vector along which a World organizes itself."*

In fact, the temporal and spatial vectors are not, for Teilhard, juxtaposed; they are brought together by the force of cosmic evolution into the organic totality: The least molecule is, in nature and in position, a function of the whole sidereal process, and the least of the protozoa is structurally so knit into the web of life that its existence cannot be hypothetically annihilated without *ipso facto* undoing the whole network of the biosphere. *The distribution, succession, and solidarity of objects are born from their concrescence in a common genesis.* Time and space are organically joined again so as to weave, together, the Stuff of the Universe.

This insight sums up, for Teilhard, not only his own vision but also what he sees as the new consciousness of mankind:

> A first point which emerges for me with a forcefulness that I cannot even dream of questioning, is that the Unity of the World is by its nature dynamic or evolutive. Here I am simply meeting in myself… the discovery of Duration which for the last century has so profoundly been modifying mankind's former consciousness of the Universe. Besides space, so staggering to Pascal, we

> now have time – not a container-time in which years are stored, but an organic time which is measured by the development of global reality. We used to look upon ourselves and the things around us as "points" closed in on themselves. We now see beings as threadless fibers, woven into a universal process.... Through its history, every being is co-extensive with the whole of duration; and its ontogenesis is no more that the infinitesimal element of a cosmogenesis in which is ultimately expressed the individuality – the face, we might say – of the Universe.

Teilhard is looking beyond the immediate descent of living species, then, to the broader scale of the evolving course of the Universe. Such a conception achieves the organic totalization of all things not on a spatial plane but in terms of cosmic past and cosmic future.

Teilhard understands his concept of cosmic, evolutionary cohesion to be well grounded, moreover, in Scientific data. He is proposing not only a "mystical intuition," not only a working presupposition, but a Scientific concept which he feels can claim significant Scientific verification. Not that all Scientists (particularly in his day) would agree; not that many particular points of difference would not arise. But, in its basic affirmation of evolutionary cohesion on a cosmic scale, Teilhard's position does accord with that of most Scientists today. As Jastrow notes, "a single thread of evidence runs from the atom and the nucleus through the formation of stars and planets to the complexities of the living organism." After a vivid and detailed account of cosmic evolution, he concludes that "man's history began billions of years before the solar system itself was formed; it began in a swirling cloud primordial hydrogen."

The common sense perspective which fragments the Universe into a disparate collection of self-enclosed entities thus clashes as much with the Scientific World-view as it does with Teilhard's vision. "The more one heeds the invitations to analyze urged on one by contemporary thought and Science," Teilhard observes:

> The more one feels imprisoned in the network of cosmic inter-relationships. Through criticism of knowledge, the subject becomes continually more closely identified with the most distant reaches of a Universe which it can know only by becoming to some degree one body with it. Through biology...the living being becomes more and more in series with whole web of the biosphere. Through Physics, a boundless homogeneity and solidarity is brought to light in the layers of matter. "Everything holds together." Expressed in this elementary form, faith in the World does not differ noticeably from the acceptance of a Scientific truth.

F. A Philosophy of Cosmic Unity

Of course it is not just on the level of Science that Teilhard advances his concept of the Universe as a cohesive, dynamic Whole. He also proposes a comprehensive, though not technically elaborated, "Philosophy of creative union." In considering the vast spectrum of Philosophical issues, he seeks "to reduce everything to the notion of union," and he aspires thereby to transcend the traditional antinomies: Thus, those innumerable difficulties vanish which every Philosophy comes up against that tries to reconstruct the World from isolated elements...instead of affirming the principle of the fundamental and substantial unity of the Universe.

Teilhard sought the ultimate ground for his "metaphysics of union" in the unification of the Divine Persons. In Trinitarian theology, he observes, we begin by presupposing God's existence as self-sufficient "supreme Being." But, for God to exist in total independence as origin and goal of everything else, it must be further assumed (in conformity with the data of revelation)...that this Center [God] is constituted by internal Trinitarian relations. In this way, the ontological principle upon which our metaphysics is based is seen to hold good even at the most profound and indeed primordial level of being: God himself, in a rigorously real sense, exists only through a process of self-unification. It cannot be our purpose here to consider the problem of founding "metaphysics" on Trinitarian doctrine, or of deducing from "ontology" the distinction of Divine persons. If such a scheme seems to overemphasize God's "self-unification" at the expense of the distinction of Persons – a tendency Eastern theologians perceive in Western theology generally – it should be noted that Teilhard is discussing, not precisely the unity of the divine nature, but rather the dynamic "self-unification" of the Persons' inner life, a notion which perhaps finds parallel in the rich Eastern theme of circumincession.

The central Teilhardian theme that "union differentiates" receives a particularly profound elucidation in this conception of the triune Godhead, "archetype of creation." New cogency is imparted to the truth that the unity of the Universe heightens rather than dissolves the unique identities of the elements. Teilhard's Philosophy of the unity of the Universe is, at any rate, deeply and solidly rooted "at the most profound and indeed primordial level of being." If the "Philosophy of creative union" is ultimately Trinitarian; if the unification of the Universe is but an image of the primordial unification of the Trinity, this can only be because there intercedes the key mediating archetype of the Body of Christ. The organic unity of the Cosmos is fundamentally Christic:

> The reader will have already seen for some time that the Philosophy of creative union is simply the development, the generalization, the extension to the entire Universe of what the Church teaches us concerning the growth of Christ. *It is the Universe conceived in function of the notion of the mystical Body.* It was in reflecting upon the mystical Body that I discovered the theory of creative union, and it is only so that it can be understood; by striving to love and hold Christ in all things.

So Teilhard's organic Cosmology is rooted in a Christology as well as a Trinitarian theology. It is also buttressed with his own peculiar ontology of being as unity, nothingness as disunity:

> Of every being we know it is true to say that the more it is divides, the less existence it has…. By dispersing, a being is annihilated. It vanishes in plurality….From all eternity God saw beneath his feet the scattered shadow of his Unity…. It was then that the superabundant Unity of life engaged, through the creation, in battle with the non-existing Multiple…. *So far as we can see, to create is to condense, concentrate, organize – to unify.*

Here two points seem to emerge which are both compelling and unambiguous. First, for a Universe dynamically evolving, the mystery of creation is more correctly formulated as a continuing process, than as an act of the past which once for all brought into existence a variety of creatures substantially the same as today. That is, the World is best seen as "in process of being created through a gradual unification of multiplicity." Secondly, the concept of being is intimately bound up with that of unity. Teilhard's is a position which Thomas Aquinas would certainly have endorsed: *ens et unum convertuntur* – being and the one are interchangeable. But, given an evolutionary Universe, Teilhard felt that this fundamental metaphysical truth needed a correspondingly dynamic expression: the more elements become unified in the course of their development, the more they attain, as it were, to being. This is a basic principle of Teilhard's implicit ontology: the greater the organic unity, the fuller the being:

Creative union is the theory that accepts this proposition: in the present evolutionary phase of the Cosmos (the only phase known to us), everything happens as though the One were formed by successive unifications of the Multiple – and as though the One were more perfect in direct proportion to its capacity to center within itself in a more perfect way at larger multiplicity. Then Teilhard spontaneously invokes the body-soul model to explicate his ontology: For the elements grouped together by the soul into the body (and by that very fact raised to a higher level of being)… "To be more is to be more fully united with more." For the soul itself, the principle of unity [is]… "To be more is more fully to unite more." For both, to receive or to communicate union is to undergo the creative influence of God… "Who creates by uniting." This has interesting implications for Teilhard's theological Cosmology and his Christology. If the order of grace does not destroy, but fulfills that of nature; if the Universe is destined to attain a full Christian realization, then it must be shaped into a Whole, an organic union in Christ. On the Christological side, if Christ's Body is to be totally fulfilled; if it is not to appear constricted and deficient in the cosmic context, then it must contain a maximum of cosmic elements – *plus esse est plura unire.*

Teilhard's theology of the cosmic Body springs organically out of his basic concept of being as maximum dynamic unity, and of truth as maximum universal coherence:

> "…the more I have thought about the magnificent cosmic attributes lavished by St. Paul on the risen Christ… the more clearly have I realized that Christianity takes on its full value only when extended (as I find it rewarding to do) to cosmic dimensions…. The more I think about it, the less I can see any criterion for truth other than the establishment of a growing maximum of universal coherence. Such an achievement has something *objective* about it, going beyond the effects of temperament."

In the Teilhardian Philosophical vision, being and truth thus find their elucidation through the categories of union and wholeness. The vision is profoundly affirmative. As the "greater," the "Whole," is vindicated, there is also asserted the primacy of supreme consciousness within that "Whole": Before embarking on a synthetic exposition of the Philosophy that supports and gives organic form to the building up of my moral and religious constructions, it may be well to bring out a number of fundamental principles or postulates in which can be seen the "spirit" in which my representation of the Universe has been conceived and in which it has developed.

i. The Primacy of Consciousness

Logically and psychologically, the first of these principles is the profound conviction that being is good: in other words.

that it is better to be than not to be;
that it is better to be more than to be less.

If we accept as an auxiliary principle that "complete" being is conscious being, then we may express this principle in a clearer and more practical form, as follows:

that it is better to be conscious than not to be conscious.
that it is better to be more conscious than less conscious.

We have here the great Teilhardian vision of hierarchical levels in the ascending, dynamic Whole: "The Universe organizes itself in a single, grand progression, somewhat untidy no doubt, but on the whole clear in its orientation, ascending from the most rudimentary atom to the highest form of living things."

This evolutionary dynamic has a direction, of course, and a scale is provided for assessing the relative value of the different elements of the Universe. This scale is constituted by rating the degree of bio-chemical complexity of the various elements, which has a "relationship of concomitance" to the level of consciousness attainable. And this coefficient of complexity "enables us to establish, among the natural units which it has helped us to 'identify' and isolate, a system of classification that is …natural and universal." Teilhard's "law of complexity-consciousness" has been subjected to much analysis and evaluation. For present purposes it suffices to note that the principle posits a Universe that is ordered and hierarchical. It affirms, moreover, that the phenomena of life and consciousness do not stand in contradiction to the rest of creation but rather rise out of a general potency of the Whole and lead to its more rigorous centration. Life, as Smulders observes,

"Becomes the supreme form of the fabric of the Cosmos, in which a fundamental law [that of]...interiorizing complexification, manifests itself at its utmost pitch with unrivalled clarity.... For life, especially human life, tinged as it is with both, the material and the spiritual, is not an anomaly in the fabric of the Cosmos; it is rather the actualization and crown of a fundamental property of that whole fabric, namely, complexification."

If man were seen as simply an alien in this World; if human consciousness were conceived as an anomaly for the Cosmos, then the organic wholeness of the Universe and its "physical" unification in Christ would appear as thoroughly bizarre concepts. But, if man and consciousness are seen as actualizing and unifying fundamental potencies of the Universe as such, then the notion of a further, decisive centration of the humanized Universe in Christ appears as an appropriated theological fulfillment of the whole of creation.

How is the Universe actuated, fulfilled, rendered whole? In the passage just cited we see the image of a unifying *fabric*; to this is often added the complementary, equally basic image of a unifying *center*. And since evolution is conceived as convergent – as conic – an additional model of totalization is proposed: that of a unifying *apex*. In this manner, the Universe is totalized by human consciousness, which binds together, centers, and crowns the whole thrust of cosmic evolution. But, humanity can fulfill this totalizing function only in an imperfect, relative, and proximate way, for men themselves must be brought together, must find a common center, and must seek a common goal. Converging evolution reaches a key new threshold in mankind, it is true; but mankind is simply, in Gray's perceptive phrase, "a new multiplicity to be united." Mankind is "a new multiplicity in search of unity, a new matter in search of spirit, a new body in search of a soul."

Of course it is Christ whom Teilhard affirms as the definitive unifier of the Cosmos. Utilizing a great variety of models, Teilhard proposes Christ as cosmic center and milieu, as quasi-formal cause, as soul of the Universe, as its substantial bond, it's Omega, its head, etc. The Universe is rendered organically unified in Christ. But, one cannot neatly compartmentalize Teilhard's thought, and we must note here that when Teilhard is sketching his Philosophy of creative union, he is already proposing a Cosmos that is radically anthropological and Christological – a Universe which is the Body of Christ: "The Philosophy of creative union is simply…*the Philosophy of the Universe conceived in function of the notion of the mystical Body.*" For "the full significance of the theory of creative union is to be found in the doctrine of the Body of Christ."

7.2.2 The Universe as Intrinsically Christic

The cosmic Body model, as we have seen, assimilates and fulfills the key Teilhardian theme of the Universe as ordered unity. Another even more prominent theme, that of the Universe as intrinsically Christic, also finds its focus in the cosmic Body model, and thus it completes the theme of unity: the Universe becomes organic whole specifically in Christ.

Teilhard repeatedly affirms that Christ binds the Universe to himself not by mere juridical title or extrinsic lordship, but rather intrinsically, "physically," "ontologically." Creation occurs in Christ and for Christ, who exercises exemplary and even quasi-formal causality over the whole. By his Incarnation, Jesus decisively unifies and assimilates the entire Cosmos. The Redemption extends in its efficacy beyond individual souls to the Universe itself, even more decisively unifying it, "super-creating" it in Christ. Creation, Incarnation, and Redemption: Teilhard directly applies all three dimensions of the Christian mystery to the Universe, thus investing them with cosmic scope and binding the Universe intrinsically to Christ.

The cosmic Body model expresses this unified, intrinsically Christic character of the Universe in a particularly striking manner, but other themes such as Christ the "animator," the "form" and "head" of the Universe, also underline, each with its own emphasis, the intrinsically Christic character of the Universe. As we have observed, these themes have been analyzed frequently for their specifically Christological significance; but they must also be studied as theology of the Universe. Cosmic Christology implies Christic Cosmology: "My road ahead seems clearly marked out; it is a matter not of superimposing Christ on the World but of 'panChristising' the Universe."

Although Teilhard never provides a fully elaborated systematic theology of the Universe in its Christic dimension, he does offer a suggestive sketch of many elements of such a theology. This sketch constitutes the speculative, abstract level which is nourished and concretized by his key model of Christ's cosmic Body.

A. The Universe as Created in Christ

Teilhard was always deeply interested in the mystery of creation. In 1918, he wrote:

> I've also felt that the problem of creation, looked at not in its present (evolutive) phase but in its first (involutive), is taking on increasing importance in my mind. What is the origin of the lower multiple? What "need" is filled by the fundamental fragmentation of being – driven from its source before returning to it? Until this problem is more or less coherently cleared up, one can't, I think, understand the worth of souls and the value of the Incarnation.

The ambiguous and problematic character of Teilhard's thought on creation is well known. Some have charged that he falsely presents matter as "eternal in itself" and the creative process as a shaping by God of pre-existing realities, like a struggle "between the One and the multiple…reminiscent of those Babylonian cosmologies…." Some decry what appears to them as necessitarianism, but others argue for the "essential orthodoxy, if not always the mode of expression, of Teilhard's argument," and they cite Teilhard's "oft-repeated intention to remain strictly within the framework of the Christian doctrine of creation…." Our interest in this intricate web of problems is limited to determining features of relevance to Teilhard's basic commitment to the

Christic dimension of the Universe. The key issue for Teilhard in analyzing the creative act is precisely the *interconnection* or relationship between God and the World. He wants to get at that relationship in a way that transcends the traditional category of efficient causality. He wants, as he put it, prayerfully to examine "the zone *where God and the Cosmos meet,"* and this "zone" is the cosmic Body of Christ.

A moment ago reference was made to alleged necessitarianism in Teilhard. It is true that he does not consider creation to be an arbitrary whim – a matter of sheer indifference to God. He does see God as "needing" creation in the sense that it mysteriously completes the Pleroma or Body of Christ. But, the "necessity" involved is the same as that involved in traditional Scotist theology: given that God wants his "masterpiece" (the Incarnate Word), a Universe is needed as context. As Teilhard expresses it, in willing Christ, God willed an entire Universe.

Some indication has also been given in the preceding chapter of the authentically Pauline character of this theme of creation in Christ. Recent and contemporary exegetes differ in the precise weight each attaches to each of the various categories they use to express the relation of Jesus Christ to the totality of creation. Thus, Lucien Cerfaux (1883-1968), seem to stress both Christ's role as goal, "knitting together" the whole Universe, and Christ's secondary efficient causality, attributed to him precisely as the God-*man*. Huby seeks something more emphatic than exemplary causality and finds it in "centrality" – Christ is for him "the supreme center of unity, harmony, and cohesion." But, it is generally the exegetes and theologians of the Scotist school who have most consistently stressed what they consider the authentically Pauline doctrine of Christ's absolute primacy, embracing a whole network of causal relationships placing the Cosmos in dependence upon the Incarnate Word.

This profound theme of the Christic dimension of creation, though richly developed by the Eastern Fathers, did not receive its full vindication in scholastic theology with the reception of such theological currents as the Franciscan, "where creation in Christ gained its place of special honor."

Teilhard himself, explicitly affirms that the Universe is created in and through Christ, and he vindicates his position by an appeal to scripture: I need only refer to the long series of Johannine – and still more Pauline – texts in which the physical supremacy of Christ [is asserted] over the Universe. I cannot quote them all here, but they come down to these two essential affirmations: "*In eio omnia constant*" (Colossians 1:17), and "*Ipse est qui replete omnia*" (Colossians 2:10; cf. Ephesians 4:9) from which it follows that "*Omnia in omnibus Christus*" (Colossians 3:11) – the very definition of omega.

Teilhard clearly feels spontaneously drawn to the thesis of the Christic dimension of the Universe because of his decisive panChristism and also because of his vivid sense that all things are radically interconnected in and organic unity. Far from being a lately arrived "propriètaire," Christ is the heart and center and key for the whole creation:

> This is the point we must bear in mind: in now case could the Cosmos be conceived and realized, without a supreme centre of spiritual consistence.... What gives the World its "gratuitous" character is precisely that the position of universal Centre has not been given to any supreme intermediary between God and the Universe, but has been occupied by Divinity himself.... Since, the Pauline Christ (the great Christ of the mystics) coincides with the universal term, omega, adumbrated by our Philosophy – the grandest and most necessary attribute we can ascribe to him is that of exercising a supreme physical influence on every cosmic reality without exception.

The pervasive and mutually complementary themes of the Universe requiring a Christ for its unification and a Christ requiring a Universe to assimilate are here presented in the key of creational theology:

> God did not will individually (nor could he have constructed as though they were separate bits) the sun, the earth, plants, or Man. He willed his Christ; and in order to have his Christ, he had to create the spiritual World, and man in particular, upon which Christ might germinate; and to have man, he had to launce the vast process of organic life (which, accordingly, is not a superfluity but an essential organ of the World); and the birth of that organic life called for the entire cosmic turbulence.

Also indicated in these lines is Teilhard's conception of creation as, not a once-for-all act by which God once posited things in a finalized form, but a dynamic, ongoing process. Creation, for Teilhard is certainly an "evolutive" process, but God brings about real novelty or "creation" at the level of each new union. Where there is no union at all there is nothing. Through union God brings his creation into being. Though the continuing process of evolution, God is bringing his creation to ever higher states of being. So Teilhard calls his brand of creationism an "evolutionary type," according to which "to create, even for omnipotence, should not be understood by us as an instantaneous act, but as a process or act of synthesis.... It is by uniting, by synthesizing, that God creates; and Christ is the key to the *mode* of this unification. This is all spelled out through a series of interlocking models which illumine from various angles Christ's unifying function: Christ is Omega, point of convergence, and magnetic, unifying pole for the Universe; he is center and axis for the Universe; and he is the soul or substantial bond of the Universe.

Christ is not "structurally detached" from creation, whose existence would be seen as decreed only consequently upon sin; nor is he a mere extrinsic exemplar. He is the very shape and ultimate substance of creation, "a kind of 'formal' cause" of creation. "Christogenesis...is itself the soul of universal cosmogenesis," and thus creation "becomes wholly Christological character." This Christocentric theology of creation represents to a significant extent a reaction against the manualistic theology of Teilhard's day, and Teilhard has no hesitation in contrasting the two:

> The learned may smile, or be angered, to hear us speak of progress. They may smugly enumerate the scandals of the present day, or argue about original sin, to prove that nothing good can come from the Earth. We may disregard these pessimists, who seem never to have questioned history, or reason, or their own hearts. But, have they the faintest suspicion, these men that their skepticism will end logically in making the World unintelligible, and in destroying our capacity to act?

Frequently Teilhard links this pessimism explicitly to a theological position "still currently presented in pious books, in sermons, and even in seminary teaching," noting that this theology is characterized by "a general almost Manichean mistrust of anything material...." Teilhard's own theology of original sin, which early occasioned great difficulty with the authorities in Rome, avoids any such denigration of the positive and Christic value of the Universe. In contrast to the manualists, Teilhard uses the doctrine of original sin to argue to Christ's cosmic efficacy and to the organic unity of the Universe in Christ. This early formulation of his argument is worth citing in full:

If Christ is to be *truly universal*, the Redemption, and hence the Fall, must extend to the whole Universe. Original sin accordingly takes on a *cosmic nature* that tradition has always accorded to it, but which, in view of the new dimensions we recognize in our Universe, obliges us radically to restate the historical representation of that sin and the too purely juridical way in which we commonly describe it being passed on.

If it is possible for the Universe to have been affected as one whole by an accident that occurred in certain souls, then its coherence "*in unitate materiae et in unitate spiritus*" must be infinitely greater than we used generally to admit. *To conform to the evidence of dogma*, the World can no longer be an agglomeration of juxtaposed objects: we must recognize it as one great Whole, welded together and evolving organically. The theoreticians of Christianity will have to overhaul the whole metaphysics of the One and the Multiple, if we wish our Philosophy to meet the demands of our theology.

If Christ is universal (if, in the other words, he is gradually consummated from all created things) it follows that his kingdom, in its essence, goes beyond the domain of the life that is, in a strict sense, called supernatural....

If this work, finally, of Christ's fulfillment is to have a meaning, is to be worth what it has cost God, the mysterious *Compound* formed by Christ and the Universe (by the Universe centered on Christ) must have a specific and unique value.... At a time when human thought is coming to recognize the Cosmos as a Whole *per se*, it would be well to devote some thought to the relationship that unites that Whole to God. We need not look far for an answer: creation by love, outward glory. But, is this all that is contained in the deposit of revelation?

This complex and not always tightly reasoned text demonstrates at least that for Teilhard original sin actually vindicates rather than precludes the assertion of the Universe's Christic dimension.

Teilhard's identification of creation with unification, insufficiently stressed by most commentators, is actually close to the heart of his whole outlook. But, this makes it all the more important that we realize the ulterior, *Christic*, foundation of this theory of creative union. To create is to unite, and the fundamental bond of union for creation is Christ. Thus, the process of creation is simply the continuing "act of forming and consummating Christ" who "sur-animates the World." The forces of creation, including man in co-operation with the Creator, are working to isolate certain energies of disintegration and to advance the forces of union, "of which the progressive sublimation, *in Christo Jesu,* is, for the Creator, the fundamental operation taking place." Of course the locus for this creative unification is the Body of Christ. Using the obviously appropriate metaphor of the tree (which abounds in his writings), Teilhard goes on to stress the organic character of the unification: And the task of the Body of Christ, living in his faithful, is patiently to sort out those heavenly forces – to extract, without letting any of it be lost, that chosen substance. Little by little, we may rest assured, the work is being done. Thanks to the multitude of individuals and vocations, the Spirit of God insinuates itself everywhere and is everywhere at work. It is the great tree… whose sunlit branches refine and turn to flowers the sap extracted by the humblest of its roots.

B. The Cosmic Implications of the Incarnation

It is only to be expected that Teilhard would link his theme of the intrinsically Chrsitic Universe with the mystery of the Incarnation itself:

> Whereas the concept "Body of Christ" is always linked in Paul's mind to Christ's redemptive death and Resurrection and only implicitly to the Incarnation, the same concept in Teilhard is almost synonymous with the Incarnation and hence closer to the Greek Fathers, whose theology developed at length the Incarnation's role in God's plan of salvation. It is because of this difference in emphasis that Teilhard finds it quite easy to reach the Cosmos directly through "Body of Christ" without mention of the Church at all.

If "Incarnation" is almost synonymous with "Body of Christ" for Teilhard, it is also deeply interrelated with the theme of creation itself – an interrelation resulting from Teilhard's Scotist stress on creation in Christ. So Teilhard can consider the two mysteries as almost interchangeable, as when he writes of the Eucharist that "through it passes directly the axis of the Incarnation, that is to say the axis of creation." More precisely, Teilhard sees the "incarnation of the Word as the final term of the process of creation," so that one ongoing development is marked by the decisive watershed of the Incarnation. Using yet another model, "part-Whole," Teilhard suggests that the Incarnation is but one aspect of the same total mystery denoted by the term "creation:" "Like the Creation (of which it is the visible aspect) the Incarnation is an act coextensive with the duration of the World." Close relationship with the Incarnation implies, of course, equally intimate connection with the Redemption. Indeed, the Redemption of creation has already begun with the Incarnation: The Universe is rent asunder; it suffers a painful cleavage at the heart of each of its monads, as the Flesh of Christ is born and grows. Like the work of Creation, which it redeems and surpasses, the Incarnation, so desired of man, is an awe-inspiring operation. It is achieved through blood.

Like St. John and the Greek Fathers, Teilhard thus sees the Incarnation as the initiation of cosmic Redemption; for the Incarnation represents not just the union of one isolated human nature with the Word but rather a cosmic event whereby, through the sacred humanity of Christ, the whole of creation finds its center, its life and light. It follows that if there are negative cosmic repercussions of original sin (which Teilhard would be the last to deny) the World is *not* on that account to be seen as fundamentally deformed. The decisive unifying force of the Incarnation more than compensates for sin's divisive havoc and makes creation a positive asset for the spiritual life: Of its nature, and as a result of original sin, it is true that matter represents a perpetual impulse towards failure. But, by nature too, and as a result of the Incarnation, it contains the spur or the allurement to be our accomplice towards heightened being, and this counter-balances and even dominates the *fomes peccati* (in Christian theology this name is attributed to concupiscence). The entire Universe is thus invested with a sort of sacramental quality; like a powerful magnetic force, the incarnate Word pulls it into saving cohesion: *The Divine Magnetism:* Christ's primordial role is to draw to himself all that, before him, moved at random.... For the Universe to subsist, *even in its natural evolution*, it was necessary above all that the dynamic soul of one and the same vigorous impetus should again be instilled into men. God chose the love of his incarnate Son as the prime mover of the restored Universe. This theology of a Christic Universe leads quite spontaneously into the concrete model of Christ's comic Body; and this logic implies that the Universe has no merely "natural" reality, unity or finality:

> ...the Incarnation so completely *recast* the Universe in the supernatural that, *in concrete fact,* we can no longer ask, or imagine, towards what Centre the elements of this World, had they not been raised up by grace, would have gravitated....the Philosophy of creative union is simply the development – generalization, extension to the Universe – of what the Church teaches us about the growth of Christ. *It is the Philosophy of the Universe expressed in terms of the notion of mystical Body.*

Given that the Incarnation does, in Teilhard's view, affect the entire Universe, the problem then arises of explaining how this influence is to be understood. We have just seen that by the image of a magnetic force Teilhard vivifies the idea that Christ is the one "final cause" organizing and orienting the character – and a different causal framework as well: that of formal causality – to clarify Christ's relationship to the Universe: Is the kingdom of God a big family? Yes, in a sense it is. But, in another sense it is a prodigious biological operation – that of the Redeeming Incarnation. As early as in St. Paul and St. John we read that to create, to fulfill and to purify the World is, for God, to unify it by uniting it organically with himself. How does he unify it? By partially immersing himself in things, by becoming "element," and then, from this point of vantage of the heart of matter, assuming the control and leadership of what we now call evolution. Here Christ is likened, not simply to a geometrical center for a circle of cosmic dimensions, nor to a magnetic pole for a universal array of filings, but (so as to communicate better the full force of the Christic-cosmic unity) as a "prodigious biological operation." In this biological operation, Teilhard goes on to say, Christ "superanimates" the whole until the final consummation, when "he will close in upon himself and his conquests" for the decisive union. "Superanimation," with its cluster of terms such as "form," "soul," and "animator," is actually subordinate to the dominant organic image of grafting, used, e.g., in his description of the Incarnation as "an operation…to graft the Person of God into the human Cosmos…." Another image subordinated to this same grafting metaphor is that of "assimilation:" "From the cosmic element into which he inserts himself," Teilhard explains, "the Word acts to subjugate all else and assimilate it to himself."

The divine "Graft" means the transformation, the divinization, not just of mankind but of the entire Cosmos:

> I see your Flesh extend throughout the entire Universe; there to be mingled with it and so extract from it all the elements that can be made to serve your purpose….
>
> To bring Christ, by virtue of a specifically organic connexion, to the heart of Realities that are esteemed the most dangerous, the most natural, the most pagan – in that you have my gospel and my mission….

This rich and mystical passage, in the course of which Teilhard also speaks of showing "the life of the lord Jesus flows through all things – the true Soul of the World," reveals a veritable cluster of key organic models. Christ's *Body* is truly cosmic – his *flesh* extends throughout the entire Universe, because by his Incarnation he has established a *specifically organic connexion* with the totality of creation, so that there is revealed *the life of the Lord Jesus flowing through all things.*

Teilhard wants this physical, organic character duly acknowledged, moreover, and all extrinsicism decisively repudiated. He decries the way in which "the organic side of the Incarnation, and in consequence its physical presuppositions or conditions, were relegated to the background," and insists that Christ is "physically and literally *he who fills all things*…the organic principle of … [the whole] harmonizing process," so that the Cosmos is "animated by his form."

Through his Incarnation, Christ thus "made Himself in some way… what would constitute a 'soul of the World.'" Certainly Teilhard is aware of the dangers involved in the use of these categories, but he is not a timid thinker, and the whole thrust of his thought leads him to affirm that even before the Incarnation became a fact, the whole history of the Universe (in virtue of a pre-action of the humanity of Christ, mysterious, but yet known to us through revelation) is the history of a progressive information of the Universe by Christ.

This same almost reckless insistence on intrinsic organicism as against extrinsicism, was noted above in our analysis of Teilhard's theology of creation. It is nonetheless important to repeat it here in, as it were, the incarnational key: Christ truly enters into the Universe in the Incarnation, becoming not merely its "lord" by arbitrary divine decree, but rather its very center, head, "form."

"Form" Why this preoccupation with formal causality? Teilhard was naturally drawn to the causality categories he knew from his manualist training. Efficient causality, while needed as a partial answer, does not suffice because "it introduces between [participated an uncreated Being] an *exteriority* which is surely exaggerated." Exemplary causality in the usual strict sense tends to suggest a model *distinct from* what is patterned upon it. And material causality, while truly intrinsic, cannot apply here, since Christ's function "is to be not a quasi-matter, a plastic or informable element, an agent of absorption, but a quasi-Soul, a plasmatic or informing element, a force of determination." Teilhard is left, then, with formal causality, which is both intrinsic and the principle of actualization.

The causality in question is not merely that of a form taken in the most general sense, but rather that of the *soul*, the form of *living* beings. In Aristotelian scholasticism, the soul not only actuates, but also animated the living being. So for Teilhard, Christ actualizes, unifies and animates the cosmic Whole as its "soul." There is still another dimension to the Aristotelian notion of form or soul which Teilhard most felicitously exploits: the form is also the intrinsic final cause or goal. True, a final cause can be purely extrinsic and its influence can consist "in nothing more than its being a good which is the term of appetite or desire." But, this is not the sort of finality Teilhard attributes to Jesus Christ:

Let us, for brevity's sake, give the name of omega to the upper cosmic term disclosed by creative union. All that I shall have to say about it may be reduced to three points:

- The revealed Christ is identical with omega.
- It is inasmuch as He is omega that He is seen to be attainable and inevitably present in all things.
- And finally it was in order that He might become omega that it was necessary for Him, through the travail of the Incarnation, to conquer and animate the Universe.

The form of man, for Aristotle, not only makes John Smith a human being; it directs all John's development *from within* towards his attainment of full human stature. So the important Teilhardian model of Christ as Omega, magnetic pole, or universal goal is not at all in conflict with complementary stress on Christ as quasi-Soul. On the contrary, intrinsic finality is an important facet of formal causality itself which deserves the explicit emphasis Teilhard gives it. Still, it is formal causality which dominates; with all due reservations made, "the word that comes nearest to a satisfactory definition of the universal influx of Jesus Christ, the Centre of the World, is 'information.'" As we have seen, Teilhard is sometimes careful to qualify his affirmation of formal causality. The question thus arises now, does such a qualification as "quasi" in the phrase "quasi-formal" empty his affirmation of all real content and literal force? In an analogous case, Karl Rahner (1904-1984), insists that his description of created grace as a "quasi-formal causality of God himself upon the created spirit" does not empty his thesis of its import: All this "quasi" implies is that this "formal," in spite of its formal causality, which must be taken really seriously, abides in its absolute transcendence (inviolateness, "freedom"). But, it does *not* imply that the statement… is a mode of speech lacking all binding force; on the contrary, it is the *quasi* which must be prefixed to every application to God of a category in itself terrestrial.

In Teilhard's case, the "quasi" does not nullify his attribution to Christ of real formal causality; but it does safeguard his thesis from gross pantheism and the crass conception of an (impossible) immediate substantial union between Christ as form and all creatures as matter. To explicate his fundamental assertion of an intrinsically Christic Universe, then, Teilhard recurs to scholastic causal categories. In his very rich but sometimes problematical conception, each causal mode complements the others (efficient, final, and formal), and each illumines another aspect of the Universe's intrinsically Christic character. But, this is not to say that Teilhard was a skilled scholastic Philosopher, or that this causal articulation of his Christic Cosmology represents the ultimate expression of his thought. On the contrary, his serious hesitations in this area are well known; he ventures here only in view of the seminary training of his colleagues, hoping by this appeal to categories they will find familiar, to evoke the deeper vision in which he is really interested. The norm of his writings is always experiential rather than speculative; in a characteristic passage, he writes concerning a negative reaction to his essay *The Priest:* "This friendly criticism has had the salutary effect of making me face the difficulties of practical life, and, incidentally, the slavery imposed on us by a certain group of accepted scholastic formulas (in particular those relating to the various forms of causality). Evidently I must find a certain orthodox way of putting things if I am to get across my "experience" without distorting or weakening it. The important thing fortunately, is that, intrinsically, the experience orthodox…." This primacy of experience makes Teilhard pass spontaneously from speculative expressions to concrete models: Christ is essentially revealed in Scripture as invested with *the power of giving to the World*, in his own person, *its definitive form*…. We must ultimately admit that there is in *natura Christi* (the nature of Christ), some universal *physical reality*, a certain cosmic extension of his Body and Soul.

It is precisely because Christ is human, that he can graft all creation into his glorified Body. Teilhard thus works out a distinctive theological anthropology with a decisively cosmic emphasis, and it is only in light of this anthropology that one can fully appreciate his cosmic Christology. Because his Universe is radically evolutionary, moreover, elements are never seen in static juxtaposition; rather, higher forms emerge from and recapitulate lower forms. All elements, but especially man, are profoundly related to the Whole:

> The first thing I saw was the Man alone can help Man to decipher the World. Up to now, Man in his essential characteristics, has been omitted from all Scientific theories of Nature.... Either through excessive admiration or lack of esteem, Man is left floating above, or left on the edge of the Universe.... This is the cause of all our present intellectual and moral difficulties. We shall never understand either Man or Nature unless, as the facts demand, we completely replace Man (without destroying him) in the heart of Nature.

Thus, "*we hold evolution in our hands*, responsible for its past to its future." "Man bears along with him the World of beings inferior to God." Just as when Teilhard explains man's rootedness in the Universe, so when he discusses man's responsibility for the Whole, Teilhard has recourse to a great variety of models which balance and complement one another. "Building the earth," e.g., should not be taken to imply that the construction remains juxtaposed to the builder. The Universe is more accurately seen as *organically converging*, and man is more properly understood as its locus of infolding: "...why not assume a Universe that, in one complete all-embracing whole, folds in upon itself until it is interiorized in a growing complexity?... Man: not simply a zoological type like the others. But, man, the nucleus of a movement of infolding and convergence...on whom and in whom the Universe enfolds itself."

For Teilhard, the traditional image of man the microcosm takes on a new and dynamic character: in the human body is focused and in-folded the entirety of the Cosmos. It may be clearer now why God, to save and fulfill the entire Universe, became *man*. Man, rooted in the whole, sums up, focuses, and recapitulates that Whole. He may not represent the highest form of intelligent life (the angels surpass him), but he does serve as focal point for the convergence of all creation, material and spiritual. Echoing St. Bonaventure and a rich patristic legacy, Teilhard seizes on man's focal position to explain the cosmic dimension of the Incarnation: Amidst all the centres of consciousness realized or capable of being realized in the World, we represent perhaps the most central.... Because men occupy this humble [sub-angelic], but *special* place, one sees why the Redeemer of all things, in order to have contact with all things, became incarnate amongst us, in the lowest of the spiritual spheres, precisely "*ut repleret omnia*." This richly seminal text suggests that if the chain of being has a hierarchical character (as traditionally assumed) according to the degree of spiritualization of the various levels, still in accord with a more profound norm more importance may devolve upon a lower but centrally situated link (humanity) because it is in that the widely variant elements of unity and multiplicity, spirit and matter, are brought together into coincidence. It is from this special center and focus that Christ realizes his plenitude.

The Word assumes a specifically human nature, then, because mankind is the focal point of universal convergence. It must be borne in mind, though, that by humanity Teilhard does not mean merely a multitude of human beings, among which the Second Person assumes one isolated place. Evolution means convergence, totalization, and the key watershed of totalization is precisely at the level of the human. Note the rich organic model Teilhard uses to explain this point:

> Under conditions of distribution which in any other phylum would have led long ago to the break-up into different species, the human vertical as it spreads out remains entire, like a gigantic leaf whose veins, however distinct, remains always joined in a common tissue. With man we find indefinite interfecundation on every level...the unique spectacle of a "species" capable of

> achieving something in which all previous species had failed. It has succeeded, not only in becoming cosmopolitan, but in stretching a single organized membrane over the earth without breaking it…. Really, I can see no coherent, and therefore Scientific, way of grouping this immense succession of facts but as a gigantic psycho-biological operation, a sort of *mega-synthesis*, and the "super-arrangement" to which all the thinking elements of the earth find themselves today individually and collectively subject.

Teilhard traces the "super-compression upon itself of the noosphere," which in turn produces a "super-organization, and that again a super-'consciousisation:' that, in turn, is followed by a super-super-compression, and so the process continues."

How is this radical totalization of mankind (and, through mankind, of the entire Universe) to find its center, ground, and point of convergence? In that prodigious, divine biological operation which is the redeeming Incarnation. Thus, mankind, totalizing the Universe, becomes itself totalized in the incarnate Christ. This deep union is realized at the spiritual level of love and knowledge, of course, but it must be recognized that there is also a specifically somatic dimension of this universal totalization. Mankind, and supremely the Son of Man, can recapitulate the *entire* creation because in man there is the coincidence of *spirit and matter*.

The ancient Hebrew conception of man mentioned earlier thus finds a resounding echo in Teilhard. Rejecting the then-common view of the body as an isolated fragment of matter separating the human individual from the rest of the Cosmos, Teilhard insists that "the Body is the very Universality of things, inasmuch as they are centred on an animating Spirit. For a soul, to have a body is to be…rooted in the Cosmos." This cosmic conception of the body, which may at first strike the Hellenized thinker as odd, has gained considerable acceptance recently through the influence of such currents as biblical theology and existential phenomenology.

Teilhard logically insists that the cosmic character of the Incarnation must be considered from this specifically somatic point of view: he himself seeks only to proclaim "the innumerable prolongations of [Christ's] incarnate Being in the World of matter... the mystery of [Christ's] Flesh, [of Christ] the Soul shining forth through all that surrounds us." Thus, the universal Christificaion implied in the very mystery of creation itself, is raised to a new level of actualization by the Incarnation, win which Christ "physically" and really unites himself to the entire Cosmos. But, this union has a specifically somatic character; and since "it is precisely in and through his Body that the Person of the Word unites himself to his creation," the union is best evoked by the model of the cosmic Body of Christ.

C. The Universe as Redeemed in Christ

Our precise concern in this section is, avoiding duplication of existing studies, to discover what light can be shed by Teilhard's soteriology on the intrinsically Christic character of the Universe. We can best begin by recalling the organic unity of Teilhard's grasp of the basic Christian mysteries: Taken in their full sense, Creation, Incarnation, and Redemption are simply facts localized at a certain point in time and space; they are truly dimensions of the World...these historical facts are simply the privileged expression of process having "cosmic" dimension.

The theme of the redemption of the entire Cosmos is, we have said, fundamental for Teilhard, who gives original sin universal scope precisely to vindicate the cosmic scope of the redemption. "The radius of Christ's Lordship and power is 'by definition' the radius of the Redemption," for Christ must emerge as the bond "*in quo omnia constant*." The Pauline reference comes naturally to Teilhard in this context.

Our question at this point is, what models does Teilhard use to elucidate this notion of cosmic Redemption? Teilhard comments that soteriology seems to have long been dominated by the model of "expiating reparation," according to which "Christ has been regarded above all as the Lamb burdened with the sins of the World, and the World above all as a fallen mass." But, from the very beginning, he argues, the tradition has offered another, radically more positive model for soteriology, that of "reconstruction" or "re-creation." He insists that this latter theme is again gaining pre-eminence because of variety of influences, including the impact of the new cosmic perspective upon the Christian consciousness. Christian salvation is thus primarily, to lead creation to its fulfillment in divine union; and for this purpose, secondarily, to eliminate the evil forces of regression and dispersion. No longer first to expiate and in addition to restore; but first to create (or "super-create") and for this purpose, in inevitable consequence, to fight against and to compensate for evil.

Teilhard's cosmic perspective thus leads him to transcribe soteriology into a fresh, major key. What must be stressed now is no longer the narrower effect of the blotting out of sin in souls, but rather cosmic super-creation: "Christ can no longer 'justify' man except by that same act super-cheating the entire Universe." Since, to create is to unify and to "super-create" is to unify decisively and establish "fulfillment in divine union," Teilhard must be said to conceive of cosmic Redemption primarily in terms of this model of decisive unification incorporation into Christ. For Teilhard, "Christ the Redeemer is, as Redeemer, also Christ the Unifier, so much so that it is not from Adam that mankind derives its real unity and solidarity but from Christ." Christ the Redeemer is Christ the principle of unity who binds up the Universe and establishes "one flesh":

> The principle of unity who saves a guilty Creation from returning to dust is Christ. By the force of His attraction, by the light of his moral and spiritual teaching, binding power of His very existence, Jesus comes to re-establish at the heart of the World the harmony of efforts and the convergence of all things. When we read the Gospel in a straightforward way we see that no ideal translates better for our understanding the *redemptive function of the Word* than the idea of the unification of all

> flesh in one same Spirit. "Unification" has a meaning that is, of course, not merely mathematical nor even metaphysical – it is specifically cosmic and Christic, so that it implies incorporation into Christ's cosmic Body of the entire course of universal evolution. In returning "to the bosom of the Father" Christ "must creatively carry the noogenesis of the Cosmos to the natural term of is maturity."

Teilhard explicates this central redemptive model of cosmic incorporation with a series of subordinate but illustrative models. Redemption is a continual compensation for and correction of the deviations inherent in cosmic evolution. It is a building up, a reconstructing, a recasting of the Universe. It means carrying forward toward convergence the evolutionary course of the Universe. This latter model finds a particularly fruitful and suggestive application in Teilhard's theology of the Cross. Teilhard wished to move away from the dominant emphasis upon expiation in defeat and solitude for the sins of souls – away from the preoccupation with condemnation of the World. He wished rather to stress the positive and cosmic significance of the Cross: In its highest and most general sense, the doctrine of the Cross is that to which all men adhere who believe that the vast movement and agitation of human life opens on to a road that leads somewhere, and that that road climbs upward. Towards the peaks, shrouded in mist from our human eyes, whither the Cross beckons us, we rise by a path which is the way of universal progress. The royal road of the Cross is no more nor less than the road of human endeavour supernaturally righted and prolonged. Once we have fully grasped the meaning of the Cross, we are no longer in danger of finding life sad and ugly. We shall simply have become more attentive to its barely comprehensible solemnity.

To sum up, Jesus on the Cross is both the symbol and the reality of the immense labour of the centuries which has, little by little, raised the created spirit and brought it back to the depths of the Divine Milieu. He represents (and in a true sense, he is) creation, as, upheld by God, it reascends the slopes of being… the Cross was placed on the crest of the road which leads to the highest peaks of creation. Jesus crucified "is not a reject: He is not defeated. On the contrary, He carries the weight of the universal course of progress with Him toward God." But, if Teilhard was able to shape a theology of the Cross with a cosmic and positive cast, it as particularly the mystery of the Resurrection which he felt vindicated the full scope of his vision. "It seemed as if he could not have enough of the Resurrection." Gray directly links Teilhard's concept of Christ's formal causality with his theology of the Resurrection. It is precisely Christ glorified, in his risen Body, who effects in a quasi-formal manner the entire Cosmos.

Like the Incarnation itself and the Passion, the Resurrection too becomes cosmic in scope – it becomes the mystery of the decisive centering of the Universe on Christ:

> We are often too inclined to regard the Resurrection as an isolated event in time, with an apologetical significance…. It is something quite other and much greater than that. It is a "tremendous" [Teilhard uses the English word for emphasis] cosmic event. It marks Christ's effective assumption as the universal Centre. Until that time, he was present in all things as a soul that is painfully gathering together its embryonic elements. Now he radiates over the whole Universe as a consciousness and activity fully in control of themselves…. When, presented with a Universe whose physical and spiritual immensity are seen to be ever more bewildering, we are terrified by the constantly increasing weight of energy and glory we have to attribute to the son of Mary if we are to be justified in continuing to worship him, it is then that we should turn our thoughts to the Resurrection.

The key to the cosmic dimensions of Christ and to the Christic character of the Universe is thus the mystery of the Resurrection; in its light Teilhard proclaims "the essential function assumed by the risen Christ at the centre and peak of Creation to bring all things to their fulfillment." It is only the risen Christ, pervading all creation and rendering it translucent, that Teilhard can truly worship: As long as I could see – or dared see – in you, Lord Jesus, only the man who lived two thousand years ago, the sublime moral teacher, the Friends, the Brother, my love remained timid and constrained.... But, now, Master, today, when through the manifestation of those superhuman powers with which your Resurrection endowed you, you shine forth from within all the forces of the Earth and so become visible to me, now I recognize you as my Sovereign, and with delight I surrender myself to you.

Through the cosmic import of the Resurrection all creation is rendered potentially instrumental for contact with Christ; the entire Universe is rendered an extension of his Body: "By virtue of the Resurrection nothing any longer kills inevitably but everything is capable of becoming the blessed touch of the divine hands, the blessed influence of the will of God upon our lives." In Christ's risen Body the entire Universe is transformed. Every created element, and in a particular way every human body, is "rigorously coextensive with the totality of space and time," but in Christ's case "this coextension of coexistence has become a coextension of domination." And the reason Christ's Body both extends to the totality of creation and dominates the whole Universe is to be traced to "the transforming effect of the Resurrection." Thus, Teilhard's theology of the intrinsically Christic character of the Universe finds its focus once again in the model of the cosmic Body, specifically the cosmic *risen* Body of Christ.

7.2.3 Conclusion

Modern man lives with a heightened consciousness of his vast Universe, a new awareness of the vital bonds which link him with the whole. This new consciousness poses a challenge to the Christian faith, to think through anew the Christian significance of the Universe. It was to this task that Teilhard dedicated his entire life. Such a Christian understanding must somehow link the Universe to Christ, God's decisive revelation. Teilhard's central thesis is that the Universe is intrinsically and organically Christic, that it constitutes the "cosmic Body of Christ." Thus, the bond between Christ and the Universe is not merely extrinsic and juridical; Christ is much more than a real estate owner or manger of creation. At the heart of his Christic Cosmology is the resolute rejection of such extrinsicism and the vigorous vindication of the Universe as cosmic Body of Christ.

An analysis of this model of cosmic Body in the light of the now advanced model methodology indicated that although it must not be taken pictorially (as must not, also, almost all theological, Philosophical and Scientific models), such a model can be richly evocative and seminal for both Christian theology and spirituality.

Teilhard's vision of the Christic nature of the Universe finds powerful expression in his earliest essays. His Writings in time of War already reveal the central crisis of his "two loves:" his self-donation to God and his total commitment to the Universe. And they spell out his resolution of this key crisis through his realization that the Universe is intrinsically Christic. Such an intuition does not garb creation in triumphalistic colors, concealing the dimension of conflict and suffering; rather, Teilhard underlines the humble, kenotic quality of Christ's cosmic presence, the torn and imperfect character of a creation still groping toward Omega.

Teilhard's early vision developed and became fully rounded through his contact with the biblical, patristic and theological heritage which affirms the cosmic Christ and the Christic Cosmos. This contact was made possible largely through his scholarly confreres who encouraged him by noting this wider context of his thought. Thus, the Semitic notion of the body as bond to all creation, the Pauline themes of creation in and through Christ, of the "Pleroma" of Christ – these and similar elements provide the biblical foundation for a Christic theology and spirituality of the Universe.

The patristic themes of recapitulation of all things in Christ, of a creation engrafted in the Word Incarnate, etc., advance this Christic conception. Duns Scotus and later Berulle both vindicate the absolute primary of Christ in the divine intentions, so that Christ is revealed as Exemplar and Prototype, Mediator, Scope and Final Cause of creation. In scholastic theologians such as Peter Galatinus (1460-1540) and Ambrogio Catarino Polito (1484-1553), both supporters of the Scotist thesis, one finds these themes focused into the explicit affirmation that all of creation is contained within the glorified Body of Christ.

In our own time Maurice Blondel (1861-1949), also a champion of the Scotist thesis, proposes a "panChristism" in which Christ appears as the ground for the organic union of the whole Cosmos, as the substantial bond of all things. It is in the context of this rich and significant Christian current that Teilhard must be studied. He corresponded and met with Blondel in his formative years; he was quite familiar with the Scotist thesis through Allegra and others; he knew the Christic vision of the Fathers and of Pauline scholoarship through such colleagues as de Lubac, de Solages, Huby, and Allegra. And he thought of himself as not merely a private student of this great current, but a member, a spokesman to the modern World of its central Christic vision of creation.

Ofcourse, each individual thinker in this Christian current brought his own unique emphasis, language, and conceptual framework to the interpretation of the Christian mystery. Teilhard's distinctive contributions to this heritage certainly include his post-Darwinian evolutionary perspective of the Universe, his affirmation that cosmogenesis is convergent and culminates in "Christogenesis," and similar original insights. Also, Teilhard emphasizes in a particularly explicit way the significance of "building the earth," of developing man's World for the true progress of the human spirit.

Teilhard's concrete and vivid model of "cosmic Body of Christ" finds its speculative complement in his interrelated concepts of the Universe as organic unity and as intrinsically Christic. He argues, on the basis of intuition, but also of Scientific presupposition and verification, that the Universe is not a mere collection of juxtaposed fragments but rather a totum, an organic *whole*. Moreover, this whole is a *dynamic* coherence in which every element is intrinsically related to every other in cosmic evolution. Man represents the highest shoot of the upper thrust of this evolution; as microcosm, moreover, man focuses and totalizes this whole. And since in the Incarnation it is precisely human nature that is assumed by the Word, Christ can thus effect the ultimate totalization and recapitulation of the Universe in the mysteries of creation, Incarnation, and Redemption.

Regarding creation, it is not that Christ comes to a pre-established Universe and merely claims juridical title to it as its lord; rather (as the Scotistic heritage insists), the very shaping, the primordial forming of creation occurs *in Christ;* thus, as Teilhard goes on to insist, Christ exercises upon the whole of creation a quasi-formal causality.

The Incarnation establishes Christ physically at the heart of the Cosmos; it thus initiates the mystery of Redemption. The Incarnation is consequently conceived in cosmic and organic terms, as an actual "taking root" in the whole, an assimilation of the whole.

The Redemption in its full extension again reveals the cosmic dimension of Christ's action. Thus, what is at issue in Christ's salvific work is not merely an expiation for the individual sins of the faithful; rather, Redemption signifies as well the "super-creation" of the Universe. Teilhard spells out this cosmic scope of soteriology in terms of the models of organic unification, of incorporation into the cosmic Body of Christ. The Universe receives its new life by being engrafted into the cosmic, resurrected Body of Christ. Thus, the central Christian mysteries of Creation, Incarnation and Redemption are seen by Teilhard as advancing phases of one divine creative-salvific action. This action brings to ever higher realization the intrinsically Christic character of the Universe.

The model of cosmic Body (and a cluster of related models) accompanies this theology, nourishing and illustrating its statement that all creation is to be seen as inserted in the full mystery of Christ.

7.3 Panikkarian Cosmotheandric Approach of the Cosmos

7.3.1 The Cosmotheandric Perspective

My contention has been that the so-called ecological sensitivity is only an appendix to the second period, and that the three real kairological moments are: a) the *primordial* or ecumenic moment, i.e., that pre-reflective awareness in which Nature, Man and the divine are still amorphously mixed and only vaguely differentiated; b) the *humanistic* or economic moment, i.e., that historical attitude in which the discriminating process of individualization proceeds from the macro - to the microsphere; and c) the *catholic* or cosmotheandric moment, which would maintain the distinctions of the second moment without forfeiting the unity of the first. Now I would like to concentrate on the description of this holistic experience rather than on its divisions.

In describing this intuition, the expression *theanthropocosmic* might sound more accurate, because *anthrōpos* refers to Man as a human being, i.e., as distinct from the Gods, while *anēr* tends to connote the male. This has not, however always been the case. Further, the word *theandric* has a venerable history in western thought and has always stood for the union of the human and the divine without confusion. Besides, the expression *cosmotheandric* is rather more euphonic than *theanthroposcosmic*.

In order to reduce my presentation to its basic elements, I shall just 1) elaborate the basis of this intuition, 2) formulate the insight, 3) consider some possible objections, and finally 4) describe how this insight sees reality.

A. Some Assumptions

The cosmotheandric vision might well be considered the original and primordial form of consciousness as the undivided vision of the totality. But, in its primordiality, it is still an innocent and undiscriminated vision, which is quickly obnubilated by the more glittering regional discoveries, whether physical or metaphysical. It is hardly astonishing to find Man almost intoxicated by is progressive discoveries of the bountiful reality of the Worlds above, around and within. The waves are indeed captivating, the undersea currents and marine fauna surely deserve our careful study, but we might now also turn our attention to the entire ocean.

It seems that envisioning all of reality in terms of three Worlds is an invariant of human culture, whether this vision is expressed spatially, temporally, cosmologically or metaphysically. One sacred text, among many others, says: "He revealed himself threefold." There is a World of the Gods, another of Men and a third of those who passed through the sieve of time; there is Heaven, Earth and the UnderWorld; there is the sky, the earth and the in-between; there is a past, the present and the future; there is the spiritual, the psychical and the corporeal, etc.

The classical tripartite division of Man as body, soul and spirit (*corpus, anima, spiritus*) could be understood as another formulation of the same intuition, provided we do not interpret it in a merely individualistic way by understanding "my" body, soul and spirit. In point of fact, none of these three dimensions are individualized or particularized. Body, soul and spirit are rather the common denominators of every real being if this latter is not sundered from its vital connections with the entire reality. The Christian dogma of the Mystical Body affirms precisely this each of us is an integral part of a higher and more real unity, the *Christus totus* (the Total Christ).

Be this as it may, it would today be an unwarranted and *kata chronic* interpretation to read our more modern categories into traditional three-storey building of these Worldviews. It would amount to a methodological error just the reverse of anachronistic exegesis. If the latter judges the present with obsolete categories of understanding, the former judges the past with present day, but equally inappropriate, patterns of intelligibility.

I am suggesting, however, that this vision has always been with us, and that it has always been the function of the wise to remind their contemporaries of the whole, and so rescue them from being dazzled by enlightening but partial insights. Yet we might wonder whether humankind ever would have attained its ability to analyze and discriminate without the one-sidedness and even exaggeration occasioned by the regional discoveries. *O felix culpa*?

Today however, this holistic vision seems to be the undimmed hope of an ever-growing number of people and the explicit goal of human consciousness. Man, who has never sought partial truths, now suspects that many traditional convictions may in fact be only partial. Man has always sought the ultimate reality, and now he suspects that by ruthlessly transcending everything he may very well leave reality behind. Man is not satisfied to attain the peaks if from there he cannot at least see the valleys as well. The entire reality counts, matter as much as spirit, goodness as much as evil, Science as much as mysticism, the soul as much as the body. It is not a question of regaining the innocence we had to lose to become who we are, but of conquering a new one.

At every level and period of human consciousness, there has always been the temptation to curtail the real, to concoct shortcuts to synthesis by eliminating whatever parts of reality consciousness could not easily assimilate or manipulate. Very early on, God was deprived of a body, and later of matter altogether, so that he became spirit only. For the same reason –viz. removing imperfections from the Perfect he was made immutable and immobile. Something similar happened to Man. Haunted by the need to preserve his "dignity," he first stripped himself of his animality, then his body and senses, and soon enough he put aside his feelings until he became a "thinking rod," a *res cogitans*, and a speaking machine. Despite the optimistic iranian-christian doctrine of the resurrection of the flesh, the perfection of Man was increasingly "spiritualized" until it called forth an understandably opposite reaction. Certainly it is better to enter the kingdom crippled or maimed than to be cast out entirely. But, this lopsided solution need not be the general rule. On the contrary, "to the man who has will always be given more, till he has enough and to spare…"

Or again, it is true that no one can serve two masters, but it is equally true that there is ultimately only one master, one whole, one reality, so that no part of the real can or should be annihilated or ignored in favour of another part. Spiritual reductionism is as deleterious as material reductionism. Our task now is to overcome any and all of these overbearing reductionisms which threaten to confine reality to but one of its constituents. Of course this can only done if we pierce through our own anthropocentric perspective in the ongoing conquest of the new innocence.

This conquest is one of the underlying assumptions of the cosmotheandric vision. Earlier we mentioned the radical relativity of all reality and distinguished this from an agnostic relativism which would eliminate any certainty and every difference. It is this *radical relativity* which stands in the background of the undivided cosmotheandric consciousness: we cannot close communication between spheres of the real. Further, this communication cannot be merely moral-link or some dim knowledge of the fact that things are related. In Aristotleian terms, the relations must be as real as the elements they relate. In other words, the ontological status of the consciousness linking the different realms of existence must have at least the same consistency as the realms it binds together. So either the Universe is made of relations as strong-and as real-as the *relata*, or the latter fall away in a chaotic, disintegrating and solipsistic Universe.

Similarly, the cosmotheandric vision also assumes an experience of the non-individualistic aspects of knowledge and eventually of the supra-individualistic subjects of the knowledge. We know, we enjoy knowing, but we are not private owners of "our" knowledge. My knowledge is real knowledge only inasmuch as it is in me, but it is not mine. Knowledge is not only communion with the object, but also communion among subjects.

Our fundamental assumptions, then, is the ultimate unity of reality: it all coheres in spite of spheres of being, degrees of knowledge, ontological falls and ontic hierarchies, a complete vision of reality cannot overlook any of its aspects or sacrifice any "lower" parts in favour of "higher" ones. No amount of distinguishing between "appearance and reality," "*paramā*rthika and *vyavahā*rika," "*ens a se* and *ens ab alio*," "the way of the wise and the way of fools," "matter and spirit," "creator and creature," "noumenon and phenomenon," "truth and illusion,".. can blind us to the fact that the other side of the coin, as were, even if not true, ultimate, existent, or whatever, still has its own peculiar degree of reality to the extent that it consistently affirms: *Brahman* is the ultimate subject of *avidyā* (ignorance). Seeing the rope (of India's famous parable) as a snake may be – is – an illusion, but the rope is real, even if it is only real in an imaginary dream. *Vidyā* (wisdom) does not consist in recognizing this World as unreal, but in dis-covering it as the mere appearance, *māyā*, the veil of (i.e., belonging to) the real.

Panikkar could try to formulate the same idea from a different angle. A glance at the history of consciousness shows it pendualting between an exaggerated unity, which swallows all variety, and an equally extreme atomism (even if couched in dualistic terms), which makes any ultimate intelligibility impossible and breaks down peace and harmony in the bargain. The great masters and probable the simple folk kept the balanced vision, but the epigones run to the extreme. The cosmotheandric experience begins to regain, on a further turn of the spiral, the positive (and not merely dialectical) middle way between the paranoia and monism and the schizophrenia of dualism. This is what Panikkar would like to show.

B. Formulation

Orthodoxies and traditionalism of every sort have for over century severely criticized modernity. They have told us that Man, estranged from the Cosmos and cut off from God, cannot survive. The cosmotheandric intuition is in this sense both traditional and contemporary. It seeks to recover Man's roots, but it goes further. First, it does not stop with Man, but penetrates to the very wellsprings of "creation." It would mean re-establishing tradition not only down to the "metaphysical era," but deeper still, to a time "before the World was formed, "when wisdom played with the children of Man and delighted in their company. Secondly, without ignoring a certain hierarchical order, this vision does not locate the centre in God - an impossible task in any case, once Man is aware it is he who does this-but strikes a balance whereby the three dimensions find their center each moment in the free interplay among them. Let me try to explicate this.

The cosmotheandric principle could be formulated by saying that the divine, the human and the earthly-however we may prefer to call them-are the three irreducible dimensions which constitute the real, i.e., any reality inasmuch as it is real. It does not deny that the abstracting capacity of our mind can, for particular and limited purposes, consider pats of reality independently; it does not deny the complexity of the real and its many degrees. But, this principle reminds us that the parts are parts and that they are not just accidentally juxtaposed, but essentially related to the whole. In other words, the parts are real participations and are to be understood not according to a merely spatial model, as books are part of a library or a carburettor and a differential gear are parts of an automobile, but rather according to an organic unity, as body and soul, or mind and will belong to a human being: they are parts because they are not the whole, but they are not parts which can be "parted" from the whole without thereby ceasing to exist. A soul without a body is a mere entelechy; a body without will an artificial reason is a mere abstraction; and reason without ill an artificially constructed mind, etc. They are constitutive dimensions of the whole, which permeates everything that is and is not reducible to any of its constituents.

What this intuition emphasizes is that the three dimensions of reality are neither three modes of a monolithic undifferentiated reality, nor three elements of a pluralistic system. There is rather one, though intrinsically threefold, relation which manifests the ultimate constitution of reality. Everything that exists, any real being, presents this triune constitution expressed in three dimensions. Panikkar is not only saying that everything is directly or indirectly related to everything else: the radical relativity or *pratītyasamutpāda* of the Buddhist tradition. Panikkar is also stressing that this relationship is not only constitutive of the whole, but that it flashes forth, ever new and vital, in every spark of the real. No word can be understood in isolation. All words are relational. God is meaningless without creature. Reality is just the other side of the ideal. Goodness implies evil. The Earth needs either water or sun or an empty space. Time needs space and vice-versa. Time betrays, exhumes (perspires) eternity. All of these relations have most often been interpreted dialectically, mainly because they are seen as binary relations. The cosmotheandric vision overcomes dialectics because it discovers the Trinitarian structure of everything-and that third dimension, the divine, is not just a "third" opposition, but precisely the *mysterium coniunctionis*. Truth, for instance, is not the opposite of error-as if only these two extremes existed. The continuum runs from the one to the other. All things are, as it were, androgynous and ambivalent because they are in fact Trinitarian. The relations which pervade the Universe penetrate the innermost chambers of every being. The cosmotheandric intuition is not a tripartite division among beings, but an insight into the threefold core of all that is, insofar as it is. Let us briefly describe these three dimensions.

a) To begin with, every being has an abyssal dimension, both transcendent and immanent. Every being transcends everything-including and perhaps most pointedly "itself," which in truth has no limits. It is, further, infinitely immanent, i.e., inexhaustible and unfathomable. And this is so not because this depth belongs to every being as such. To place limits on being – *qua* being-is to destroy it. To isolate a being-were this even possible-would amount to stifling it, killing it, cutting the umbilicus which unites it to being. In harmony with the greater proportion of human traditions, I call this dimension divine, but this does not imply that another name would not or could not do. The basic perception here is the infinite inexhaustibility of any real being, its ever-open character, its mystery-if we allow the word in this connection-its freedom, another language might say. Through every real being breathes a wind of reality, a *prāṇa*, as it were, permeating every fibre of that being and making it real not only by connecting it with the entire reality, but also by suspending it over a fathomless ground which makes growth, life and freedom possible. Everything that is, is because it shares in the mystery of Being and/or Non-Being, some may prefer to say.

This divine dimension is not an umbrella superimposed over beings, nor a merely extrinsic foundation for them, but the constitutive principle of all things, comparable to the Thomistic act of existence which confers existence on beings without being, properly speaking, an ingredient of "being." This means that God does not enter into a *formal* composition of a being because, in this terminology, God is not a formal principle (*causa formalis*) nor is real being reducible to its form. Everything that there is, is sat.

Were it not for this dimension, ultimately no change would be possible, for there would be no "room" for it. Or again, were it not for this dimension, every particular change would amount to a total transmutation of the changing being, so that nothing would really change because there would be no continuity whatsoever. Some systems understandably prefer to call this dimension nothingness, emptiness, the vacuum that makes all the rest possible. Were it not for this dimension, any change would entail a total alienation, for no being would be flexible enough to allow for both variation and continuity.

b) Every real being, further, is within the range of consciousness; it is thinkable, and by this very fact tied up with human awareness. Again, there is no need here to quibble over words or with them. We cannot speak, or think, or affirm anything whatsoever-positively or negatively-about anything which is not connected with our consciousness. The very act of affirming or negating anything establishes a connection, if none were there already. We may speak about a hypothetical astronomical body of unknown chemical constitution orbiting some unknown sun. Yet this sentence makes sense only insofar as it speaks from within known parameters projected onto an equally knowable hypothesis. In so many words, the waters of human consciousness wash all the shores of the real-even if Man cannot penetrate the *terra incognita* (unknown land) of the hinterland-and by this very fact, Man's being enters into relation with the whole of reality. The entire field of reality lives humanized in him. The transparent character of consciousness belongs not only to the Man who knows, but also to the object known. We could call this a dimension of consciousness may be, it is manifest in and through Man. Even if we defend the possibility of a consciousness utterly independent of Man, this very affirmation-made by any human being-already contravenes such an independence.

This does not mean that everything can be reduced to consciousness or that consciousness is everything. The cosmotheandric insight declares precisely that the three constitutive dimension of the real are not mutually reducible; hence the material World and the divine aspect are irreducible to consciousness alone. And yet both are pervaded by, and in a certain sense co-extensive with, consciousness. As the Fathers of the Church liked to say in the commentaries on the book of Exodus, he can see only the back of God, when he has already passed; we can discover God's "footprints," but we cannot see God face-to-face. Or as Philosophers have often observed: matter is matter because it is opaque to the mind. So too, the individual thing *qua* individual is not knowable, the Cosmos is Cosmos because it is not Man or Spirit, and so on. This human dimension of reality does not mean that a particular entity, about which Man is not aware, or not yet aware, does not exist or is not real. It does not mean, for example, that Pluto did not exist before 1930, it as real as a probable planet since the beginning of this century, and as a possible one for at least two millennia. It was real as a possible celestial body since Man discovered the possibility of celestial bodies, and it was real as a body or a being insofar as body and being have ever been objects of consciousness. Even a hypothetical discourse on Pluto as a non-being relates it to human consciousness by this very ontic opacity.

The natural and unavoidable question still remains: did Pluto exist as a celestial body before human beings existed on Earth? No one denies that we can, and Panikkar would add that we must, think that Pluto existed, like all the other planets, long before human life was possible on Earth. In other words, Pluto is thinkable as an astronomical body whose existence is independent of human consciousness. But, its very thinkability already relates it-though not necessarily causally-to human consciousness.

All this does not mean, obviously, that Pluto-or any other being, for that matter-has to be known or thinkable by any or every conscious human being. It simply means that thinkability and knowability as such are features of all that is.

As a result of the experiments of Piaget and others, we may accept that a child in his "preconceptual" period does not assume that a watch hidden by a handkerchief still lies underneath it. Moreover, he does not even explore this possibility by lifting up the cloth. But, he soon learns that the watch is there, and this comes as a major discovery. Panikkar suspects that the adult is still deeply affected by this discovery and makes the same unconscious assumption when he deals with a fundamentally new awareness, namely intellectual consciousness: we assume that Pluto was there even before we lifted up the handkerchief of opaque distance by means of the telescope, as if consciousness were exactly the same as sensory awareness. Panikkar is not saying that Pluto was not there before its "discovery." He says that the problem does not arise before it is a meaningful problem.

Just as in the first dimension Panikkar was not affirming that every being is divine, so here he is not affirming that every being is conscious, either by making that particular being the subject, the substance, the *hypokeimenon* (the underlying thing), the hypostasis of the divinity in the first case or of consciousness in the second. It all depends on what we mean by a being: its private property (what that being alone "possesses," excluding all the rest) or what makes it unique (its inclusive uniqueness): its differentiation (from other) or its identity (with itself). In other terms, it is all a question of whether we use the principle of singularity or the principle of individuality to determine what a being is. He says, however, that every being has a constitutive dimension of consciousness, even if my understanding of that being does not hypostasize consciousness in "it," but somewhere else-in "me" knowing "it," for instance, or in consciousness in general. He is not only saying that we could not know a being if it were not somehow related to consciousness, but also that this relation is constitutive of that very being. Consciousness permeates every being. Everything that is, is *cit*.

Were it not for this dimension, reality would not be knowable and awareness would be a superimposed and extrinsic characteristic.

c) Every being, finally, stands in the Worlds and shares its secularity. There is nothing which enters human consciousness without at once entering into relation with the World. Again, this relation is not merely external or accidental: anything that exists has a constitutive relation with matter/energy and space/time. Even if we grant the possibility of an extramundane existence, even if we accept the reality of an atemporal and acosmic mystical experience, not only are all such figures of speech Worldly ones, but the very act of negating any relation with the World already constitutes a relation, albeit a negative one. In a word, extra- or ultra-mundanity is already a secular feature and has the *saeculum* as its referent.

For example, let us assume that truth and angels are real entities, each in its proper order. Both have a Worldly dimension. An epistemological concept of truth, as well as an ontological idea of truth, can only be meaningful within a World, i.e., within the range of Worldly experience-even if we extrapolate afterwards. Furthermore, truth, insofar as it belongs to epistemology, is not only connected with Man's mind, but with Man's objects, material or imaginary, which also already belong to this World. A metaphysical truth-whatever this may be-is only true if it is really *kata*-physical. Something similar can be said regarding a "heavenly" angel. Even if we disregard the etymological fact that "angel" means and envoy, one sent precisely to Men and to the Earth, the very existence of an angel, an *asura*, a *deva*, an *apsara*, a spirit, is linked to the destiny of Man and the World, and thus intimately related to that World. Even if we say that an angel is above matter and beyond space and time, these references already tie it to our World.

One of the most valuable hypothesis that the economic moment has furnished is the division of reality into a clear and cogent domain of spiritual ideas and a material precipitate of that intellectual domain. Plato in Greece and Śankara in India could be adduced as exemplars-differing scholarly interpretations of these two thinkers notwithstanding. But, this pattern of intelligibility is ultimately reductionistic and has its limits. It divides reality into two, and the cleft-even if it is considered only epistemological-soon proves insurmountable. The cosmotheandric vision, by contrast, would consider this third dimension an equally constitutive element of every being. There are not two Worlds. There may be as many distinctions and ontological gradations as we deem necessary, but ultimately there is only one reality-despite the drawbacks of this latter term, which in fact stresses the res, the cosmic dimension. Everything that is, is *res* and *ānanda*.

Is Panikkar saying that God is Worldly or abolishing the distinction-so dear to civilized Man-between Nature and Culture? Or between World and Person? No. He is not abolishing these distinctions, not even entering no into a discussion of them . He is only saying that a God without the World is not a real God, nor does he exist. He is saying that this cosmic dimension is not superfluous appendix to the other two dimensions, but equally constitutive, both of the whole and of each real part of the whole.

We mentioned earlier the correlation between *microcosm* and *macanthropos*, which is also one of the pillars of the Upanisadic experience. To each part of the human body corresponds a part of the material Universe. This correlation is essential in *tantra*, but equally present in the West. Man can become everything not only because he can grasp everything, but also because he is in perfect correlation with the material World. The relationship could not be more intimate. And it is a two-way intercourse: "If Man is a microcosm, the World is a macanthropos." For this reason interpreters of the Bible noted that after Man's creation God did not say that it was good, as on other days of creation, because Man was already understood to share in the very destiny of the Universe.

A powerful metaphor used by a zen master may give us another glimpse into this intuition of the polar unity between Man and Nature. Describing the effect of the discipline of simplifying one's life, he says, "Here is shown bare the most beautiful landscape of your birthplace." Perhaps only one's separate, not just a beautiful parcel of land or indeed anything "outside" of us; but part and parcel of ourselves, an extension or rather a continuation of our very being. Such a landscape is more than geography and even more than history: it is one's self; it is the very body or embodiment of one's own feelings, of our own most personal discovery of the World, of the environment-which not only "shapes" our lives, but actually *is* our proper field of existence. The roots which link us to the World lie there, it is there that we are in touch with the umbilicus which still gives us life and makes us insincere, and where some faint hope of attaining a new innocence still remains. That place is part of me, just as I am part of that place. There is and artists of every sort may be more sensitive to this feeling-they are our antennae - but the most ordinary person is surely open to its power.

Panikkar is saying that a purely immaterial being is as much an abstraction as an exclusively material one, and thus that a monistic spiritualism is as one-sided as a monistic materialism. He is saying that there are no disembodied souls or disincarnated Gods, just as there is no matter, no energy, no spatio-temporal World without divine and conscious dimensions. This does not mean that God has a body *like* ours. Even superficially, no two bodies are the same; by analogy, God's body differs from ours. On the other hand, it does mean that God is not without matter, space, time, body, and that every material thing that is, is God's, or more precisely, God's thing, God's own World.

Were it not for this spatio-temporal dimension, reality simply would not exist. Everything would be but the dream of a nonexistent dreamer who has only dreamt about the dream about the dream, without ever actually having dreamed at all. Were it not for matter and energy, or space and time, not only would human discourse and thinking be impossible, but God and consciousness could also recede into sheer nothingness and meaninglessness. The final foundation for the belief that something exists is that the World exists; the ultimate basis for Man's hope is the existence of the World. Whatever answer one may give to the ultimate *why* of Gottfried Wilhelm Leibniz (1646-1716) and Martin Heidegger (1889-1976), the question rests on the Worlds which sustains it and makes the asking possible. Why anything exists can be a question only if that *why* exists, i.e., if it already "sticks out" of nothingness.

C. Some Objections

All this may encounter to main objections. The first would say that by connecting everything intrinsically to everything else, we divest things of their individuality and toss everything indiscriminately into the same sack. The second objection would assert that it is simply false to suppose that one being could not exist without another.

In the final analysis, however both objections are based on a deficient epistemology. The first says that *A is-not B*, when it wants and needs only to say that *A is not-B*. The second objection claims to move from a *could-not* or *can-not* in the logical realm of thinking to an *is not* in the ontological realm of existence. Panikkar thus explains:

When we think, we may follow either of two patterns of intelligibility, primarily governed by the principles of non-contradiction and identity. Elsewhere he argued that the bulk of modern western thought is governed by the primacy of the principle of non-contradiction and that something similar could be said regarding indic culture and the principle of identity. Applying the principle of non-contradiction, we tend to isolate "things" and thus truncate their total reality by artificially severing them from what they really *are*. The limit of any being is Being itself-to use a certain terminology-and if we stop short of this (Being), we cripple the reality of that particular being. Following the principle of non-contradiction. A is the more A, the more it can be distinguished and separated from non-A. We know here by differentiation, Science and scission.

Applying the principle of identity, we tend to be blind to differences, throwing together really different dimensions of the real and confusing identity with the denial of differences. Following the principle of identity, A is the more A, the more it is identified with itself. We know here by identification, participation and union. There is no need to stress further that identity and difference are correlative. The one implies the other as much as they are mutually exclusive. Panikkar can only differentiate two things if he can show that they are not like each other.

He submits that the time has come to integrate these two principles. Every knowing process is a discriminating enterprise, but it has equally a synthetic function. This is to say that in order to know what beings are, we should not maim the very being they are. On the other hand, we also have to leave room for the differences. Only the combination of the two principles can provide a satisfactory answer in which identity is not annihilated by difference, or difference swallowed up in identity.

An elephant is not a man, but both *are*, though in different ways. The elephant is and the man *is*, but the one is not the other. The elephant is not-man and the man is not-elephant, but it would be incorrect to say (or to think) that the elephant *is-not* man or the man is-not elephant. Precisely because we cannot sever the *is* from the elephant or from the man, we cannot manipulate things in this way. Man implies that man-is. So we may say that *man-is* cannot be identified with *elephant-is*; but denying humanness to the elephant (the elephant is not-man) does not at all entail denying its is-ness (the elephant still is). In this sense we cannot say "the elephant is-not man." The *is* distinguishes as much as it unites them.

Most theistic systems, to put another example, affirm the difference between God and his creatures by stressing his transcendence; but they will equally affirm God's *sui generis* identity with creation by underscoring his immanence. God is more immanent to any creature-most systems will affirm-than the creature's own identity, so that if we were to subtract God from that creature, the latter would collapse into utter nothingness.

What Panikkar is saying is that the links which connect everything with everything else constitute those very things. When affirming that a piece of bread is cosmotheandric insofar as it is real, for instance, he is not saying that it is a piece of bread *plus* many other things, viz., a part of God and a portion on Man, thereby blurring all differences. He is saying that the piece of bread is a *piece* of bread, which implies first of all that it is a piece and not the totality of bread. He says, further, that bread is also a piece of all those things which serve as bread or food. The real bread of the piece of bread is more than an isolated monad, and its "breadness" (if by this we understand all that distinguishes it from non-bread) does not exhaust all that the bread *is*. The piece of bread is the bread of the piece, and this bread of the piece is the *is* of the bread. The "is" of the piece of bread is intrinsically connected with everything that is. To be sure, the piece of bread is a piece of Being and has to be dealt with as such. But, individualizing the piece-whatever piece-cannot and must not excommunicate it from the communion of beings and its *sui generis* participation in Being. Analytical thinking, important as it is, cannot overshadow the fact that it conveys meaning only within a given synthetic framework, whether conscious or not.

Panikkar would like to linger for a moment with this example and allow it also to exemplify the meaning that the Eucharist acquires from this perspective. The consecration of the bread is not so much the transformation of the bread into Christ as the transformation of Christ into bread. The consecrated bread does not cease to be bread. On the contrary, it becomes integral bread, a bread that contains the entire reality, a bread that is divine and material and human at the same time. It is the revelation of the cosmotheandric nature of reality. When we break bread in everyday life, we tend to be forgetful of this fact, and we alienate ourselves from this integral experience. The Eucharist reminds us of the whole and makes it real for us: "This is the Body of Christ." It is well known that this very expression indicated primarily the

Church, i.e., the Body of believers, the community of all Men. The Mystical Body does not mean just a small group of humans. It extends to the "breadth" of the entire Universe in its proper status. That this proper status is said to be reached at the end of time amounts to one interpretation which depends on a certain Cosmology, namely that which understands the *eschaton* in historical terms, and the "end" of time as the fullness of time. We may come to have a tempiternal understanding of this fullness, however, which would allow the *presence* of the whole to fill our lives-precisely in the present.

The answer to the second objection has to do with the nature of the mind which cannot, in and of itself, distinguish between the "actuality" and the "possibility" of any entity without an external empirical criterion. No amount of thinking about a possible 100 rupees enables me to know whether the money is actually in my pocket or not. On the other hand, we often tend to extrapolate without proper foundation, that is, to impose on the sphere of existence what belongs only to the realm of the ideally or intellectually thinkable. Here there seems to be a *metabasis eis allo genos*, a severe dislocation of genres which occasions misunderstanding. All this is said, recall, in order to obviate the objection which maintains that whereas some beings cannot be without another, there do exist some beings which cannot exist without a heart, but a living heart can exist without oak trees. And although an oak tree requires appropriate soil, it does not demand the existence of human justice. Panikkar does not deny that a being *could-be* or even *can be* without another. He does not deny that birds *could-be* without oceans, although they could not be without air. He must however insist that we are not dealing here with mere possibilities but with actualities, so that if beings A and B exist at all, there is in point of fact no A without B or any B without A, even if one or both *could-be* without the other. We should take seriously the fact that the knowledge of what is does not coalesce with the prediction of what could be. Let us consider an extreme case: a theistic system may assert that while there is no World without a creator, there *can be* a God without any creation.

A theist can certainly *think* of a God who does not require the existence of any creatures in order to be real, but this "God" does not exist because the actual God, the God that in fact exists, *is* God with creatures. That God "can be" (without creatures) is a phenomenological feature of God, not an ontological statement about "him."

A further phenomenological remark may be pertinent here. A rigorous *epoche* works in to direction: it brackets the eidetic intuition from the burden of existence, thus freeing essences from the pangs of existential birth, but it also liberates existences from responsibilities beyond their competence. In a theistic conception God may very well be defined phenomenologically as *id quo mais cogitari neiquit*, "that than which nothing greater can be thought." Further, God can be described as that "necessary being" which can exist, by itself (i.e., which does not need any other being in order to exist), whereas the creature or contingent being can be defined as that which can exist only *ab alio*, only if grounded in another or in something else. We would then have to say that a phenomenological analysis of our consciousness when thinking "God" or "creature" yields self-sufficiency in the first case and non-self-sufficiency in the second. A necessary being without creatures is thinkable, a contingent being without a Ground is unthinkable. We could further add that a necessary being *can* exist without creatures and a contingent being *can-not* exist without a ground of existence. This may help to clarify our concept phenomenologically. It might even help us to recognize the validity of a qualified ontological argument, but it cannot justify extrapolation into the existing Universe or into the Universe of existences. In other words, the statements "God can be without World" and "World cannot be without God" may be valid phenomenological observations, but they are not ontological affirmations about God or World.

Similarly, although one can think of a World without humans, this in no way proves that there is such a World without humans. It proves one can *think* of such a World, but it does not prove its existence. In fact, such a World (without humans) does not exist. Someone could retort that certainly this is the case no, but millions of years ago there *was* an astronomical Universe without human beings. Without entering into polemics by declaring that the concept of time implied here is neither convincing nor valid, and without invoking The Theory of Relativity in order to deny such an absolute diachrony, one can respond, first, that the statement itself operates in a human consciousness in which World and Man coexist and, secondly, that if we introduce the past we have to introduce the future as well, which invalidates the objection. If we affirm: "There was time, t1, in which there was a Universe without humans," we have to complete the statement by saying that from the perspective of time t1, "there will be a time, t2, in which the Universe will be with humans." Now our point is precisely that the time of which we are conscious in one way or another is t = t1 + t2, for t1 and t2 are only partial times. So we may still say: "There is no time, t, in which the Universe is without humans." Time is not only time past.

Yet the *pūrvapakṣin* might then retort that he was merely claiming that "There *was* a time without humans" and not that "there *is* such a time." This objection can be met by relaying that this was the only past from the perspective of the *present* (in which there is no World without humans). This amounts to affirming: "Now, we can imagine a *was* (an empty time, as it were, for no Man was there) in which there were no human beings, but there was a World." And this is true only as a *was*, not as an *is*. Which is why we instinctively say: "There *can* be a time in which there is an Earth and no humans, but as far as we are concerned, there is in truth no Worlds without humans."

Now however, as said earlier, Panikkar should like to present this cosmotheandric principle with the minimum of Philosophical assumptions. And the minimum here is that reality shows this triple dimension of an empirical (or physical) element, a noetic (a psychical) factor, and a meta-physical (or spiritual) ingredient. By the first he means the matter-energy complex, the Cosmos; by the second, the *sui generis* reflection on the first and on itself; and by the third, the inherent inexhaustibility of all things: the cosmic, the human and the divine.

D. Dimension

Panikkar has spoken of three, although different, dimensions of one and the same reality. The metaphor "dimension" is intended to help overcome the monistic temptation of constructing a simplistic modalistic Universe, viz. a Universe in which all things are but variations and modes of one substance. At the same time, it represents an attempt to overcome the pluralistic temptation of positing two or more unbridgeable elements, substance or groups of reality which have only external or casual, and ultimately accidental links with one another. Without denying differences, and even recognizing a hierarchical order within the three dimensions, the cosmotheandric principle stresses the intrinsic relationship among them, so that this threefold current permeates the entire realm of all that is.

This intuition ultimately results from a mystical experience and as such is ineffable. It is not an analytical conclusion. It is rather a synthetic vision which coordinates the various elements of knowledge with the knower, and then transcends them both. But, in the long run it is the fruit of a simple and immediate insight which dawns upon Man's awareness once he has glimpsed the core where the knower, known and knowledge meet.

a) In this version, the World is not a habitat or an external part of the whole or even of myself. The World is simply that greater body which I only imperfectly notice because I am generally too concerned with my own particular business. My relationship with the World is ultimately no different from my relationship with myself: the World and I differ, but are not two separate realities, for we share each other's life, existence, being, history and destiny in a unique way. My hand is not my heart; I can live without hands but not without heart. My World does not coalesce with your World; I can live without having realized many of my relations with this World, but not if I lack all of them. In our unique and idiosyncratic ways we share the entire World but, as the ancients loved to say, we "speculate," we are a reflection, an image of reality. This is what it means to be the image and likeness of the Creator. And this is why everything *speaks* of "him" - because he speaks everything. There *is*, certainly, no World without Man or Man without World.

Rejecting the World and reducing reality to God and the soul is the typical "spiritualist," or rather the Gnostic, temptation. Gnosticism can preach salvation in and through knowledge only because it has resigned itself to saving only the soul, the spiritual part on Man and the Cosmos. To do so, it must condemn matter and even exclude the World completely: there is no "new Heaven and new Earth."

The World is not only the glory of the Lord, it is also the World of Man. They belong together. Matter is as enduring as Spirit, although both may need to pass through the purification of death in order to rise again. Recovering our links with the World is not a question of having, but of being. The Earth will belong not to the powerful, or the resourceful, or those who are superior to it; but to the meek, the gentle children of Earth.

Something similar could be said regarding God and the World. The Cosmos is not just matter and convertible energy. The Cosmos has life, the Cosmos is on the move and, like Man, has also a dimension of *plus*, a "more," which is in itself and yet does not come from a restricted, abstract "more," The Cosmos is not an isolated chunk of matter and energy; it is the third dimension of the total reality. A Cosmos without Man and consciousness would not be and is not, certainly, the Cosmos we inhabit. A Cosmos without this divine urge, this dynamism built into its innermost core, is surely not the Cosmos we experience, the proper garb of every actual theophany. And he repeats, for those who are allergic to certain words, that this vision is not limited to a particular Philosophical or religious conception of reality.

b) God is not the absolute Other (regardless of the Philosophical difficulty) inherent in this formulation: absolute transcendence is contradicted by the very thought of it). Nor is God the same as us. He says that God is the ultimate and unique "I", that we are God's "thous," and that our relation is personal, Trinitarian and non-dualistic. But, the cosmotheandric vision does not need to be couched in such terms. It is enough to say that

Man experiences the depth of his own being, the inexhaustible possibilities of and for relationship, his non-finite (i.e., infinite) character-for he is not a closed being and cannot put limits on his own growth and evolution. Man discovers and senses an inbuilt *more* in his own being which at once belongs to and transcends his own private being. He discovers another dimension which he cannot manipulate. There is always more than meets the eye, finds the mind or touches the heart. This *ever more*-even more than perceiving, understanding and feeling-stands for the divine dimension.

Traditionally, this *more* has also been experienced as a better and most of the time as an *other*, as the mystery of the Beginning and the Beyond, i.e., as the Eternal and Infinite (or Supertime and Superspace). Here is not the place to set up a model for the divine. The cosmotheandric myth-as one is tempted to call it-clearly excludes a rigid monism or an unqualified atomism, as much as it excludes deism and anthropomorphism, but it does not exclude the wide range of systems that try more or less successfully to encompass the rich variety of the given without sacrificing that variety for the sake of unity, or oneness for the sake of multiplicity.

God is not only the God of Man, but also the God of the World. A God with no cosmological and therefore no cosmogonic functions could not be God at all, but a mere phantom. God is that dimension of more and better for the Worlds as much as for Man. Not only Man, but also the Cosmos is unachieved, not finished, in-finite. The Cosmos does not expand mechanically or unfold automatically; it also evolves, grows, moves toward an ever new Universe. Not only are theo-logy and meta-Physics representing all-embracing disciplines-necessary; but now, more than ever, theo-Physics has its place.

c) Man here is ultimately more than an individual. Man is a person, a knot in the net of relationships not limited to the spiritual "thous," but reaching out to the very antipodes of the real. An isolated individual is incomprehensible and also unviable. Man is only Man with the sky above, the Earth below, and his fellow beings all around. But, just as "individualizing" the human being is tantamount to cutting the umbilical cord which gives him life, so isolating Man from God and the World equally strangulates him. There is no Man without God or without World.

Perhaps we run into a semantic problem here. Perhaps these three names or groups of names should be reserved for the exclusivity features of their respective dimensions. If so, the divine would stand for what is neither human nor cosmic, the human for what is neither divine nor cosmic, and the cosmic for what is neither human nor divine. But, how then do we link the three together? How do we explain the extra - or super-human urges of Man? Or the creative power of the Cosmos? Or the humanizing bent of the divine? To be sure, it is all only a way of speaking, but just as surely do modern Man's idioms require a thoroughgoing revision, indeed, a new language. Man does not become less human then he discovers his divine calling, or the Gods lose their divinity when they are humanized, or the World becomes less Worldly when it bursts into life and consciousness. Perhaps we are saying that Man is at the crossroads, because the real is precisely this crossing of these three dimensions. Every real existence is a unique knot in this trefoil net. Here the cosmotheandric vision of reality stands for the holistic and integral insight into the nature of all that there is.

An old mandala could perhaps help to symbolize the cosmotheandric intuition: the circle. There is no circle without a centre and a circumference. The three are not the same and yet not separable. The circumference is not the centre, but without the latter the former would not be. The circle, itself invisible, is neither the circumference nor the centre, yet it is circumscribed by the one and inscribed around the other. The centre does not depends on the others, since it is dimensionless, yet it would not be the centre-or anything at all, for that matter-without the other two. The circle, only visible from the circumference, is matter, energy, the World. And this is so because the circumference, Man, Consciousness and encompasses it. And both are what they are because there is God, a centre, which alone-i.e., qua God, as the ancients would put it-is a sphere whose centre is everywhere and whose circumference is nowhere.

How shall we call the complete mandala? We should distinguish the divine, the human and the cosmic; the centre should not be confused with the circumference, and this latter should not be mixed up with the circle, but we cannot allow separation. After all, the circumference "filled in," and the centre acts as the very "seed" of the other two. There is a "circuminsession," a *perichorēsis* of the three.

In the ecumenic age, the Cosmos acted mainly as the centre; because this attitude was ecstatic, it could be cosmocentric, for Man was not totally aware of himself and his special position in the Universe. Thinking was mainly a passive activity-precisely because Man thought it was passive. But, when we become aware that the World is not the centre, we also begin to look for the real centre and circumference. This marks the transitional phase of theocentric conception, until Man finally realizes that it is he who has enthroned God in and as the centre.

In the economic phase, Man becomes more and more the centre; because this moment was enstatic, it was bound to become anthropocentric, for Man was conscious of being the measure of all things and thus of his central position in the Universe. Thinking became active-precisely because Man became conscious of his mental activity. But, as we gain perspective on various arcs of the circumference, we discover that it is not a straight line and we begin to look for a possible centre-or centres-of the curvature. No wonder that this problematic centre was sought in a multitude of ways and not easily found, for one segment of the circumference yields a different centre from that calculated from any other sector of the circumference. Apparently we are not all on the same circumference, until we go far enough..... and share the same mythical horizon.

The cosmotheandric vision does not gravitate around a single point, neither God nor Man nor World, and in this sense *it has no centre*. The three coexist, they interrelate and may be hierarchically constituted or coordinated-the way ontological priorities must be-but they cannot be isolated, for this would annihilate them.

This cosmotheandric intuition Panikkar has been trying to describe, though expressed rather Philosophically, represents, the emerging religious consciousness of our times. Modern Man has killed an isolated and insular God, contemporary Earth is killing a merciless and rapacious Man, and the Gods seem to have deserted both Man and Cosmos. But, having touched bottom, we perceive signs of resurrection. At the root of the ecological sensibility there is a mystical strain; at the bottom of Man's self-understanding is a need for the infinite and un-understandable. And at the very heart of the divine is an urge for time, space and Man.

7.3.2 Transhistorical Consciousness

In a more contemporary way of speaking about the consciousness, we could say that it amounts to experiencing the sacredness of the secular. Panikkar means by secularity the conviction of the irreducible character of time, i.e., the sense that Being and time are inextricably connected. Time is experienced as a constitutive dimension of Being; there is no atemporal being. *Sacred secularity* is an expression meaning that this very secularity is inserted in a realty that is not exhausted by its temporality. Being is temporal, but is also "more" and "other" than this. Now this "more" is no mere juxtaposition-as if eternity, for instance, would arrive "after" time, or as if a supra-temporal Being were temporal "plus" something else or merely atemporal. Similarly, this "other" is not another Being which does not share temporality. Panikkar would use the word *tempiternity* to express this unity. Employing another neologism, Panikkar has called *cosmotheandrism* the experience of the equally irreducible character of the divine, the human and the cosmic (freedom, consciousness and matter), so that reality-being one-cannot be reduced to a single principle. This is, in Panikkar's opinion, the basis for a change which is truly pluralistic.

If we take pluralism not as a political strategy but as a word representing the ultimate structure of reality, we shall have to overcome the assumption of a single pattern of intelligibility. At this level, all words break down. It may be that there is only one scheme of intelligibility, but we cannot postulate it a priori. It may also be that there is a peculiar awareness of dimensions of reality which simply does not fit into the category of intelligibility. We may be aware of Matter or of the Spirit and yet be unable to call them intelligible-not only de facto, because *we* cannot (*quoad nos*) know it, but *de iure* (*quoad se*), because they do not belong to the order of intelligibility.

The underlying hypothesis of monotheism is that there is a Supreme Mind to which all things are intelligible, so that if *quoad nos* beings are not transparent, *quoad se* i.e., for God-all reality is intelligible. It would not be fair to criticize this metaphysical hypothesis by underscoring the dangers of manipulation and the abuses it has led to in all sorts of caesaropapisms, totalitarianisms and colonialisms, East and West. The problem is of a deeper nature.

To say that we are beginning to witness the end of history does not have to mean the end of Man. Yet the ordeal is going to have historical proportions, precisely if we are to bring history to a close. In this crucible of the modern World, only the mystic will survive. All the others are going to disintegrate: they will be unable to resist either the physical structures or the psychical strains. And this disintegration will include the so-called middle classes which for the moment can eat adequately and do not try to take a stand on any slippery decision-making platforms.

The mystic, or at least a certain kind of mystic, has a transhistorical experience. He or she does not situate thing along the course of linear time. Theirs is a vision which includes the three times: past, present and future. An example is the difference between the popular belief in the Semitic religions of a "creation" at the beginning of the World, understanding this creation as an event situated in the past, and the interpretation often given by metaphysicians and mystics: that the "creation" and "conservation" of the Universe by God are not two separate acts; and that creation is a continuous process. Scholastic theology affirms that the simplicity of God obliges us to say that the very act by which

God begets the Son creates the World. The eternal intra-trinitarian process and the temporal extra-trinitarian act ultimately coalesce in their source. In this vision, the fulfillment of my life does not need to depend on the fulfillment of the historical future of my nation, people, race or even of humankind. Panikkar is somewhat independent of the structures of historical events. If the end of life is the destruction of all *karmas* still binding one to the temporal flux, then the meaning of human life no longer lies n the historical fulfillment of a mission but in the realization of the human being.

Pre-historical Man was fearful of Nature, but he managed in his own way to come to terms with Mother Earth or the Earth Goddess. Now Big Brother and his twin, technology, are frightening historical Man, who tries desperately to cope with them. Pre-historical Man had to take his distance from Nature, so to speak, in order to survive as Man. It is this alienation from Nature that made him Man and differentiated him from the animals-for better or worse. Modern, i.e., historical, Man has now to separate himself from *the System* in order to live as Man. It is this salutary severance, this weaning from the System that will differentiate those who succeed in preserving their humanness from the robots, victims of the System: ants, work addicts, cogs in the megamachine, "bits" identified by number in the ubiquitous computers' memory banks. Withdrawal from the System does not necessarily mean flight into the mountains or mere escapism from history. It certainly does mean a pilgrimage to the "high places" of the human spirit and the human Earth, as well as an overcoming of the historical obsession. But, it also means keeping one's hands and heart free to help fellow beings on their way to this new conscientization. Perhaps we could call it *Realization*.

Here are some of the traits of this Realization: Nonhistrical consciousness sees life mainly in the interplay between the past and the present; the future has hardly any weight. Historical consciousness is busy discharging the past into the future; the present s just the intersection of the two. Transhistorical consciousness attempts to integrate past and future into the present, past and future are seen as mere abstraction. Not only has the two-storey building of pre-historical Man collapsed, but the one-storey building of historical Man is also a shambles. The two-storey building as the cosmological image of traditional religions: now and here are only the time and place for the struggle to attain the happiness of salvation elsewhere and after.

Human life is more than just an accretion from the past and a projection into the future. It is both (and together) the *ex* and the *sistence* which constitute our being. This is why only by in-sisting on the ex-sistence are we saved. And this is the experience of contemplatives. They live the present in all its in-tensity and in this tension discover the in-tentionality and in-tegrity of life, the tempiternal, ineffable core which is full in every authentic moment.

The democratization of modern consciousness, the levelling down of the hierarchical structure of the Universe, destroys the belief that salvation or realization is a privilege. Man wants the fulfillment of life not only here and now for the select few, but for everybody. This means that there is now emerging a new myth that the fullness of life-or more simply, its meaning-has to be attained not only in this World, as the mystics have always stressed, but for everyone. This salvation, understood as human fulfillment, cannot be tied to, or belong to, one race, one culture, or one religion. Modern conScience feels that it has to be universal, within reach of everybody. Yet it is obvious that this is not the case; a substantial proportion of the five billion humans have not even reached the minimum level of the *humanum*. It is this impasse that fosters the emergence of transhistorical consciousness on a societal level, once the great temptation is resisted: the fall into hedonistic indulgence in the merely temporal moment by those who can selfishly afford it. This may be said to be the traditional touchstone of authentic spirituality. Escapism from the people, instant self-gratification, selfish elitism and blindness to the historical predicament of Man would be just the opposite of the transhistorical consciousness Panikkar is describing.

Summing up, the background of pre-historical Man in the *theoCosmos*: he finds himself in friendship and confrontation with the *numina*, the natural and divine forces. His scenario is the divinized Cosmos. He lives mainly turned toward the past. He worships his ancestors.

The horizon of historical Man is *history*: he finds himself in collaboration and struggle with human society of the past, present and future. His World is the human World. He lives mainly turned toward the future. He worships the God that shall be.

The emerging myth of the transhistorical Man assumes a more or less conscious *theanthropocosmic* vision of the Universe: he finds himself, in varying degrees of harmony and tension, within a cosmotheandric *reality* in which all the forces of the Universe-from electromagnetic to divine, from angelic to human-are intertwined. He lives mainly in the present. He is very cautious in worshipping. If at all, he would reverence the intersection of past and future, of the divine and the human.

Pre-historical Man has *fate*. He is part and parcel of the Universe. Historical Man steers *destiny*. He predestines here he stands. He arranges his own life. Tranhistorical Man lives his *life*. He is involved in the total adventure of reality by participating in the portion "allotted" to him or by willingly shaping the part that he is.

The pre-historical mentality does not have to justify Man's existence to itself or to others. The human beings simply lives, like any other living being. Historical consciousness has to justify, i.e., to prove, the value of Man's existence by his *doing*, i.e., by creating or producing his own World with its values. Modern Man is a worker. Transhistorical Man has lost both the pre-historical naiveté and the historical optimism/pessimism. He feels the urge to be what he s supposed to be by occupying his proper place in the Universe.

The World of transhistorical Man, his environment, is the cosmotheandric Universe. The renewed interest in astrology, for instance, is due not merely to the desire to know what will happen, how a marriage or a business will develop, but to the increasing awareness that personal destiny is linked both with the fate of society and with the adventure of the entire Cosmos. As another example, we may cite the renewal of popular religiosity and the proliferation of so many new religious movements expressing people's thirst to connect again not only with the human World but with the Universe at large, where humans are not the only conditioning forces. The destiny of Man is not just an historical existence. It is linked with the life of the Earth (ecological interlude) and with the entire fate of reality, the divine not excluded. God or the Gods are again incarnated and share in the destiny of the whole Universe. We are all in the same boat, which is not just this planet Earth but the entire mystery of life, consciousness, existence. *Love* is the supreme principle, the linking force which brings everything together. But, we have already hinted at the main reason for the awakening of such consciousness: life has to make sense even when all the idols-progress, civilization, peace, prosperity, paradise-fail. To make virtue of such a necessity does not make the virtue any less real, once it truly achieved. We could formulate the same fundamental intuition from a personalistic perspective. All Men want to reach salvation. Panikkar takes this statement to be a quantified tautology. We could describe three fundamentally different interpretations or experiences of this salvation, according to the predominant degree of consciousness. In most religions we find the three types, although with differing emphases. For purposes of our discourse, we may call one nirvana, the other *sotēría* and *mokṣa* the third.

Nirvāṇa, as the name indicates, would suggest here a "blowing out," an exhaustion of the burning material, an escape from the structures of the prison of space and time and thus of matter. I save myself by allowing *samsāra*, this World, to fall quietly away, even if to do so I must put up with it for the time being and do my duty. My salvation consists in the realization that I was already immortal, except that I was enmeshed in this trap of matter. The examples here would run from Plato and the Gnostics to Mahāvira and the Vedāntins. They cross religious boundaries, because the source could be said to be the personal experience that my being s ultimately pure consciousness (or simply a soul) and that this consciousness or soul has nothing to do with my body or, ultimately, with matter.

Sotēría, as the name indicates, implies a being whole and healthy, protected and well. It entails a belief in the possibility of transforming the structures of space and time into something that will provide Man with the very fullness of his being. One is saved when one reaches that condition of a New Heaven and a New Earth here the deep and authentic nature of everything will shine forth in its true state and make manifest the universal order: personal, cosmic or divine. Immortality is not something which belongs to one's nature but something that belongs to the redeemed structures of the transformed Universe. It has to be not only conquered but recreated, as it were. It is a new creation. The examples here would run from Paul and the Christian Fathers to Abhinavagupta and the Tantrikas. They cross religious boundaries because the source could be said to be the personal experience that my being is a mixture of spirit and matter that has not yet arrived at its complete fusion, and that this integration is ultimately the very meaning of reality.

Now it is clear that if the ideal of salvation is *nirvāṇa*, the historical development of the World is a very secondary process, relevant only insofar as it touches one's self directly, making one suffer or giving one enough to eat and live on, so that one may pursue the real goal of one's life. On the contrary, if the ideal of salvation is *sotēría*, the historical development of the World impinges directly on my own realization and that of all my fellow beings. To be engaged in the historical process of transforming humankind is the means for salvation.

Traditional religious have been inclined to interpret salvation as *nirvāṇa* in a more or less radical or qualified manner. So traditional Christians would consider this World not as an obstacle, perhaps, but as a means to attain the other, the real one. Modern movements such as Marxism and Humanism have been inclined to interpret salvation as *sotēría* in a more or less radical or qualified manner. The great crisis of our times is that *nirvāṇa* has ceased to be credible to a great part of the World, mainly to that part of humankind which has been touched by the ideology of modern Science. And, at the same time, *sotēría* has equally lost its credibility for a great part of humankind presently facing the no-exit of the present paneconomic ideology. Is there any way out of the dilemma? Is there a transhistorical human experience above and beyond the nonhistorical *nirvāṇa* and the historical *sotēría*? If *nirvāṇa* is fundamentally transcendent, and *sotēría* immanent, *mokṣa* could be the code for this rather nondualistic interpretation of the problem. The people of the World thirst for this integral liberation, not only from the chains of an unjust social order but equally from the limitations of a confining, selfish ego.

In sum, transhistorical consciousness is not worried about the future because time is not experienced as linear or as an accumulation and enrichment of moments past, but as the symbol of something which does not exist without Man but cannot be identified with him, either. It is neither the City of God nor the City of Man that transhistorical Man is about to build. He or she would rather concentrate on building to completion the microcosm that is Man, both individually and collectively: mirroring and transforming the macrocosm altogether.

Separated, any one of these three modes of consciousness is insufficient to bear the burden of being human. Not unlike the androgynous character of Man (in spite of the differentiation between male and female), these three modes are all intertwined in human life, although kairologically distributed. Man is embarking upon a new venture, about which we know only that we allow the internal dynamism of our deepest being to express itself, without projecting beforehand what we are to do and to be. We are creatively participating in the very existence of the cosmotheandric reality.

The cosmotheandric vocation is a calling to the inner discovery of a lifestyle that is not exclusively historical. You do not postpone everything for the future, you do not become entangled in the World of means (always the irresistible temptation of technology). Panikkar calls this transhistorical consciousness, the mystical awareness? It is a consciousness which supersedes time-or rather which reaches the fullness of time, since the three together, then I am the contemporary of Christ as well as of Plato, the end of the World has already come, or rather is constantly coming... along with its beginning. Then my individuality touches everything and everybody and yet I *am* all the more: *aham Brahman*. The end of the World will come before some of you die, said Christ. "Today you shall be with me in Paradise. " Then (i.e., now) resurrection and also reincarnation make sense. The meaning of life is not something you can make a career out of, nor yet something you can postpone discovering until after death. And this is the paradox: I am then everybody and everything-but from a unique angle, so to speak.

Sharing in the unfolding of Life, assisting at the cosmic display of all the forces of the Universe, witnessing the deployment of time, playing with the dynamic factors of life, enjoying the mysteries of knowing and no less the mystery of living, waking not haunted by the doing of the day ahead, but gifted with the being bestowed in the present, not wanting oneself to succeed at the price of other's defeat, or wanting to "distinguish" oneself by doing something "extra"-ordinary, as if the ordinary were not enough, just walking in the divine Presence, as the ancients used to say, being conscious of the systole and diastole, of the World, feeling the very assimilation and disassimilation of the Cosmos on both the macro - and the micro-cosmic scales, lending sensitivity to the stars and atoms, being the mirror of the Universe and reflecting it without distorting it, suffering as well in one's own flesh the disorders of the World, being oneself the laboratory where the antibodies or medicines are created, not being unaware of the forces of evil or the trends of history, but not allowing oneself to be suffocated by them either, each of us overpowering these demons in our own personal lives, understanding the songs of the birds, the sounds of the woods and even all the human noises as part of the vitality of reality expanding, living, breathing in and out, not just to go somewhere else (and never arrive), but just to be, to live, to exist on all the planes of existence at the same time: the tempiternal explosion of the adventure of Be-ing..... *this is transhistorical existence.*

7.3.3 Toward a New Cosmology

To this point, we have been emphasizing the relationship with individual things. But, this is not the whole story. It still remains for us to build a total relationship with the Earth, planet Earth as a whole, and the entire astrophysical and subatomic reality as a Universe.

What is most striking here is both the lack of, and the need for, a new Cosmology. We know we cannot do without one, and yet we also know that we do not today have a single convincing candidate. Modern Science in general, and Physics in particular, refuse-and rightly so-to provide us a complete picture of the World, to offer an explicit Cosmology. Yet, in spite of the sober claims of the best Scientist, the popular imagination and the pop-Science literature are constantly serving up a potpourri of "interesting" titillations of a Scientific World-picture. Another proof *ad hominem* that Man is not only a logical being, but a mythopoetic one as well.

To discover that the same "natural" laws rule in the astrophysical and subatomic Worlds encourages the idea of a unified Cosmos, but the mathematical substructure it offers as the real unity seems only a lifeless, featureless uniformity. And to revert to pre-Scientific ideas like the Earth as a big animal, or cities with their own guardian angels, or plants with their particular spirits, etc., will not do for modern Man. The idea of the World as a whole can also be a splendid abstraction, and nothing else, a kind of theoretical omega point required as little more than a mental hypothesis to coordinate our thinking. And again, to be led by simple ecological considerations, respectable as such motives may be in response to the material and economic havoc wrought by technology upon the physical environment, will not suffice either.

Panikkar is afraid that stressing this pragmatic aspect too greatly will only lead to more refined and subtle ways of exploiting the Earth. At first, it was done brutality and without consideration;

now, with precautions, recycling and cajoling-but nevertheless exploiting her as if we remained her lords and masters.

The modern western World has undertaken a thoroughgoing deanthropomorphization of the meaning of the word *God*. It has also tried to deontologize God. In the same process, Man has equally devitalized the Earth. The Earth has been left for dead by the same token that the Heaven has been deserted. Modern Man seems to have forgotten what the Vedas, the Bible and the Chinese Classics affirm: that Heaven and Earth share the same destiny. With Heaven fading away, the Earth become no longer a living Being, but simply matter and energy; and the forces of nature are no longer living spirits and qualities, but merely "attributes" of nature.

Important as this purification of the ideas of Heaven and Earth may have been, it has had an unexpected side-effect; Man has been converted into an isolated being without partners, superiors or inferiors. Heaven has become a human project, a more or less heuristic ideal; and the Cosmos, little more than a condition of human existence. But, neither Heaven nor the Cosmos have any reality of their own. This is the radical humanism of our times. It has converted Man into an isolated *Dasein* - with neither a *Da* (here, there) where to rest, nor a *Sein* (being, essence) which to be.

In a certain sense, such a process brings a very positive acquisition. Perhaps modern western Man needed to deeply enter this experience of excruciating isolation and solitariness in order to rediscover with a higher degree of awareness, on a new curve of the spiral, that the three dimensions-the divine, the cosmic, and the human-all belong to the real and interpenetrate one another, so that everything has anthropomorphic features, as well as divine and material dimensions. A totally deanthropomorphized God could not be real, just as there can be no totally dehumanized Universe. Both the cosmic and the divine are irreducible dimensions of the real which cannot be co-opted by Man, although they meet in Man, just as Man meets in them.

7.3.4 Cosmotheandric Spirituality

Panikkar suggests some milestones for this new awareness of a terrestrial spirituality. For heuristic purposes, he divides into paragraphs what is simple and corresponds to a single and simple vision. And, for the sake of brevity, he does not elaborate all the ramifications of this insight.

First, this cosmotheandric insight has to emerge spontaneously. A new innocence is required here. Legal impositions or moral constraints will not suffice, important as these human disciplines may be on their own terrains. But, spirituality cannot, ultimately, be legislated or commanded. It has to germinate freely in the very depths of our being. The proper soil is the myth.

Second, such spontaneity entails that this spirituality keep itself independent, so far as possible, from Philosophical and Scientific hypotheses. The criterion for the authenticity of a myth is its meta-Philosophical and meta-Scientific character. A myth is polyvalent and polysemic. For many people today, God and Science are no longer myths, but ideologies, i.e., it will function whether we follow one ideology or another.

Third, the Earth is neither inferior to Man nor superior. Man is neither the boss of this World, nor just a creature, the product of a cosmic Womb. The Earth is also not "equal" to Man. Equality assumes a higher genus of which the two species are precisely equal specimens. Man and the Cosmos, to the contrary, are ultimates, and thus reducible neither one to the other nor to a higher entity. The relation is non-dualistic. Both are distinct, but not separable. My head is distinct from me, yet cannot be separated from me. It would cease to be what it is, and so would I. The head is essentially the head *of* a body. The metaphor of the body may still be powerful: we do not treat our bodies as something other, although we discover their otherness: *aliud non alius*.

Fourth, our relation with the Earth is part of our self-understanding. It is a constitutive relationship. To be entails being *in* and *with* the World. I do not treat my stomach independently of my body, or of myself. I am convinced that what is best for my stomach is also best for me-although sometimes I may set my sights on the maximum instead of the optimum and overeat or drink too much. Our relationship with the Earth is similar, once this total awareness has dawned. We don't so much need a pragmatic recycling as a living symbiosis, a mutual rejuvenation, a spiral movement. If there are entropic phenomena in the Universe, there are equally syntropic ones-the vital ones.

At the height of European individualism, to save one's soul as the greatest concern. A more mature spirituality discovered that the business of saving our individual souls was neither a business nor a real salvation, because such individualistic souls do not exist: we are all interconnected, and I can reach salvation only by somehow *incorporating* the entire Universe in the enterprise. *Auctis augendis*, Panikkar says that the cosmotheandric spirituality makes us aware that we cannot save ourselves without *incorporating* the Earth in the same venture-and, *minutis minuendis* (every person represents and symbolizes all of reality), God as well.

Fifth, with this kind of spirituality, the pan-monetary ideology is overcome. One does not live just to eat, but when we eat properly we live and let live, and life circulates. We do not work in order to earn money or to acquire commodities, but because human activity is part of human and cosmic life and sustains the entire organism. Accumulation implies a peculiar relationship to time. Money gives power, but power above all over the uncertain future. The cosmotheandric spirituality sees fulfillment not so much in some future time as in a wider space that incorporates the "three times."

Sixth, this spirituality overcomes the dichotomy between so-called nature mysticism as a lower form of union with the World, and theistic mysticism as a supposedly superior form of God. Nature is nothing if not *naturata* (begotten), and God equally remains and abstraction if not *naturans* (begetter). If I climb the highest mountain, I'll find God there, but likewise if I penetrate the depths of an apophatic Godhead I shall find the World there. And in neither case will I have left the heart of Man. The "creation" of the World does not need to mean that the "creator" has gone away. Nor does the "incarnation" of God need to mean exclusive "hominization" in a single individual. The entire reality is committed to the same unique adventure.

Finally, this spirituality would heal another open wound for modern Man: the chasm between the material and the spiritual and, with this, between the secular and the sacred, the inner and the outer, the temporal and the eternal. It is not a question of blurring differences, but of realizing interrelations and becoming conscious of interdependencies and correlations. Man does not have a double citizenship, as it were-one here below and another above, or for later on. He or she is here and now the inhabitant of an authentic reality that has many mansions and presents many dimensions, but which does not slice human life into sections, either in time or in space, or for the individual or for society. Service to the Earth is divine service, just as the love of God is human love.

All that remains is for us to spell it out in our own lives.

7.3.5 The Christophanic Experience

Christophany, as Panikkar states, is not a simple extension of Christology that attempts to explain—and even understand—the "fact" of Christ. Since, it is more experiential, christophany concentrates its attention on the light in which Christ manifests himself to us. In this way we discover that not only do many of Jesus' statements create scandal by shaking our habits, but they seem to originate in a different vision of the World.

One striking example of this is Jesus' Eucharistic speech (John 6:22-67). Scientific Cosmology does not help here. If we restrict ourselves to such a scheme, the speech makes no sense; it could be accepted only as metaphor, and even "with a grain of salt." The same could be said of the Cosmology of Jewish contemporaries of Jesus. They were "right" to be scandalized. We are dealing here with a dilemma of which we are not always conscious.

In order to accept in a human way freely and consciously and fact or event, we must seek to understand it intellectually. The famous problematic of Tertullian, *credo quia absurdum* ("I believe because it is absurd") is generally misunderstood; its *quia* ("because") does belong after all, to the order of reason. It gives us a reason to believe. The dilemma consists in this: because of the intellectual process of acceptance, we must either integrate such a fact into our vision of the World of modify that vision. To take one significant example, most medieval scholastics who believed in the saying *philosophia ancilla theologiae* ("Philosophy as the handmaid of theology") did not take into account the fact that the theology of the time was no more that an essentially Aristotelian-Plantonic Philosophy that served to undergird and constituted the basis of Christian dogma. In adhering to the Hellenic Cosmology it converted theology into *ancilla philosophiae* ("the servant of Philosophy"). Even those who defend a *theilogia crucis* ("theology of the cross") and are ready to insult reason, end up building another castle based on another Philosophy, as happened with the earliest protestant theology.

The christophany that Panikkar wishes to introduce resolves the dilemma by accepting the second part that is, by modifying its vision of the World. This is possible only if the faith that has allowed the reality of Christ to be revealed to is strong enough to overturn the habitual parameters of our understanding: again we encounter the *antisrophe* that we have noted before, an *antistrophe* that is more profound than Nietzsche's *Umwertung* ("transvaluation [of values]").

The problem is central. The manifestation of Christ, the epiphany that stands at the basis of christophany, is so powerful that, inasmuch as it does not reenter the categories of the rational mind, it unsettles a merely rational cosmovision. Luther, among many others, had seen and suffered this dilemma, which in fact caused his antipathy to scholasticism inasmuch as he believed that its "theology" was only Greek wisdom, "foolishness before God" (1 Corinthians 3:19). In brief, christophany requires, in addition to the two eyes we use to deal with everyday experience, a third eye, which faith alone can open. The faith that moves mountains (Matthew 17:20) and dominates the plants and the elements

(Matthew 20:21; Luke 17:6; Mark 11:22) may well modify our cosmovision.

What then is the change that is necessary to bring to "our" cosmovision?

The question makes no sense because Worldviews are not changed at will: they constitute the omnicomprehensive myth that produces meaning and makes things and events coherent with its distinctive vision of the World. To allow this new vision to spring forth constitutes the great challenges of our times.

A cosmovision does not constitute the concept of the World we construct (Cosmology) as much as the vision we have of reality as it presents itself to us, as we see it in a vital relationship that constantly moves between objectivity and subjectivity. The cosmovision changes as our eyes our categories of understanding.

Christophany is the fruit of such "seeing," which then seeks to express itself in comprehensible language and draws insight form tradition itself, the fruit of a perception of the *phania* of Christ.

The problem is of capital importance. Panikkar has already referred to the atheistic hypothesis of the superfluous God: after all, the Universe functions, regardless of whether or not God exists. This transcendent, absent God is completely useless. The same may be said of Christ. If "the mystery of Christ" leaves our cosmovision unchanged, it remains imply a private affair of "the faithful," with no real bearing on the World. Christophany's challenge and task are to present a vision of the Universe in which the mystery of Christ finds its place. Otherwise, everything is reduced to pious and meaningless pharses.

The challenge is real. In what do we place our trust? In the words, for example, that tell us that Christ has risen, or in Scientific categories that present the resurrection as a collective hallucination? If our "faith" is only belief in the words of others, it obviously cannot be accepted by the human intellect. If there has been a personal experience, however, it will try to find a suitable language that will be understandable only within a determinate cosmovision. The challenge is no light matter.

Two variant interpretations can lead us to the heart of what *manere* ("to remain" one in the other) could mean. We might call one anthropological, the other Philosophical.

The first is the universal phenomenon of falling in love. The vision of the person loved is transformed, though others don't see what the person in love sees.

Te second, which is also a universal phenomenon, can be expressed by saying that everyone is open to transcendence. Each of us has a certain consciousness that in fat there is something else, something greater than what we can grasp by sight. It has frequently been noticed, however, that something of this transcendence descends into inner depths. Of man and we speak of the immanence of the divine. God, the sacred, the numinous, or whatever we wish to call it, remains then in us it is *immanent*. There is a *manere* of God in each of us. This creates a certain reciprocity: God is in us and are in God. Paul, echoing Greek wisdom, preached to the Athenians that in God "we live and move and have our being" (Acts 17: 28).

One need only cite the first (untranslatable) phrase of the *Īśā-upaniṣad*: "Everything that moves in this changing World is entwined by God."

But, this is not yet the christophanic experience, which is neither merely "human" like the first nor exclusively "divine" like the second. On the contrary, the christophanic experience reveals to us that, when they are authentic, the first is not merely human nor the second solely divine. In the christophanic experience it is neither God who remains in us nor we in him; it is rather a theandric or eucharistic presence that penetrates us and remains in us, and we in it. On that one hand, it is similar to the anthropological experience of falling in love, but with a difference: the christophanic experience is not a mere human presence. It is the human and the divine in a union that is unique. On the other hand, it is a mutual *manere*, which assumes the nature of the two experiences just described. Here, in experiential form, is what various doctrines later elaborate. The encounter with Christ partakes of the encounter with both the person lived and the divine. Without the falling in love, without the falling in love, without the silence of the *Abgrund* ("abyss"), there is no christophany no Christic manifestation. Christian mysticism presents this polarity, which is not free of tensions. Those who are inclined to knowledge, to *jñāna*, will see the divine aspect; those more sensitive to love, to *bhakti*, will see Christ's humanity as central.

7.3.5.1 Christophany is the Symbol of Divine, Human, and Cosmic Reality

The entire cosmotheandric experience is implicit here to divine, the human, and the World. Christ's function is not limited to "redeeming" humanity but embraces the restoration of the World; the cosmic *mandala* (both *orbis* and *mandala* mean circle).

"Whoever sees me sees the Father" (John 14:9). Jesus Christ is pure transparence, the Way. At the same time, whoever sees Jesus Christ sees the prototype of the complete man, the *totus homo.* Whoever discovers Jesus Christ experiences eternal life that is, the resurrection of the flesh and therefore the reality of matter, of the Cosmos (material Universe). Jesus Christ is the living symbol of divinity, humanity, and the Cosmos. Whatever experience does not entail these three dimensions can hardly be called a living encounter with the young rabbi who one night told Nicodemus that man's new birth must spring out of water (matter) and the Spirit (John 3:5-6).

In Jesus Christ the finite and the infinite meet, the human and the divine are joined. In him the material and the spiritual are one, and also the male and the female, high and low, heaven and earth, the historical and transhistorical, time and eternity. From the historic-religious point of view the figure of Christ could be described as that of a person who reduces to zero the distance between heaven and earth, God and man, transcendent and immanent, without sacrificing either pole which is precisely the principle of *advaita*. Jesus prayed, "That they be one" (John 17:21).

If, as we have said, we separate the figure of Christ from the Trinitarian mystery, we fail to grasp the meaning of christophany. In this respect one may speak of the "radical Trinity" as a complement to the intuition of the unity between the immanent and the "economic" unity. The immanent Trinity would be God's mystery "within" (*ab intra*) the divine interiority, of whole the economic Trinity would be the action directed "externally" (*ad extra*), the "work of creation" (*opous creationis*), especially as it refers to humanity. After Tertullian this distinction became of the fear of falling into pantheism, as a famous thirteenth-century text asserts: *Inter creatorem et creaturam non potest similitude notaari, quin inter eos major sit dissimilitude notanda* ("Between the creator and the creature no similarity can be noted without calling attention to the dissimilarity, which is greater").

To keep us from forgetting the Trinity, Karl Rahner formulated the thesis that "te economic Trinity is the immanent Trinity," and immediately added, "and vice versa." Some theologians criticize this "vice versa" because they hold that it contradicts the Lateran Council's affirmation cited above. Without entering into the heart of that discussion now, I would like to underscore again the difficulty that Western thought has experienced in admitting that a-dualism could exist between monism and dualism. "The Father is equal to the Son," the trinitarian doctrine asserts, because everything that the Father is he gives to the Son without holding anything back, yet the Son is not the Father; otherwise he would not be the Son, and the immanent Trinity would vanish. According to the Council of Toledo, *Quod enim Pater est, non ad se, sed ad Filium est; et quod Filius est, non ad se, sed ad Patrem est; similiter et Spiritus Sanctus non ad se, sed ad Patrem er Filium relative refertur: in eo quod Spiritus Patris et Filii predicator* ("What the Father is, he is no for himself, but for the Father; in the same way the Holy Spirit does not refer to himself but to the Father and the Son: therefore is called the Spirit of the Father and the Son").

It is worth saying that the nondual *advaita* to which I refer is neither a dialectical negation of duality nor a secondary act of the intellect or perhaps better, the human spirit. Rather, it is a direct vision that transcends rationality (without denying it.) I do not intend to say that duality comes "first" and is subsequently denied but that we see relationality immediately "before" any duality. In this sense we may also call it "non-unity." The constitutive relational nature of reality or, better, its corelationality cannot be characterized as either unity of duality. In fact, both the latter are no more than what human thought requires when it breaks out of the primordial silence from which it originates.

The way in which the radical Trinity manifests itself in Christ presents us with the nondualist unity between the divine and the human (the *theandric* mystery of Easter theology). But, the human being, too, constitutes a between spirit and body, and each of us exists in the corporeality proper to material things. The "three" (the "divine," the "human, and the "material") go together with neither confusion nor separation.

I have called this experience the *cosmotheandric* or the *theanthropocosmic* intuition. At times this intuition has been misunderstood, as if it were a question of three substances. Again, Christ remains the central symbol. Christ is one, and not a union of "three' elements, even though we can and must acknowledge this tridimensionality in him, well as in the whole of reality. It is enough to remember that the traditional vision of Jesus Christ has always recognized in him the harmonious conjunction of these three dimensions of the real, even though every period and every person accentuates now one, now the other element of the triad.

Maximus the Confessor writes that in Christ the five great "conjunctions" are realized: the masculine with the feminine (Galatians 3:28), the World of the damned with paradise (Luke 23:43); the terrestrial World with heaven (Acts 1:9-11), the sensible with intelligible things (Ephesians 4:10), created with uncreated nature.

Rather than a *coincidential oppositorum,* Jesus Christ has been described as the reconciliation between the divine and the

Universe, the one who has called upon those who believe in him to act in "the service of reconciliation" (*diakonia tēs katallagēs,* in 2 Corinthians 5:18). Thus, overcoming "otherness" could be experienced as the *mysterium coniunctionis* (the sacrament of conjunction), as the center of the cross as *quaternitas perfecta* ("fourfold perfection"). In fact, Christ is more the "conjunction" than "coincidence." For in him all Christian teachings are conjoined. As we have said, creation cannot be separated from the incarnation, nor the incarnation from the Trinity.

St. John Damascene emphasizes that we "do not have to say that man bas become God but rather that God made himself man." This has been a great difficulty for monotheism. Now can Being, absolutely one and simple, become anyone whatsoever? Let us repeat is again: the incarnation makes no sense except in the Trinity.

If we separate Jesus Christ from the Trinity, his figure loses all credibility. He would then be a new Socrates or any other great prophet. If we separate Jesus Christ from humanity, he becomes a Platonic ideal of perfection and frequently an instrument for dominating and exploiting others by becoming a God. If we separate his humanity from his actual historical journey on this earth and his historical roots, we turn him into a mere Gnostic figure who does not share our concrete and limited human condition.

The conjunction of these three elements constitutes the task of christophany for our age which emerges into a *mythos*.

7.3.6 The Emerging Mythos

We have been saying that only a holistic insight into the nature of reality will orient us in the jungle of multiple opinions and specialized branches of knowledge. We have, further, suggested the cosmotheandric insight as a possible hypothesis for such an enterprise. Finally, we have concentrated on the role and nature of the Divine among the mentioned triad of Cosmos, Man, and God while being careful not to sever this dimension from the whole of reality. We will now try to relate this vision to our World. It is the World in which we live, in which we believe we live, and which offers the context for our ideas about God and Man. The predominant Worldview of our times is the Scientific Cosmology, but this Cosmology is a product of the modern culture and is not the only vision of the World. The immensity of the topic allows only for some sketches.

All too often Philosophers and thinkers have remained in the lofty realm of ideas and have shunned consciously or unconsciously delving into the "real World" in parlance not only of common people but also of the Scientific community. The well known and highly criticized gap between theory and praxis exists also between what we call the humanities and what is labeled as the natural Sciences. The incursions of Philosophers have reached into sociological fields, but more rarely into the technological realm. We cannot offer immediate solutions, but we cannot avoid the problem. We should look for hints of some fundamental areas for change in our Worldview, or in what Panikkar calls our *World-mythos*.

7.3.7 Cosmology and Kosmology

Although the modern Scientific Cosmology has triumphed over the old cosmologies, the modern vision has not corrected many errors of the old cosmologies, but rather seems to have merely displaced or found functional substitutes for certain key elements. Therefore, in order to stress continuity, on the one hand, and novelty, on the other, Panikkar has chosen to change the ordinary spelling of the new Cosmology (to Kosmology) instead of introducing any new name. By Kosmology, Panikkar understands Science in the holistic sense. Kosmology is a *kosmos-legein*, a "reading" of the kosmos, the disclosure of the World to our human consciousness by means of all forms of knowledge we may possess. It is mainly understood here in the sense of the subjective genitive: the *logos*, the word of the kosmos that Man should try to hear and to understand by attuning himself to the music of this World, to the mysteries of the kosmos. We are aware that the kosmos speaks differently to different cultures and that Man hears and interprets this *logo* in many ways. It deals with how Man envisions the Universe, with how the kosmos displays itself to Man, and with the experience that Man has of the Universe of which we happen to form part and that leads us to discover the real Universe in which we live. It aspires to a knowledge of the kosmos in a manner similar to the way theology aspired to a knowledge of God and thus claimed to have saving power. The novelty of this cosmotheandric kosmology is that it also claims to possess saving power for the fullness of Man, a microcosm. It tries to understand and interpret, more or less profoundly, whatever enters into the field of our consciousness.

The new kosmology Panikkar is envisioning is neither an updating of the old "Worldviews" nor a mere reform of the new Cosmology, but a transformation of both. Be that as it may, in stressing the difference between kosmology and Cosmology he is trying to dispel a crypto-Kantian assumption regarding Scientific cognition: There is no World as in a "World in itself." The word "Worldview" may be misleading. The word tends to make us assume that it is all a question of different views of the same World, a World that is "obviously" described by "our" Cosmology. If we are also World and not only in the World, then we cannot eliminate the subjective factor of the Cosmos, but neither can we dispense with its objective aspect.

Man is not totally objectifiable. Man is a subject, a subject of understanding, even a subject of self-understanding, and this self-understanding belongs to the essence of Man. Self-understanding is not only my understanding of myself, but is also all the understandings that our fellow beings have of themselves. The kosmos is not a mere object of epistemology. Kosmos and Man belong together, and human self-understanding cannot be severed from the World in which Man lives. The historical experience of Man is also a kosmological factor. Hence, the importance of the predominant Scientific Cosmology, which we cannot peremptorily dismiss without painting ourselves into a solipsistic corner.

The new kosmology cannot be idealistic; it cannot be a result of the mind alone. Modern man has had too much experience of the hardness of life, the resistance of matter, and the objectivity of Science to put everything on the side of the subject. But, it cannot be materialistic either. To begin with, Science is too conscious of its own limits and limitations. The numinous appears everywhere, each new answer opens up scores of new questions, and human experience has been too painful to permit everything to be reduced to a mechanistic dialectic – projecting into the future what it cannot answer now.

Here metaphysics does not mean what is behind (or underneath) this physical World. The *meta* is not epistemological but ontological; it points to a World, which is not a concept but a symbol in the sense that the symbol is prior to subject-object epistemological knowledge. As we said earlier, a symbol is symbol only for those who recognize it as a symbol. I could sum it up by saying that the kosmos of traditional kosmology is a symbol, whereas the Cosmos of Cosmology is a concept. It is a methodological error to assume that ancient kosmologies, for instance, did not know anything about those distant galaxies invisible to the naked eyes because they did not have a clear concept of them. They knew "them" as part of this World, which had room for the unknown and even the unknowable beyond. Eschatological reflection, for instance, as a metaphysical ingredient of some kosmologies, did not refer to an astronomic big-bang coming to an end, but to the end of creation in its metaphysical meaning. It is naïve to consider our ancestors mentally retarded because they did not know today's marvelous physical Sciences. They lived in "another" World. I should add that for the new kosmology the World is both symbol and concept. At this juncture we can simply say without further elaboration that the World is neither one nor two. Each World presents an *advaitic* relationship with the people living in it.

There is order in the Universe. Indeed, there is an amazing and stupendous order. One does not need to descend into the awesome abyss of the atoms, or to ascend to the dizzying heights of the galaxies to discover it. One does not need to adduce an "anthropic cosmological principle" or a "cosmic blueprint" to be convinced of it. It suffices to watch a child, to smell a flower, to rest at night, to talk with a friend, to be a potter, a shoemaker, or to engage in agriculture. Nobody can deny that there is a design; one need only look. The design is everywhere. We have only to read the signs. Now, the rational mind cannot stop here, and not fully experiencing (enjoying) the design jumps by deduction (according to some) or by induction (in the opinion of others) to the designer, in response to which the atheist will make every effort to criticize the logical cogency of the arguments.

Yet the designer is nowhere to be found. It is even problematic to infer a designer. The principle "any effect requires a cause" is a mere tautology: an effect is that which requires a cause. To recognize something as an effect begs the question. It presupposes already that it comes from a cause. Nor should we forget that the so called proofs for the existence of God are neither mathematical nor ontological. Otherwise the existence of God would depend on the power of our calculus or the strength of our (contingent) being. These "ways" merely show that the belief in God is not against reason. Even if we have arrived at such a designer, this creates as many problems as it solves. We have to artificially sustain this designer, hide its faults, excuse its nonappearance, explain its absences, and defend this supreme Being whom nobody has ever seen – or at least justify his existence (*theodicea*). After all we have seen, it should be sufficiently clear that contesting the existence of a transcendent designer does not mean maintaining the atheistic position and declaring that the design has come about by spontaneous generation, sheer chance, or mere probability. On the contrary, the design is so marvelous that it is its own revelation.

It is crude anthropomorphism to assume a designer, and it is crude mechanistic attitude to presuppose that there has to be a cause behind it all. Ultimately, such attitudes signal a lack of contemplation. One of the most elaborated contemporary studies on these subjects is The Anthropic Cosmological Principle. There is a Universe, our authors (Barrow and Tipler) say. This Universe is the actual one, but we cannot know for sure whether there are not also many other Worlds, even an infinite number of them. Ultimately, it would not matter, since modern Science would understand it in terms of "all collections of laws and particles which ever did, does, or ever will exist." This may be the cosmological monotheistic Universe of modern Science, but it is certainly not the Universe of the kosmologies that have been the habitat of the World's civilizations for millennia. Panikkar tackles here the minor question for the authors, but an eye-opener for us. They write: "Although the FAP [Final Anthropic Principle] is a statement of Physics and hence, ipso facto has no ethical or moral content, it nevertheless is closely connected with moral values, for the validity of the FAP is the physical precondition for moral values to arise and to continue to exist in the Universe..."

Yet in defining the FAP the authors say: "Intelligent information-processing *must* come into existence in the Universe, and, once it comes into existence, *it will never die out*." I have added the emphasis to show that the condition of not containing any *ought* or its equivalent is not fulfilled, even in sentences about physical assumptions. The "must" in this definition makes it an imperative sentence. I am not minimizing the importance of the Anthropic Principle, but am pointing to this welcome contradiction to indicate that previous compartmentalization of disciplines and specialties is no longer possible. The Anthropic Principle is moral and may even be one of the foundations of morals – and therefore cannot be proven by Physics alone. Try as we might, we can no more separate morals from Science than we can sever Science from theology. Barrow and Tipler correctly insist that "no moral values of any sort exist in a lifeless Cosmology." But, this unification under the aegis of Reason is precisely the cosmological monotheism I am criticizing: the "Big Bang" (God?) was at the Beginning.

A Trinitarian kosmology is not longer monotheistic. The trinity is not three substances. This would be tritheism. The Trinity is pure relation, and we are also incorporated in this relationship, as the Christian Incarnation affirms. This Trinitarian view may, on the one hand, enter into conflict with the prevalent Scientific Cosmology, while, on the other hand, it may offer a more positive solution than that of mutual respect at the price of total separation between the Scientific and the religious realms.

The Trinitarian symbol is enlightening. The Divine is real, a real but different dimension of the Universe, neither independent nor separable. This dimension pervades everything, because nothing is without this dimension. It is not directly detectable, as a body is, or intelligible, as an idea may be. Otherwise we could reduce the Divine to a material or intelligible reality. Yet Man constantly discovers that the "more" and "different" is not an addition or a separation, but, as it were, an ingredient of reality itself. Something similar should be said regarding Man and the Cosmos. Consciousness as well as Matter pervades everything, and nothing is without these dimensions. There is a *perichōrēsis* between the three. The Divine contains, and is everything, but so are Man and the World as well. Each is the Whole, and not just in a particular mode. The three are not merely modalities of the real. The puzzle, if it were one, cannot be solved statically. As three beings, it is a flat contradiction – one is not three. As one being, it comes to no more than modalism. Yet reality is neither one nor three. What we have is a "complex" reality, because we see it from one particular vantage point, precisely from the human one. The one is by "becoming" the others, and also vice versa. The traditional expression in terms of the Christian trinity is that the One is by begetting and inspiring the others, and the others are by being begotten and inspired. We may want to look for better metaphors, but the point is to try to understand this *fluxus quo* of reality itself, as the very rhythm of being. If we look at reality in this dynamic way, we may say that every being is an I, a Thou, and an It. The new mythos will certainly contain elements from all the strata of humanity, but it will need a glue, so to speak, a leading thread, a dynamic force that will meld old and new into something we cannot yet properly foresee. Panikkar believes that the cosmotheandric insight may have sufficient traditional elements, and just enough of a revolutionary character, to serve as that catalyst for hope. Indeed, the cosmotheandric trinity is not an ideology but a myth. It therefore does not and could not claim to inform only one creed, a single religion, a homogeneous set of beliefs, a unified World culture, or anything of the sort.

A myth allows for communication and discussion; it allows for quarrels and helps in overcoming misunderstandings. Although it provides a language, it does not automatically create unanimity or consensus. By its very nature a myth is polysemic, and therefore not incompatible with pluralism.

Summing up: a new mythos may be emerging. Signs are everywhere. Panikkar has already given many names to fragments of this dawning: cosmotheandric insight, sacred secularity, kosmology, ontonomy, radical relativity, and so on.

General Conclusion

In the study of Cosmos we reflect about the World and our place in it. Others are less obvious, appearing as problems only to those willing to think very hard about highly abstract questions. There are a series of questions about "the World." We assume that the World includes everything that there is – that is, all that exists. The first and largest part, "What are most general features of the World?," includes readings on the problem of universals, the nature of particular things and the manner of their persistence through time, rival theories of the passage of time, absolute space and incongruent counterparts, causation, and a budget of paradoxes.

It is notoriously hard to provide a satisfactory account of what our World is. Certain twentieth-century coinages like "meta-Philosophy" and "meta-psychology" encourage the impression that our World is based on the study of metaphysics that somehow "goes beyond" Physics. The best approach in understanding the Cosmos as meant by "metaphysics" is by way of the concepts of appearance and reality. It is a commonplace that the way things seem to be is often not the way they are, that the way things *apparently* are is often not the way they *really* are. We might say that one is engaged in "metaphysics" when one is attempting to get behind all appearances and makes attempt to describe things as they really are.

The metaphysician's aim is to make assertions that strictly and literally describe reality and which can, with sufficient effort, be understood by anyone whose intellect is equal to the task. Metaphor may play a heuristic role in metaphysics – as in Physics or economics or comparative linguistics – but metaphor must be banished from the metaphysician's "finished product." To say these things is not to say that the metaphysician (necessarily) regards the metaphorical as inferior to the literal; it is merely to demarcate what belongs properly to metaphysics.

Is metaphysics, so conceived, possible? – that is, is it possible to "engage in metaphysics" in the above sense and to reach any interesting or important conclusions? Various Philosophers have argued that metaphysics is impossible. The thesis that metaphysics is impossible comes in what might be called strong and weak forms. The strong form of the thesis is this: The goal is not there, since there is no Reality to be described; all the statements we have called metaphysical are false or meaningless. And is hard to see how all metaphysical statements could be simply false. If one metaphysician says that everything is material and another says that it is false that everything is material, then, if their statements are meaningful, one or the other of them must be true. The weak form of the thesis is this: The goal is there, but we human beings are unable to reach it, since the task of describing Reality is beyond our powers; metaphysical statements are meaningful, but we can never discover whether any metaphysical statement is true or false (or discover anything else interesting or important about the class of metaphysical statements).

How does the World exists at all instead of the nonentity which might be imagined in its place? "Apart from man," says Schopenhauer, "no being wonders at its own existence." When man first becomes conscious, he takes himself for granted, as something needing no explanation. But, not for long; for, with the rise of the first reflection, that wonder begins which is the mother of metaphysics, and which made Aristotle say that men now and always seek to philosophize because of wonder — The lower man stands in intellectual respects the less of a riddle does existence seem to him ... but, the clearer his consciousness becomes the more the problem grasps him in its greatness. In fact the unrest which keeps the never stopping clock of metaphysics going is the thought that the non-existence of this World is just as possible as its existence.

Philosophy stares, but brings no reasoned solution, for from nothing to being there is no logical bridge. Attempts are sometimes made to banish the question rather than to give it an answer. Those who ask it, we are told, extend illegitimately to the whole of being the contrast to a supposed alternative non-being which only particular beings possess. These, indeed, were not, and now are. But, being in general, or in some shape, always was, and you cannot rightly bring the whole of it into relation with a primordial nonentity. Whether as God or as material atoms, it is itself primal and eternal but if you call any being whatever eternal, some Philosophers have always been ready to criticize you with the paradox inherent in the assumption. Is past eternity completed? They ask: If so, they go on, it must have had a beginning; for whether your imagination traverses it forwards or backwards, it offers an identical content or stuff to be measured; and if the amount comes to an end in one way, it ought to come to an end in the other. In other words, since we now witness its end, some past moment must have witnessed its beginning. If, however, it had a beginning, when was that, and why?

It is not probable that the reader/student will be satisfied with any of these solutions, and contemporary Philosophers, even rationalistically minded ones, have on the whole agreed that no one has intelligibly banished the mystery of *fact*. Whether the original nothing burst into God and vanished, as night vanishes in day, while God thereupon became the creative principle of all lesser beings; or whether all things have foisted or shaped themselves imperceptibly into existence. You leave the logical riddle untouched, of how the coming of whatever is, came it all at once, or came it piecemeal, can be intellectually understood. Nevertheless, within experience, phenomena come and go. There are novelties; there are losses. The World seems, on the concrete and proximate level at least, really to grow. So the question recurs: How do our finite experiences come into being from moment to moment? By inertia? By perpetual creation? Do the new ones come at the call of the old ones? Why do not they all go out like a candle?

Who can tell off-hand? The question of being is the darkest in all Philosophy. It might have been true that nothing ever existed: no minds, no atoms, no space, and no time. When we imagine this possibility, it can seem astonishing that anything exists. Why is there a Universe? And things might have been, in countless ways, different. So why is the Universe as it is? These facts cannot be causally explained. No law of nature could explain why there are many laws of nature, or why these laws are as they are. And, if God created the World, there cannot be causal explanation of why God exists. Since, our questions cannot have causal answers, we may wonder whether they make sense.

How should we choose between these explanations? The many-Worlds hypothesis is more cautious, since it merely claims that there is more of the kind of reality we know. But, God's existence has been claimed to intrinsically more plausible. By 'God' we mean a being who is omnipotent, omniscient and wholly less arbitrary, than the existence of many complicated and specific Worlds. If such a God exists, however, why is the Universe as it is? It may not be surprising that God chose to make life possible. But, the laws of nature could have been different, so there are many possible Worlds that would have contained life. It is hard to understand why, with all these possibilities, God chose to create *our* World. As we shall see, there may be other answers to this problem. But, we have larger questions to consider. I began by asking *why* things are as they are. We must also ask *how* things are. There is much about our World that we have not discovered. And, just as there may be other Worlds like ours, there may be Worlds that are very different.

In the remainder of this Conclusion, I have made an attempt to give some content to the very abstract remarks we have made about the nature of metaphysics by examining a particular metaphysical problem. It would seem – that there is nothing to choose between our World: is it Physics? Or is it metaphysics? – As long as the reader considers to think that it is not the question with the problem of choosing one discipline but considering the manner in which I have understood the Cosmos. I have strongly suggested (at least in the exposition and the development of the Cosmos) a Christian outlook and context paved to journey to seek the Cosmos. The efforts made to reflect, study, and contribute in laying the problem and characteristics of the Cosmos is/was basically to present a Philosophical stance in approaching the reality of the Cosmos. Therefore, the terminologies, concepts, jargon leads me to deal with the metaphysical possibility of understanding and grappling with the reality of the Cosmos.

Thus, the proposition I make in this Book, is a thesis based on key concepts and important topics such as speculative mode, fundamental concepts, Philosophical premises, phenomenological assumptions, Scientific theories and metaphysical claims. The sequence in which the chapters have been outlined cannot be rationalized logically. However, it does propose a certain sense of continuum in its exposition. The language might sound arbitrary for those who have no basis in Philosophy, epistemology and metaphysics. Therefore, the reader/students ought to be convinced and eschewed with commitment without buttressing and being ostentious about the subject of Cosmology.

Bibliography

Barrow, John D. and Frank J. Tipler. *The Anthropic Cosmological Principle*. Oxford: Oxford University Press, 1988.

Berry, Thomas and Brian Swimme. *The Universe Story: From the Primordial Flaring Forth to the Ecozoic Era*. San Francisco: Harper San Francisco, 1992.

Berry, Thomas. *The New Story*. Chambersburg, Pa.: Anima Books, 1978.

Burrell, David B. *Aquinas: God and Action.* London: Routledge and Kegan Paul, 1979.

Carrel, Alexis. *Man the Unknown*. London: Burn & Oats, 1961.

Copleston, Frederick. *A History of Philosophy*, 9 Vols. New York: An Image Book, 1994.

Dasgupta, Surendranath. *A History of Indian Philosophy.* 5 Vols. Madras: Macmillan Press, 1932.

de Chardin, Teilhard. *Man's Place in Nature: The Human Zoological Group*. Translated by René Hague. New York: Fontana Books, 1966.

de Chardin, Teilhard. *Science and Christ.* Translated by René Hague. London: William Collins Sons & Co. Ltd, 1968.

de Chardin, Teilhard. *The Divine Milieu.* New York: Harper Torchbooks, 1957.

de Chardin, Teilhard. *The Future of Man*. Translated by Norman Denny. London: William Collins Sons & Co. Ltd, 1964.

de Chardin, Teilhard. *The Phenomenon of Man*. New York: Harper & Row, 1959.

de Chardin, Teilhard. *The Phenomenon of Man*. New York: Harper Torchbooks, 1961.

de Chardin, Teilhard. *The Phenomenon of Man*. Translated by Bernard Wall. New York: Harper & Row, 1959.

de Chardin, Teilhard. *The Prayer of the Universe: Selected from Writings in Time of War*. Translated by René Hague. New York: Fontana Books, 1973.

de Marneffe, J. *Contemporary Christian Philosophy*. Madras: University of Madras, 1971.

de Smet, R. V. "Sankara and Aquinas on Creation," *Indian Ecclesiastical Studies* 11(1972): 236.

de Smet, Richard. "Origin: Creation and Emanation." *Indian Theological Studies*. 15/3 (1978): 266-279.

Dougherty, Kenneth. *Cosmology: An Introduction to the Thomistic Philosophy of Nature*. New York: Graymoor Press, 1956.

Fergusson, David A. S. *The Cosmos and the Creator: An Introduction to the Theology of Creation*. London: SPCK, 1998.

Frost, S. E. *Basic Teachings of the Great Philosophers: A Survey of Their Basic Ideas*. New York: Anchor Books, 1962.

Glenn, Paul. *Cosmology: A Class Manual in the Philosophy of Bodily Being*. New York: Herder & Herder, 1957.

Hagens, Van Bernard (Translated). *Cosmology*. Sonada: Salesian College, 1972.

Haldar, M. K. *Studies in Whitehead's Cosmology*. Delhi: Atma Ram & Sons, 1972.

Hale, Robert. *Christ and the Universe*. Edited by Michael Meilach. Chicago: Franciscan Herald Press, 1973.

Haught, John F. *The Cosmic Adventure: Science, Religion and the Quest for Purpose*. Paulist Press, New York, 1984.

Hawking, Stephen. *A Brief History of Time: From the Big Bang to Black Holes*. New York: Bantam Books, 1988.

Jaki, Stanley L. *Cosmos and Creator*. Edinburgh: Scottish Academic Press, 1980.

Kozhamthadam, Job. *Philosophico-Scientific Reflections of the Cosmos*. Pune: JDV College, 1975.

Laird, John. *Theism and Cosmology*. New York: Books & Library, 1969.

MacKay, Donald M. *Science and the Quest for Meaning: A Clear and Reasonable Discussion Exploring the Compatibility of Scientific Knowledge and Christian Faith*. Michigan: William B. Eerdmans Publishing Company, 1982.

Mercier, Jean L. "The Problem of Creation." in *The Philosophy of the Absolute Reality*. Bangalore: ATC Publications, 2000.

Moltmann, Jürgen. *God in Creation*. Philadelphia: Fortress Press, 1993.

Panikkar, Raimon. *Christophany: The Fullness of Man*. Translated by Alfred DiLascia. New York: Orbis Books, 2007.

Panikkar, Raimon. *Invisible Harmony: Essays on Contemplation and Responsibility*. Edited by Harry James Cargas. Minneapolis: Augsburg Fortress, 1995.

Panikkar, Raimon. *The Cosmotheandric Experience: Emerging Religious Consciousness*. Edited by Scott Eastham. Delhi: Motilal Banarsidass, 1998.

Panikkar, Raimon. *The Rhythm of Being: The Gifford Lectures*. Maryknoll: Orbis Books, 2010.

Panikkar, Raimundo. *A Dwelling Place for Wisdom*. Translated by Annemarie S. Kidder. Westminster: John Knox Press, 1993.

Panikkar, Raimundo. *Colligite Fragmenta: For an Integration of Reality*. Villanova: University Press, 1978.

Panikkar, Raimundo. *The Trinity and the Religious Experience of Man*. Madras: The Christian Literature Society, 1970.

Panikkar, Raimundo. *The Unknown Christ of Hinduism*. London: Darton, Longman and Todd, 1968.

Panikkar, Raimundo. *Worship and Secular Man*. Maryknoll: Orbis Books, 1973.

Peach, J. V. *Creation and Cosmology*. London: Burns & Oates, 1965.

Perumalil, Augustine. *Religious Cosmologies*. Delhi, Cambridge Press, 2007.

Rahner, Karl, Cornelius Ernest and Kevin Smyth (Editors). *Sacramentum Mundi: An Encyclopedia of Theology*. 8 Vols. Bangalore: Theological Publications in India, 1975.

Raven, Charles E. *Teilhard de Chardin, Scientist and Seer*. London: Collins Press, 1962.

Rideau, Emile. *Teilhard de Chardin: A Guide to His Thoughts*. Translated by R. Hague. London: Collins Press, 1967.

Savary, Louis M. *Teilhard de Chardin: The Divine Milieu*. New York: Paulist Press, 2007.

Soares, G. "The Theological Significance of Modern Cosmologies," *Indian Ecclesiastical Studies* 2 (1963): 102

Sterba, James P. (Series Editor). *Metaphysics: The Big Questions*. Edited by Peter van Inwagen and Dean W. Zimmerman. USA: Blackwell Publishers, 1998.

Trefil, James. *The Moment of Creation*. New York: Charles Scribner's Sons, 1983.

Whitehead, Alfred North. *Process and Reality*. Edited by David Ray Griffin and Donald W. Sherburne. New York: The Free Press, 1978.

Index of Subjects

D

E

F

G

I

Q

R

S

U

Index of Authors